LIFELONG LEISURE SKILLS AND LIFESTYLES FOR PERSONS WITH DEVELOPMENTAL DISABILITIES

LIFELONG LEISURE SKILLS AND LIFESTYLES FOR PERSONS WITH DEVELOPMENTAL DISABILITIES

by

Stuart J. Schleien, Ph.D., CTRS
Professor and Division Head
Recreation, Park, and Leisure Studies
School of Kinesiology and Leisure Studies
University of Minnesota, Minneapolis

Luanna H. Meyer, Ph.D.
Professor, School of Education
Chair, Doctoral Program in Special Education
Coordinator, Inclusive Elementary and
Special Education Program
Syracuse University, Syracuse

Linda A. Heyne, Ph.D., CTRS
Coordinator, Inclusive Recreation Project
Institute on Community Integration
University of Minnesota, Minneapolis

and

Bonnie Biel Brandt, M.A.
Regional Training Coordinator
University Affiliated Program
College of Education
University of Guam, Mangilao

with invited contributors

·P A U L·H·
BROOKES
PUBLISHING Cº

Baltimore • London • Toronto • Sydney

Paul H. Brookes Publishing Co.
Post Office Box 10624
Baltimore, Maryland 21285-0624

Typeset by Brushwood Graphics, Inc., Baltimore, Maryland.
Manufactured in the United States of America by
Maple-Vail Book Manufacturing Group, Binghamton, New York.

Library of Congress Cataloging-in-Publication Data
Lifelong leisure skills and lifestyles for persons with developmental
    disabilities / by Stuart J. Schleien . . . [et al.].
        p.   cm.
    Includes bibliographical references and index.
    ISBN 1-55766-147-2
    1. Developmentally disabled—Recreation.   2. Leisure—Study and
teaching.   3. Leisure—Study and teaching—Activity programs.
    I. Schleien, Stuart J., 1956–
GV183.5.L54   1995
790.1'96–dc20   94-37005
                                                                      CIP

British Library Cataloguing-in-Publication data are available from the British Library.

CONTENTS

LIST OF TABLES

LIST OF FORMS

ABOUT THE AUTHORS

Stuart J. Schleien, Ph.D., CTRS, School of Kinesiology and Leisure Studies, University of Minnesota, 224 Cooke Hall, 1900 University Avenue, S.E., Minneapolis, MN 55455. Dr. Schleien is Professor and Division Head in Recreation, Park, and Leisure Studies, with a joint appointment in Special Education, at the University of Minnesota. Internationally recognized for his service and scholarly contributions in the fields of therapeutic recreation and special education, Dr. Schleien was the recipient of the Researcher of the Year Award by the Minnesota Recreation and Park Association and the Educator of the Year Award by the Minnesota Arc. He is the author of more than 75 journal articles, research monographs, and book chapters, and has written six books in the areas of inclusive community recreation and outdoor education, lifelong leisure and friendship skills development, and therapeutic recreation. He has presented his work throughout the United States and Canada, and in Australia, England, Israel, and Sweden.

Luanna H. Meyer, Ph.D., School of Education, Syracuse University, 150 Huntington Hall, Syracuse, NY 13244. Dr. Meyer is Professor of Education, Chair of the Doctoral Program in Special Education, and Coordinator of the Inclusive Elementary and Special Education Program at Syracuse University. Her research has focused on inclusive schooling, children's peer relationships, nonaversive behavioral intervention, and educational change. She has published more than 100 books, book chapters, and journal articles, and has lectured extensively in the United States as well as in Canada, New Zealand, Poland, Israel, and Australia. She currently co-directs the New York Partnership for Statewide Systems Change and is Director of the Consortium for Collaborative Research on Social Relationships.

Linda A. Heyne, Ph.D., CTRS, University of Minnesota, 109 Norris Hall, 172 Pillsbury Drive, S.E., Minneapolis, MN 55455. Dr. Heyne is Coordinator of the Inclusive Recreation Project at the Institute on Community Integration, University of Minnesota. For the past 10 years she has directed her efforts toward including individuals with disabilities in community recreation environments. Dr. Heyne has served as integration facilitator of an inclusive recreation program for children and youth with disabilities at the Jewish Community Center of the Greater St. Paul Area, as well as coordinated multiple therapeutic recreation grant-supported projects at the University of Minnesota.

Bonnie Biel Brandt, M.A., University Affiliated Program, College of Education, University of Guam, UOG Station, Mangilao, GU 96923. Ms. Brandt is Regional Training Coordinator for the University Affiliated Program at the University of Guam and a private educational consultant in the Western Pacific. Over the past 10 years she has provided services to the Guam Public School System, the University of Guam, the College of Micronesia, and many programs serving individuals with disabilities in the region. Her professional efforts have focused on program development, systems change, and family advocacy.

ABOUT THE CONTRIBUTORS

John Dattilo, Ph.D., CTRS, 223 Hardman, Department of Recreation and Leisure Studies, University of Georgia, Athens, GA 30602. Dr. Dattilo is Associate Professor in the Department of Recreation and Leisure Studies at the University of Georgia. He is the author of *Inclusive Leisure Services: Responding to the Rights of People with Disabilities* (1994), *Leisure Education Program Planning* (1991), and *Behavior Modification in Therapeutic Recreation* (1987).

Beverly Rainforth, Ph.D., PT, P.O. Box 6000, School of Education and Human Development, State University of New York at Binghamton, Binghamton, NY 13902. Dr. Rainforth has worked as both a physical therapist and a special education teacher for preschoolers and school-age children with disabilities. Currently she is Associate Professor of Special Education at the State University of New York at Binghamton.

Ronald P. Reynolds, Ph.D., CTRS, 923 W. Franklin Street, P.O. Box 2015, Department of Recreation, Parks, & Tourism, Virginia Commonwealth University, Richmond, VA 23284. Dr. Reynolds is Professor and Coordinator of Therapeutic Recreation at Virginia Commonwealth University, Richmond, Virginia. He has been the editor of two journals related to therapeutic recreation, and has co-authored two textbooks and a study guide for the national certification exam in therapeutic recreation.

John E. Rynders, Ph.D., 255 Burton Hall, Department of Educational Psychology, University of Minnesota, Minneapolis, MN 55455. Dr. Rynders is Professor in Special Education at the University of Minnesota where he specializes in mental retardation and early education/special education. He is experienced as a teacher of persons with disabilities of all ages and as a researcher on topics such as early intervention/family support and inclusive programming. Dr. Rynders has published numerous articles and was awarded the Theodore Tjossem Outstanding Research Award by the National Down Syndrome Congress in 1992 for his work with persons who have Down syndrome and their family members.

Nancy A. Staur, M.A., CTRS, Dowling Urban Environmental Learning Center, 3900 West River Parkway, Minneapolis, MN 55406. Ms. Staur has taught kindergarten through sixth-grade students with and without special needs lifelong leisure skills and adapted physical education in inclusive classrooms.

Jennifer York, Ph.D., PT, 101 Pattee Hall, Department of Educational Policy and Administration, 150 Pillsbury Drive, S.E., University of Minnesota, Minneapolis, MN 55455. Dr. York is Assistant Professor in the College of Education at the University of Minnesota. She is currently Coordinator of Interdisciplinary Studies at the Institute on Community Integration and is the director of several inclusive education projects. For the past 15 years she has focused on issues of cross-disciplinary collaboration to support the inclusion of individuals with developmental disabilities.

FOREWORD

*L*ongitudinal Leisure Skills for Severely Handicapped Learners: The Ho'onanea Curriculum Component, by Bonnie Biel Wuerch and Luanna M. Voeltz, was an advanced and creative look at leisure education for young people with developmental disabilities. I have used the *Ho'onanea* curriculum as a
resource frequently since it appeared in 1982. I also have shared my copy and recommended it to practitioners on many occasions as I have worked with them on a preservice and inservice basis. I was very
pleased to find out from the authors that the original version was undergoing an update.

The original authors, Bonnie Biel Brandt (formerly Wuerch) and Dr. Luanna Meyer (formerly Voeltz),
who initially worked together in Hawaii, have been joined by two other extremely talented authors and certified therapeutic recreation specialists (CTRS), Drs. Stuart J. Schleien and Linda A. Heyne from the University of Minnesota. This collaborative effort now brings together four authors who are leaders in the
fields of leisure education and developmental disabilities. These individuals are all deeply committed to the
enhancement of quality of life for all persons with developmental disabilities, including commitment to
inclusive leisure/recreation services within schools and communities. Their commitment is evident in their
writing, which is based on considerable practical experience working with persons with developmental disabilities, teachers, families, and community recreation providers.

In *Lifelong Leisure Skills and Lifestyles for Persons with Developmental Disabilities,* the authors have
brought the original information into the 1990s. The expanded focus of this sequel is apparent in the new
title emphasizing the lifelong nature and positive lifestyle changes leisure education can bring for persons
with developmental disabilities. Readers familiar with the *Ho'onanea* curriculum will notice many updates
and extensions and new information reflecting the evolution of issues and services from the early 1980s
into the 1990s.

With new and updated information comes the possibility for an expanded audience of readers and
users of this information. I believe this expanded volume will be appealing and useful to all practitioners,
as well as those professionals working to prepare practitioners involved in all aspects of leisure education.
Anyone interested in committing to age-appropriate, inclusive leisure education in schools, homes, and
neighborhoods, as well as community leisure/recreation, will find this book to be an excellent resource.

Crucial issues and activities, some new and some extensions of those raised in the first book, are
brought to light in this volume. First, and perhaps foremost in many respects, leisure/recreation for persons
with developmental disabilities is presented here as an important part of *enhanced quality of life*. As individuals with developmental disabilities increasingly are included in regular places such as regular schools
and classrooms, homes in regular neighborhoods, stores and services in their communities, and real community job sites with co-workers without disabilities, it becomes more apparent that they still may have
large amounts of "free time" and are in need of leisure education to learn to use that time in life-enhancing
ways. With that as a basis, many other issues and activities are discussed and practical suggestions are
offered.

Throughout this volume, emphasis is placed on persons with developmental disabilities needing
leisure/recreation skills that are useful in *inclusive school, home, and community environments*. This
emphasis is infused throughout the text in many ways, including a new set of instructional sequences useful across environments; for example, there are new sequences for Game Boy (instead of the former Atari
home video system), which might be used at home as well as in the community, and the addition of aerobics, which typically involves a community recreation environment with peers without disabilities. The
importance of *choice making* based on individual preferences as well as family preferences is made more
salient in this volume. Enhanced participation in leisure/recreation by individuals with more significant,
multiple disabilities is included now. This is especially evident in new information on using microswitch
technology and other individualized adaptations to enhance meaningful partial to full participation of all
persons, including those using auxiliary communication for choice making and participation. The impor-

tance of meaningful *friendships* in the lives of persons with developmental disabilities and the relationship of inclusive leisure/recreation opportunities to friendship building in school (e.g., the Dowling Friendship Program in Minnesota) and community are considerably enhanced in this sequel. The importance of *involving family members and/or care providers* in all aspects of planning and implementation has been expanded here as well. As in the first version of this curriculum, the importance of not only the acquisition of leisure/recreation skills, but the *maintenance and generalization* of those skills, is apparent throughout this volume.

Lifelong Leisure Skills and Lifestyles for Persons with Developmental Disabilities is an excellent and greatly enhanced and expanded resource in leisure education. It represents what we now know as "best practices" in leisure education. It should be extremely useful for anyone interested in enhanced leisure skills for persons with developmental disabilities across inclusive school, home, and community environments.

Susan Hamre-Nietupski, Ph.D.
Division of Curriculum and Instruction
The University of Iowa
Iowa City

PREFACE

*F*ree time involves what we do when we are free from other responsibilities. It represents choices; we may choose what to do, with whom to spend free time, and where free time will be experienced. While leisure and recreation involve personal choice, friends, and enjoyment, they also must involve learning skills so that one can participate socially and appropriately. Most individuals can perform at least fairly well in a variety of activities of their own choosing. Leisure skills are developed naturally as children and youths effortlessly explore their environments with their peers. Others, particularly individuals with significant disabilities, often do not have the skills to engage in appropriate and independent play. They are left with much time with little to do and a limited number of individuals with whom to participate in activities. There are many individuals who need direct support to develop a broad repertoire of leisure skills. These individuals must be provided with ongoing opportunities to expand their leisure and social repertoires in home, school, and neighborhood environments. This book is written to support the wide array of potential *audience* leisure educators who could support such activities and experiences. Parents, siblings, teachers, classmates, recreation professionals, and playmates/friends can all serve in this critical role to help ensure a life full of choices, active participation, and enjoyment. This book is written to help you facilitate this quality of life.

This sequel, entitled *Lifelong Leisure Skills and Lifestyles for Persons with Developmental Disabilities,* formerly *Longitudinal Leisure Skills for Severely Handicapped Learners: The Ho'onanea Curriculum Component,* is the product of the collaborative efforts of several individuals with and without disabilities, their families, practitioners, and researchers during a period of more than 7 years. All of these individuals contributed conceptual and practical input into the nature of this work and were directly involved throughout the various stages of development, field testing, and validation of the recreation and sports activity instructional sequences in home, school, and community environments throughout Hawaii, Minnesota, and New York.

The original *Ho'onanea* curriculum development project began in the late 1970s when the Department of Special Education at the University of Hawaii, the Special Education Center of Oahu (a private school serving children and youths with significant disabilities), and the Special Education Department of Waipahu Intermediate School (an integrated public school) combined their efforts. Almost a decade later, Dr. Luanna Meyer (formerly Voeltz) approached Dr. Stuart J. Schleien with plans for this sequel. Together, Meyer, Schleien, Bonnie Biel Brandt (formerly Wuerch), and newcomer to the project, Dr. Linda A. Heyne, enthusiastically brainstormed their ideas for an expanded and updated version of the original product.

The results of these collaborative efforts include a revised curriculum that contains several new recreation and sports activities that reach well beyond the classroom. These new commercially available activities can be implemented in homes, communities, and classrooms. For example, the pottery or aerobics instructional sequences are designed for use in neighborhood recreation centers, YMCAs, Jewish Community Centers, and other recreation environments. Other new activities have been designed and validated with individuals with significant disabilities, including teaching leisure and social skills to replace severe challenging behaviors.

In addition to the broader scope of activities, we have addressed in great detail the involvement of family members, community recreation professionals, and others close to the individual as key players in the leisure education process. The original chapter addressing leisure development by parents in the home, as well as the activity selection information, has been expanded. A new chapter on inclusive community recreation programming (with Dr. John E. Rynders and Nancy A. Staur) has been added. Almost all of these additions and revisions are based on our many years of working directly with families, teachers, and community recreators.

Dr. John Dattilo helped shape Chapter 6 into a state-of-the-art piece on preferences and choice instruction. Drs. Jennifer York and Beverly Rainforth have written a comprehensive new chapter concerning ecological assessment strategies, adaptations, and the use of microswitch technology to promote independent play. While continuing to be grounded in the principles and practices of systematic instruction, Chapters 3 (Skill Acquisition) and 8 (Implementation Strategies) have been significantly revised to reflect inclusive educational practices and to incorporate recent information on maximizing incidental learning opportunities. Finally, Dr. Ronald Reynolds, former editor of the *Therapeutic Recreation Journal,* completes this sequel with a thought-provoking look into the future for leisure skills programming for individuals with developmental disabilities. We believe that these authors, representing the fields of therapeutic recreation, special education, adapted physical education, and physical therapy, have contributed significantly to this project.

ORGANIZATION OF THIS VOLUME

This book is designed to provide teachers, recreation professionals, parents, and other potential leisure educators with the information and guidelines necessary to successfully implement the *Lifelong Leisure Skills and Lifestyles* curriculum component with individuals with disabilities. It is, of course, assumed that the information and guidelines will be expanded and adjusted by the leisure educator to fit not only the unique abilities and needs of specific participants, but also the unique abilities and needs of the leisure educator.

The nine chapters of this sequel are organized according to the major steps and decisions the leisure educator must make in implementing this curriculum. Chapter 1 provides the background and philosophy of leisure education in general and the *Lifelong Leisure Skills and Lifestyles* program in particular, and the roles of the leisure educator. Chapter 2 describes the step-by-step process used to select the 10 leisure activities in this book, as well as provides guidelines to help the leisure educator identify other activities appropriate for participants at home, in school, and in the community. Chapter 3 details the instructional objectives, environments, and procedures that have been proven effective in accomplishing the program's goals. Chapter 4 includes validated task-analyzed skill sequences for the 10 leisure activities, including 6 activities that were not included in the first version of this curriculum. A few of these activities are oriented toward physical activity and could be participated in and enjoyed across home, school, and community environments. Chapter 5, a new addition to this sequel, focuses on specific adaptations that may be necessary to implement in a leisure education program to accommodate people with various motor and sensory disabilities. These strategies have been field tested across children and adults with significant and multiple disabilities. Special branches, teaching procedures, and modifications for individualized problems are described in detail. Chapter 6 emphasizes a systematic approach to ensuring that participants learn how to make activity choices during their free time and generalize leisure skills from highly instructional situations to leisure environments that are naturally occurring. Chapter 7 was written to help the leisure educator facilitate participation in inclusive community leisure environments. Special emphasis is placed on ways to structure the social dynamics of the program to promote relationships. Chapter 8 describes how teachers, parents, and recreation professionals can incorporate leisure education instruction into their ongoing activities in classroom, home, and community environments. Preparing the leisure environment, scheduling the necessary opportunities to learn, and monitoring the instructional program are highlighted. Focus groups are described to illustrate how key players collaborate across leisure environments to overcome obstacles and facilitate the success of participants. Chapter 9 describes the in-home instruction component, which allows for differing levels of parent and/or caregiver participation in an individual's leisure education depending on parent and/or caregiver preferences, resources, and capabilities. The Epilogue takes a thought-provoking look at the future of leisure service delivery to individuals with disabilities. It examines the influences of contemporary movements in society and human services on the provision of leisure services. Following a comprehensive bibliography, the appendices contain a list of vendors and purchase prices of the materials for the 10 leisure activities used in the program and copies of the forms, assessment instruments, and activity illustrations discussed in the text for the leisure educator to reproduce for his or her own use.

To conclude, we have attempted to build upon the highly successful *Ho'onanea* curriculum by developing an alternative to other models in therapeutic recreation and leisure education. What we offer is a recreation activities curriculum that is designed specifically with individuals with developmental disabilities in mind. We incorporated the values and perceptions of individuals with disabilities, their parents and care providers, and teachers and recreation professionals. Processes to enable learners who cannot speak or who have significant cognitive or multiple disabilities to communicate their activity preferences have been incorporated throughout the book. We continue to build upon systematic instructional strategies and behavioral strategies to help expand people's repertoires with lifelong, age-appropriate, generalizable, and enjoyable activities. Finally, we place added emphasis on context and lifestyle issues as critical supports for the establishment of personally meaningful leisure repertoires of value to the person, family, and friends. We believe that you will find many uses for *Lifelong Leisure Skills and Lifestyles for Persons with Developmental Disabilities*.

ACKNOWLEDGMENTS

We would like to express our gratitude to various individuals who participated in the research and development of this book. We appreciate their creative thoughts and most generous cooperation. We wish to give special thanks to the contributors of the various chapters of this volume, including our colleagues and friends Dr. John Dattilo, Dr. Ronald Reynolds, Dr. John E. Rynders, Ms. Nancy A. Staur, Dr. Beverly Rainforth, and Dr. Jennifer York. Also, we are extremely grateful to Dr. Susan Hamre-Nietupski for her ongoing consultation with us and her uplifting foreword to the book.

The original project, *Ho'onanea,* began as the combined effort of the Department of Special Education at the University of Hawaii, the Special Education Center of Oahu (SECO), and the Special Education Department of Waipahu Intermediate School. In addition to providing major input into the original grant proposal that was funded to develop the curriculum component, professional staff from both SECO and Waipahu Intermediate were intensively involved throughout the first 2 years of this work, with these two schools serving as field-test sites for the development and validation of the initial versions of the activities' task analyses and curriculum implementation procedures. For this sequel, it is critical that we acknowledge Dr. Jeffrey Raison and Ms. Micky Pearson, from the Dowling Urban Environmental Learning Center, Minneapolis Public Schools, for their administrative and programmatic support of this project. Many of the activities that are described in this edition originated under their leadership.

A number of therapeutic recreation specialists and other professionals were helpful in the development of this work. Their creative ideas are infused throughout the chapters and activity curriculum. We express our appreciation to Dr. Lynn Anderson, Jonathan Balk, Maurice Fahnestock, Dr. Rick Green, Dr. Jennifer Mactavish, Tip Ray, Kathy Strom, and Ezell Voeltz.

Credit for a taxing and excellent job of typing and manuscript preparation is owed to Teri Anderson.

Special thanks are also extended to Roslyn Udris, Production Manager for Paul H. Brookes Publishing Co., for overseeing the production of this book.

Finally, a very special thanks is due to the individuals who learned these leisure activities and to their families and other individuals close to them who thought the activities were important enough in many cases to provide crucial assistance in transferring these skills to their home and neighborhood environments.

To my lovely family: Dana, Jenna Lillian, and Jason David
To Daonté and Steven
To the children and families who have generously contributed to the development of these pages
To Mariko and Jay

LIFELONG
LEISURE SKILLS
AND LIFESTYLES
FOR PERSONS WITH
DEVELOPMENTAL DISABILITIES

Chapter 1

A LEISURE EDUCATION CURRICULUM COMPONENT

leisure: a. freedom or spare time provided by the cessation of activities: 1) free time as a result of temporary exemption from work or duties; 2) time at one's command that is free of engagements or responsibilities. b. a period of unemployed time.

play: to engage in recreational activity, amuse or divert oneself; suggests an opposition to work; it implies activity, often strenuous, but emphasizes the absence of any aim other than amusement, diversion, or enjoyment.

What is leisure? What is play? According to *Webster's Third New International Dictionary* (1986), *leisure* refers to an individual's "free time"—time when a person can do what he or she prefers to do. Leisure time should be distinguishable from nonleisure time, and this distinction can be made by looking at the specific environments where leisure and nonleisure time take place. For example, when an individual is working and must perform a particular job, we can readily predict where the person will be working as well as the times of day and days of the week during which he or she will be working. Similarly, when children are in school, we have a fairly good idea of the kinds of activities we would expect to see them doing as part of their educational program. Neither school nor work meets the definition of leisure time, as specific responsibilities are prescribed and specific tasks must be carried out. There may be brief periods of time during the workday—breaks—or the school day—recess—when assigned tasks are temporarily suspended and individuals are free to do as they wish within certain guidelines. But generally speaking, jobs and school programs do not allow us to decide how to spend our time; nor do they let us vary greatly from what is expected in those environments.

Sometimes environments provide both leisure and nonleisure opportunities in varying amounts. Throughout our lifespan, for example, the home environment requires the performance of various household tasks as well as provides numerous opportunities for leisure activities. Each member of a household may be responsible for certain chores—those chores might need to be done at prescribed times (e.g., cooking dinner) or whenever it is convenient to do them (e.g., doing the laundry or vacuuming the rugs). As long as those chores are completed to the satisfaction of the members of that household, the remaining time is available for leisure. Community environments may also represent a combination of responsibilities and free time. Stores may be places to shop for groceries and other needed household goods, but a shopping mall can also be a place to "window shop" and simply hang out with friends as a way of passing a free Saturday afternoon.

There are certain periods during the lifespan in which individuals are more likely to find larger blocks of leisure time in a variety of environments. Infants and young children are not usually assigned major responsibilities or duties, and their entire day may thus appear to consist of leisure wherever they happen to be. Even when they begin school and their educational activities start to occupy more of the school day, younger children have significant opportunities for playtime during an already short school day. Furthermore, times for learning also resemble play; that is, teachers of very young children are taught to use structured and imaginative play, and learning centers select materials that are highly motivating and with which children would choose to play. In addition, teachers closely monitor children's involvement in play as the context for educational activities. As children grow older, leisure time decreases and structured activities are more frequently scheduled into what was previously free time. For example, recess is replaced by scheduled academic lessons. Schoolwork even extends beyond the school day as homework is assigned and occupies increasing percentages of afterschool and weekend hours.

Responsibilities at home also change as we grow older. Young children are less competent to perform household chores and, therefore, are likely to be excused from many duties. However, teenagers in the household may carry important responsibilities; they may also receive clear messages that they are free to do as they wish when their jobs are done. Finally, for an adult, full-time employment further restricts time available for leisure—until retirement, when full-time leisure begins for a period of time that can potentially extend for 20 or more years.

Leisure time, therefore, involves what we do when we are free from other responsibilities. It also represents certain choices. First, we may choose what we do with our free time. We can also decide with whom to spend it. Those choices vary within different environments and domains. We may have friends at work, but our choice of friends is somewhat limited by whom our employer decides to hire. Friends are also made at school, but an administrator determines class schedules and teachers may decide who sits next to whom in the classroom. We may or may not make friends with other students in the classroom, and existing friends may or may not share classes with us. Teacher decisions on grouping and seating arrangements can have an important positive impact on children's friendships (Meyer & Henry, 1993) as well as restrict friendship choices. However, after school and on weekends, particularly as we grow older, we can choose whom to telephone and invite to play tennis, shop at the mall, or watch a video at home. Yet, again, these choices are almost invariably restricted by the opportunities made available to us.

What we do can be as important to our leisure time as with whom we do it. What do people do during leisure time? As children mature and learn how to establish friendships with their peers, they actively develop a personal repertoire of recreation activities to draw on during free time with those friends. Indeed, friendships may be made based on shared leisure preferences—two children who like to play video games may enjoy one another's company more than two children who do not share any such interests with one another. Some leisure choices involve solitary time—time to be alone and time to do preferred activities without any need to negotiate shared interests. A family may value time spent together in mutually enjoyable activities, but family members also appreciate times when each individual is free to pursue a personal interest. Indeed, parents may expect their children to become increasingly independent in occupying their leisure time without the need for parental involvement and supervision—either alone or with a peer, at home or outside the home. For any of this to happen, children must have a repertoire of leisure and recreation activities, and each of these activities involves a certain set of skills.

Therefore, whereas leisure and recreation involve personal enjoyment, friendships, play, and choice, they also involve learning skills, that is, *how to play*. Most children and adults can readily name a variety of play behaviors that they can do fairly well and enjoy doing. For most children, it may appear that a leisure repertoire develops "naturally" and no instruction is necessary. Parents, recreation professionals, and educators may, however, underestimate the extent to which children without disabilities learn and are taught to play, and they may not fully recognize the "play instruction" that is provided to children by "leisure educators," such as parents, siblings, teachers, classmates, and recreation professionals. One of the major arguments for inclusive schooling, for example, is that unless children with significant disabilities attend school with their classmates without disabilities, they will be deprived of the myriad of natural opportunities available to children and youth to learn social and play skills throughout their school careers (Meyer, 1991; Schleien, Cameron, Rynders, & Slick, 1988).

Most children seem to develop effortlessly a repertoire of leisure and recreation activities to use in different situations, with different family members and/or friends, and in different environments. Other children may seem to be at a loss under certain circumstances, or may even seem unable to entertain themselves under any circumstances. A child's parents may gradually become aware that, whereas an older sibling grew increasingly able to occupy his or her free time independently and constructively, this child cannot be left alone or with a friend even in what would seem to be the most enjoyable of play situations. Children and youth with significant disabilities may need direct support to develop a repertoire of play skills. More time and instructional power may be needed to establish these skills, just as is the case for other skill areas. In addition, it is important to ensure that these young people are also afforded the opportunities to develop leisure and recreation repertoires that are readily available to their peers without disabilities at school, in the neighborhood, and at home. This book is written to support such activities for these children and young people.

INFLUENCE OF LEGISLATION AND POLICY

Beginning in the mid-1970s, the need to provide recreation/leisure services for individuals with disabilities has received increased attention from lawmakers. For example, PL 94-142, the Education for All Handicapped Children Act of 1975, and its recent reauthorization, PL 101-476, the Individuals with Disabilities Education Act (IDEA), feature therapeutic recreation as a related service for persons with disabilities. Therapeutic recreation is devoted to facilitating the development, expression, and maintenance of an appropriate leisure lifestyle for individuals with physical, mental, emotional, or social limitations (National Therapeutic Recreation Society, 1982). Published federal regulations for rehabilitative services such as Section 504 of the Rehabilitation Act indicate the importance of recreation programs for individuals with disabilities. Several states' developmental disabilities plans designate recreation/leisure as a priority area for children and adults with developmental disabilities. Moreover, the President's Committee on Mental Retardation included recreation/leisure/social skills instruction as 1 of its 10 priority areas.

Viewed from another perspective, because large numbers of formerly institutionalized individuals have returned to their respective communities, it is important for them to have appropriate recreation and leisure skills for improving their quality of life and to prevent reinstitutionalization. At the same time, for individuals still living in large, residential facilities who have not yet been placed in family-style homes, acquisition of recreation skills is a positive avenue for developing collateral skills in social/friendship, motor, cognitive, and vocational domains. In other words, improved leisure skills pave the way for living in a less restrictive environment in the community.

WHAT TO TEACH IN LEISURE EDUCATION

Play activities or behaviors are organized into activity groupings or subsets that are often related to specific environments or skill levels of the individual (e.g., playing bocce is a lifelong sport typically for park and other outdoor environments). Being able to characterize how individuals spend their leisure time and identifying what an individual's actual leisure-time environments are like are important to the design of any leisure education program. This is particularly critical to the development of a lifelong leisure repertoire, which implies having access to a variety of activities and opportunities across the lifespan. But what does that variety look like? In their schema for leisure education, Wehman and Schleien (1981) grouped leisure skills into object manipulation (toy play), games, hobbies, and sports, and proposed that different skill levels are needed for different types of activities. Others have associated play with a domain or an environment, rather than a type of behavior, which is likely to be characterized by recreation/leisure activities appropriate to those environments (Ford et al., 1984). This book offers a perspective that recognizes the intersection of leisure with other domains, such as the combination of type of activity, people, and environment proposed for the leisure domain by Ford et al. (1989). This approach requires planning in each of the following goal areas (see Chapter 8 for the complete *Scope and Sequence* chart, which highlights these six major goal areas that characterize leisure and recreation opportunities):

School and extracurricular   Examples include looking at books (kindergarten), participating in sports (high school), and taking elective classes (transition ages 19–21 and adults).

Activities to do alone at home and in the neighborhood   Examples include reading and looking at books (primary), listening to music (middle school), and writing cards and letters (high school and adults).

Activities to do with family and friends at home and in the neighborhood   Examples include playing board games at different "levels" (e.g., Junior Trivial Pursuit for intermediate ages and Trivial Pursuit or Balderdash for high school and adult ages).

Physical fitness   Examples include participating in an exercise routine (primary), playing a sport regularly (middle school), and lifting weights (transition ages 19–21 and adults).

Activities to do with family and friends in the community   Examples include going to a fast-food restaurant (middle school) and going to a shopping mall with friends (high school and adults).

Activities to do alone in the community   Examples include going to the public library (all ages) and going for a drive (high school and adults).

Each of these orientations emphasizes a common feature of leisure and recreation: the value of play for individual development, adjustment, and personal enjoyment.

WHY LEISURE EDUCATION IS IMPORTANT

There is a great deal of evidence regarding the benefits of play and appropriate leisure activities (Dattilo, 1991; Meyer, Evans, Wuerch, & Brennan, 1985; Schleien, Green, & Heyne, 1993; Voeltz, Wuerch, & Wilcox, 1982; Wehman & Schleien, 1981). The following are some of the variables that relate to quality of life:

Play participation and increased leisure skills are related to increases in skill level in a variety of other curriculum areas. As a function of participation and instruction in play, collateral skill development has been documented for children in other areas such as language; problem solving; cognition; personal-social behavior; gross and fine motor skills; and, in older and higher functioning children, academics such as reading comprehension and mathematics (Voeltz & Apffel, 1981; Wehman & Schleien, 1981). The theory and writings of Vygotsky in particular highlight the potential value of play as the context for social interactions between children. Vygotsky (1978) and recent educational theorists building on his writings have proposed that virtually all higher order cognitive functions are facilitated through children's social interactions (Tharp & Gallimore, 1989). Play may be especially well suited to providing enhanced development in collateral skills because it allows continued practice of behaviors in a comfortable and pleasurable context (Schleien, Heyne, & Dattilo, 1995; Wehman, 1977; Wehman & Schleien, 1981).

Increases in play skills are related to decreases in negative and inappropriate excess behaviors. Unstructured time or "down time" can be risky because there are more opportunities for problem behaviors to occur—either by the child alone or during negative interactions with other children and adults. Children are not likely to remain inactive during free time; they need stimulation of some kind. If they do not have the skills and opportunity to engage in appropriate leisure and recreation activities during "down time," they are more likely to engage in higher rates of self-stimulatory behavior or other actions that are familiar and stimulating. For some individuals with significant disabilities, this may include engaging in excess behavior, such as stereotyped mannerisms, acting-out, or even self-injurious behavior. Constructive play has been shown to be negatively correlated with such excess behavior (Meyer, Evans, et al., 1985; Schleien, Kiernan, & Wehman, 1981). There are data documenting decreases in such problem behaviors as a function of implementing a positive or curricular approach to restructure the environment to teach alternate, incompatible positive behaviors (Gaylord-Ross, 1980; Kissel & Whitman, 1977; Meyer & Evans, 1989). Leisure activities have been documented as filling this programming need effectively.

Constructive use of leisure time is related to the success of persons with significant disabilities living in community environments. Parents and professional care providers in living environments often express dissatisfaction with the way people with significant disabilities use their leisure time, including a general feeling that young children are constantly "under foot" and cannot be left unsupervised for any length of time (Katz & Yekutiel, 1974; Marion, 1979; Van Deventer et al., 1981). The availability of respite care and access to a variety of community opportunities are identified by parents as major supports for keeping their children at home rather than seeking out-of-home placements (Cole & Meyer, 1989). Follow-up studies related to afterschool needs indicate that, in the past, persons with significant disabilities have had a restricted range of leisure activities; they were typically involved in passive pastimes such as watching television (Kishi, Teelucksingh, Zollers, Park-Lee, & Meyer, 1988). Furthermore, the types of leisure and recreation activities that had been supported in many school programs, such as bowling and other group sports including Special Olympics, simply were not available to individuals once they became adults and finished school unless they were independent in those skills (Dattilo, 1991; Schleien & Meyer, 1988). There is longstanding literature in developmental disabilities that relates success in community placements to adaptive behavior and, particularly, to the absence of a need for constant supervision (Cunningham & Presnall, 1978; Eyman & Call, 1977). If a leisure education program can prepare young people with significant disabilities to deal constructively and enjoyably with breaks in routine and free time in general, and thus reduce the need for supervision and control by others, community participation and inclusion could be greatly enhanced (Schleien & Ray, 1988).

Having a repertoire of enjoyable and preferred leisure and recreation activities is essential for quality of life and the development and maintenance of positive relationships with family and friends. Children and adults without disabilities enjoy access to a variety of play and leisure activity pursuits. These range from extracurricular school programs to community recreation programs offered after school, on weekends, and during the summer throughout the school years. These may be offered in formal clubs and recreation environments (e.g., parks, YMCAs, Jewish community centers, dance halls) for adults. No one is expected to justify his or her need to "play," and everyone has ample resources to enjoy preferred activities during breaks in designated responsibilities and tasks. Play should, perhaps, be ultimately justified simply as play. In the past, special educators, therapeutic recreation specialists, and adaptive physical educators focused on teaching students with significant disabilities the various skills that increase adaptation to the needs and demands of others and the environment. Just as persons without disabilities have the right to engage in preferred leisure-time activities during their free time, persons with disabilities must be guaranteed the same right.

As children grow older, they experience increased opportunities and support (chauffeuring by parents, taking the bus, driving a car, etc.) to get together with friends at one another's homes and in the community. Even computer dating services exist to assist people in locating partners and spouses. Clearly, any personal relationship—friendships, best friends, family, and intimate relationships with partners and spouses—are nurtured by opportunities to share enjoyable leisure time with one another and to explore mutual interests and activities. If a child with significant disabilities has no leisure skills and interests, or is prevented from participating in the kinds of leisure and recreation opportunities enjoyed by his or her peers, that child is also effectively being barred from many opportunities to develop friendships and other meaningful personal relationships. Surely, few dimensions of an individual's life could be as essential to the quality of that life as personal relationships with family and friends.

EXISTING PROGRAMS IN THE LEISURE DOMAIN

Longitudinal Leisure Skills for Severely Handicapped Learners: The Ho'onanea Curriculum Component (Wuerch & Voeltz, 1982), the first version of this curriculum, was undertaken to address particular leisure needs that were not adequately addressed in existing leisure curricula and programs. Some of the features of available programs that may continue to be problematic and/or be limited in their usefulness include:

1. The emphasis is on instruction for organized recreation and physical education activities outside the home and school or in specialized leisure environments, such as camping, swimming, Special Olympics, and field trips. These prescribed activities always require special organization, group participation, transportation, supervision, and continual expense. Such requirements seriously limit generalization to other environments, and these activities are often of limited usefulness to persons with significant intellectual disabilities in dealing constructively with daily leisure time. Little attention is given to activities that can occur across environments and in environments where many nonleisure activities are regularly conducted.
2. Programs designed for persons with disabilities emphasize instruction for group activities accompanied by organizational demands and dependence on additional resources. Special Olympics, for example, requires a substantial investment of money and volunteer time. Although many individuals continue to participate in such organized group activities, significant blocks of time in daily life do not conveniently fit into such slots. Leisure time includes periods when self-initiation is required and when other participants are not necessarily available.
3. Most available curricula assume entry-level skills higher than those of persons with significant disabilities and they lack adaptive alternatives for students with multiple, visual, motor, or hearing disabilities. Even specially prepared curricula are most often designed for per-

sons with moderate cognitive disabilities and require extensive branching for persons with severe and profound cognitive disabilities.

4. Available information still primarily emphasizes toys and games that are developmentally, but not chronologically, age appropriate for teenagers and adults. It is degrading for an adolescent or adult to play with a "baby toy" or a game that is clearly marked on the box "ages 3–6" (e.g., Candyland). Alternative activities must be identified that can be mastered with few entry-level skills and still be maximally useful for a number of years or throughout life.

5. The activities that are age appropriate and most likely to be encouraged are overwhelmingly passive ones, such as listening to music and watching television and videos. Other more active options are available to young people with significant disabilities to help broaden their leisure repertoires.

6. Available adapted activities are often predicated on relatively homogeneous functioning levels by all participants. For example, Special Olympics activities are designed for persons of similar skill levels competing against one another. Even the more recent "integrated" activities supported by Special Olympics (e.g., Unified Sports) are explicit in requiring that participants without disabilities be *matched* in skill level with participants who have disabilities. Activities are needed that can be enjoyed by two or more participants with differing skills, for example, a teenager with significant disabilities and a classmate or same-age neighbor who does not have a disability but is a friend.

7. Most materials that are designed for and that might be enjoyed by persons with multiple and significant disabilities are prohibitively expensive and difficult to obtain. Unlike the leisure materials available for children without disabilities—which may be inexpensive or expensive, but are readily available in most retail stores or at a friend's house—those suggested for persons with significant disabilities tend to require specialized knowledge of retail sources accessible only through special catalogs and often at considerable expense. In addition, because such materials are so specialized, they may not interest same-age peers or family members.

8. Available curricula tend to approach leisure education as an *instructional program* issue, rather than emphasizing the *affective dimensions* of one's leisure activities repertoire. A prevailing emphasis on skill performance can take the fun out of any activity, as many adults without disabilities can attest when asked why they no longer play the piano or run 10-kilometer races competitively, two activities that occupied major blocks of time throughout their school years. Furthermore, just as children without disabilities may compliantly engage in extracurricular activities identified for them by their parents and teachers, but choose to abandon those activities when they become autonomous, students with significant disabilities who are taught activities chosen by someone else are unlikely to enjoy those activities later in life. The end result will be a repertoire of "leisure" activities that the individual with disabilities views much like work and would virtually never engage in unless forced to do so. A commitment to choice making, preferences, and personal enjoyment must be a primary focus of any leisure activities curriculum component with lifelong implications.

9. None of the previously available curricula, including *Longitudinal Leisure Skills for Severely Handicapped Learners: The Ho'onanea Curriculum Component*, seriously acknowledged and explored leisure as the context for developing and supporting friendships and other meaningful personal relationships with peers. Ensuring that the leisure activities taught are age appropriate is an important first step in this process, but this is only the first step. Without participation in inclusive recreation, social, and educational activities, children and youths with disabilities are not afforded the variety and quality of opportunities for learning to play for *friendship's* sake. This also means that family input is critical to ensure that friendship

opportunities are culturally valued and sustainable at home, in school, and in the child's neighborhood once formal instruction has ended.

DEVELOPMENT OF THE LIFELONG LEISURE SKILLS CURRICULUM

The first version of this curriculum began as a federally funded project to develop and validate a leisure activities curriculum component that met the following three major goals:

1. For adolescents with significant disabilities, the goal was to demonstrate the acquisition of a repertoire of leisure activity skills that were age appropriate and readily available. Because the selected activities were already enjoyed by peers without disabilities, this shared repertoire was to enhance these individuals' positive relationships with family and friends.
2. The second goal was to develop a process to establish and support choice-making skills to ensure that individuals were learning and enjoying preferred leisure activity skills that they would choose during unstructured play periods of free time.
3. The goal for teachers, recreation professionals, parents, and other care providers was to facilitate a process of cooperative planning by all of the people involved in a leisure education component that would reflect a primary commitment in principle and practice to the purpose of leisure and play in an individual's life.

The project was referred to as *Ho'onanea*, which is Hawaiian for "to pass the time in ease, peace, and pleasure; to relax, absorbed, contented" (Pukui & Elbert, 1986). The original curriculum component was designed around a core of 10 leisure activities that were field-tested with 50 adolescents with disabilities who attended five different schools in Hawaii. The project was focused on designing a curriculum for adolescents because there seemed to be few materials available for teenagers with significant cognitive impairments compared with very young children. The disabilities of the original sample of students included mental retardation requiring extensive support, autism, severe emotional disturbance, and severe multiple disabilities.

The original curriculum component described in *Longitudinal Leisure Skills for Severely Handicapped Learners* was designed to meet particular leisure education needs of individuals with significant disabilities related to community adjustment in a variety of environments. It was not intended to address the full spectrum of leisure/recreation environments that should be systematically addressed. Instead, it focused on preparing young people to engage appropriately in leisure activities (all involving object manipulations) that would be appropriate for use during varying amounts of free time and that would occur throughout the day and in different environments. Such time periods could range from a few minutes to several hours in length, and might be referred to as "free time" (i.e., blocks of unobligated time that are either planned or occur sporadically) or "down time" (i.e., usually shorter segments of time that are breaks in scheduled routines or assigned tasks, such as brief time periods between instructional activities in the classroom). They might also occur in such environments as the home, school, a friend's house, or in the community. Finally, the activities in the original curriculum were primarily indoor, individual, and dyadic (intended for use by the individual and perhaps one other peer without disabilities playing together), and did not involve activities oriented toward physical activity.

This revised version of the curriculum includes 4 of the original 10 activities—6 of the activities were deleted because they are no longer available or popular, or because they are not appropriate for lifelong participation. In their places, six new activities have been added that emphasize peer play, community participation, and building lifetime skills, and that introduce an element of physical activity. These activities have been field tested with individuals with significant disabilities in community recreation and school programs throughout New York, Minnesota, and Michigan. Whereas we continue to emphasize developing a leisure repertoire that is age appropriate across the lifespan—rather than particular to the play of young children, and, thus, no longer appropriate when the young person becomes a teenager—many of these activities can indeed be started during the elementary school years. We have also expanded the focus of the curriculum to include new material on community leisure services and community recreation activities. Furthermore, this curriculum incorporates recent information about combining systematic instruction and opportunities for incidental learning in inclusive environments. At the same time, we have retained our focus on the design of a comprehensive, systematic leisure education program for individuals with significant disabilities. We do not assume that context (being in typical schools, classrooms, neighborhoods) or relationships with peers without disabilities are sufficient for a person with a significant intellectual impairment to master the skills involved in choice making or play—direct intervention and instruction are needed as well. Whereas we maintain that it is important to teach participation in leisure activities that are both enjoyed by peers without disabilities and readily available in the community, we also recognize that some participants present complex motor and sensory needs that must be accommodated. Therefore, a chapter has been added about incorporating most promising practices in integrated therapy with guidelines for adapting materials and instructional procedures.

Finally, as noted above, this book reflects a major focus on leisure-time activities as the context for developing friendships and supporting a variety of positive social relationships. Rather than leaving this outcome to chance, Chapter 8 describes a "focus group" process with an exemplary case study representing our most recent work on supporting friendships and positive relationships with others.

ACTIVITIES IN THE LEISURE EDUCATION CURRICULUM

Ten activities were selected and are presented in this curriculum to address the leisure education needs of students with significant disabilities at home and in the community.

Aerobic warm-ups	Pinball
Connect Four	Pottery
Jenga	Remote control vehicle
Magic Mitts (Scatch)	Simon
Nintendo Game Boy	Target games

These particular activities were selected as representative of those enjoyed by children, adolescents, and adults without disabilities during free time in typical leisure situations at home, at school, and in the community. We have provided detailed (and field-tested) task analyses only for these activities, but teachers, recreation professionals, and family members are encouraged to select similarly appropriate materials and activities that might be available in the future or might be particularly prominent in a certain region or community. The general instructional and support procedures described throughout this book can be used to design programs to teach any new leisure activity.

It was mentioned earlier that most existing play curricula involve activities that are appropriate for very young children; therefore, the activities cease to be typical when the individual grows older. A particular focus of both the first and the current versions of the curriculum is to identify materials and interactions that are considered appropriate throughout the lifespan. This means that instruction and activities that are started at an early age will continue to meet leisure-time needs as the child matures. To this end, activities were selected that are appropriate free-time activities for both young children and adults and that are adaptable for use in a variety of ways by participants who exhibit varying skill levels. Thus, the activities can be enjoyed at elementary and secondary age levels as well as throughout adulthood.

Our judgments that these activities are appropriate for use by teenagers with significant disabilities in particular are supported by our involvement with focus groups (see chap. 8, this volume) and two social validity evaluation procedures: 1) a field test was conducted in Hawaii public schools in which teenagers without disabilities participated with teenagers with significant disabilities in dyadic interactions that involved use of the leisure activities in this curriculum (this program attracted a range of teenagers without disabilities, who identified the activities as similar or identical to those that they engaged in with their "best" friends without disabilities) (Meyer & Kishi, 1985); and 2) in a study in which teenagers without disabilities, parents, and teachers made judgments about the appropriateness of the activities and behaviors exhibited by a sample of teenagers with significant disabilities, we found that the materials were judged appropriate and that youths who had been instructed to play appropriately with the materials were rated higher than both the same youths before instruction and youths who had not received instruction (Voeltz, Wuerch, & Bockhaut, 1982). Selection of the materials included in this book was based on feedback over the years regarding *Longitudinal Leisure Skills for Severely Handicapped Learners*, as well as input from our focus groups of teenagers and parents in Minneapolis, Minnesota, and Syracuse, New York, that the new list included socially popular and acceptable activities for teenagers and young adults in particular. The age appropriateness of the activities is supported by self-report and personal observation that peers without disabilities do indeed engage in these activities during their free time.

SKILL LEVEL REQUIREMENTS OF THE LEISURE EDUCATION CURRICULUM

The 10 activities in this curriculum were identified on the basis of their extreme skill level flexibility. Each of the instructional sequences was designed to include an entry-level phase that could be characterized as requiring no prerequisite skills in order for instruction to begin. The curriculum component was not designed only with persons who require minimal support in mind, nor do we assume that the participant will exhibit no motor or sensory disabilities. On the contrary, it was our intention to address the particular needs of individuals who have significant cognitive disabilities, and who may also exhibit one or more sensory or motor disabilities. Therefore, our original field-test sample of 50 teenagers, as well as the young people with whom the new activities have been field tested, include persons with very significant disabilities.

The participants with whom we have worked represent a range of functioning levels. The intent was to provide for each activity a set of instructional sequences that would progress from an activity component that could be used immediately with less skilled individuals to "higher" levels of play. Later, these same sequences could be used with less skilled individuals and more highly skilled individuals, as well as with friends without disabilities interacting with peers who have significant disabilities. Similarly, adaptations to accommodate motor and sensory disabilities were also validated in actual use with participants who have multiple disabilities; these are described in detail for both individual activities and across activities in Chapter 5, which focuses on integrated therapy applied to leisure education needs.

The original focus of this curriculum component was to meet a need in the lives of teenagers with significant disabilities and, to some extent, that continues to be our major emphasis. There are more materials and activities currently available for younger children with disabilities and for individuals with less significant disabilities than there are for teenagers and adults with significant disabilities. But even as our intention was to design a curriculum component to address the needs of these teenagers and adults, we also wish to offer a caveat: Teachers, parents, recreation professionals, and other care providers need to apply the "long view" to support the acquisition of new skills by young people with significant disabilities. Just as it has been short-sighted to teach play activities to young children that become stigmatizing once those children become teenagers, it would be equally short-sighted to teach exclusively "teenage" things that cannot be accessed beyond the secondary years. We have attempted to emphasize activities that have a *long life*—activities that can be enjoyed by young children, teenagers, and adults alike. This is a difficult and demanding order, and it should not preclude every child's participation in certain activities that their same-age peers enjoy even if they are quickly obsolete. Children should be allowed to be children regardless of whether they have disabilities. Yet, when we do engage in structured and systematic instructional efforts, we should take on the responsibility of looking into the future on behalf of the child. We must ensure that precious instruction time is not devoted exclusively to activities that meet the needs of the present only. Given the likelihood that children with significant disabilities will have increased natural opportunities for inclusion in daily activities enjoyed by children without disabilities as they attend inclusive community recreation programs and schools, we optimistically chose to assume the long-term view in writing this book. Thus, the emphasis in *Lifelong Leisure Skills and Lifestyles for Persons with Developmental Disabilities* is on leisure activities that address both current *and* future leisure environments.

PARENTAL INPUT AND CHOICE

Another major emphasis of this book is its focus on the personal preferences of both the participant and his or her family. Our emphasis on parental input throughout the decision-making and leisure instruction process is integral to even the initial assessment sequence. Because we have identified activities that should be maximally accessible at home and in the community, it is essential that these are indeed the types of activities that the participant's parent(s) values and will make available at home. They should, in fact, be the types of activities that other family members enjoy. Prior to implementing any leisure education curricular component for an individual, the recreation professional or teacher must coordinate planning with the family and other care providers to ensure that they have a commitment to follow through with leisure opportunities when leisure skills develop.

Finally, the individual's personal preferences are accommodated throughout the design and implementation of the leisure education plan. This begins with an assessment procedure to assist in the initial selection of activities that the individual truly enjoys, rather than those that someone else decides would be "good for him or her." We assume that if the individual has selected an activity that he or she truly prefers, no persuasion or artificial incentives are necessary to encourage engagement in that activity during free time. Finding a reliable way to identify personal preferences of persons with significant disabilities is a difficult process when the individual has few communication skills and is not known to communicate particular choices. Thus, the procedures we developed (see Chapter 6) can also be used to identify and teach the expression of choices in other domains as well as in leisure education.

The Participant Interest Inventory procedure (Form 2.3, Chapter 2) can be used at any time during instruction as well when it seems necessary to check whether a change in interest might have occurred. For example, a participant could appear interested in a new activity during the initial inventory procedure, but after a few weeks of instruction, the individual may have changed his or her mind about the activity (accompanied by no progress on the skill acquisition sequences). Repeating the interest assessment procedure provides a quick check on whether preferences have remained the same or they have changed. In addition, the choice instruction procedures (see Chapter 6)—built on the foundation of personal preferences—incorporate strategies that: 1) teach individuals to initiate leisure activities appropriately, 2) promote spontaneous and meaningful choices of activities during leisure time, and 3) provide the leisure educator with an independent measure of preferences and enjoyment that can assist in making future instruction decisions. These choice instructional procedures have been validated through field testing and single-subject experimental investigations (Meyer, Evans, et al., 1985; Voeltz & Wuerch, 1981b). Furthermore, the choices that participants make as a function of these instructional procedures can be reliably correlated with meaningful leisure experiences by the individual.

Chapter 2

APPROPRIATE LEISURE
ACTIVITIES SELECTION

*B*efore a participant can be taught to function independently during leisure time, the leisure educator (e.g., certified therapeutic recreation specialist, parent/guardian, classroom teacher) must identify and select activities and materials appropriate for the participant and describe how these activities will be used by him or her. The leisure activities and their instructional objectives described in this book were selected and field-tested using a problem-solving approach. By implementing this approach, a leisure educator can identify and select activities that are appropriate for individual participants in particular recreation environments.

IDENTIFYING POTENTIAL LEISURE ACTIVITIES

Activities that are already in the participant's school, home, and/or community, as well as those that can be easily purchased from nearby stores or through catalogs, should be examined first. At this point in the selection process, the leisure educator does not have to evaluate each activity according to a strict set of criteria; he or she need only make a "best guess" as to whether or not the activity will meet the leisure functioning needs of the participant. The leisure educator should ask, *"What existing leisure activities might the participant enjoy and interact with during his or her free time in current and future leisure environments?"* regardless of whether the participant currently possesses the skills needed to manipulate these materials.

In answering this question, the leisure educator should consult people who spend time with and know the participant—parents and other individuals close to the participant, siblings, teachers, therapeutic recreation specialists, adaptive physical education specialists, physical therapists, speech pathologists, and so forth. Because much of the leisure time of individuals with developmental disabilities often occurs in the home, an assessment of parental preferences for their child's recreation activities is often crucial to the success of any leisure education program (Schleien & Ray, 1988; Voeltz & Apffel, 1981). Environmental resources (e.g., space, finances, transportation); people resources (i.e., individuals with whom the participant spends his or her leisure time); and family values and preferences for specific types of activities (i.e., those frequently enjoyed and thought to be worthwhile by family members) all determine, to some extent, the number of opportunities the participant will have to practice and continue to enjoy learned leisure skills (Ford et al., 1989; Rynders & Schleien, 1991; Schleien & Ray, 1988; Voeltz & Wuerch, 1981a; Wehman & Schleien, 1980a).

For example, parents and other individuals close to the participant should be asked:

1. What leisure activities are already in the home, including other family members' toys, games, and equipment?
2. What leisure activities does the participant appear interested in, even if he or she does not currently know how or is not permitted to do them?

3. What does the participant currently do during his or her free time?
4. What are the participant's favorite activities?

It may be helpful to parents if the participant's classroom teacher provides them with a list of specific leisure activities already available in the classroom or under consideration for purchase. Then, parents could be asked to estimate their son's or daughter's interest in these activities and to rate their appropriateness as potential leisure activities.

This parental information can be obtained informally through the usual communications between the teacher and parents, or the teacher may want to be more formal and use the Home Leisure Activities Survey (Form 2.1). The teacher may send this survey home for the parents to complete and return, or he or she may conduct a telephone interview and record the parents' responses on the form.

ASSESSING THE ACTIVITY'S APPROPRIATENESS

Once an array of potentially appropriate activities has been identified, the leisure educator should then assess the appropriateness of each activity according to a set of criteria that relate to "educational best practices." Using the Leisure Activity Selection Checklist (Form 2.2), the leisure educator can determine if an activity is appropriate for a particular participant or group of participants and can compare the relative appropriateness of various activities. On this checklist, 14 criteria are arranged into three broad areas of concern: 1) lifestyle, 2) individualization, and 3) environmental.

The *lifestyle* criteria focus on selecting leisure activities that would be considered appropriate by society—activities that would be regarded as valid and worthwhile by the people with whom the individual with a disability comes into contact. This area of concern addresses the need for activities and skills that could increase the opportunities for a participant with a disability to take part in the more complex leisure activities and social interactions that exist in the community. Thus, the questions in this area ask about the activity's appeal to peers without disabilities and its adaptability to the types of play situations and relationships with peers and care providers that are likely to be encountered by persons with *and* without disabilities.

The *individualization* criteria focus on selecting leisure activities that meet the unique needs and skill repertoires of participants with disabilities. This area of concern is the one usually emphasized, focusing on the entry-level skills and the disabilities of participants. Whereas the selected activities are, therefore, usually appropriate for these levels and abilities, this emphasis has, unfortunately, often led to the selection of either preschool toys or expensive specialized equipment—neither of which peers without disabilities are likely to play with during their leisure time. Implicit in these individualization criteria is our belief that, regardless of a participant's current functioning level, chronological age–appropriate activities should be made available. It would probably be unrealistic to suppose that a person with a developmental disability can always interact with such age-appropriate activities in the same manner and to the same degree as his or her friends without disabilities; however, through specific skill instruction and/or modifications to the materials and procedures, or even to the goals and instructional objectives themselves, varying skill levels can be accommodated and each individual can participate maximally.

Individualization concerns also address the need for activities that are not only appropriate for the participant's chronological age, but also encourage the participant to be actively involved in play. In this way, we rely on the activity materials themselves to prompt and maintain appropriate interactions between participants rather than on instructional cues and positive reinforcement provided by the leisure educator. This requires the identification of activities that have their own reinforcing characteristics, and are, therefore, most likely to hold the person's interest, such

Home Leisure Activities Survey

Participant: _Dana Johnson_ Date: _9/5/94_ Completed by: _Suzanne Johnson (mother)_

1. Please list any leisure activities available in your home, including other children's toys and games, in which your child has shown some interest.

   Connect Four, Jenga, Nintendo Game Boy, puzzles, toy piano

2. What are your child's favorite leisure activities?

   puzzles, playing ball, swimming, going for rides in the car

3. What does your child typically do during his or her free time?

   watch TV, play with puzzles, listen to the radio, scribble with paper and crayons

4. Can you list some indoor or outdoor activities your family enjoys doing together? (Please list these by beginning with those you most prefer.)

   camping, fishing, horseback riding

5. Are there any special space or transportation needs that we should consider in planning leisure or recreation activities for your child?

6. People resources: Are there other people in the home who spend leisure time with your child? Who are they and what would you like your child to be able to do with these persons? _Dana's brother and 2 sisters play with her — I'd like Dana to be able to sit for maybe 15 minutes without breaking and grabbing toys. She also will tantrum and cry when she can't get her way, which makes her hard to get along with._

7. Which of these activities are available in the home?

✓ Nintendo Game Boy	— Pottery	— Simon
— Pinball Games	— Remote Control Toys	— Target Games
✓ Jenga		
— Magic Mitts (Scatch)		
✓ Aerobics		
✓ Connect Four		

8. Please assign a rating to each activity to indicate how interesting you think your child would find the activity.

   1 = not very interesting; 2 = somewhat interesting; 3 = very interesting

3 Nintendo Game Boy	3 Pottery	2 Simon
2 Pinball Games	2 Remote Control Toys	1 Target Games
3 Jenga		
3 Magic Mitts (Scatch)		
1 Aerobics		
3 Connect Four		

9. Which of these activities is your child permitted to play with?

✓ Nintendo Game Boy	✓ Pottery	✓ Simon
✓ Pinball Games	✓ Remote Control Toys	✓ Target Games
✓ Jenga		
✓ Magic Mitts (Scatch)		
✓ Aerobics		
✓ Connect Four		

10. Which of these activities do you feel are appropriate leisure-time activities for your child?

✓ Nintendo Game Boy	✓ Pottery	✓ Simon
✓ Pinball Games	✓ Remote Control Toys	✓ Target Games
✓ Jenga		
✓ Magic Mitts (Scatch)		
✓ Aerobics		
✓ Connect Four		

Leisure Activity Selection Checklist

Participant: __Dana Johnson__ Date: __9/10/94__ Completed by: __Amy Selemister__

Instructions: For each activity circle "yes" or "no" for each criterion. Tally the number of "yes" responses for each of these subsections and record them on the appropriate line. Tally the overall score for each activity. Activities that receive a score of 11 to 14 points are generally considered appropriate for instruction.

	Game Boy Activity	Connect Four Activity	Jenga Activity
Lifestyle: A concern for selecting activities that are socially valid and that will facilitate typical play and leisure behaviors, as well as provide opportunities for increasingly complex interactions.			
1. *Age Appropriateness.* Is this activity something a peer without a disability would enjoy during free time?	yes · no	yes · no	yes · no
2. *Attraction.* Is this activity likely to promote interest of others who frequently are found in the participant's leisure-time environments?	yes · no	yes · no	yes · no
3. *Environment Flexibility.* Can this activity be used in a variety of potential leisure-time situations on an individual and group basis?	yes · no	yes · no	yes · no
4. *Degree of Supervision.* Can the activity be used under varying degrees of caregiver supervision without major modifications?	yes · no	yes · no	yes · no
5. *Longitudinal Application.* Is use of the activity appropriate for both an adolescent and an adult?	yes · no	yes · no	yes · no
Individualization: Concerns related to logistical and physical demands of leisure activities on current and future environments and free-time situations.			
1. *Skill Level Flexibility.* Can the activity be adapted for low- to high-entry skill levels without major modifications?	yes · no	yes · no	yes · no
2. *Prosthetic Capabilities.* Can the activity be adapted to varying disabilities (sensory, motor, behavior)?	yes · no	yes · no	yes · no
3. *Reinforcement Power.* Is the activity sufficiently novel or stimulating to maintain interest?	yes · no	yes · no	yes · no
4. *Preference.* Is the participant likely to prefer and enjoy the activity?	yes · no	yes · no	yes · no
Environmental: Concerns related to logistical and physical demands of leisure activities on current and future environments and free-time situations.			
1. *Availability.* Is the activity available (or can it easily be made so) across the participant's leisure environments?	yes · no	yes · no	yes · no
2. *Durability.* Is the activity likely to last without need for major repair or replacement of parts for at least a year?	yes · no	yes · no	yes · no
3. *Safety.* Is the activity safe (i.e., would not pose a serious threat to or harm the participant, others, or the environment if abused or used inappropriately)?	yes · no	yes · no	yes · no
4. *Noxiousness.* Is the activity not likely to be overly noxious (noisy, space consuming, distracting) to others in the participant's leisure environments?	yes · no	yes · no	yes · no
5. *Expense.* Is the cost of the activity reasonable? That is, is it likely to be used for multiple purposes?	yes · no	yes · no	yes · no
Area of Concern Scores 1. Lifestyle 2. Individualization 3. Environmental	5 / 3 / 4	5 / 4 / 5	5 / 4̶5̶ / 5
Total Activity Score	12	14	14

16

as materials that produce lights, sounds, movements, tactile sensations, and so forth. We refer to these materials as "reactive" materials. Thus, the questions in this area ask about the activity's intrinsic appeal to the participant, personal preference for the activity, and its adaptability to various levels of skills and participation.

The *environmental* criteria focus on selecting leisure activities that can be easily used in a variety of leisure environments and situations. This area of concern addresses the need for activities whose logistical and physical demands do not overburden the leisure educator to such an extent that it becomes more trouble to have the participant play with these activities than not to play with them. Thus, the questions in this area address such practical matters as the activity's cost, availability, durability, safety, and potential for disturbing other people who are with the participant.

To use this checklist, the leisure educator must rate each activity on all 14 criteria and then determine those activities that may be appropriate, which are generally those activities that receive 11 points or more in the total activity score. The leisure educator may even rank the activities by comparing the scores and dropping those on the low end of the scale. However, if there are one or more criteria that are particularly relevant to an individual's unique characteristics, such as the adaptability potential of an activity for an individual with mobility problems, the leisure educator must make sure that any activity selected scores high in these areas.

ASSESSING PARTICIPANT INTEREST

The Leisure Activity Selection Checklist (Form 2.2) can inform a leisure educator whether or not an activity is appropriate for a participant's age and skills. It also takes into consideration whether or not the activity is something the participant will actually enjoy and prefer. It is critical that the activities used in the instruction sessions be preferred or of high interest because we assume that a student will be more likely to choose from and play independently with activities he or she prefers—important goals of this curriculum. The third step the leisure educator should take in selecting leisure activities, therefore, is to assess a participant's interest in those leisure activities already rated as appropriate. Assessing the preferences of persons with disabilities may be easy when they have strong preferences and make them very obvious by expressing them verbally or grabbing and seeking out one activity and wandering away from another activity. Assessment can, however, be more difficult with persons with severe developmental disabilities for two reasons. First, they often have difficulty expressing and communicating their likes and dislikes. Their disabilities may limit their means of communication and increase the time it takes them to respond. Their responses may also be regarded as inappropriate—either excessive or imperceptible—by others around them. Second, persons with significant disabilities may have difficulty identifying their feelings and discriminating between emotions due to restricted language repertoires and the fact that their emotional needs often are not incorporated in their educational programs. The Participant Interest Inventory (Form 2.3) provides a simple yet effective method of obtaining information about the activity preferences of participants with developmental disabilities and is especially suitable for nonvocal participants.

This inventory is based on the assumptions that: 1) inner feelings are reflected in outward behaviors, and 2) there is a correlation between the level of interest and enjoyment and certain outward behaviors. If a person moves toward the play materials, it is assumed that he or she is interested in them; if a person moves away, it is assumed that he or she is not interested in them. If a person smiles when the activity lights up, it is assumed that he or she is enjoying the activity; if the individual frowns, it is assumed that he or she is not enjoying the activity. Furthermore, if a person does not display any of these opposing types of behaviors and ignores the activity's presence, it is not really known whether that person likes or dislikes the activity, but it

Participant Interest Inventory

Participant: Dana Johnson

Instructions: For each activity, complete each of the sentences below by placing the number of the description that best matches the participant's behavior in the appropriate box for that activity.

	Game Boy	Connect Four	Verga	Magic Mitts	Pinball
Date	9/10/94	9/10/94	9/10/94	9/10/94	9/10/94
Rater	Amy	Amy	Amy	Amy	Amy
A. For this participant's usual level of *interest* in play materials, he or she is: 1. Not as interested as usual 2. About as interested as usual 3. More interested than usual	3	3	3	3	3
B. For this participant's usual level of *physical interaction* with materials (pushing control buttons, turning knobs, putting things together, etc.), he or she is: 1. Not as busy as usual 2. About as busy as usual 3. Busier than usual	2	3	3	3	3
C. For this participant's usual *affective* behaviors (smiling, signs of enjoyment, etc.), he or she seems to be: 1. Enjoying this less than usual 2. Showing about the same amount of enjoyment as usual 3. Enjoying this more than usual	3	3	3	3	3
D. For this participant's usual level of *looking or visual regard* of an activity, object, or person, he or she is: 1. Not looking as much as usual 2. Looking as much as usual 3. Looking more often or longer than usual	3	3	2	3	3
E. Compared to this participant's *usual behavior* during a short period of time with minimal supervision, he or she is: 1. Engaging in more negative behavior than usual 2. Engaging in about the same amount of negative behavior as usual 3. Engaging in less negative (or off-task) behavior than usual	2	3	2	3	3
Activity Interest Scores: (Total the numbers in each column)	13	15	13	15	15

18

is often assumed that such indifference is more of a negative than a positive response to the activity.

To assess a participant's preferences accurately, the leisure educator must know that participant's behavior very well. The items in the inventory do not quantify the observable behaviors—the amount of time the participant interacts with the activity, the number of times he or she touches the pieces, and so forth—because the range, rate, and frequency of behaviors exhibited by persons with disabilities vary so much (as they do for anyone). Whereas 1 minute of interaction may be the usual level of play for one participant, 15 minutes may be the norm for another. Therefore, it is up to the leisure educator to make the comparisons with the participant's usual behaviors and to quantify these behaviors on the inventory. In addition, if a participant's reactions are usually slow and/or imperceptible, the leisure educator must be even more keen in his or her observations. If a participant has a significant motor disability, a slight stiffening of the body when the play material emits a sound may be the person's only acknowledgment of the activity's presence. For a participant who usually does not touch or even face such materials, a brief side glance may be the only sign that he or she prefers an activity. In fact, we have discovered that self-stimulatory behavior with the leisure materials (e.g., repeatedly tapping the top of the pinball machine) may be a communicative response to a preferred activity.

To make an accurate assessment, the leisure educator must also be aware that behaviors that might be considered negative in other situations may actually be positive in this situation because they indicate preference for an activity. This inventory purposely tries to avoid placing value judgments on the types of interactions with the activity shown by the participant. Whether a participant displays such positive behaviors as stacking one wooden Jenga block upon another as hoped for in the instructional objective, or displays such negative behaviors as mouthing the block or repetitively banging it on the table, all of these behaviors should be counted as "touching" the activity. For the purpose of this assessment, the leisure educator should distinguish between the negative behaviors that *do not relate* to the activity. Thus, if the participant is engaged in a self-stimulatory behavior (e.g., body rocking) without looking at or touching the activity, the leisure educator *should not* complete the inventory. However, if the participant is rocking his or her body while looking at the activity, the leisure educator *should* complete the inventory. Granted, it is not always easy to tell whether a participant is or is not looking at an activity while he or she is body rocking, and a leisure educator may well wonder if a participant really knows what object is being banged on the table. Yet, results from a study conducted by Voeltz and Wuerch (1981b) suggest that although some self-stimulatory behaviors (body rocking, finger flicking, arm flapping, etc.) are correlated with low levels of interest and appropriate play, other self-stimulatory behaviors involving the leisure activity materials (e.g., repetitive banging of Lego pieces on the table, ritualistic finger tapping on top of the pinball machine) are often correlated with both high levels of attending to the leisure activities and preference (see also Meyer, Evans, Wuerch, & Brennan, 1985). For participants who are being introduced to a particular activity for the first time and who cannot be expected to know how to manipulate the materials appropriately without direct instruction, these self-stimulatory behaviors may actually show interest in the activity and represent attempts to play rather than negative behaviors in need of intervention.

Of course, the leisure educator should judge when negative behaviors, even if they are related to the activity, become too intense and must be stopped even before the 2 minutes of observation are finished. The leisure educator should never tolerate destructive behaviors that are likely to result in injury to the participant and others around him or her, or that are likely to cause damage to the environment or leisure activity.

At least three different leisure activities should be rated on the inventory by the leisure educator. If many appropriate activities have been identified and the leisure educator does not wish to assess a participant's interest in all of them, the leisure educator may simply make a "best guess" or use any information supplied by the parents or others to determine which three to five activities to inventory. Factors such as illness, medication, and behavior incidents preceding exposure to the activities may greatly influence a participant's behavior during these observation sessions. Therefore, to ensure that decisions regarding a participant's preferences are based on a representative sample of behavior, the leisure educator should schedule these observation sessions appropriately.

To assess a participant's leisure interests, it is often beneficial for individuals from a participant's home, school, workplace, and/or community to work together. For example, parents can either simultaneously observe and rate the participant with a teacher in the classroom or conduct another Participant Interest Inventory (Form 2.3) in the home. Parental involvement should be encouraged because parents are likely to be most familiar with the way the participant expresses interest and enjoyment, as well as how the participant typically behaves during play situations.

The activities that score the highest on the inventory are most likely to be the activities that the participant prefers; therefore, the leisure educator should proceed to instruct the participant on how to play with these activities. Once instruction is underway, however, the leisure educator may occasionally repeat (e.g., once per month) the Participant Interest Inventory to evaluate whether or not a particular activity still interests the participant. This is especially useful when, despite instructional program changes, the participant does not progress in acquiring the necessary skills or the participant's behavior becomes resistive. If the participant's interest in the activity rates lower in this second assessment than in the initial one, the leisure educator may decide to discontinue instruction on that activity. Unlike other curriculum areas where it is unlikely that an instructor would cease instruction simply because a participant resists the activity or displays uncooperative behavior, in leisure education, clues regarding a participant's lack of interest *should* signal a need to find another activity, because it is imperative that the activities taught are preferred and enjoyed by the participant.

ASSESSING CURRENT LEISURE FUNCTIONING

Once appropriate and preferred leisure activities are identified, the fourth step in the selection process is to assess the participant's current skills and functioning level, and compare them with the skills needed for appropriate and independent interactions with the activities. Two different assessment procedures can be applied to provide the leisure educator with this information: 1) conduct a discrepancy analysis (Certo, Schleien, & Hunter, 1983; Ford et al., 1989), and 2) baseline on a predetermined instructional sequence.

A discrepancy analysis is most useful when a written sequence of skills describing normalized appropriate activity interactions is not available, and when it is used with *chained* leisure activities. In chained leisure activities such as pinball games, Game Boy, and various target games, the skills and sequences in which they must be performed are quite rigid. The participant must learn to perform a complete list of responses in precisely the order specified or else the activity will not work. For example, in pinball games, the machine must be turned on, a ball must be released into the playing area, and the flippers must be manipulated when the ball is within the designated striking range.

Because these chains of individualized behaviors are seldom conveniently organized in sequences that progress from easy to difficult, more traditional baseline procedures that assume this progression in an instructional sequence would not be applicable. Instead, the leisure educator exposes the participant with a disability to the same activity, attempts to elicit performance of each step, and notes *discrepancies* between what the participant can currently do versus how each step is performed by a skilled peer. Thus, in a discrepancy analysis, there may not be any crucial sequence of instructions, but the discrepancies mark those skills or steps in the behavior chain that require instruction and/or adaptations so that the participant can learn to play independently in the activity. In some cases, the adaptation involves bypassing a step or starting the game over a second time rather than continuing on to steps that require maximum support.

A discrepancy analysis is also useful for identifying leisure-related support skills—skills required for initiating a leisure activity, choosing an activity to play with, maintaining and caring for activity materials, and so forth. By observing what the participant does immediately before and after participating in the activity, the leisure educator can include in the participant's program those related support skills that the participant lacks.

When a written instructional sequence of skills for a leisure activity already exists, the leisure educator may be able to use traditional baseline procedures to assess the participant's current functioning level. In this curriculum, task analyses are already provided for several chained leisure activities (target games, pinball games, Game Boy), and the leisure educator does not need to observe the performance of a participant without a disability on each of the steps of the task analysis.

Progressive leisure activities also lend themselves well to a baseline assessment procedure. Progressive activities, such as Simon, remote control vehicle, Jenga, Connect Four, pottery, and aerobics, are more flexible than chained activities in the sense that an instructional sequence can be specifically designed to progress from easy to difficult. There are identifiable key responses necessary for appropriate interactions with progressive activities, but there are not necessarily any "correct" ways to play these games or manipulate these materials. For example, stacking is a key response that must be repeatedly used in playing with Jenga, but many different shapes may be built with the same pieces. A task-analyzed instructional sequence can be deliberately designed for these activities as a series of phases and steps within each phase that progress from easy to difficult. The purpose of baselining on these activities is to determine within this hierarchy of phases the particular phase at which the participant cannot perform the steps independently and therefore requires leisure skills instruction.

A common method of conducting a baseline is to take a "best guess" at the participant's placement within the phases and then probe forward and backward between phases. A strategy we recommend is to begin with a phase the leisure educator expects the participant to be able to do successfully. This provides the individual with opportunities for success during a baseline session. Baselining is essentially a testing situation, and, as such, is potentially stressful for participants with long histories of failure. It is, therefore, important that the leisure educator reward attending behavior, subtle response attempts, and cooperation interactions. The leisure educator should always keep in mind that leisure is a time for enjoyment. Table 2.1 outlines the recommended baselining procedures used to assess a participant's placement with the phases of the progressive leisure activities included in the curriculum component found in Chapter 4.

DEVELOPING GOALS AND OBJECTIVES

At this point in the selection process, the leisure educator should have a clear idea of which leisure activities to implement with a particular individual and how that person functions in these activities. Yet, before the leisure educator can effectively teach functional and appropriate play skills, he or she needs to develop and select goals and instructional objectives appropriate for that participant. In this final step in the selection process, the leisure educator should ask, "After I instruct the participant, what should that participant be able to do with the activity that he or she cannot do now?" If the participant is school age, the answers to that question can then be incorporated into the participant's individualized education program (IEP). For an adult,

Table 2.1.   Guidelines for conducting a baseline session for progressive activities

1. Arrange an instructional environment as specified in the instructional procedures for the particular activity.

2. Provide a general cue indicating free time and model the sequence or responses listed under the first phase of the task analysis.

3. Provide the cue a second time and also cue the participant to play with the activity.

4. Allow a few seconds for the participant to initiate interactions with the activity.

    a. If the participant does begin playing, observe and record the participant's responses that match any of the responses in the phase.

       If the participant correctly performs 80% (or whatever percentage the leisure educator decides on) of the responses on the first attempt, move to the next phase and repeat the process until the participant fails to meet the criterion.

       Begin instruction on the first step of the phase below the 80% criterion. (For the exception, read p. 32 about backward chaining.)

    b. If the participant does not initiate play, do not score any responses.

       Begin instruction on Step 1 of Phase I. (For the exception, read p. 32 about backward chaining.)

---

these goals and objectives could become part of the individualized habilitation plan (IHP) or individualized program plan (IPP).

Educational goals are broad statements describing in general terms the intended outcomes of the person's participation in a leisure education program. An instructional objective is also a statement of the intended participant outcomes; however, the objective differs from the goal mainly in its scope and specificity. An instructional objective provides the details of how a goal is operationally defined for each participant, and it focuses on a reliable, measurable, and/or observable participant behavior that may be only one example of all the possible behaviors encompassed by the goal. One goal of the *Lifelong Leisure Skills and Lifestyles* curriculum is that the participant will learn how to enjoy a leisure activity. This goal can be made more specific by a variety of instructional objectives, such as: 1) the participant will look at and touch the leisure activity, 2) the participant will look at and smile at the activity while a peer manipulates the materials, or 3) the participant will participate in the activity in the exact manner as a peer without a disability.

The overall goal of this leisure education curriculum component is that the participant will acquire and then use appropriate leisure skills that will enable him or her to make personally meaningful leisure choices. Yet, the term *appropriate* is a relative term. Ideally, it would be defined to imply that the participant would learn to play in exactly the same manner as a peer without a disability; however, this is not always a realistic goal for participants with developmental disabilities because of significant cognitive delays (e.g., the participant cannot count points and keep score) or sensory and motor impairments (e.g., the participant cannot grasp and manipulate a playing piece).

When these disabilities must be considered in formulating goals and objectives, the leisure educator should first analyze the activity to determine the minimum skills necessary for the participant to enjoy and independently interact with the activity. For example, counting the number of points scored in a pinball game is not crucial to playing the game, but turning the machine on, pulling and releasing the ball-release knobs, watching the balls' movements, flipping the flippers, and turning the machine off *are* essential component skills. In addition to minimizing the number of steps, the leisure educator may also identify alternative ways to manipulate the activity materials or modify the materials themselves so that the participant can still play in a functional manner and independently. For example, for a participant with cerebral palsy who cannot hold a Game Boy system with one hand while manipulating the buttons and controls with the other, the system unit can be stabilized by gluing Velcro to the back and sides of the unit as well as to a slanted or vertical display board at the appropriate eye level for the participant.

Even with these modifications, however, sometimes *appropriate* cannot be defined to include complete independence for a particular participant. In some instances, it may be necessary to redefine the participant's use of the activity to reflect partial participation (Ford et al., 1989). In these cases, the leisure educator must identify the maximum number of skills the participant is able to learn as well as ways to help the participant gain access to the enjoyable aspects of the activity. The parent, teacher, therapeutic recreation specialist, or peer without a disability can then assist the participant with any skills he or she cannot perform independently. Whereas this is a positive strategy to ensure that a participant is not excluded from enjoying a truly preferred activity, it should not be a substitute for finding at least some leisure activities that the participant can enjoy and play with independently.

When the leisure educator determines the skills that a participant needs to learn, he or she must also specify the conditions and criteria for mastery of those skills. The more precise the instructional objective—details about the materials and assistance given to the participant, the environment in which the participant is expected to perform the skills, the acceptable level of performance the participant will display—the easier it is to collect data and use these data to evaluate the participant's performance accurately and make instructional decisions.

In determining the conditions and criteria, the leisure educator should be specific enough so that two people could agree (i.e., reliability) as to whether or not the objective has been met. The conditions, however, should be written to reflect authentic leisure situations or the natural play environment, not merely instructional environments. For example, rather than "Given a one-to-one instructional environment with the participant seated at an individual work station and the cue 'stack the Jenga blocks'. . . ," the leisure educator might state: "Given a naturally occurring free-time period during the participant's day and one of the cues 'free time,' 'go play,' 'pick something to play with'. . . ." Likewise, performance criteria should be written to reflect the actual performance demands of a particular participant's leisure-time situations and activities. Independent participation in some activities requires a high degree of accuracy for the activity to work. For example, the participant must press a colored lens within 5 seconds or the Simon game will not progress. For such activities, the leisure educator might establish the criterion of "90% of the trials correct." For activities such as Jenga, where there is no one correct way to play and there are many objects to build, the leisure educator might want the criterion to reflect a response (stacking blocks, removing blocks from stack, loading stacking tray, etc.) for a duration that corresponds to the participant's usual length of free time. For example, "Given free time during the school day, a verbal cue indicating that the participant can play ('free time,' 'go play'), and a participant decision to play with Jenga, the participant will independently acquire the activity materials and play appropriately (load tray, remove blocks, stack blocks) for 10 minutes."

The instructional objectives included in Chapter 4 for the 10 activities constituting the *Lifelong Leisure Skills and Lifestyles* curriculum are provided merely as starting points for the leisure educator to use when writing instructional objectives for his or her students. These instructional objectives are broadly stated and are not intended to be adopted as presented here. The leisure educator should include specific conditions and performance criteria, and the final objectives should reflect a consideration of the unique needs and preferences of the individual, the naturally occurring conditions associated with the participant's free time, and the actual performance demands of these situations and the particular activity.

The selection of appropriate leisure activities can be a very time-consuming process; however, if the leisure educator lays the groundwork carefully so that the activity and the participant are well matched before any leisure skills instruction takes place, the instruction will be more effective and beneficial.

Chapter 3

INSTRUCTION FOR
SKILL ACQUISITION

This chapter provides the leisure educator with the methods and strategies for teaching participants with significant disabilities to appropriately use the leisure-time activities of this curriculum component. Specific instructional procedures and a task analysis, with possible branches and modifications, are given for each activity after the general strategies are described. If the leisure educator chooses other activities for a leisure education program, he or she can also use these procedures and task analyses as guidelines. In addition to the information included here on providing systematic leisure instruction to learners who require a great deal of assistance to acquire skills, we have also included some general guidelines to support incidental learning and practice in leisure skills through play with same-age peers and friends.

FREE TIME AND ACTIVITY CUES

The ultimate purpose of leisure activities instruction is to teach the participant to play in age-appropriate ways—without the supervision or direction of a parent or individual close to the participant—with preferred leisure activities whenever free time occurs. This means that the first critical skill for the participant is recognizing that free time is available. Once this free-time period is recognized, the individual must also have a strategy to indicate activity preferences during that free time.

The cues that generally indicate the existence of free time can be extremely subtle (e.g., absence of any other activity, cessation of a task or stimulus). Others are more straightforward (e.g., a parent tells his or her child to "Go play" or "I'm busy making dinner. Please entertain yourself for awhile, okay?"). Learners with significant cognitive impairments may not readily learn to play in response to the more subtle cues that free time exists, and may require some prompting indefinitely to initiate leisure activities appropriately. In the original *Ho'onanea* field tests, we were able to teach virtually all individuals—regardless of the severity of their intellectual disability—to initiate play in response to a verbal or nonvocal communicative cue such as "You have free time" or "Play." This expectation is most likely to be realized if such generalized cues for leisure-time activity are systematically incorporated into the participant's leisure education program from the very beginning of instruction. Therefore, prior to conducting leisure activities instruction, the leisure educator, in collaboration with parents, care providers, and other professionals such as therapeutic recreation specialists and adapted physical education teachers, should identify a generalized cue or set of cues that will be used consistently to prompt leisure activities instruction and naturally occurring free-time situations. Such cues should be used to begin each skill acquisition or choice instructional session and should also be used across environments (home, school, and community) to facilitate generalized responding.

Prior to instruction, the leisure educator must also decide how the participant will be taught to indicate his or her activity preferences. Individuals who can talk or sign can simply be taught to name the activities they want for play in spoken or sign language. The leisure educator begins each instruction session and each trial within the session by providing the generalized cue indicating free time and following that cue with the name of the leisure activity scheduled for instruction. For example, the leisure educator might say or sign, "Free time, let's play with the Game Boy." Even if an individual uses a nonvocal communication system (but is not profoundly hearing impaired), this verbal cue should be paired with the nonvocal stimuli on the assumption that the participant might well be able to learn to discriminate such cues, which have maximum utility across a variety of environments.

Participants who are nonverbal should be taught an alternative nonvocal strategy, such as pointing to a picture of the activity. We have used this procedure successfully with many students who have severe to profound cognitive disabilities. In such instances, the teacher says, "Free time, let's play Game Boy" during each instruction session and trial within an instruction session, while simultaneously presenting the Game Boy and a picture of the Game Boy to the participant. Throughout skill instruction on the Game Boy, the picture of the Game Boy materials are placed next to or above the actual unit. Eventually, after repeated pairings, the leisure educator should begin to fade the actual activity materials and begin a session by simply providing the generalized verbal cue, the activity names, and the activity picture. In Appendix C, we have included drawings of the leisure activities included in this curriculum. The leisure educator can photocopy these drawings, color them, laminate them for longer wear, and bind them together with a ring holder to create a picture book. Or, the instructor could take photographs of the actual materials and laminate those for use in the picture book.

WARM-UPS

Leisure education should be carried out in a relaxed atmosphere if we are to be consistent with the purpose of leisure activities—to enjoy oneself. Yet, whenever an individual presents considerable instructional needs, there is a risk that the introduction of the structure implied by "skill acquisition instruction" can result in a stressful situation for that person. If this occurs, it threatens the nature of leisure education and could seriously interfere with the individual's ability to enjoy any of the activities being taught. An analogy might be a piano player who is actually quite skilled, but who was compelled to take piano lessons for many years under parental pressure and who had a piano teacher who was a rigid "task master," emphasizing skill development at the expense of enjoyment. Consequently, our piano player might actually detest playing the piano, and seldom—if ever—view it as an activity for relaxation or personal enjoyment during free time. Another individual whose parents and piano teacher somehow avoided most of the "work" cues that might have been associated with learning scales and practicing fingering could have a completely different attitude, and might be found happily playing the piano for personal enjoyment whenever the occasion presents itself. Behavioral principles can explain this relationship between one's learning history and a particular activity: Whenever anxiety, pressure, and a demand situation is associated with an event, that event is likely to become aversive. Because of this, we recommend the use of a warm-up procedure to create a positive mood prior to leisure education. Indeed, for some individuals whose instructional history is replete with difficulty and failure—or who typically exhibit challenging behavior whenever instruction demands are made—the warm-up procedure might be continued indefinitely as the lead-in to more incidental teaching techniques for acquiring a new skill (see Meyer & Evans, 1989, for more detailed procedures regarding the implementation of such procedures to teach leisure activities as alternatives to problem behaviors).

Warm-ups are brief 2- to 3-minute free-play interactions between the leisure educator and the participant during a leisure activity. The leisure educator demonstrates how to use the activity materials appropriately. During this demonstration, the participant should be reinforced for attending to the activity materials, but the instructor should also engage in considerable warm, pleasant commentary about playing with the game or materials; this commentary should not be "contingent" in the behavioral sense, but should represent noncontingent positive affect about the situation. Then, the leisure educator should encourage (but not force) the participant to touch, explore, and manipulate the leisure materials. After conducting an initial warm-up with the activity materials, the leisure educator can begin instructing the participant on the steps of the specific task analysis. The behaviors and approximations to the responses listed in the task analysis should be reinforced. If the participant's or leisure educator's interactions with the materials produce an auditory, visual, or tactile stimulus, the participant's attention should be directed to the stimulus and then immediately reinforced with friendly commentary.

Warm-ups provide the leisure educator with the opportunity to begin an instructional session on a fun, positive note. They are also useful in introducing a participant to a newly purchased leisure activity before the instructor begins any formal instruction. Or they can provide a brief break in the course of a structured instruction session: The instructor should monitor participant reactions carefully and switch to this "warm-up" mode whenever the individual shows signs of anxiety or stress. Remember, learning anything new, even a play activity, can be stressful and generate the same personal fear of failure aroused whenever we are confronted by a challenge. By monitoring an individual's mood carefully and responding to that mood, the leisure educator can also use warm-ups to help prolong the duration of a participant's attention, make instruction more enjoyable, and provide opportunities for parallel and cooperative play between the leisure educator and the participant in preparation for peer play. Warm-ups (or wind-downs) also help end instruction sessions. Finally, of course, because these activities are intended to be *play*, and play does generally involve behavior that looks like fun and may even appear to be "off-task," friendly bantering and brief warm-ups throughout instruction should actually be a major strategy to model what play really is for the participant.

SHAPING ATTENDING BEHAVIORS

During an instruction session, it is extremely important that the participant attends to the activity materials. If he or she does not pay attention to the activity materials, or will not even look at them, then the leisure educator must shape attending behaviors as well as teach the steps of the task analysis. We caution against teaching attending behaviors as an isolated skill prior to actual activity instruction, as was once done in structured programs (e.g., teaching an individual to respond reliably to a cue to "Look at [an item]" before he or she would be taught how to use the item). Regardless of whether or not a participant can be taught attending skills in isolation, the procedure has several drawbacks that make its use inappropriate in leisure instruction. For example, and most important, this procedure teaches the participant to pay attention and respond to the instructor and the instruction environment instead of the actual leisure materials. This focus may be acceptable for certain academic skills, but when teaching play skills, the long-term goal is self-initiated play in a noninstruction environment where a leisure educator is not present. Therefore, it is crucial that attending behaviors depend on the leisure activity, not on the instructor and instruction environment.

The guidelines listed in Tables 3.1 and 3.2 are used to effectively shape the attending behaviors of persons with significant disabilities.

TASK ANALYSIS

A task analysis is the identification of all of the necessary participant responses or component skills and the sequence in which these responses or skills must occur for appropriate interactions

Table 3.1.   Shaping attending behaviors early in instruction

---

1. Before beginning an instruction session, demonstrate the activity for the participant. Emphasize the reinforcing characteristics of the activity.

2. During an instruction session, do not ask the participant to attend to the materials. Instead, shape the desired response by:

    a. Waiting for the participant to come on-task and to orient his or her body toward the materials. Immediately provide a reinforcer for this behavior, however brief it is. Then begin instruction.

    b. Gradually increasing the criterion for reinforcement and the duration of time on-task until the participant is being reinforced for attending to the task rather than simply coming to the task.

    c. Ignoring nonattending behaviors. Do not make eye contact with the participant, do not touch the participant, and do not reinforce the participant for looking at the instructor rather than at the materials unless this behavior is part of the instructional procedures.

    d. For the participant who never naturally orients his or her body to the activity, try placing a high-preference reinforcer (e.g., a piece of cereal or candy) on the leisure materials. Prompt the participant so that he or she orients his or her body to the activity and allow the individual to have the reinforcer. Gradually fade out the reinforcer. (Note: This procedure should only be tried as a last resort!)

---

with the activity or other player(s). It provides the leisure educator with the content of the skill acquisition instruction sessions, telling him or her exactly what the participant must do, step by step, to meet an instructional objective.

Prior to providing any instruction on an activity, the leisure educator must develop a task analysis that is appropriate for the particular participant or must individualize an existing task analysis by using the following procedures:

1. Analyze the component skills required for the participant to meet the instructional objective.

    Instructional objective: Given a remote control vehicle and track, the participant will move the vehicle making a U-turn on 80% of the trials during two consecutive instruction sessions.

    Component skills:

    Turn the vehicle on.

    Place the vehicle on a track or on the ground or floor.

    Operate the remote control forward/reverse switch.

    Operate the remote control steering wheel to make the necessary turns.

    Turn the vehicle off.

2. Determine the appropriate sequence of the component skills.

    Step 1:   Turn the vehicle on.

    Step 2:   Place the vehicle on a track or on the ground or floor.

    Step 3:   Press the button on the hand control to "forward" and hold in position.

    Step 4:   As the vehicle moves forward, turn the wheel on the hand control to the right so the vehicle makes a U-turn.

Table 3.2.   Shaping attending behaviors later in instruction

---

1. When the participant begins to initiate correct responses, reinforce sustained attention only.

2. Eliminate reinforcement for attending as soon as the participant begins initiating correct performance. By then, the natural cues and consequences of the activity itself should prompt and reinforce the individual's interactions with it.

3. If the participant is not attending during an instruction session, ignore him or her and do not allow manipulations of the leisure materials. Remove them if the participant begins to "fool around" or behave inappropriately.

Step 5: Turn the wheel to the left to straighten the vehicle.

Step 6: Release the button on the hand control.

Step 7: Turn the vehicle off.

3. Break the component skills and sequence of performance into instructional units (steps) appropriate to the particular participant's skills and attention span.

Step 1: Slide the power switch located under the vehicle to the "on" position.

Step 2: Place the vehicle on a track or on the ground or floor.

Step 3: With the nonpreferred hand, press the button on the hand control to "forward" and continue to hold it in that position during the next maneuver.

Step 4: With the preferred hand, turn the wheel on the hand control to the right so that the vehicle makes a semicircle around the cone marking the track.

Step 5: Turn the wheel to the left so that the vehicle straightens out and moves ahead.

Step 6: Release the "forward" button.

Step 7: Slide the power switch to "off."

In developing a task analysis, the leisure educator should actually play with the leisure activity many times to analyze and sequence the component skills required of the participant. In fact, the authors of this book have often asked their own children or their colleagues' school-age children to help with this "task"! To specifically adapt a task analysis for a particular participant, the leisure educator must also be prepared to modify steps as needed to accommodate learning style and to make decisions about the "size" of an individual step based on past learning performance by an individual. For many participants, the task analysis must also include social behaviors, or other leisure-related support behaviors, whenever the play activity involves playing with one or more peers (see our example in Form 3.2 where the game Connect Four is played by two teenagers, one of whom has a significant disability).

Because the task analysis tells the leisure educator precisely what the participant must be taught to do and in what sequence, it is critical that it is accurately written down in a format that provides the leisure educator with an easy reference during instruction sessions. The leisure educator can use the Steps of the Task Analysis form (Form 3.1) to record the steps he or she decided to teach. The number of steps the instructor records on any given form depends on the number of steps in the task analysis. However, if a participant is only working on acquiring a few steps of the task analysis (i.e., "partial participation")—perhaps other steps will be performed by a peer—the leisure educator may want to record only those steps to save time. Any embedded social skills should also be included in the sequence if they are targeted for participant acquisition. Whatever the number of steps and teaching methods used, the leisure educator should always record the steps on the form in the same way, by beginning at the *bottom* of the form with the first step. The instructor writes the first step of the task analysis on the bottom line, numbered 1 on Form 3.1, the second step on the next-to-bottom line, numbered 2, and so forth. With most teaching methods, the instructor reads the steps and collects data starting from the bottom of the page and progresses upward. However, if the instructor uses a backward chaining teaching method (see p. 32), he or she reads the steps and collects data starting from the top of the page and progresses downward. Form 3.2 (Skill Acquisition Data Record) provides an example of how a specific data collection form can then be designed to accommodate selected data collection needs (see details below).

TEACHING METHODS

The leisure educator must determine not only *what* to instruct but also *how* best to instruct the participant. There are many instructional methods, and the instructor should use whatever

Steps of the Task Analysis

Participant: _Dana Johnson_   Activity: _Simon_

1. Slide the On/Off switch to "on."
2. Slide the Game Selector switch to "1."
3. Slide the Skill Level switch to "1."
4. Press the Start button.
5. Look at the lighted lens and/or listen to its sound.
6. Press the same lens within 5 seconds. If a matching error occurs, press the Start button, look at the lighted lens and/or listen to its sound, and press the same lens within 5 seconds.
7. Slide the On/Off switch to "off."
8.
9.
10.
11.
12.
13.
14.
15.
16.
17.
18.
19.
20.
21.
22.
23.
24.
25.
26.
27.
28.
29.
30.

Skill Acquisition Data Record

Participant: Jerome
Skill Sequence: Play Connect Four with a Peer
Leisure Educator: Lillian Meister/Sun Skalko

Level of Assistance Key

I = Independent	FP = Full Physical
V = Verbal	X = Partial Physical
PP = Partial Participation	M = Point or Model

Date and Initials[a]

Steps in Activity Sequence	LM 9/18	SS 9/24	SS 10/1	LM 10/7	SS 10/13	LM 10/22	SS 10/30	LM 11/15			% Correct[b]
10. Place game pieces in box and return box to shelf.	10 X	10 X	10 PP	10 X	10 X	10 I	10 I	10 I	10	10	
9. Indicate preference to play or not to play another game.	9 M	9 M	9 M	9 M	9 I	9 M	9 M	9 I	9	9	
8. Congratulate other player when game is completed.	8 V	8 V	8 V	8 V	8 V	8 V	8 V	8 V	8	8	
7. Pick up correct color checker and place into playing frame.	7 X	7 X	7 M	7 FP	7 M	7 X	7 I	7 I	7	7	
6. Take turns playing with peer.	6 PP	6 PP	6 PP	6 PP	6 PP	6 PP	6 PP	6 PP	6	6	
5. Choose red or black checkers.	5 M	5 M	5 I	5 I	5 I	5 I	5 I	5 I	5	5	
4. Check release lever for position to hold checkers in frame.	4 PP	4 PP	4 PP	4 V	4 V	4 V	4 I	4 I	4	4	
3. Sit across from peer and organize game box to play.	3 PP	3 PP	3 PP	3 PP	3 X	3 X	3 X	3 X	3	3	
2. Walk to shelf and retrieve game.	2 V	2 V	2 M	2 M	2 I	2 I	2 I	2 I	2	2	
1. Indicate preference to play Connect Four.	1 FP	1 FP	1 M	1 M	1 I	1 I	1 I	1 I	1	1	

[a] One data probe should be collected at least once every 2 weeks for each activity sequence.

[b] Percentage of steps performed independently (I).

method(s) suits both the situation and the participant. Regardless of what method of direct instruction is used, leisure education is greatly enhanced by frequent and meaningful opportunities for incidental learning while playing with the leisure materials with peers, siblings, and classmates who do not have disabilities (Rynders et al., 1993). First, these are naturally occurring opportunities for free time that involve time with friends (or perhaps family members). Nothing could be a more successful leisure education outcome than evidence that the participant can and does play with the materials in a manner that seems satisfactory to his or her peers. Second, peers most effectively reinforce or discourage the appropriate positive and negative play and social behaviors, respectively, which would have to be artificially consequated by an adult instructor. Finally, if the leisure educator can comfortably "let go" and not worry about how perfectly the individual is playing with peers even before he or she has mastered a particular task analysis for an activity, peer play offers multiple "trials" for practice in a highly motivating situation that could not possibly be carried out by even the most intensive of programs. It also helps to remember that these play interactions are most likely the context for developing friendships and other relationships between individuals with disabilities and their peers without disabilities.

For systematic instruction by the leisure educator, two basic teaching methods are *total task instruction* and *individual step instruction*. In the former, the leisure educator focuses on the total task and provides instruction on all of the steps in a skill sequence during each trial of every instruction session, even if the participant does not meet the performance criteria for all of the steps. In the latter, the instructor focuses on the individual steps and provides instruction on a step in a skill sequence for as many trials and instruction sessions as are necessary for the participant to meet the performance criteria for that step.

If the leisure educator does use individual step instruction, he or she must also decide whether to use a *forward chaining* or *backward chaining* procedure to link the individual steps into a sequence. In forward chaining, the leisure educator begins instruction on Step 1, and the participant repeats this step over and over until he or she meets the performance criterion for that step. The leisure educator then proceeds to Step 2 and provides whatever instruction is necessary for the participant to perform Step 1 and Step 2 according to the performance criteria for those two steps. The next step in the skill sequence is added after the individual masters the previous steps. Instruction continues until the participant is able to perform the entire skill sequence during a trial.

Backward chaining is the reverse procedure; that is, instruction begins on the last step of the skill sequence. The leisure educator performs the task from Step 1 until the last step, then instructs the participant to perform the last step. Once the participant masters the last step according to the performance criteria for that step, the next-to-the-last step is added to the instruction. After performing the task from Step 1 to the next-to-the-last step, the leisure educator instructs the participant to perform the next-to-the-last step and then the last step. As the instruction sessions continue, the instructor does fewer and fewer steps, and the participant does more and more of them, until he or she is able to perform the entire skill sequence in the appropriate order beginning with Step 1. In many instances, backward chaining can be more motivating for participants than forward chaining, and therefore more successful, because the participant reaches the natural reinforcer (i.e., the most reinforcing part of the activity) immediately after his or her own performance of the final sequence of the activity.

In our field tests, however, we have relied heavily on total task instruction rather than individual step instruction. By moving through the entire sequence as smoothly as possible, the participant is exposed to multiple trials of "partial participation" in the entire play activity, including all the natural reinforcing events of the activity itself (Baumgart et al., 1982). A total task method provides the participant with maximum exposure to the activities' natural reinforcements, including shapes, sounds, lights, movements, and so forth, as these are interspersed throughout the skill sequences or clustered toward the later steps. Furthermore, especially for the chained activities, total task instruction allows for maximum independent participant performance. In these activities, individual steps usually do not have the same degree of difficulty, nor do they follow an easy-to-difficult sequence. That is, steps that are "easy" or "difficult" for the participant are interspersed throughout the activity; forward or backward chaining entails mastering the next step in the sequence regardless of its difficulty level for the participant.

In contrast, a total task approach allows the individual to master steps as he or she goes along—according to that individual's natural learning curve—and simultaneously allows for more help on those steps that are more difficult for the participant. An individual may already know how to perform some steps and/or may learn steps midway in the sequence before learning the first or last steps. During each trial, therefore, a total task format gives the participant an opportunity for independence and practice on the steps he or she already knows as well as instruction on the steps he or she has not yet mastered.

While this format appears to lead to the most rapid participant progress, it is not critical that total task instruction be adopted in order to successfully implement this curriculum. What is important is that the leisure educator uses whichever method he or she selects consistently and that the method matches participant needs. Also, if individual step instruction is preferred, it is critical that the participant perceives the activity as enjoyable through repeated exposure to the activity's reinforcing characteristics.

INSTRUCTIONAL CUES

To help the participant correctly carry out the steps listed on the task analysis during the instruction session, the leisure educator should provide instructional cues, as necessary. Instructional cues refer to information provided to the participant before an action is performed. These cues are an addition to information naturally provided by the environment, and they reflect a difference in intensity, duration, or frequency (Falvey, Brown, Lyon, Baumgart, & Schroeder, 1980; Heyne & Schleien, 1994).

One of the goals of this curriculum is that the participant with significant disabilities learns to play in response to cues that normally occur during leisure time and with leisure activities. For example, when a parent tells his or her child to "Go and play," it is hoped that the child will select an activity, get a toy off the shelf, and play independently with the toy. However, individuals with significant disabilities may not know how to choose and manipulate the materials appropriately. They may not know how to take their cues either from the people around them (another reason why inclusion is so important—it provides these individuals with many opportunities to watch and see what their peers do) or from the activities themselves, especially during the initial contact with the leisure activities. By providing assistance and systematically pairing instructional cues with the naturally occurring ones, the leisure educator can provide the participant with significant disabilities the extra information needed to learn these leisure skills.

There are numerous types of instructional cues available to the leisure educator. Those that have been used successfully in our work are listed in Table 3.3.

When the leisure educator selects instructional cues for use in the instruction sessions, he or she should keep several things in mind. Instructional cues vary in the amount of information they provide as well as in their usefulness for individual participants. It is critical that functional instructional cues be selected for use during instruction. Not all types of cues are functional for all individuals. For example, verbal cues might be appropriate for a person who demonstrates good receptive language skills, but a participant who does not demonstrate such skills probably will not benefit from verbal cues because they would not necessarily provide him or her with the additional information needed to perform the steps of the task analysis correctly. In such an

Table 3.3   Types of instructional cues

1. Priming, physical assistance, manual guidance, or physical prompts	The leisure educator places his or her hands and/or body in direct physical contact with the learner's, and puts the participant through the correct performance of a response. It is critical that the participant's hands and/or body are in direct contact with the activity materials and that the movements of the participant's hands and/or body, not the instructor's, create a change in the materials.
2. Gestural cues, gestures	The leisure educator motions or moves his or her hands or body to suggest a response—for example, pointing to the pinball game's "on" switch to assist the participant with the first step of the task analysis: "Turn the power switch to 'on.'"
3. Instructions, verbal cues	The leisure educator addresses statements or words (in the participant's primary language and communication system) directly to the individual to assist with a response; for example, finger spelling instructions for an individual with dual sensory impairments.
4. Modeling, demonstrations	The leisure educator demonstrates an appropriate response for the participant.
5. Match-to-sample cues, pictorial cues	The leisure educator presents the participant with a visual or tactual representation of the direct response; for example, showing sequenced pictures of how to start the Game Boy.
6. Redundant cues, color coding	The leisure educator highlights difficult discriminations or makes characteristics of the activity materials more salient; for example, adding a color cue to indicate orientation to a particular Game Boy cartridge.

instance, physical assistance or a gesture would be a more functional cue for the leisure educator to use. Likewise, if an individual is extremely tactilely defensive, the instructor is likely to have difficulty relying on physical assistance.

In determining what kind of instructional cues might be functional for a particular individual, the leisure educator should consider: 1) the participant's prior response to different assistance modes, 2) the participant's language and communication skills, and 3) parent or care provider input.

Instructional cues also vary in terms of their intrusiveness or artificiality. Often instructional cues are presented in a hierarchical organization based on their perceived level of intrusiveness, ranging from most to least intensive cues in the following order: physical assistance, modeling, gestures, redundant cues, match-to-sample cues, verbal cues. The leisure educator is instructed to adhere to this hierarchy by always providing the least intrusive cue first—the verbal cue—and resorting to a physical assistance cue only if all "less intrusive" cues fail to generate an appropriate response from the participant. Indeed, instructors are told to provide the next level of cue, one after the other, until the participant correctly performs the step.

Whereas this procedure and variations of prompting hierarchies (see, for example, Sulzer-Azaroff & Mayer, 1977, pp. 206–212) have long been regarded as effective in teaching learners with severe intellectual disabilities, we have found it far more useful to reference the natural environment in making a decision about which cue to use. Our preference is to use the cue that seems least intrusive for the environment and the situation, as well as the cue that seems least likely, logically, to encourage the participant to look to the wrong source for information in the future. Thus, a verbal cue in which the instructor—who is totally artificial to the situation—tells the participant what to do might actually be the *most intrusive* cue in a natural environment. In contrast, a gentle push at the elbow—called a partial physical prompt and regarded as far more intrusive than a verbal prompt in most hierarchies—could be considered a *less intrusive* cue in many environments and situations in the real world. We also found that rather than waiting for the participant to make mistakes and become confused, a quick prompt that blends readily into the natural situation, using a zero time-delay procedure that is gradually faded, is most supportive of positive participant involvement. Waiting for an individual to fail to respond or to intervene with negative or challenging behaviors when the participant does not know what to do seems far less preferable than giving the extra bit of assistance until the participant has had ample trials to learn what the next step is.

The implementation of a time-delay prompting procedure, which can result in errorless learning, is really quite simple. First, a "natural" prompt that seems the least intrusive to the situation is identified; for example, pointing to the control on the Game Boy. Next, a schedule of "time-delays" is instituted as follows: For the first 10–20 trials, the instructor follows the natural cue for a next step with the predetermined natural prompt—pointing to the control—before any error, performance delay, or challenging behavior can occur. After 10–20 trials, the instructor waits 2 seconds before delivering the pointing cue, then delivers the cue, which in turn prompts the participant's correct response. After 10–20 more trials, the teacher waits 3–4 seconds before delivering the pointing cue. Generally, by the time the time delay has been increased to 5 seconds (sometimes as many as 10 seconds), the participant has mastered the behavior. When this occurs, it will be immediately evident to the instructor because the participant will suddenly intervene with the correct response before the instructor can deliver the "time-delayed" prompt.

We have found few situations where any application of a prompt hierarchy seems appropriate. Instead, the leisure educator should carefully evaluate the participant's performance in previous instruction sessions and on previous instruction trials along with an analysis of the kind of prompt that seems natural to the activity and the environment. The leisure educator should then plan this prompt into the instructional sequence, using a time-delay procedure to fade the prompt, and thus give only the type and amount of assistance needed by the participant to successfully perform the steps of the task analysis.

The instructor must always incorporate a plan to *fade* any prompts being provided to the participant that will simply not be available outside of an instruction session. It is very easy for an instructor to get "hooked" on providing unnecessary instructional cues for a variety of good intentions—desire for the participant to always experience success, desire to be needed by the participant, and so forth. Ultimately, even the best intentions result in a participant's lack of independence and conflict with the goal of this curriculum. The leisure educator should always strive to provide enough assistance so that the participant can successfully perform a step, while removing any intrusions (additional cues, reinforcements, corrections) as rapidly as possible. It is hoped, for example, that the participant will eventually turn the wheel on the remote control not because the instructor tells him or her to do so, but because the participant can see that if he or she does not adjust the vehicle's direction, it will become trapped into a corner and no longer move.

There is a delicate balance between providing enough assistance and, at the same time, remembering that all instructional cues must be eliminated before one can consider the participant as having truly acquired a new leisure skill. If some continuing assistance is needed, the instructor must strive to identify someone in the natural environment who can provide it—a peer, perhaps, or someone at the site where the leisure activity takes place. These individuals will presumably always be present in the participant's leisure environments in the future, whereas the leisure educator may not be. It is also critical that instruction continues to aim for the primary goal of leisure education—enjoyment. Again, if the leisure educator becomes the "focus" of the instruction sessions, that is, more salient and reinforcing to the participant than the leisure materials themselves, the leisure educator's presence may distract the participant's attention and ultimately lessen his or her enjoyment of the materials and activity.

However, it would be perfectly natural for a young person with a disability to be distracted by the presence of a peer—who is becoming a friend—while playing a game in the community. As long as the extra assistance is being provided by someone who is likely to be a continuing feature in the individual's world, and a friend is even central to one's leisure time, such prompts may not interfere at all.

POSITIVE REINFORCEMENT

Positive reinforcement is used in conjunction with instructional cues to teach the participant how to use the leisure activity appropriately. Defined as the presentation of a consequence or event following a specified response that increases the likelihood of that response's reoccurrence, positive reinforcement is a powerful tool in teaching individuals both *what* manipulations of the leisure materials are appropriate and *when* different manipulations or responses should be made.

Reinforcers can be anything—a smile, a pat on the back, a compliment, a promise to go out for a burger later, money, a favorite toy, or even access to free time. Things are termed reinforcers by their effect on someone's behavior or responses. This definition may seem obvious, but all too often instructors select consequences that seem reinforcing to them, but do not function as reinforcers for the participants.

Several procedures have been developed for determining functional reinforcers, but common sense may be the best path to making decisions on behalf of particular individuals. People who know the participant well can generally list the things he or she likes and dislikes. The ability to generate this list would most likely be limited only by restricting the list to stereotyped reinforcers such as a hug, a favorite food, grades, or money. Encourage the participant's parents, friends, and classmates to brainstorm everything they think that he or she likes, no matter how unorthodox some items might appear, and the list may be surprising. It is also helpful to identify reinforcers with features that are intrinsic to particular leisure activities. For example, certain games may include music, which may be reinforcing to an individual who enjoys music. Knowing the characteristics of the leisure activities helps in the selection of an activity that feeds directly into a preference. Table 3.4 presents guidelines for using positive reinforcement in a leisure education program.

Any artificial reinforcers that are extrinsic to the leisure activity or environment and that are introduced by the leisure educator to help with instruction must be eliminated before the participant can be said to possess a functional leisure skill. Similar to the application of instructional cues and assistance procedures, the participant should initially receive lots of reinforcement from the instructor and others, both to increase appropriate responses and to expe-

Table 3.4.   Guidelines for using positive reinforcement

1. Use functional reinforcers that are age appropriate, easily provided, of brief duration, and whose presentations do not distract the participant from the task.
2. During the initial instruction sessions, provide reinforcement for every correct response, regardless of whether it is an assisted response or an independently performed response.
3. During the initial instruction session, provide reinforcers immediately after performance of a correct step or response.
4. During the initial instruction session, also reinforce the participant's attending and cooperating behaviors.
5. As the participant consistently performs the steps with increased independence and begins to enjoy the natural reinforcements provided by the leisure activity itself, begin fading the reinforcements provided by the leisure educator.

rience enjoyment with the activity. However, as instruction progresses, the participant should begin to be reinforced solely by the consequences provided by the leisure activity itself or play with peers in the leisure activity rather than by the instructor.

If the leisure educator does find it necessary to "add" reinforcers to the instructional situation, such as a smile or verbal comment after correct responses, these should be faded by gradually and systematically decreasing the frequency, intensity, and/or duration of such social reinforcers. For example, the instructor might comment on every other response rather than every movement the participant makes. It is equally important to fade any reinforcers directed to maintain attending, in-seat behavior, taking proper care of the materials, and so forth. In fact, it is just as important to fade any artificial consequences as it is to use effective instructional procedures in the first place. A failure to do either will result in the same outcome—an individual who is dependent on adult care providers for typical activities of daily living.

CORRECTION OF ERRORS

During skill acquisition, the leisure educator should carefully assess the participant's needs for instructional cues and positive reinforcement while considering the learner's prior performance, entry skills, and interests to ensure that the need for corrections is minimal. However, the participant will still make occasional errors in performing the steps listed in the task analysis, and the correction procedures described in Table 3.5 are recommended.

When a performance error does occur, it is essential that the participant discriminate the difference between a correct response and what he or she did. In part, this is accomplished if the leisure educator immediately interrupts the trial with a brief, unemotional statement such as, "No, that won't work. Let's try this way instead." For individuals with limited receptive language skills, the instructor should also remove the participant's hands from the activity. Care should be taken not to be overly negative when errors do occur, so as to disassociate leisure education from the previous failure experiences a participant may have had. At the same time, it is

Table 3.5. Correction procedures

Procedure A (recommended when using individual step instruction)
1. Immediately interrupt the participant's incorrect response.
2. Repeat the instructional cue paired with the activity cue that preceded the incorrect response.
3. Give whatever additional assistance is necessary to ensure a correct response by the participant.
4. Immediately reinforce the correct response.
5. Repeat the procedure, this time fading the additional assistance, to provide additional practice on the missed step.
6. If the participant meets the performance criterion for that step, continue on to the next step in the task analysis.

Procedure B[a]
1. Immediately interrupt the participant's incorrect response.
2. Go back two steps in the task analysis and give the appropriate instructional cue for that step.
3. Have the participant repeat the two steps and the missed step, providing enough assistance to ensure correct responses on all three steps.
4. Reinforce each correct (assisted and unassisted) response.
5. Repeat the procedure to provide additional practice on the missed step.
6. Continue on to the next step in the task analysis.

[a]From Bellamy, Horner, & Inman's (1979) work on vocational instruction procedures; recommended when using total task instruction.

essential that corrections are qualitatively different from instructional cues and positive reinforcement. This is especially true for participants who rely primarily on physical prompts and corrections, such as individuals with dual sensory impairments.

Leisure education presents the instructor with a unique situation with respect to the correction of errors. "Mistakes" are often very normal aspects of engaging in leisure activities. For example, incorrect matching of the sequence of signals may be a natural part of a video game, and few individuals are able to complete every sequence presented in such a game: Starting over is part of the game! Also, by definition, leisure implies fun and enjoyment. Because we can take what was meant to be a game so seriously that all the fun is taken out of it, we must avoid the temptation to become too concerned about "accuracy" or "winning" during leisure activity instruction. How many of us would choose leisure activities that require perfect performance or require us to win every game? Because of this, the leisure educator must handle errors that occur during instruction sessions somewhat differently than he or she would, for example, during instruction on a vocational task. Participants should be taught to recognize errors and either to self-correct or to begin a new game in a good-natured way when they make a mistake they cannot correct. They should also learn to laugh during their efforts, which is another reason for peer play as an essential component to leisure education.

The 10 leisure activities task analyzed in the next chapter specifically include procedures for teaching participants how to deal with different types of incorrect responses (e.g., the participant is taught to restart the game for Game Boy). These strategies are either outlined in the activity's instructional procedures or have been incorporated directly into the task analyses.

INCIDENTAL TEACHING AND PEER RELATIONSHIPS

If a careful job is done of identifying leisure activities that are age appropriate for individuals with disabilities, these participants will acquire the kinds of activities enjoyed by their peer group. If this is the case, the participant will have increased opportunities to play with peers as he or she acquires increased skills with activities that are considered popular. Many of the readers of this book are parents, and as parents we can imagine many things we do not want our children to do under the influence of their peers. But the reality is that a peer group is central to development and essential to enjoying meaningful personal relationships beyond the immediate family. Toys, games, and organized recreational activities provide a context for individuals to get to know one another and become friends. A person with a disability is missing out on an important part of life if he or she is not involved with those toys, games, and organized recreational activities.

In our work at the University of Hawaii, the University of Minnesota, and Syracuse University with community recreation agencies and area public schools, we developed and validated strategies to support positive play and peer relationships between individuals with and without significant disabilities (Green & Schleien, 1991; Heyne, Schleien, & McAvoy, 1993; Meyer, 1992; Meyer & Putnam, 1988; Rynders & Schleien, 1991; Rynders et al., 1993). Our approach to involving peers without disabilities in the lives of individuals with disabilities is to focus on supporting friendships and other positive interpersonal *peer* relationships between these individuals. Past efforts have involved using peer tutors to supplement instruction for learners with disabilities, but this seems to us to represent the addition of yet another "authority" figure in the lives of participants, quite possibly at the expense of a more typical friendship-type relationship (Meyer, 1991). Alternatively, giving people the chance to play together using their newly acquired leisure interests and skills could enrich their social lifestyles. These leisure situations also provide countless "practice trials" in a comfortable environment that matches the true intent of leisure time—doing something enjoyable.

Based on our experiences in supporting friendships, we have the following suggestions to offer as general guidelines to support play and leisure activities:

• Individuals without disabilities do not need a great deal of information about disabilities in order to participate with, enjoy, and be a friend to a peer with disabilities. What they may need is limited information to aid understanding of similarities and otherwise "unpredictable" behaviors and to feel more comfortable with these peers. This information should most likely focus on specific adaptations needed by a particular individual, such as how to manipulate a friend's wheelchair safely and how their peer communicates.

• Leisure educators are models for interactions between individuals. Whenever differential treatment is modeled, for example, and a participant with disabilities is allowed to do things that no one else would be allowed to do, a powerful message is being communicated: that the individual is, in fact, *different*. Leisure educators should help all participants become comfortable with having reasonable expectations for social behavior—the same kinds of expectations they would have for their peers without disabilities. For example, hair pulling need not be tolerated at any time. Young children in particular can seem overly accommodating in allowing themselves to be treated in a manner that they would never allow with a peer without a disability. Indeed, natural peer consequences for unacceptable behavior appear to be powerful motivators for positive behavior in inclusive leisure environments.

• Individuals without disabilities must be taught how to interact with peers who have disabilities. They do not need to memorize any facts about syndromes or learn to agree with positive attitudinal statements; what they need is specific information about how their friend communicates, moves, and manipulates the leisure materials.

• Rather than assuming that the leisure educator will show peers without disabilities what to do, these individuals should be asked for ideas about adapting games and activities or about new activities that they enjoy and that they believe their new friend could also learn to do and enjoy. Leisure educators will be pleasantly surprised at their creativity and problem-solving abilities.

• Leisure educators should reinforce appropriate play and social interactions through their best instructional practices in all domains. For example, competitive goal structures are being increasingly replaced by cooperative structures in sports and other games (Rynders & Schleien, 1991; Rynders et al., 1993). Similarly, academic instruction can emphasize cooperation, joint problem solving, critical thinking, sharing, and other positive social and self-regulatory goals through models such as cooperative learning (Putnam, 1993). The incorporation of playful cooperative learning groups in classroom academic activities in an inclusive school program can also create the social context for the development of meaningful friendships between children that will carry over into their leisure activities at home and in the neighborhood.

• If individuals are familiar with one another in a community recreation center, YMCA or YWCA, or school classroom, recreation professionals, teachers, and parents need to "let go" and not allow overprotectiveness to limit the social experiences of participants with even the most significant disabilities. Just as we allow typical children to take increasing risks in order to lead a normal life, individuals with significant disabilities have to be allowed to do things, including play with their peers, without constant intrusion by adults when it would not be age appropriate for this to occur with any other individual. Indeed, allowing individuals to begin such activities under the general supervision of adults in neighborhood recreation activities and at school is the perfect way to begin this process. Do not interfere! What the participants do together when they play the game may not look exactly like an instruction session, but think twice before interrupting or intervening if no harm seems to be done and everyone is having a good time.

Most children and youth survive and thrive on the thousands of "incidental teaching" trials in social and play behaviors offered by their peer groups throughout the developmental period. Participants with disabilities in inclusive environments finally have access to these incidental learning opportunities, and it behooves adults to allow these new relationships to develop without turning every peer interaction opportunity into another instructional situation.

DATA COLLECTION AND PROGRAM CHANGES

A participant's performance during the instruction sessions can tell the leisure educator whether or not the instructional cues and positive reinforcers are helping the participant increase his or her play skills. Collecting such skill acquisition data on a probe basis is necessary before an instructor can make any informed decisions about progress, needed program revisions, or even mastery of the leisure activity goal.

Data Collection

The steps of the task analysis are the participant responses that the leisure educator should observe and record on the Skill Acquisition Data Record (Form 3.2). The example shown on the data record illustrates a participant's performance on a leisure activity goal involving appropriate play with the game Connect Four with a peer. The data record allows the leisure educator to record individual response performance as well as to graph overall achievement on the activity sequence. Each number from 1 to 10 (10 at the top) at the far left corresponds to a step in the task analysis sequence for which the instructor is keeping a record. Each vertical column of numbers on the data record represents a complete trial (for this sheet, the instructor can record 10 trials). It is not necessary to collect continuous data on participant performance every time a trial is conducted; as in the example provided, data were collected on a probe basis approximately once each week. This seems to be adequate to monitor performance, and the instructor can always collect more frequent probes if he or she has any reason to suspect that the program needs to be revised. The actual activity sequence should, of course, occur at least several times weekly regardless of whether data are being collected on performance. In fact, we recommend that activities involving peer play occur several times for every time that data are collected to ensure that the participants involved do not associate the activity with being monitored by an adult.

To collect data using Form 3.2, the leisure educator simply notes the participant response and level of assistance needed for each trial. In the example, Jerome is making steady progress in mastering his objective to play Connect Four with his peer. Also, his task analysis includes certain social skill steps as well as steps involved in manipulating the game materials. On the first two trials, he was not independent on any of the steps but exhibited considerable variability in the type of assistance needed. By the third data probe, he was performing Step 5 independently ("choose red or black checkers"), a behavior he maintained consistently from that point on. Two probes later he was also performing Steps 1 ("Indicate preference to play Connect Four"), 2 ("Walk to shelf and retrieve game"), and 9 ("Indicate preference to play or not to play another game") independently. After another two probes, Jerome mastered two more steps; he added one more on the next probe; and 2 months into the instructional program he was at the 70% level overall in completing the various steps of the task analysis.

The data record also includes information that should be useful for problem solving. The level of assistance key is used to record exactly what type of instructional cue was used for each step, including independent response, verbal, partial participation, full physical, partial physical, and point or model. The leisure educator records his or her initials and the date of the data probe at the top of each trial. For each step, the leisure educator then records the symbol for each cue. Noting who carried out the instruction session could also be important information; for example, Jerome had severely self-injurious behavior, which could be quite different in the presence of different instructors. Thus, certain programs were conducted by two different individuals at different times to see any performance patterns associated with particular adults on particular activities. Reading the data across the row for any one step in the task analysis can reveal problems or a lack of progress, as well as show mastery. For example, Jerome does not appear to be making any progress on Step 8 ("Congratulate other player when game is completed"). In this example, this was a concern for the leisure educators because of Jerome's lack of peer interaction. Thus, an instructor could decide that either this particular step needs to be modified further or a different level of assistance should be explored rather than only the verbal cue being used.

Data Evaluation and Program Changes

Prior to each session, the leisure educator should review the data he or she has collected on participant performance during previous instruction sessions to help determine what types and amounts of instructional cues and positive reinforcements should be provided during the instruction session. The leisure educator should also evaluate the participant's performance data on a weekly basis to decide whether or not the participant is progressing, and, if not, should determine the types of instructional program changes that need to be made. Table 3.6 presents decision rules for evaluating participant performance and for determining program changes, and Table 3.7 presents some guidelines for modifying the task analysis.

Mass trials instruction is repeated instruction of only one step of the task analysis. In some instances, where a particular step shows no progress, mass trials instruction can be an effective way to teach difficult steps (Bellamy et al., 1979). It may be particularly useful when the participant is performing all but one step of a skill sequence, and when neither branching the step nor redesigning the task analysis has worked. However, the repetition of a step associated with repeated failure is a potentially negative situation. The leisure educator should therefore make mass trials instruction extremely reinforcing and should avoid errors during those sessions. By using an errorless learning procedure involving fading of the instructional cue through time-delay (see earlier discussion in this chapter), the instructor can avoid creating a problem situation that might eventually lead to a lack of interest in the entire leisure activity. Procedures for conducting mass trials instruction appear in Table 3.8.

SKILL MAINTENANCE

When the participant's performance matches the criteria in the leisure activity's instructional objective, the leisure educator should stop providing skill acquisition instruction sessions on that activity. Of course, the activity itself should still be made available to the individual during choice instruction sessions (see Chapter 2) as well as during naturally occurring leisure situations.

Skill maintenance probes should also be scheduled for all of the activities the participant has acquired. These probes allow the leisure educator to determine whether or not the participant

Table 3.6.   Decision rules for evaluation of participant performance

1. Prior to each instruction session, review all data on the participant's performance.

2. If, after 1 week of instruction and collection of data only on independent versus assisted responses, there is no improvement in performance, begin collecting data on the types of instructional cues given.

3. Study the data for any changes in the hierarchical levels of the instructional cues necessary for correct responses. If there is an indication of some increased independence, such as a verbal cue replacing a physical assist, continue the same instruction.

4. If there is no indication of some increased independence, consider one of the following program changes:

    a. Change the type(s) of positive reinforcement.

    b. Change the frequency of positive reinforcement.

    c. Change the type(s) of instructional cues.

    d. Change the instructor.

    After making the program change, continue instruction for at least five instruction sessions.

5. If there is still no change, branch the task analysis into smaller units of participant responses. For possible alternative procedures, consult the branches given in the discussion of the specific activity. Make a program change and continue instruction for approximately 10 instruction sessions.

6. If progress is still not evident, consider this lack of progress as an indicator of participant lack of interest and discontinue instruction on the activity. Readminister the Participant Interest Inventory (Form 2.3) to identify a new preferred leisure activity; be sure to include in the inventory the activity on which the participant failed to progress to see if his or her interest decreased from the initial assessment. Such a decrease would further support a decision to discontinue instruction on that activity.

7. When the data show progress on some or most steps of the task analysis, but a consistent lack of improvement on one particular step, consider one of the following:

    a. Branch the step into smaller units of participant response.

    b. Implement mass trials instruction procedures (see Table 3.8) for the step.

    c. Assess the instructional objective in relationship to the participant's entry skills and capacities to perform the required responses and do whatever is necessary for successful performance—redesign the task, include a prosthetic device, aim for partial participation, and so forth. If partial participation is the most likely decision, determine whether a peer or friend can perform the step during play with the participant, instead of requiring an adult's assistance.

Table 3.7.   Guidelines for task analysis modification

1. Is the size of a step or phase appropriate?

    • If it is too large, can the step or phase simply be branched into smaller participant responses?

    • If it is too narrow, can related participant responses be combined into a unit that results in some functional change in the activity?

2. Does a participant's specific disability (e.g., a significant motor impairment) preclude performance of a step or phase? If so:

    • Can another functional response be identified to replace the step or phase?

    • Can the activity be redesigned to either eliminate the step or phase or make it easier to perform?

    • Can a prosthetic device be identified?

3. Is partial participation a more appropriate objective?

    • Can those steps or phases that the participant is capable of performing independently be identified?

    • Can a process be developed to make performance of the missing steps as natural as possible by a peer or friend without disabilities?

Table 3.8. Mass trials instruction procedures

1. Identify the step of the task analysis and the participant's response that is presenting difficulties.
2. Schedule additional 5-minute instruction sessions for that step, if possible, at several times during the day.
3. Begin and end each mass practice instruction session with warm-ups.
4. Arrange the instruction so that the trials in the instruction session occur fairly rapidly; the participant receives enough assistance to perform at least 75% of the trials correctly (Bellamy, Horner, & Inman, 1979); and the leisure educator reinforces every correct response.
5. Collect data on every trial, indicating the types of instructional cues if they are given by the instructor.
6. When the participant performs the step at the 75% level without any instructional cues during two consecutive sessions, discontinue mass practice.
7. While mass practice is being implemented, continue the regular instruction sessions for the leisure activity to ensure that independence is maintained on other steps and that the sequence of the steps is not forgotten. During the regular instruction sessions, provide total assistance on the step presenting the difficulties until the criterion level is met in the mass practice instruction sessions.

can still perform the leisure skills at the criterion level. As a general rule of thumb, the skill maintenance probes should occur once every 2 weeks after the participant has mastered an instructional objective and, after 1 month, on a monthly basis. After several months of skill maintenance, the leisure educator may decide to conduct the probes every 2 months or so.

To conduct a formal skill maintenance probe, the leisure educator arranges the instruction environment as he or she did during skill acquisition instruction sessions and gives the participant a general cue indicating free time, the leisure materials, and a cue to participate in the activity. Using the task analysis and its accompanying data sheet, the instructor then observes the participant and records the data on his or her performance. No instructional cues or positive reinforcers should be given. If the participant plays appropriately and independently, the leisure activity should remain on a maintenance schedule. If he or she does not perform at the criterion level, the instructor must decide whether or not to conduct additional skill acquisition instruction to bring the participant's performance back up to criterion level. Before actually beginning additional skill acquisition instruction, the educator could informally interview the participant's parent(s) or a friend who frequently participates with the individual to see if they have noticed any loss of skills. The decision of whether or not to conduct additional instruction should also be influenced by the assessment of the participant's continuing preference for the activity as well as by other instruction demands. It may be that the activity was fine at the time, but not very motivating to the individual. It may also be that the participant's friends indicate that no one really likes that game anymore. In such cases, it is better to move on to teaching new activities than to force the issue. Again, because this is the leisure domain, it is perfectly appropriate for preferences to govern behavior.

Skill maintenance probes may also be conducted more informally as part of the choice instruction sessions. These sessions more closely resemble a naturally occurring free-time situation and, as such, are extremely suitable for probing skill maintenance. The leisure educator simply collects data on the steps of the task analysis when the participant performs them for the probe and, in addition, collects the narrative data required for a choice instruction session.

Careful implementation of these procedures can be time consuming for the leisure educator, but he or she should keep in mind that these procedures have been demonstrated to be effective in teaching even those individuals with the most significant disabilities how to engage in leisure activities appropriately—an important step toward their enjoyable use of leisure time independently and with family and friends.

Chapter 4

LEISURE EDUCATION CURRICULUM

TEN ACTIVITIES

*T*his chapter presents descriptions of 10 popular, commercially available activities that are age appropriate for participation across the lifespan. They are appropriate for use in multiple environments—at home, at school, and in the community. Most families will find them affordable and enjoyable. These 10 field-tested activities include:

- Aerobic Warm-Ups
- Connect Four
- Jenga
- Magic Mitts (Scatch)
- Nintendo Game Boy
- Pinball Games
- Pottery
- Remote Control Vehicle
- Simon
- Target Games

This curriculum contains four activities (Pinball Games, Remote Control Vehicle, Simon, Target Games) that were included in the original *Ho'onanea* curriculum. Six of the original activities (Electronic Music Stick, Lego, Lite-Brite, Marble Rollway, Portable Bowling, TV Video Games) have been omitted, however, either because they are no longer available or popular or because they are not appropriate for lifetime participation. These activities have been replaced by six new activities (Aerobic Warm-Ups, Connect Four, Jenga, Magic Mitts [Scatch], Nintendo Game Boy, and Pottery), as well as an updated version of electronic target games in the Target Games activity. These additions offer increased opportunities for participation in leisure activities in the community and for planning for lifetime enjoyment.

All the activities in this curriculum follow a similar format. Each activity begins with an introduction that discusses the value and appropriate usage of the activity. The introduction is followed by a listing of *Materials*, including suggestions for materials for possible adaptations. Next, the section *Entry Motor Skill Level and Possible Adaptations* is provided. This section identifies skills (e.g., ability to stand or sit in a stable position, head and trunk control, eye–hand coordination) that a participant would need to participate in the activity, as well as suggestions for adaptations to facilitate maximum participation. The following section, *Instructional Environment*, describes the physical environment of the activity and the positioning of the participant(s) and play materials, as well as any other considerations related to physical arrangements.

The next section, *Instructional Procedures*, recommends strategies for teaching the activity to individuals with a range of ability levels. Some of the instructional procedures apply specifically to activities, such as teaching a participant to stack Jenga blocks in a loading tray. Other instructional procedures, although also activity specific, apply more generally across the entire

45

curriculum. These general instructional procedures may include recommendations for providing verbal or modeling cues, offering physical assistance, structuring activities to encourage social interaction and friendship, or promoting partial participation (see chap. 5, this volume, for a full description of strategies for partial participation).

At the heart of each activity description is the *Task Analysis*. A task analysis or series of task analyses (presented in "phases") is outlined for specific instructional objectives. Examples of instructional objectives are "Given enrollment in an aerobics class, the participant will pre-pare for participating in the class" or "Given the Star Trek game, the participant will manipulate the Game Boy system controls to advance the starship and shoot spaceships or rocks using either torpedoes or lasers." As noted in Chapter 2, instructional objectives are offered as starting points, and, in most cases, a leisure educator will need to rewrite specific conditions and perfor-mance criteria to match an individual's unique instructional needs and preferences. Most task analyses conclude with *Skill Level Adaptations*, which offer suggestions for adapting task analy-ses to reflect varying participant skill levels.

Data on participant skill acquisition can be recorded for all the activities on Form 3.2, Skill Acquisition Data Record. Form 3.2 (appearing as a filled out version for two teenagers playing Connect Four on p.31, and as a blank version in Appendix B) should be used to list what the leisure educator regards as critical steps in the task analysis that will be monitored for the participant. As a general rule, this data record should include steps for: 1) initiating play at appropriate times and choice making, 2) gathering materials, 3) assembly of the system, 4) starting a selected game, 5) engagement and active participation with the game, 6) termination of the game and use of the sys-tem, and 7) putting materials away. Even if the player only partially participates in most steps and requires full assistance on many, it will be important to record this information and to periodical-ly ensure that the player is given the opportunity to initiate those steps that have previously required help. We do not recommend collecting data on actual game performance, such as points earned or games won. These data would be ineffective to collect, and more importantly, such cri-teria miss the mark: The reason for playing the games is to occupy one's leisure time in enjoyable and socially appropriate ways. Monitoring the steps we suggest will allow one to measure attain-ment of these leisure-time goals.

Aerobic Warm-Ups

*P*rior to engaging in physical activity, it is important to loosen and stretch one's muscles. This activity, aerobic warm-ups, focuses on participating in calisthenic exercise movements that would typically be included in an aerobics class offered by a community recreation center (Municipal Park and Recreation Department, YMCA or YWCA, Jewish Community Center) or community education program. Aerobic warm-ups have the potential for providing participants with numerous benefits. Calisthenic exercise can promote cardiovascular endurance, muscular strength, flexibility, improved body image, self-esteem, and overall physical fitness and health. The exercises presented in this activity description may be performed within the context of a class (as described here), therefore providing regular opportunities for social interaction, or they can be performed at home or in the backyard in preparation for such activities as walking or jogging around a lake with a friend, playing softball, bicycling, dancing, skiing, ice skating, or rollerblading.

Materials

Enough space to allow freedom of movement, music cassettes or compact discs (CDs), cassette or CD player, full-size mirror, exercise mat(s)

Additional materials for possible adaptations: masking tape, chalk, paper

Entry Motor Skill Level and Possible Adaptations

To engage in aerobic warm-ups, a participant needs: 1) the ability to stand or sit in a stable position, 2) head and trunk control, 3) free range of motion at shoulders, and 4) the ability to coordinate leg and foot movements. For a participant with physical limitations, a physical therapist should be consulted for appropriate positioning, movement, and mobility.

If a participant has difficulty knowing where to place his or her feet during a routine, masking tape or chalk may be applied to the floor to mark correct foot placement. When shifting positions is required, placement of the feet may be numbered in sequence on the floor. Also, initially footprints may be drawn on a piece of paper or on the floor with chalk to illustrate foot positions. As the participant learns the correct exercise pattern, the footprints should be removed.

Typically, an aerobics instructor organizes various exercise routines to music, approximating dance. As participants progress in their warm-ups, the instructor can incorporate the movements into simple dance routines to musical accompaniment. For a participant who has difficulty keeping up with a fast-paced piece of music, movements may be performed at "half-time"; that is, instead of performing one movement for each beat of music, the person may perform one movement for every two, three, or four beats, as appropriate. Exercising to music can serve as a lead-up activity to dancing at parties, school, ballrooms, night clubs, discos, or other social gathering places in the community.

Instructional Environment

1. Instruction should take place in an area large enough (e.g., aerobics studio, dance studio, gymnasium, multipurpose room) so that the participants have freedom of movement. Participants should be spaced at about an arm's length or more apart to avoid accidental contact with each other. The space should be cleared of all potentially distracting objects to enable participants to focus their attention, as in an "active meditation," on specific movements and muscle groups.
2. Depending on a participant's abilities, he or she may sit in a wheelchair or a specially adapted chair that provides the necessary head, trunk, and leg support. A participant may also stand on a prone stander, in a standing box, or on a tilt table. For someone who does not require specially adapted support, but who lacks balance or endurance, a straight-backed chair may provide sufficient support. Care must be taken so that all sitting positions (e.g., cross-leg, long-leg, kneeling, or C-sitting) are performed with the back as straight as possible.
3. Exercise mats should be available to provide the necessary cushion for participants' movements and to aid in the prevention of injury.
4. Most aerobics or dance studios have floor-length mirrors covering at least one wall. Watching oneself perform aerobics in a mirror can contribute to acceptance and appreciation of one's body, spatial awareness, the synchronization of one's movements with those of other participants, and a refined performance of exercise routines.
5. The aerobics space may be arranged for circuit training to provide opportunities to exercise specific muscle groups. That is, in circuit training several exercise stations are set up where participants perform a designated exercise for approximately 1–2 minutes before rotating to the next station.
6. Aerobic and calisthenic exercise routines generally include a variety of bending and stretching movements. Each time an exercise is performed, a participant should perform it at least 10 times per set, for one to three sets, resting briefly between sets.
7. If a participant uses a wheelchair, the leisure educator should make certain that the community center or community education facility, parking lot, classroom, washrooms, and drinking fountains are wheelchair accessible.

Instructional Procedures

1. During most aerobics exercises, the instructor provides directions and performs the exercise and dance routines in the front of the room facing the participants, and provides ongoing verbal and modeling cues naturally within the context of the class. If a participant is not able to follow the directions and modeling of the instructor independently, another person

(leisure educator, peer, friend) would need to provide additional cues and prompts based on a least-to-most intrusive instructional hierarchy. That is, the leisure educator (or peer or friend) would provide an extra verbal cue. If the participant responds correctly, then the leisure educator provides immediate reinforcement (e.g., verbal praise, pat on back) and moves on to the next step of the task analysis. If the participant does not respond correctly, then the leisure educator repeats the verbal cue and models the correct response. The leisure educator may stand next to, in front of, or facing the participant (whichever position is most conducive to instruction) and perform the step with him or her. If the participant still does not respond correctly, then the instructor repeats the verbal cue and physically guides the participant through the correct response. This instructional sequence is repeated until the participant is able to follow the instructor's directions and modeling independently, or, if that is not possible, is able to continue through partial participation.

2. To physically assist a participant during an exercise, the leisure educator should stand behind or to the side of the participant and provide hand-over-hand physical guidance as needed. As the participant's proficiency increases, the leisure educator should stand back, only moving closer to assist in those skills the participant has yet to acquire.

3. For most participants, the addition of music enhances and encourages participation. It also provides a natural cue for beginning and ending the activity. As noted earlier, some participants may not be able to keep up with fast-paced music. In this case, participants may perform one movement for every two, three, or four beats, as needed, instead of one movement per beat. As the participant gains proficiency, gradually increase the tempo at which the movement is performed.

4. If a circuit training arrangement is used, the instructor should determine, before the class, the total number of stations, the amount of time to be spent at each station, the number of repetitions ("reps") per exercise, and the types of exercises based on the participants' abilities and needs.

Task Analysis: Aerobic Warm-Ups

Phase I: *Instructional Objective:* The participant will prepare for participating in an aerobics class.

Step 1: Before leaving home, dress in proper attire (workout clothes) to participate in the aerobics class.

Step 2: Enter the community recreation center or community education facility.

Step 3: Locate and proceed to the room where the aerobics class is being held.

Step 4: Enter the room.

Step 5: Acknowledge the other participants and the instructor.

Step 6: Locate the coat rack and proceed in that direction.

Step 7: Take off coat and hang it on a coat hanger (or place it with other belongings).

Step 8: Find a spot on the floor, approximately two arm lengths from the nearest participant(s).

Step 9: While waiting for the class to begin, engage in light conversation with other participants and the instructor.

Step 10: When the class begins, listen to and follow the verbal directions of the instructor.

Skill Level Adaptations: Access to the facility for a participant who uses a wheelchair needs to be screened before the first class meeting. Wheelchair access to the facility may be provided via a ramp and reserved parking, and access to the classroom may be provided via ramps or elevators. Also, washrooms and drinking fountains must be physically accessible.

A peer or friend may either travel to the facility with a participant or meet a participant at the front door of the facility. This person could initially assist a participant in Step 3 (locating the classroom), Step 6 (finding the coat rack), Step 8 (finding a position on the floor), and Step 9 (interacting with other participants and the instructor). As the participant becomes more familiar with the surroundings and the other people, assistance in these steps can be faded and the participant can take the lead in completing these tasks. The peer or friend (or leisure educator) may also need to be available to assist the participant in understanding the instructor's directions. This person could provide additional verbal cues, modeling, or physical assists as appropriate for the type of assistance to which the participant is most responsive and as appropriate for the instructional cue hierarchy described above. Care needs to be taken so that the participant does not become dependent on additional cues and assistance, but rather attempts to attend and respond directly to the instructor's directions.

Phase II: *Instructional Objective:* At the aerobics instructor's directions, the participant will engage in a relaxation exercise.

Step 1:   Listen to and follow the instructor's directions and modeling throughout the class.
Step 2:   Lie on the floor face up approximately two arm lengths from the nearest participant(s).
Step 3:   Relax the entire body for 1–2 minutes.
Step 4:   While relaxing, inhale deeply and exhale slowly in a regular pattern.
Step 5:   Tighten the entire body for 20 seconds, continuing to breathe.
Step 6:   Relax the body again for 1–2 minutes, continuing to breath deeply and regularly.
Step 7:   Tighten the entire body again for 20 seconds, continuing to breathe.
Step 8:   Relax the body again for 1–2 minutes, continuing to breathe deeply and regularly.
Step 9:   Stand to an upright position.
Step 10:   Jump up and down and shake the body for 1–2 minutes.
Step 11:   Attend to the instructor for further directions.

Skill Level Adaptations: To set the atmosphere for relaxation, the exercise routine should be accompanied by calm music played at a slow, even tempo. Remind participants to continue breathing throughout the entire sequence. It is appropriate to inhale during relaxed states and to exhale during more vigorous movements.

Phase III: *Instructional Objective:* At the aerobics instructor's directions, the participant will perform underhand arm extensions in time to music.

Step 1:   Listen to and follow the instructor's directions and modeling.
Step 2:   Stand with arms at sides and palms facing forward.
Step 3:   Lift arms forward and upward 1 foot from the body and hold the position for 3 seconds.
Step 4:   Return arms slowly to sides.
Step 5:   Rest arms for 1–3 seconds.
Step 6:   Lift arms forward and upward 2 feet from the body and hold the position for 3 seconds.
Step 7:   Return arms slowly to sides.
Step 8:   Rest arms for 1–3 seconds.
Step 9:   Lift arms forward and upward directly in front of the body and hold the position for 3 seconds.
Step 10:   Return arms slowly to sides.
Step 11:   Rest arms for 1–3 seconds.

Skill Level Adaptations: By adding finger flexion to the underhand arm extension routine, this exercise approximates the motion that is used in throwing horseshoes and in bowling. The amount of time the underhand extension is held in position and the arms are at rest may be adjusted to suit a participant's individual needs.

Phase IV: *Instructional Objective:* At the aerobics instructor's directions, the participant will perform overhand arm extensions in time to music.

Step 1:   Listen to and follow the instructor's directions and modeling.
Step 2:   Stand with arms at sides and palms facing back.
Step 3:   Lift arms forward and extend them upward toward the ceiling, palms facing forward.
Step 4:   Lower arms 1 foot and hold the position for 3 seconds.
Step 5:   Return arms slowly to upward position.
Step 6:   Hold position for 1–3 seconds.
Step 7:   Lower arms to 2 feet from the body and hold the position for 3 seconds.
Step 8:   Return arms slowly to upward position.
Step 9:   Hold position for 1–3 seconds.
Step 10:   Lower arms to directly in front of the body and hold position for 3 seconds.
Step 11:   Return arms slowly to upward position.
Step 12:   Hold position for 1–3 seconds.
Step 13:   Lower arms completely to rest by sides.

Skill Level Adaptations: This exercise approximates the "spike and serve" action used in a volleyball activity and the casting of a fishing line.

Phase V: *Instructional Objective:* At the aerobics instructor's directions, the participant will perform side arm extensions in time to music.

Step 1:   Listen to and follow the instructor's directions and modeling.
Step 2:   Stand at least two arm lengths away from the nearest participant(s).
Step 3:   Extend arms out in front of the body and lock fingers and hands to resemble an elephant's trunk.
Step 4:   With back held straight, swing arms 1 foot to the left, looking left as you swing.
Step 5:   With back held straight, swing arms 1 foot to the right, looking right as you swing.
Step 6:   Swing arms to left and right as high as possible.
Step 7:   Continue locking fingers and hands, extended outward in front of the body.
Step 8:   Bending forward slightly, swing arms 1 foot to the left, looking left.
Step 9:   Bending forward slightly, swing arms 1 foot to the right, looking right.
Step 10:   Swing arms to left and right as high as possible.
Step 11:   Bending forward slightly, swing arms forward away from the body.
Step 12:   Bending forward slightly, swing arms back toward the body.
Step 13:   Swing arms downward between legs, looking downward.
Step 14:   Swing arms upward away from the body, looking forward.
Step 15:   Wait for further directions from the instructor.

Skill Level Adaptations: This movement approximates striking a ball as in games such as croquet, hockey, and golf. To approximate the ball strike in such games as softball, badminton, and tennis, this exercise could be modified by positioning the arms a few feet in front of the body and then swinging to the right and left.

Phase VI: *Instructional Objective:* At the aerobics instructor's directions, the participant will perform toe touches in time to music.

Step 1:   Listen to and follow the instructor's directions and modeling.
Step 2:   Stand with legs slightly apart in a comfortable position (avoid locking knees), with back straight.
Step 3:   Bend forward slowly about 1 foot and extend both arms to reach for toes.
Step 4:   Return to upright position.
Step 5:   Bend forward slowly about 2 feet and extend both arms to reach for toes.
Step 6:   Return to upright position.
Step 7:   Bend forward slowly until body is at a 90° angle and extend both arms to touch toes.
Step 8:   Repeat Steps 3 through 7 as directed by the instructor.
Step 9:   Wait for further directions from the instructor.

Skill Level Adaptations: Toe touches are beneficial for promoting trunk and leg flexibility. Toe touches may also be performed from a seated position. To promote social interaction, two participants could sit opposite each other with their legs extended and toes touching. The participants could then try to touch the fingertips of the other person. Next, the participants could try to hold the other person's hands or to give each other a "high five."

All of these simple movement exercises may be performed to music. The tempo of the music should be varied to peak interest. A complete warm-up routine would include a variety of toe touches and bending and stretching movements for all parts of the body, including the neck, shoulders, and calves.

Phase VII: *Instructional Objective:* At the aerobics instructor's directions, the participant will prepare to leave the class and facility.

Step 1:   Relax for a few minutes to "cool down."
Step 2:   Interact socially with the other participants and the instructor, if appropriate.
Step 3:   Locate the coat rack and proceed in that direction.
Step 4:   Remove coat from the coat hanger and put coat on.
Step 5:   Say good-bye to the instructor and the other participants, and/or walk with participant(s) to parking lot.
Step 6:   Exit the facility.

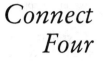

Connect
Four

Connect Four: The Vertical Checkers Game is played like a combination of checkers and tic-tac-toe. The game is inexpensive (less than $12), making it affordable and accessible for almost any family or leisure educator. Furthermore, the instructions are printed in both English and Spanish. Connect Four is easy to assemble and play, and individuals with very different ability levels can fully participate in and enjoy the game. The action of the game involves two players taking turns dropping their individual checkers into a plastic grid through slots at the top of the grid, causing the checkers to stack vertically. As columns are filled with checkers, rows and diagonals take shape. Each player attempts to be the first to line up four checkers of the same color (red or black) in a horizontal, vertical, or diagonal row, while preventing the other player from doing so.

As with many games, the rules can be modified in various ways to individualize the game. Both the materials and the action of the game—black and red checkers dropping through slots to form interesting visual displays—appear to be intrinsically reinforcing. Even the assembly of the grid, and particularly the release of all the checkers at the end of the game, can be motivating to participants. Because the game involves turn taking and can accommodate individuals of different skill levels, Connect Four is an excellent interactive game for a person with significant intellectual impairments or multiple disabilities playing with a peer without disabilities. Finally, a video version of Connect Four is available for use with an Apple computer; therefore, leisure educators who already have access to this equipment can use both the manual and the computer versions with participants.

Materials

Connect Four: The Vertical Checkers Game by Milton Bradley (the game consists of a plastic grid, two end supports, and black and red checkers [21 each])

Additional materials for possible adaptations: the box base or cover, modeling clay, Play-Doh

Entry Motor Skill Level and Possible Adaptations

The grid is assembled in a vertical position by inserting its sides into the notched edges of the two end supports. When the sliding lever is at the bottom of the grid, it holds the checkers in place in the grid; when moved to one side, it allows the checkers to fall through the bottom of the grid. In order to play the game as intended by the manufacturer, a player must have: 1) head and trunk control, 2) the ability to hold a stable position, 3) fine pincer grasp for the checkers and the release lever, and 4) sufficient eye–hand coordination to insert the checkers into the grid at the top.

If a participant has difficulty picking up the checkers from a flat surface, the checkers could be positioned at an angle on a change holder. If a player does not have a pincer grasp to hold the checkers and release the lever, a therapeutic recreation specialist or occupational therapist should be consulted to determine whether a modified pincer grasp, gross palmar grasp, or supported pincer grasp would be preferable for his or her fine motor development. For a participant with unsteady movements that make it difficult to keep the grid in place, Play-Doh or clay can be used to stabilize the end supports on the table surface; alternatively, a peer without a disability could hold the grid for the participant during each turn.

Placing the standing grid into the game's container box during play will prevent the checkers from scattering when released at the end of each game. If a player cannot grasp and manipulate the sliding lever without support, an extension can be glued over the lever to provide more surface to grasp. The grid itself should also be stabilized.

Instructional Environment

The participant should be seated at a table across from another player with the leisure educator close enough to provide any necessary support. Depending on the participant's abilities, he or she may use a wheelchair equipped with a tray or specially adapted seat with a table. Or, the participant may stand on a prone stander, in a standing box, or on a tilt table. In each case, the other player should be positioned across the playing surface facing the participant.

In some instances, it may be necessary to avoid proximity to any hard playing surface. One participant we worked with who enjoyed this game a great deal could not be positioned at a table or similar hard surface as he engaged in severe head banging and face slamming when close to such surfaces. Learning a variety of alternative activities to occupy his time and attention was part of this young man's program, so we could not wait to teach Connect Four until after his self-injurious behaviors no longer posed a threat to his safety. Thus, in this case, the inverted game box containing the game was placed on a peer's lap who sat knee-to-knee facing the participant during play.

Instructional Procedures

1. Assembling the grid when Connect Four begins and releasing the checkers when each game ends are steps that are as interesting and reinforcing to many participants as the game itself. Thus, these steps should be included in the initial teaching sequence. Another preparation activity that can support both academic skill development and engagement in the game is to participate in sorting the red and black checkers, giving all the checkers of one color to a partner and keeping those of the other color. The level of independence on these steps depends on the individual participant's characteristics.

2. Precisely because Connect Four is a game intended for two players who take turns, it provides an ideal context for teaching and supporting the incidental learning of many social

skills. There are several opportunities for choice making, including: a) choosing to play Connect Four, b) choosing either red or black checkers, c) choosing which column to use for each checker, and d) repeating these choices several times throughout any one game. Turn taking is an essential rule of the game and can also be practiced by taking turns releasing the checkers after each game. A participant can also learn to reinforce others by congratulating the other player as each game is completed (regardless of whether or not anyone "won"). In addition, because assembly and disassembly are not complex tasks, the participant can fully participate in both gathering and putting away materials.

3. Rather than focusing on actually making rows of four checkers of one color, the goal of the activity should be individualized to meet participant needs. For players who are practicing reach and grasp movements and eye–hand coordination, playing Connect Four can provide as many learning trials as the outdated, nonfunctional mass practice of placing pegs in a pegboard or stringing beads. An appropriate goal for a participant with a significant cognitive disability may be to attend to cues and recognize when a column is full. Mastery of this goal can be validated through observation that the participant no longer attempts to insert another checker into a full column but moves to one with available space. For another participant, the goal might be to partially participate in all motor movements and visually attend to the checker motions. In every case, the activity goal should include social skills development, including sharing, turn taking, smiling at and congratulating a peer, and indicating preference.

Data Collection and Monitoring Mastery

Form 3.2 (p. 31), Skill Acquisition Data Record, has been partially completed to illustrate how the leisure educator might record probe session data on selected, critical steps of the task analysis for initial play. Ten steps have been identified as targets for this participant, and these are listed on the data record from bottom to top at the far left under "Steps in Activity Sequence." We recommend collecting probe data on each goal once every 2 weeks; this data record would accommodate approximately 5 months of data. As can be seen from the key at the top right, each response is recorded for one of six levels of assistance: 1) independent, 2) verbal, 3) partial participation, 4) full physical, 5) partial physical, or 6) point or model.

Task Analysis: Begin Connect Four

Instructional Objective: Given the Connect Four game, the participant will actively participate in playing manual Connect Four with a peer under minimal supervision by the leisure educator.

Step 1:   Indicate preference to play Connect Four.
Step 2:   Walk to shelf and retrieve game.
Step 3:   Sit across from peer and organize game for play.
Step 4:   Check release lever for centered position to hold checkers in frame.
Step 5:   Choose red or black checkers.
Step 6:   Take turns playing with peer.
Step 7:   Pick up correct color checker and place into any available slot on grid.
Step 8:   Congratulate other player when game is completed.
Step 9:   Indicate preference to play or not to play another game.
Step 10: Place game pieces in box and return box to shelf.

Skill Level Adaptations: For a participant who uses a wheelchair, the game should be stored in a location and at a height that allows access, and the task analysis should be modified to reflect use of the wheelchair to retrieve and put away the game. For the young man we described earlier who initially could not be positioned near a hard table-top surface, the game was positioned on the leisure educator's or a peer's lap for Step 3 of the instructional sequence. Later, when his self-injurious behavior was no longer a threat, Step 3 involved setting up the game on a table top of his choice.

For a participant who is fully supported during the activity, a peer can hold the grid near eye level and even slant it so that a participant with significant motor impairments can visually scan the checker display throughout the game. Once inserted at the top, the checkers cannot slide out of the grid until the release lever is moved at the bottom of the grid, which makes it possible to position the grid at whatever angle is necessary.

As with many of the games and activities in this curriculum, it is not necessary to be concerned about who wins or loses each game according to the manufacturer's criterion of four checkers of the same color in a row. The primary purpose of participation in the activity is to learn and enjoy activity-focused peer play, as well as to enable the development of eye–hand coordination and various motor, self-management, and social skills.

Task Analysis: Assembly of Connect Four

Instructional Objective: Given the Connect Four game box, the participant will assemble the game for play.

Step 1:   Take the lid off the box and place it upside down on your lap or on a table surface, putting the bottom of the box inside of it.

Step 2:   Pick up one of the blue end supports and turn it so that the notched edge is facing you.

Step 3:   With your other hand, pick up the yellow grid and fit the two prongs on one side of the grid into the notches of the end support.

Step 4:   When the side of the grid is flush against the notched edge of the end support, hold the grid at the top with one hand and the end support at its middle with the other hand. Slide the grid down and the edge up so the two pieces lock in place.

Step 5:   Hold the grid in one hand. With your other hand, pick up the remaining blue end support with the notched edge facing you.

Step 6:   Fit the two prongs on the other side of the grid on the remaining end support.

Step 7:   When this side of the grid is flush against the notched edge of the end support, hold the grid at the top with one hand and the end support at its middle with the other hand. Slide the grid down and the edge up so these two pieces lock in place.

Step 8:   Position the game box between you and your partner, and stand the grid upright in the box.

Step 9:   Check that the position of the release lever at the bottom of the grid is in the center locked position so that the checkers will not fall out.

Step 10:   Locate the checkers and sort them by red and black.

Step 11:   Choose a color, a turn, and begin play.

Jenga

*J*enga is an inexpensive game that is appropriate for many age groups, from elementary school–age children through adults. It can be played by any number of players or alone. Jenga encourages turn taking and social interaction with other players, as well as the development of eye–hand coordination and fine motor skills. Jenga has the advantage of being a simple, straightforward game that is easy to understand and uncomplicated to play; at the same time, it is challenging and reinforcing for people with varying skill levels. The game is available for less than $15, and is relatively small and compact for easy portability.

Jenga contains 54 rectangular wood blocks that measure approximately 3″ × 1″ × 1/2″ each. The materials are durable and unbreakable, and should be able to withstand rough play. To play Jenga, the blocks are stacked in a loading tray to form a "tower." The players then take turns carefully removing blocks, one by one, from anywhere below the top of the tower, and then stacking them on top of the tower to build it ever precariously higher. The object of the game is to see how high the tower can be constructed without falling.

Although the manufacturer intends the "winner" to be the last person to take a turn without making the tower tumble, Jenga can be played to emphasize enjoyment, cooperation, and socialization, rather than winning. As the manufacturer suggests, the person who causes the tower to fall can have the privilege of setting up the tower in the loading tray for the next game (thus avoiding the potential stigma of being the "loser"). In addition, players can provide encouragement and feedback to each other throughout the game.

Jenga provides many opportunities for choice making. Besides choosing to play Jenga instead of another leisure activity, with each turn, participants select which particular wood block to remove from the tower and where to stack it on top of the tower.

Materials

Jenga by Milton Bradley, which includes 54 wood blocks and 1 plastic loading tray to construct the tower before play begins

Additional materials for possible adaptations: Velcro strips, glue, playing board, clay or Play-Doh

Entry Motor Skill Level and Possible Adaptations

To play Jenga as designed by the manufacturer, the participant must have: 1) the ability to maintain a stable position, 2) head and trunk control, 3) fine pincer grasp and release, and 4) sufficient eye–hand coordination to remove blocks from the tower and restack them.

If a participant is not able to perform a pincer grasp to remove and stack the wood blocks, he or she may indicate (point with finger or wand) to a peer which block to manipulate and reposition. When stacking blocks into the loading tray, a participant may use a modified pincer grasp, supported pincer grasp, or gross palmar grasp to pick up the block and hand it to a peer who can then place it into the loading tray. (An occupational therapist, therapeutic recreation specialist, or physical therapist should be consulted to determine which style of grasp would be preferable for the player's fine motor development.)

To facilitate filling the loading tray with blocks, the tray may need to be stabilized. This can be accomplished by first gluing one side of a Velcro strip to each end of the base of the loading tray. Next, glue the other sides of the two Velcro strips to a flat, stable playing board at the same distance apart (approximately 10″) as the Velcro strips on the loading tray. When the loading tray is filled with blocks, care needs to be taken while loosening the tray from the Velcro fasteners. An alternative for stabilizing the loading tray would be to affix clay or Play-Doh to the corners of the base of the empty tray, and to press the base of the tray firmly and securely onto the table, board, or playing surface.

Instructional Environment

The participant should sit at a table with the tower of blocks, or loading tray and pile of blocks, directly in front of his or her body. Other players may sit next to or across from the participant. If the participant needs physical prompts or assistance from the leisure educator, the educator should stand near the participant so he or she is able to offer assistance easily, but unobtrusively.

Depending on the player's abilities, the player may use a wheelchair equipped with a tray or a specially adapted seat with a table. Or, the participant may stand on a prone stander, in a standing box, or on a tilt table. In each case, the other players can pull their chairs close to the participant and playing surface to play the game.

Instructional Procedures

1. Setting up the Jenga tower can be as reinforcing to the players as actually playing the game. A participant may fill the loading tray alone (suggested by the manufacturer) or players may take turns filling the tray together. If a participant has considerable difficulty in handling and manipulating the blocks, however, filling the tray may become tedious and time-consuming for all the players. In this case, the first time the game is played, a peer can demonstrate how to construct the tower in the loading tray so the players can experience the reinforcing fun of playing the actual game as soon as possible. The next time the game is played, the leisure

educator will need to gauge how much assistance a participant needs to reconstruct the tower while still retaining the appeal of the activity.

2. As a game intended for two or more players, Jenga provides many opportunities for social interaction and turn taking. Players take turns removing and stacking blocks. They may also take turns aligning the blocks in the loading tray. While playing the game, players can acknowledge each other, smile at each other, offer each other feedback and encouragement, and congratulate the person who positions the last piece before the tower falls. To establish a cooperative goal and avoid having a winner and a loser, players can work together to set new records for building the tallest tower.

3. Because constructing the initial tower and playing Jenga are not complex tasks, a player with an adequate pincer grasp and good eye–hand coordination can participate fully in both of these activities. A player who is less skilled in these areas can still enjoy the game through partial participation.

4. For participants who need to strengthen their pincer grasps or develop eye–hand coordination, playing Jenga provides multiple opportunities for practicing reach, grasp, and release skills within the context of an age-appropriate leisure skill. A physical therapist, occupational therapist, or therapeutic recreation specialist should be consulted to ensure the promotion of these skills. For extra practice in these skills, it is appropriate to play Jenga alone. For added interest, the solo player can try to top his or her record height before the tower collapses, or try to build the tower higher in a shorter amount of time.

5. If a participant is unable to perform a pincer grasp, the leisure educator or peer can employ a hand-over-hand or finger-over-finger physical assist to help the participant pick up and release the wood blocks.

Task Analysis: Setting Up the Tower

Instructional Objective: Given the 54 Jenga blocks and a loading tray, the participant will fill the tray with blocks to construct a tower for playing Jenga.

Step 1: Select Jenga from among at least two leisure activities.

Step 2: Retrieve game from the shelf where it is stored.

Step 3: Remove loading tray and wood blocks from box and place them on the table.

Step 4: Set box aside.

Step 5: Place the base of the loading tray securely on the playing surface, with the long open side of the loading tray directly facing you and the open end of the loading tray on the right.

Step 6: To begin placing the first row of blocks in the loading tray, pick up one wood block with the preferred hand using a pincer grasp.

Step 7: Place one of the long, narrow ends of the first block, face down, square into the left hand base of the loading tray.

Step 8: Pick up a second wood block using a pincer grasp.

Step 9: Place one of the long, narrow ends of the second block face down on top of the exposed long, narrow end of the first block.

Step 10: Pick up a third wood block using a pincer grasp.

Step 11: Place one of the long, narrow ends of the third block face down on top of the exposed long, narrow end of the second block. (The first row of blocks is now complete.)

Step 12: To begin the second row of blocks, pick up a fourth wood block using a pincer grasp.

Step 13:   Place one of the short, narrow ends of the fourth block face down in the newly cre-
           ated left corner of the loading tray farthest away from you, with the wider side of the
           block flush against the first row of blocks.
Step 14:   Pick up a fifth wood block using a pincer grasp.
Step 15:   Place one of the short, narrow ends of the fifth block face down and next to the fourth
           block, with the wide side of the block flush against the first row of blocks.
Step 16:   Pick up a sixth wood block using a pincer grasp.
Step 17:   Place one of the short, narrow ends of the sixth block face down and next to the fifth
           block, with the wide side of the block flush against the first row of blocks. (The sec-
           ond row of blocks is now complete.)
Step 18:   Repeat Steps 6 through 17 until all 54 blocks are loaded into the loading tray (18
           rows).
Step 19:   Carefully tilt the right end of the loading tray full of blocks up and counterclockwise
           until the tower stands upright directly in front of you.
Step 20:   Adjust and realign blocks as necessary to stabilize the tower.
Step 21:   With the left hand, carefully slide the tray away to the left to allow the tower to stand
           by itself. (Use the right hand to stabilize the pieces.)
Step 22:   Set the loading tray aside to begin playing Jenga.

Skill Level Adaptations: For a participant who uses a wheelchair, store Jenga in a location and at a height that provides easy access to the game. The task analysis should be modified
to reflect the use of a wheelchair to retrieve the game and set up the tower.

     As noted earlier, a peer (or peers) may provide assistance to a participant who has difficulty
manipulating the blocks. For example, the participant could point to a particular wood block
(with a finger, stick, pencil, or head wand) that he or she wants loaded into the tray and indicate
where the block should be positioned. A peer could then do the actual picking up and placement
of the block. In addition, a peer could assist the participant in manipulating the block pieces by
providing finger-over-finger or hand-over-hand physical assistance in grasping and releasing the
blocks.

Task Analysis: Playing Jenga

Instructional Objective: Given the tower of Jenga blocks, the participant will take turns removing a block from below the top story of the tower and stacking it on top of the tower.

Step 1: Decide which player should go first. (The manufacturer suggests that the player who builds the tower should go first, with play continuing to the left of the first player.)

Step 2: Take turns with your partner(s) selecting a wood block to remove from anywhere below the top story of the tower.

Step 3: With the index finger of the preferred hand, gently push one short, narrow end of the selected block toward the middle of the tower so the other end of the block protrudes away from the tower and can be easily grasped.

Step 4: Using a pincer grasp, gently pull the protruding end of the block out and away from the tower with the preferred hand, without causing the tower to fall. (If any other blocks are knocked out of place, straighten them using one hand only.)

Step 5: Decide where to place the block on top of the tower.

Step 6: To gain a more secure grasp, reposition the fingers to pincer grasp the narrow sides at the middle of the block.

Step 7: Extend your arm to position your hand above the desired spot on top of the tower.

Step 8: Gently lower your arm to place the block in the desired spot on top of the tower. (As intended by the manufacturer, each turn ends 10 seconds after a block has been stacked or as soon as another player touches another block.)

Step 9: Continue taking turns with your partner(s), removing and stacking blocks, until the tower finally collapses. (The manufacturer indicates that a pro can build a tower as high as 36 stories or more!)

Step 10: If desired, play another game of Jenga by refilling the loading tray.

Step 11: Load the tray with Jenga blocks.

Step 12: Insert the tray in the box.

Step 13: Close the box and return it to the storage shelf.

Skill Level Adaptations: When loading the tray with blocks, a peer (or peers) may assist a participant who has difficulty removing and stacking blocks. Similar to the adaptations for the previous task analysis, a participant could indicate (point with finger, stick, pencil, or head wand) which block to remove or stack, and the peer could then perform the task. In addition, finger-over-finger or hand-over-hand physical assistance in grasping would be appropriate at the discretion of the leisure educator.

To remove and stack blocks, and for Step 4 that involves straightening blocks that are knocked loose, the manufacturer's rule states that only one hand should be used. This rule may be modified to allow two-handed use for a participant who would not be successful using only one hand. Step 8 may also be modified to allow more than 10 seconds to pass before a turn is complete.

If a participant uses a wheelchair, the task analysis should be modified to reflect the use of the wheelchair during play and when returning the game to the storage shelf.

Winning the game should be deemphasized in favor of promoting social interaction, enjoyment, and cooperation. Through playing Jenga, participants can learn to greet each other, take turns, initiate and maintain conversation, help each other with physically handling the game pieces, praise the successful stacking of blocks, and work together to load the tray for a new game.

Magic Mitts
(Scatch)

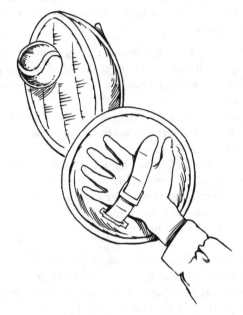

*M*agic Mitts, or Scatch, is a catch-and-throw ball game that can be enjoyed by friends and family of all ages. Magic Mitts can be adapted to varying skill levels, and can be played indoors or outdoors. To play Magic Mitts, two or more participants throw a light-weight, felt-covered ball back and forth, catching the ball with a Velcro-faced mitt strapped to the back of their hands (thus requiring no palmar grasp to hold the mitt). Magic Mitts can develop throwing and catching skills, eye–hand–foot coordination, depth perception, visual tracking, and physical conditioning, as well as social and interpersonal skills. The game allows for active recreation by players who need to work on synchronizing their small and large skeletal muscles. Magic Mitts, and other similar games, are inexpensive (about $6), and the rules can be easily modified to create interesting variations of the activity.

Materials

Magic Mitts by Sportcraft (or similar game such as Scatch), which includes one felt-covered rubber ball (similar to a tennis ball) and two flat, circular, Velcro-faced mitts with adjustable straps

Additional materials for possible adaptations: Velcro strips, glue, board, tongs, reaching device, masking tape

Entry Motor Skill Level and Possible Adaptations

To play Magic Mitts as intended by the manufacturer, a participant must have: 1) the ability to move about freely and/or the ability to stand or sit in a stable position, 2) head and trunk control, 3) sufficient eye–hand coordination to accomplish visually directed throwing and catching, 4) free range of motion at shoulder, 5) release at end of arm swing, 6) sufficient strength to throw the ball, and 7) whole-hand grasp.

The Velcro-faced Magic Mitts are ideal for a participant who would have difficulty grasping and holding a traditional paddle. The mitt simply straps to the back of the open hand and can be adjusted easily to any hand size. If a participant has difficulty using the Magic Mitt to catch the ball, larger mitts may be substituted (Remco Toys offers a larger Catch Glove).

If a participant has difficulty manipulating even the larger mitt, then Velcro strips may be glued to a board that is positioned near (within reaching distance of) the participant. When indoors, the board could be angled against a wall; when outdoors, the board could lean against a tree. With this arrangement, a peer or family member could throw the ball toward the board and the participant could remove the ball from the board and return the throw to the other player. If a participant has difficulty removing the ball, the leisure educator could provide tongs or a reaching device to facilitate retrieval, as well as be sure that the Velcro-covered board is within sufficient reaching distance.

Instructional Environment

1. Magic Mitts can be played indoors or outdoors—in parks, playgrounds, schools, front and backyards, and other neighborhood environments.
2. The distance between the players should be determined prior to each instruction session based on the participant's overall throwing and catching abilities. Initially, the distance between players should be at least 1 foot less than the participant's height. If the participant has the ability to learn an overhand throw, a distance of $1^{1}/_{2}$–2 feet between the players will help ensure success in directing the throw. As the participant's ability to throw the ball improves, the distance between players can gradually be increased.
3. In the initial stages of instruction, masking tape can be applied to the ground or floor to mark the distance between players. The participant should be instructed to stand behind this line while he or she is throwing and catching the ball. As instruction progresses, the masking tape should be removed and the participant should be taught to stand at a designated distant point without marked lines.
4. Depending on the participant's abilities, he or she may sit in a wheelchair or a specially adapted chair. The participant may also stand on a prone stander, in a standing box, or on a tilt table.

Instructional Procedures

1. Each participant should retrieve his or her own mitt from the equipment bag or shelf and put the mitt on his or her nondominant catching hand to allow throwing the ball with his or her dominant throwing hand. Initially, one player may act as lead thrower, providing instructional cues, encouragement, and reinforcement to the other player. The ball may be thrown either underhand or overhand, depending on the participant's ability to throw the ball. Participants should be encouraged to throw the ball at a slow to moderate speed, and to aim it directly at the other player's mitt.
2. Prior to instruction, the leisure educator should determine the most appropriate throwing and catching distance between the players based on the participants' preferences and skills. The leisure educator can initially mark the throwing distance between players by affixing strips of masking tape to the floor or ground. A slender rope, string, or other long, flexible object could also be used. (The players should be encouraged to participate in performing this task.) The distance between players needs to be reassessed by the leisure educator as instruction proceeds and performance improves.
3. Prior to instruction, the leisure educator will need to decide whether the participant should throw the ball using an underhand or overhand motion. If the participant has a good grasp

and control of the ball, the leisure educator may consider starting him or her on Phase II, which provides instruction on the overhand throw. The skill that is typically easier, the underhand throw, is outlined in Phase I. Depending on the individual participant's needs and potential for experiencing success, the leisure educator may change the phase of instruction as needed.

4. Several sets of Magic Mitts may be purchased to enable more than two players to play the game at the same time. Having several sets of the game available also gives players access to extra balls during the game; therefore, when balls are accidentally thrown outside the playing area, the players can avoid spending an inordinate amount of time chasing and retrieving them. Of course, for some participants, requiring such gross motor movements is desirable. The leisure educator needs to assess the amount of gross motor movement that is appropriate for each participant.

5. Intended by the manufacturer as a game to be played by two or more players, Magic Mitts provides many opportunities for social interaction and the development of friendships and other relationships. Players can provide each other encouragement, pointers, feedback, "high fives," and discussions of the game afterward. They can make decisions together about how far apart they should stand or how fast to throw the ball, they can help each other retrieve and pick up stray balls, and they can invent novel games with new rules.

Task Analysis: Magic Mitts

Phase I: *Instructional Objectives:* Given a Velcro mitt and felt ball, the participant will throw the ball toward the mitt of the other player using an underhand toss. When the other player throws the ball to the participant, the participant will catch and retrieve the ball from the mitt.

Step 1: Choose to play Magic Mitts from among at least two leisure activities.
Step 2: Retrieve Magic Mitts from shelf or equipment bag.
Step 3: Pick up the mitt with the preferred hand.
Step 4: Insert the fingers of the nonpreferred catching hand between the back of the plastic mitt and the Velcro strap, palm down, leaving the thumb free.
Step 5: Using a pincer grasp with the preferred hand, pull the free end of the Velcro strap to tighten the strap securely but comfortably around the nonpreferred catching hand.
Step 6: Pick up the ball with the preferred throwing hand, using a whole-hand grasp.
Step 7   Stand at an appropriate distance from the other player; face the player.
Step 8: Swing the arm down and backward to an underhand throwing position.
Step 9: While watching the other player, swing the arm upward and forward, releasing the ball when it is aligns in front of the body and is pointed toward the other player.
Step 10: Check the throw (and catch) by looking at the other player or at the place where the ball fell.
Step 11: The other player catches the ball and removes it from the mitt.
Step 12: Watch the other player as he or she throws the ball toward you.
Step 13: Visually track the ball as it comes toward you, positioning your mitt to catch the ball.
Step 14: Catch the ball.
Step 15: Look at the ball attached to the mitt.
Step 16: With your preferred throwing hand, remove the ball from the mitt using a whole-hand grasp. (If the ball is not caught with the mitt, look at where the ball fell and bend over to pick up the ball with the preferred throwing hand.)
Step 17: Resume the throwing position. Face the other player and continue to throw and catch the ball using Steps 6–16 of this task analysis.

Phase II: *Instructional Objectives:* Given a Velcro mitt and felt ball, the participant will throw the ball toward the mitt of the other player using an overhand throw. When the other player throws the ball to the participant, the participant will catch and retrieve the ball from the mitt.

Step 1:   Choose to play Magic Mitts from among at least two leisure activities.
Step 2:   Retrieve Magic Mitts from shelf or equipment bag.
Step 3:   Pick up the mitt with the preferred hand.
Step 4:   Insert the fingers of the nonpreferred catching hand between the back of the plastic mitt and the Velcro strap, palm down, leaving the thumb free.
Step 5:   Using a pincer grasp with the preferred hand, pull the free end of the Velcro strap to tighten the strap securely but comfortably around the preferred nonpreferred catching hand.
Step 6:   Pick up the ball with the preferred throwing hand, using a whole-hand grasp.
Step 7:   Stand at an appropriate distance from the other player; face the player.
Step 8:   Move the arm over head and backward to an overhand throwing position.
Step 9:   While watching the other player, swing the arm downward and forward, releasing the ball when it is aligned in front of the body and is pointed toward the other player.
Step 10:   Check the throw (and catch) by looking at the other player or at the place where the ball fell.
Step 11:   The other player catches the ball and removes it from the mitt.
Step 12:   Watch the other player as he or she throws the ball toward you.
Step 13:   Visually track the ball as it comes toward you, positioning the mitt to catch the ball.
Step 14:   Catch the ball.
Step 15:   Look at the ball attached to the mitt.
Step 16:   With the preferred throwing hand, remove the ball from the mitt using a whole-hand grasp. (If the ball is not caught with the mitt, look at where the ball fell and bend over to pick up the ball with the preferred throwing hand.)
Step 17:   Resume the throwing position. Face the other player and continue to throw and catch the ball using Steps 6–16 of this task analysis.

Branch For Step 9, Phase II: Magic Mitts

Problem 1:   The participant does not watch the other player while throwing the ball; therefore, he or she does not throw the ball to the participant.

Instructional Objective: The participant will watch the other player continuously—from the point at which the arm is moved into the throwing position to the point at which the ball is released—on four out of five trials for three consecutive sessions.

Instructional Procedures:

1. This branch is designed to be used within the context of the task analysis as a parallel objective to the phase in which the participant is being instructed. Collect data on the steps performed independently by the participant and on the number of trials in which the participant watches the other player.

2. Position yourself next to the player to whom the participant is throwing the ball, which should be at whatever distance the participant is currently using during instruction. On giving the verbal cue, "(Name of participant), watch (name of other player)," point to the other player with the index finger.

3. Systematically increase the distance between yourself and the other player until you are standing next to the participant.

4. Initially, reinforce the participant every time he or she watches the other player while throwing the ball. As you move closer to the participant, more emphasis should be placed on the ball successfully reaching the other player's mitt. This can be done by pairing the two responses—"Good watching, (name of participant). You threw the ball right to (name of other player)'s mitt." This continuous reinforcement should be reduced to reinforcement only for throwing the ball to the other player.

Problem 2:   The participant does not release the ball.

Instructional Objective: The participant will move his or her arm appropriately and will open his or her fingers to release the ball.

Instructional Procedures:

1. This branch is designed to be used independently of the task analysis. Follow the procedures for mass trials (see Table 3.8) and record data on the number of trials in which the ball is released independently.

2. Tilt the Velcro-covered board at a slight angle against the wall at the participant's eye level. Instruct the participant to stand or sit in a chair in front of the board.

3. Instruct the participant to hold the ball with a whole-hand grasp in the preferred throwing hand at eye level.

4. Physically prime the flexing of the wrist and the release of the ball. Pair this physical assistance with the verbal cue, "Throw the ball." Reinforce the successful release of the ball.

5. When the participant begins to release the ball without physical priming, incorporate the arm movements for the appropriate underhand or overhand throw the participant is using in the skill acquisition instruction sessions. This can be done by physically guiding the participant at the elbow and shoulder to move the arm.

6. When the participant meets the criterion of three out of four successful releases, begin to systematically increase the distance between the participant and the board until the distance is 2 feet. Begin reinforcing the participant for hitting the panel board.

7. The distance between the participant and the board should be $1^1/_2$–2 feet when the released ball falls within 6 inches of the board on 60% of the trials.

Problem 3:   The participant releases the ball, but releases it too late so that it hits the floor.

Instructional Objective: The participant will throw the ball—releasing it at the maximum extension position when the hand is farthest from the body and at about eye level—on two out of three trials for three consecutive sessions.

Instructional Procedures:

1. This branch is designed to be used within the context of the task analysis as a parallel objective to the phase in which the participant is being instructed. No additional data sheet is needed for this branch.

2. Position the participant close enough to the other player to ensure success. As the participant's accuracy improves, increase the distance between the players.

3. For participants who respond well and immediately to verbal cues, a signal such as "Now" may be used to teach the participant when to release the ball. Stand as close to the throwing arm as possible to ensure the accuracy of the signal. Prior to beginning this correction pro-

cedure, explain to the participant both the nature of the problem and why the cue is being used.

4. For participants who respond better to physical assistance, use your own arm to block the follow-through movement of the participant's throwing arm. This block should result in the release of the ball at the appropriate time. The block should be paired with a verbal cue such as "Now" and should be faded as quickly as possible.

Problem 4:   The participant does not throw the ball with sufficient velocity to reach the other player.

Instructional Objective: The participant will throw the ball with sufficient strength to reach the other player on two out of three trials for three consecutive sessions.

Instructional Procedures:

1. This branch is designed to be used within the context of the task analysis as a parallel objective of the phase in which the participant is being instructed. No additional data sheet is needed for this branch.
2. Initially, the distance between the participant and the other player should be close enough to ensure success. The distance may be increased as the participant's strength increases or technique improves.
3. Position the participant so that the nonpreferred foot opposite the throwing arm is slightly in front. The participant's body should be angled so that the throwing arm and shoulder are farther from the other player than the opposite arm and shoulder.
4. As the participant brings his or her arm forward to throw the ball, assist him or her in rotating the shoulder and upper portion of the body on the throwing side as well as in bringing them forward. This should increase the power of the throw.
5. While modeling may be sufficient for those participants with good imitation skills, others may require full physical assistance. Concentrate on developing the shoulder movement prior to coordinating the shoulder and arm movements.

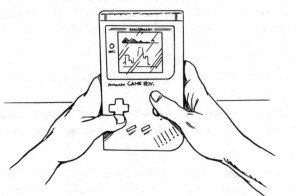

Nintendo Game Boy

*T*he Nintendo Game Boy Compact Video System is widely available and has become popular among children as well as adults. Similar to television video games, Nintendo's Game Boy System can be used with any one of dozens of game cartridges that cover a range of interests and, within any given game, varying degrees of difficulty. The games can be played alone or two Game Boy Systems can be linked to allow two people to play together. The auditory, visual, and activity/task challenges of the various games combine to give the Nintendo system almost universal appeal. Because of the size and resolution of the small screen display, the Nintendo Game Boy System is probably not appropriate for very young children or preschool children. Older children with significant special needs who attend to the visual and auditory stimuli, however, can enjoy the system regardless of cognitive level. In the broader community context, playing Nintendo Game Boy is viewed as age appropriate across the lifespan.

The compact video game system has many advantages over the older television video games and coin-operated video computer games found in arcades. First, it is relatively affordable—once the Game Boy System is purchased (at less than $100), the individual game paks are quite reasonable. More than 150 games are already available on the Nintendo system, and new games are continually marketed based on current themes. Therefore, many families are quite willing to purchase the Nintendo system (if they do not already own it for a sibling). Rather than being an expensive adaptive toy of interest to only the young person with a disability, the Nintendo Game Boy System appeals to siblings and parents as well. In fact, because not everyone in a particular neighborhood or peer group will have the system, owning the Game Boy can provide an opening for the development of a friendship network for a child with disabilities as potential friends are invited to share in a valued activity of mutual interest.

For a participant with a disability, the portability and small size of the system make it ideal for use in a variety of home, school, and community leisure environments, either alone or with a friend or family member. The optional earphone attachment also allows participants to play the game(s) without distracting or disrupting others. Therefore, a student or employee who has finished his or her work could use the Game Boy during a scheduled break without interfering with ongoing activities in the room. Similarly, a participant could be taught to play the Game Boy on the bus or in other public environments involving a lengthy wait time that had previously been associated with disruptive behaviors. Saving a participant's favorite game for a lengthy bus ride between home and school could be an effective replacement for aggression and stereotyped behaviors that emerge in such unstructured situations. Finally, the Game Boy System is durable and can take a fair amount of abuse; it should survive travel back and forth, an occasional fall to the floor, and being left unpackaged around the house.

Materials

Nintendo Game Boy Compact Video Game System, which includes the Game Boy System unit with one game pak, earphones for digital stereo sound, video link cable for simultaneous multiple player use, and four "AA" batteries

Additional materials used in our task analyses are:

1. Game Boy Rechargeable Battery Pack/AC Adapter
2. Game Boy Compact Carrying Case (holds unit plus four game paks, cable, headphones, and instruction booklets) with belt loop for secure hands-free carrying
3. Star Trek game cartridge
4. Boxxle game cartridge
5. Tetris game cartridge (included with the system)

No tools are needed to assemble the system. Additional materials for possible adaptations: individually adapted game pak cartridge containers; Velcro attachment to stabilize Game Boy System on table surface for play through partial participation with another individual.

Entry Motor Skill Level and Possible Adaptations

To use the activity as intended by the manufacturer, the participant must have: 1) the ability to maintain (or be maintained in) a stable position, 2) head and trunk control, 3) isolated finger and thumb movements for pushing the control buttons, and 4) the ability to grasp and stabilize the entire unit with the other hand.

If isolated finger or thumb movements are difficult for the participant, a peer can use a hand-over-finger partial participation technique. With this technique, the peer holds the individual's hand and pointed finger or thumb lightly over the controls, and encourages movement without actually prompting it. Once the individual touches a button or control, the peer pulls the finger or thumb back a short distance to be in a position for the next response.

If the participant lacks the ability to hold the Game Boy System with one hand while manipulating the buttons and controls with the other, the Game Boy System unit should be stabilized. To do this, glue Velcro on both the back and sides of the unit and on a slanted or vertical display board positioned within sight of the player at slightly below eye level. This will allow the unit to be stabilized once the game pak cartridge is inserted. The advice of an occupational therapist, therapeutic recreation specialist, and/or physical therapist should be sought on appropriate body posture, hand grasp, thumb use, finger-pointing strategies, and height/angle of the Game Boy System for optimal play by a participant who has physical disabilities.

The Game Boy System is perhaps more interesting auditorially than it is visually, unless the player is more sophisticated and is responding to the visual cues on the small screen indicating game status. Thus, we have found that Game Boy may still be interesting to a player with a visual impairment who cannot see the screen but is motivated by the auditory responses of the various games. Concomitantly, Game Boy is likely to be enjoyed by an individual with a hearing impairment whose overall skills are relatively high. Game Boy will be less interesting—and probably ignored—by a person who has little functional hearing and significant cognitive delay, regardless of visual acuity.

Instructional Environment

The player should be positioned so that he or she can either hold the Game Boy unit close to and slightly below eye level or see and reach the unit attached to a display board at that level. The leisure educator or peer should be close enough to provide any necessary assistance, including facilitating finger pointing and thumb use of the control buttons.

Depending on the player's ability, he or she may be seated at a table or desk or in a wheelchair equipped with a tray (and possibly a display board), or, if possible, in a casual or straightback chair found in the home, school, work, or community environment where the game will be played. He or she may also stand on a prone stander, in a standing box, or on a tilt table with a tray at the proper height for use of the unit.

The various materials should be available, and the leisure educator should have the player partially participate in assembly and in inserting the game cartridge even if the player is not expected to perform these steps at the present time. (Indeed, we recommend postponing instruction in the assembly task analysis [later in this activity description] until after the participant has learned to enjoy one or more of the games.) Similarly, the player should be allowed to partially participate in putting materials away after play is over. Finally, no matter what the player's individual skill level, every player should participate in choice making during the activity; for example, choosing Game Boy from among different leisure activities and choosing one particular game pak cartridge over another.

Instructional Procedures

1. Participants who are just beginning to learn how to play a video game should begin with the Game Boy System fully assembled. We recommend that the leisure educator or peer perform the initial steps of the assembly task analysis with the partial participation of the player. Two separate assembly task analyses are included here—one for use with the Rechargeable Battery Pack/AC Adapter and the other for use with batteries.
2. The Nintendo Game Boy Compact Video Game System is sufficiently flexible and sensorily reinforcing to accommodate widely varying skill levels. An adult without disabilities will find each game as challenging as he or she wishes to make it (e.g., none of us has finished the complete sequence of "puzzles" in the Boxxle game). We have also observed a 3-year-old who scored few points but nevertheless enjoyed playing the games. Because the actual outcomes of each person's involvement with Game Boy are "private" and the outward appearance of playing with the system is virtually identical across all skill levels, no one should be embarrassed by his or her performance. Thus, the system is an ideal leisure skill for players with significant cognitive disabilities. For maximum benefit and participation, the initial goals for these players should be to teach them the required play responses, such as making choices, putting cartridges in the unit, turning the game on, pushing the start button on cue, and using the controls to create action on the screen. We recommend that leisure educators or peers not be concerned about whether the player succeeds in actually scoring points. For those participants who are more capable cognitively, performance accuracy will be enhanced through incidental learning, individual effort, and peer play—just as it is for anyone else. Thus, success on mastery of this activity is not defined by accuracy or skill level, but by engagement and participation.
3. Regardless of skill level, it is important that the participant be actively involved in choice making, both in selecting the Game Boy System over an alternative activity and in selecting one game pak cartridge over another. We have written each of the following specific task analyses for Star Trek, Tetris, and Boxxle so that they begin with the choice of a game cartridge.

4. During instruction in use of the Game Boy game paks, the leisure educator or peer should rely upon the Game Boy System unit speaker to hear the sound effects rather than using the earphones. The sound effects and music often provide major cues for moving on to the next step in any given game. Thus, it is important that the leisure educator hear these auditory signals to help cue the participant.

5. The task analyses are written so that the participant learns to play the games individually. Even if a peer is the person providing assistance, focusing the initial sessions with the Game Boy System on play with a game pak by the participant with disabilities will facilitate maximum involvement and mastery of important steps. After a few sessions, the leisure educator is encouraged to incorporate turn taking and cooperative play into the use of the Game Boy System, whereby players with and without disabilities would share one unit and game.

Data Collection and Monitoring Mastery

As noted earlier, Form 3.2 should be used to list what the leisure educator regards as critical steps in the task analysis that will be monitored for the participant. As a general rule, this data record should include steps for: 1) initiating play at appropriate times and choice making, 2) gathering materials, 3) assembly of the system, 4) starting a selected game, 5) engagement and active participation with the game, 6) termination of the game and use of the system, and 7) putting materials away. Even if the player only partially participates in most steps and requires full assistance on many, it will be important to record this information and to periodically ensure that the player is given the opportunity to initiate those steps that have previously required help. We do not recommend collecting data on actual game performance, such as points earned or games won. These data would be ineffective to collect, and more importantly, such criteria miss the mark: The reason for playing the games is to occupy one's leisure time in enjoyable and socially appropriate ways. Monitoring the steps we suggest will allow one to measure attainment of these leisure-time goals. (The reader should note that data on participant skill acquisition can be recorded for all 10 of the activities in this chapter by completing Form 3.2, Skill Acquisition Data Record. A blank version of this form is included for the Game Boy activity on the following page. A blank version also appears in Appendix B. A completed version for Connect Four appears on page 31. It is not included for any of the other activities.)

Task Analysis: Star Trek

Instructional Objective: Given the Star Trek game, the participant will manipulate the Game Boy System controls to advance the starship and shoot spaceships or rocks using either torpedoes or lasers.

Step 1: Select the Star Trek cartridge from among at least two choices of leisure activities.

Step 2: Partially participate in removing the cartridge from its box and inserting it in the Game Boy System unit.

Step 3: Hold the assembled Game Boy System unit, with Star Trek cartridge inserted, in the right or left hand.

Step 4: Use an individualized strategy to push the switch at the top left (behind the screen) to the "on" position.

Step 5: Watch the screen and listen to the Star Trek theme music.

Step 6: When the Star Trek theme music stops, locate the two small gray buttons centered near the bottom of the Game Boy System under the screen. Press the gray button on the right (with the word "start" printed under it) three times until a small arrow flashes on the screen (it will be next to the word "start").

Step 7: Press the gray button on the right again. A man will appear on the screen and his mouth will move as if he is talking. When his mouth stops moving, press the gray button again, then press the gray button two more times.

Skill Acquisition Data Record

FORM 3.2

Participant: _____
Skill Sequence: _____
Leisure Educator: _____

Level of Assistance Key		
I = Independent		FP = Full Physical
V = Verbal		X = Partial Physical
PP = Partial Participation		M = Point or Model

Date and Initials[a]

Steps in Activity Sequence											% Correct[b]
10.	10	10	10	10	10	10	10	10	10	10	
9.	9	9	9	9	9	9	9	9	9	9	
8.	8	8	8	8	8	8	8	8	8	8	
7.	7	7	7	7	7	7	7	7	7	7	
6.	6	6	6	6	6	6	6	6	6	6	
5.	5	5	5	5	5	5	5	5	5	5	
4.	4	4	4	4	4	4	4	4	4	4	
3.	3	3	3	3	3	3	3	3	3	3	
2.	2	2	2	2	2	2	2	2	2	2	
1.	1	1	1	1	1	1	1	1	1	1	

[a] One data probe should be collected at least once every 2 weeks for each activity sequence.
[b] Percentage of steps performed independently (I).

Step 8: When words appear on the screen, wait until they stop and press the gray button again. Do this every time that words move and then stop on the screen. The gray button will need to be pressed six more times in all before the man appears again.

Step 9: The man's mouth will move every time he talks. Each time he stops talking, press the gray button again. You will need to press the gray button four more times in all to make a map appear.

Step 10: When the map changes and the starship starts to fly (it moves across the screen from left to right), try to shoot anything that flies or moves in front of the starship. The starship can be hit eight times by space rocks or spaceships before it will blow up and the game ends (a new game will then start).

Step 11: The black cross control button has four parts—a top, bottom, left, and right—and controls the movement of the starship on the screen. Use the left thumb to work this control. To move the starship up, push the top part of the black button. To move it down, push the bottom part of the black button. To move it backward, push the left part of the black button. To move the starship forward faster, push the right part of the black button.

Step 12: To fire a laser, use the right thumb or forefinger to press the top rose-colored button that is farthest to the right (it has an "A" printed under it). To fire a torpedo, use the right thumb or forefinger to press the lower rose-colored button that is to the left (it has a "B" printed under it).

Step 13: Fire the torpedoes (you have only four of them) and lasers whenever anything appears directly in front of the starship. If you do not fire, the rock or spaceship will hit you.

Step 14: Continue moving the starship on the screen using the black button and firing the lasers and torpedoes until the game ends and a new game starts.

Step 15: When finished playing, push the button behind the screen to the left "off" position and remove the Star Trek cartridge.

Skill Level Adaptations: Some players will find Steps 6–9 difficult to do and/or they will be easily distracted during these steps, which involve reading text on the small screen (for those who play the game as intended). We recommend that the leisure educator or peer perform these steps for the participant, preferably using partial participation with the leisure educator or peer using hand-over-hand assistance to push the button the necessary number of times and at the correct times. Once the Star Trek game begins, the action should be sufficient to maintain active involvement and interest.

Note that it is not necessary to be concerned about the accuracy or "score" obtained on Steps 10–14. The primary, or perhaps, only response expected of the participant will be manipulation of the buttons and attention to the screen. Peers without disabilities and participants with disabilities who have more skills may be motivated to develop accuracy skills and improve their scores, but the development of this level of play can appropriately be supported through incidental learning, individual effort, and peer play.

Task Analysis: Boxxle

Instructional Objective: Given the Boxxle game, the participant will manipulate the Game Boy System controls to move the figure and boxes within the walls on the screen.

Step 1: Select the Boxxle cartridge from among at least two choices of leisure activities.

Step 2: Partially participate in removing the cartridge from its box and inserting it in the Game Boy System unit.

Step 3:   Hold the assembled Game Boy System unit, with Boxxle cartridge inserted, in the right or left hand.

Step 4:   Use an individualized strategy to push the switch at the top left (behind the screen) to the "on" position.

Step 5:   Watch the person pushing boxes on the screen and listen to the Boxxle theme music play through at least once. (Note: The theme will repeat indefinitely.)

Step 6:   When ready to play, locate the two small gray buttons centered near the bottom of the Game Boy System under the screen. Press the gray button on the right (with the word "start" printed under it) three times until the music changes and two figures appear on the screen.

Step 7:   Watch the screen while the two figures walk toward one another, a heart moves to the top of the screen, and the words "Please take my gift" appear above the two people.

Step 8:   When the music changes again, watch the screen: A man will appear inside walls within three boxes.

Step 9:   Locate the black cross control button, which has four parts—a top, bottom, left, and right. This controls the movement of the man on the screen, including the man pushing a box from one place to another whenever he is behind the box and there is no obstacle.

Step 10: To move the man to the right, use your left thumb to push the right part of the black button.

Step 11: To move the man to the left, use your left thumb to push the left part of the black button.

Step 12: To move the man down, use your left thumb to push the bottom of the black button.

Step 13: To move the man up, use your left thumb to push the top of the black button.

Step 14: Repeat Steps 10–13 as often as desired.

Step 15: When the man and/or boxes are "trapped," push the gray "start" button two times to begin a new game.

Step 16: Repeat Steps 10–13 until finished playing.

Step 17: When finished playing, push the button behind the screen to the left "off" position and remove the Boxxle cartridge.

Skill Level Adaptations: As with the Star Trek game, it is not necessary to be concerned about whether the participant succeeds in moving the boxes to the target locations on the screen in Steps 10–13. The primary, or perhaps only, response expected of the participant is manipulation of the buttons and attention to the consequent movements of the man and the boxes on the screen. Peers without disabilities and participants with disabilities who have more skills will be motivated to move the boxes as intended, but the development of this level of play can be supported appropriately through incidental learning, individual effort, and peer play.

Task Analysis: Tetris

Instructional Objective: Given the Tetris game, the participant will manipulate the Game Boy System controls to change the position of block segments as they fall from the top to the bottom of the television screen.

Step 1:   Select the Tetris cartridge from among at least two choices of leisure activities.

Step 2:   Partially participate in removing the cartridge from its box and inserting it in the Game Boy System unit.

Step 3:   Hold the assembled Game Boy System unit, with Tetris cartridge inserted, in the right or left hand.

Step 4:   Use an individualized strategy to push the switch at the top left (behind the screen) to the "on" position.

Step 5: Watch the screen and listen to the Tetris theme music.

Step 6: When the music stops, the screen image will change. Watch the blocks fall from the top of the screen into position at the bottom.

Step 7: When all the blocks have fallen, the Tetris display screen will appear again. Locate the two small gray buttons centered near the bottom of the Game Boy System under the screen. Press the gray button on the right (with the word "start" printed under it) two times and the game will start.

Step 8: The black cross control button has three parts that will move the falling blocks. Use the left thumb to push the left part so that the falling block will move left. Use the right thumb to push the right part so that the falling block will move right. Use the right thumb to push the bottom part to make the blocks fall faster.

Step 9: The two rose-colored buttons under your screen to the right of the Game Boy System unit will turn the boxes around. Push one and then the other button and listen to the sound effects as the blocks are falling.

Step 10: Repeat Steps 8 and 9 until all the blocks have fallen, the theme changes, and the screen shifts to a display that says, "Game over. Please try again."

Step 11: Press the gray "Start" button again and repeat Steps 8–10 until the game is over.

Step 12: When finished playing, push the button behind the screen to the left "off" position and remove the Tetris cartridge.

Skill Level Adaptations: Again, the purpose of the game should not be to obtain a high score or "win," but to actively participate and enjoy the game. Participants who possess the ability to improve their performance accuracy can learn to do so through incidental learning, individual effort, and peer play.

Task Analysis: Assembly of Game Boy

Instructional Objective: Given the Game Boy System and a selected game pak, the participant will assemble the Game Boy System for play.

Version One: For use with batteries (without adapter)

Step 1: Detach the Velcro closing to open the cover on the Game Boy Compact Carrying Case.

Step 2: Grasp the Game Boy System and pull it from its pouch.

Step 3: Put the Game Boy System on your lap or on a table top.

Step 4: Unsnap the top front pouch on the Game Boy Compact Carrying Case and choose a Game Boy cartridge box. Put the case on your lap.

Step 5: Open the Game Boy cartridge box by holding it on both sides with one hand and pressing the button that sticks up from the box with the thumb on your other hand, then pull apart the top and bottom of the box and remove the cartridge.

Step 6: Put the empty cartridge box back into its pouch on the carrying case, and put the case aside.

Step 7: Pick up the Game Boy System in one hand, and turn it so that the back is facing you (the side with no screen or buttons).

Step 8: Pick up the cartridge so that the picture is upright and facing you (other cues include the arrow under the picture pointing down and the indentation along the top of the cartridge above the picture).

Step 9: Push the cartridge into the long thin hole behind the screen until it will go no further and does not stick out from the Game Boy System at the top.

Step 10: Turn the Game Boy System around so the screen is facing you and hold it in the preferred hand.

Step 11:   If desired, put the earphone plugs into your ears and plug the round end into the small hole at the bottom of the Game Boy unit.

Step 12:   With the nonpreferred hand, use the index finger to push the switch at the top left (behind the screen) to the "on" position.

Step 13:   If the Game Boy System is working, the tiny red battery light to the left of the screen will switch on and the picture on the screen will move briefly (the word "Nintendo" appears at the top and moves to the middle). Then there will be a display with music and sound effects for the particular game pak chosen.

Step 14:   When the music stops or after the theme has played for the selected number of times, locate the two small gray buttons centered near the bottom of the Game Boy System under the screen. Press the gray button on the right (with the word "start" printed under it), closest to the rose-colored buttons. For most games, press this button only once. For Star Trek, press the button three times. A small arrow will be flashing next to the word "start" or "play" on the screen. You are now ready to play.

Version Two: For use with the Rechargeable Battery Pack/AC Adapter

Step 1:   Take the Game Boy Rechargeable Battery Pack/AC Adapter (leave both connecting cords for this unit attached during storage) and locate the AC wall plug.

Step 2:   Grip the plug and connect it to the wall socket.

Step 3:   Place the adapter on your lap or on a table top (select one for entire task).

Step 4:   Detach the Velcro closing to open the cover on the Game Boy Compact Carrying Case.

Step 5:   Grasp the Game Boy System and pull it from its pouch.

Step 6:   Place the carrying case within reach but out of the way.

Step 7:   Hold the Game Boy in the right hand so that the screen is on top, facing you.

Step 8:   With the left hand, put the small round end of the wire on the adapter (the wire that is not plugged into the wall) into the hole on the left side, at the top near the screen.

Step 9:   Put the Game Boy System on your lap or on a table top.

Step 10:   Unsnap the top front pouch on the Game Boy Compact Carrying Case and choose a Game Boy cartridge box. Put the case on your lap.

Step 11:   Open the Game Boy cartridge box by holding it on both sides with one hand and pressing the button that sticks up from the box with the thumb on your other hand, then pull apart the top and bottom of the box and remove the cartridge.

Step 12:   Pick up the carrying case, put the empty cartridge box back into its pouch in the carrying case, and put the case aside.

Step 13:   Pick up the Game Boy System in one hand and turn it so that the back is facing you (the side with no screen or buttons).

Step 14:   Pick up the cartridge so that the picture is upright and facing you (other cues include the arrow under the picture pointing down and the indentation along the top of the cartridge above the picture).

Step 15:   Push the cartridge into the long thin hole behind the screen until it will go no further and does not stick out from the Game Boy System at the top.

Step 16:   Turn the Game Boy System around so the screen is facing you and hold it in the preferred hand.

Step 17:   If desired, place the earplugs into your ears and plug the round end into the small hole at the bottom of the Game Boy unit.

Step 18:   With the preferred hand, use the index finger to push the switch at the top left (behind the screen) to the "on" position.

Step 19:   If the Game Boy System is working, the tiny red battery light to the left of the screen will switch on and the picture on the screen will move briefly (the word "Nintendo" appears at the top and moves to the middle). Then there will be a display with music and sound effects for the particular game pak chosen.

Step 20: When the music stops or after the theme has played for the selected number of times, locate the two small gray buttons centered near the bottom of the Game Boy System under the screen. Press the gray button on the right (with the word "start" printed under it), closest to the rose-colored buttons. For most games, press this button only once. For Star Trek, press the button three times. A small arrow will be flashing next to the word "start" or "play" on the screen. You are now ready to play.

Pinball
Games

*P*inball games are very appropriate for establishing independent and generalized play behaviors. They produce novel visual and auditory stimulation, which are characteristics likely to reinforce participants with significant disabilities and maintain their interest. Because pinball games are popular among children as well as adults without disabilities, and can be played either in a group or alone, this activity offers participants with disabilities of all ages a skill that will remain appropriate throughout their lives. It also encourages interactions with participants without disabilities. Pinball games can be found in many community environments, such as arcades, bowling alleys, shopping centers, and airports. They are widely available in various styles—table top, free-standing, and commercial—and at various prices.

Materials

Pinball machine (regulation or table top) with the following minimal features: pull-knob ball shooter, field of play with bumper areas that light up and make sounds when in contact with the ball, and dual flippers operated by pushing buttons on the sides of the machine

Additional materials for possible adaptations: large ball-type knob; modeling clay; pencil or page turner; reacher adaptor and grip

Entry Motor Skill Level and Possible Adaptations

To use the pinball machine as intended by most manufacturers, a participant must have: 1) the ability to maintain a stable position, 2) head and trunk control, 3) sufficient strength to pull against a spring-loaded ball release, and 4) the ability to apply finger or whole-hand pressure over flipper buttons. In addition, for pinball machine models that have a ball shooter in the shape of a hook and a reset dial, the participant must also have: 1) the ability to independently hook his or her finger onto the ball shooter, and 2) independent finger use to turn the reset dial. Other machines require at least a palmar grasp to pull the ball shooter knob.

If the participant has difficulty manipulating the machine, the leisure educator can attach the following materials to the machine: 1) a large ball-type knob attached over or in place of the ball shooter so that a whole-hand grasp can be utilized, 2) modeling clay added to the ball shooter and/or flipper buttons to build them up, 3) a pencil or page turner to turn the reset dial, and/or 4) a reacher adaptor and grip to extend the player's reach toward the machine.

Instructional Environment

The participant should be positioned so that the front of the machine is centered directly in front of the participant's body. To physically assist a participant with little or no manipulation skills, the leisure educator should stand either in front of or behind the participant and be able to touch the player and the machine. As the participant's proficiency increases, the leisure educator should be positioned farther away and move closer only to help with those skills the player still has to acquire.

Depending on the participant's abilities, he or she may sit in a wheelchair equipped with a tray or in a specially adapted seat with a table. Or, the participant may stand on a prone stander, in a standing box, or on a tilt table with a tray positioned at an appropriate height in front.

Instructional Procedures

1. It is crucial that the leisure educator match the instructional objective he or she selects with the participant's level of functioning. There are some participants for whom the entire task analysis would be appropriate, and a phase to operate a coin-slot machine would help to generalize to community environments. For participants who have little or no numerical skills, Steps 2 and 22 of the task analysis dealing with counting the points scored can be eliminated. For these participants, the instructional objective should focus on the minimal skills required for independent play: pulling the shooter and some degree of ability to visually track the ball (Steps 4–6, 8). For participants with short attention spans or interfering behaviors, steps of the task analysis may be broken down into smaller units. In the initial trials, the leisure educator can provide instruction only on the first ball and Steps 1–9 of the task analysis, then add the second ball and Steps 10–15, and, finally, the third ball and Steps 16–23.
2. Activities such as pinball games that require the player to use two hands also require the leisure educator to use two hands when giving physical assistance. This may make accurate data collection difficult if a procedure designed to handle this situation is not planned in advance. When the participant's skill level is relatively low, it is fairly easy to record on the data sheet the steps he or she independently performs as they occur or soon after they occur. However, when the participant becomes more proficient but still requires physical assistance on a few steps such as flipper use, it may be easier to record the steps he or she misses during a trial. After the trial is over, the leisure educator can then record the independently performed steps.
3. Errors made while playing with the pinball machine are difficult to correct because the game is fast, and interrupting the game at the point of error may not always be possible. For a participant with a high level of receptive language, the leisure educator should point out the error after the ball is out of play. On the next ball, the leisure educator should give a verbal cue prior to the missed step. For a less-skilled player, the leisure educator should turn the game off at the point of error and wait until the ball rolls out of play to prevent the player from making further contact with the game. The leisure educator should then begin a new

trial and give the necessary assistance to ensure that the participant performs the missed step correctly.

4. Prior to instructing a participant who engages in high levels of self-stimulatory behaviors, procedures should be established to control such behaviors:

    a. If a participant engages in self-stimulatory behaviors by pressing the flipper buttons repeatedly while the ball is in the upper bumper area or after the ball has rolled out of play, teach the participant to keep his or her hands on the sides of the machine with his or her fingers or palms held over the flipper buttons. If such behaviors continue, see the Branch for Step 9 for more detailed procedures.

    b. If a participant displays behaviors that interfere with the correct performance of the task or give the appearance of being highly inappropriate, turn the machine off. Because access to all lights, noise, and motion—the intrinsically reinforcing properties of the activity—are therefore removed, this procedure is a mild form of "time-out" (which should be used with discretion).

    c. If the lights and sounds emitted by the machine provoke self-stimulatory behaviors and/or physiological reactions (e.g., seizures) in a participant, make minor modifications to the machine to control the magnitude of stimulation being emitted. For example, cover the light with tape and/or do not allow the player to turn the machine on or press the counter reset button (even turned off, the machine can still function adequately).

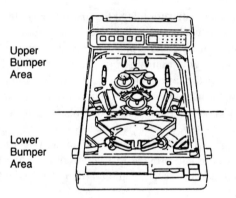

Upper Bumper Area

Lower Bumper Area

Task Analysis: Pinball Games

Instructional Objective: Given a regulation or table-top pinball machine, the participant will engage in appropriate interactions with the machine as stated in the following task analysis.

Step 1:   Turn the power switch to "on."
Step 2:   Press the counter reset button so that the number in the "particle count" window is "00000."
Step 3:   Turn the reset dial clockwise until the number 3 appears in the "ball in play" window.
Step 4   Place finger in the shooter slot.
Step 5:   Pull the shooter all the way out until the first ball rolls in front of the shooter.
Step 6:   Release the shooter so that the ball moves into play.
Step 7:   Place hands on the sides of the machine with fingers or palms over the flipper buttons.
Step 8:   Watch the ball as it passes through the upper bumper area.

Step   9:   When the ball drops into the lower bumper area, press the flipper buttons with fingers or palms to keep the ball in play.

Step 10:   When the ball is out of play, place finger in the shooter slot.

Step 11:   Pull the shooter all the way out until the second ball rolls in front of the shooter.

Step 12:   Release the shooter so that the ball moves into play.

Step 13:   Place hands on the sides of the machine with fingers or palms over the flipper buttons.

Step 14:   Watch the ball as it passes through the upper bumper area.

Step 15:   When the ball drops into the lower bumper area, press the flipper buttons with fingers or palms to keep the ball in play.

Step 16:   When the ball is out of play, place finger in the shooter slot.

Step 17:   Pull the shooter all the way out until the third ball rolls in front of the shooter.

Step 18:   Release the shooter so that the ball moves into play.

Step 19:   Place hands on the sides of the machine with fingers or palms over the flipper buttons.

Step 20:   Watch the ball as it passes through the upper bumper area.

Step 21:   When the ball drops into the lower bumper area, press the flipper buttons with fingers or palms to keep the ball in play.

Step 22:   After the third ball has been played, count the number of points that appears in the "particle count" window.

Step 23:   Turn the power switch to "off."

Branch for Step 8: Pinball Games

Problem: The participant does not track the movements of the ball after it leaves the shooter.

Instructional Objective: The participant will visually track and locate the ball after it leaves the shooter.

Instructional Procedures:

1.   Present the machine to the participant with the power off.
2.   Deliver an instructional cue indicating the ball's initial location, and deliver a verbal cue, "Watch the ball. After you show me where the ball is, we can play the game."
3   Pull the shooter so that the ball moves into play.
4.   Lift up one end of the machine so that the playing surface is parallel to the table and the ball stops moving.
5.   Instruct the participant to point to the location of the ball. If the participant has been visually tracking the ball, he or she should be able to locate the ball within 5 seconds. If the participant does not appear to be visually tracking the ball, shoot the ball into play, and, without stopping the ball from moving, assist the participant in tracing the ball's movement with his or her finger.
6   Reinforce the participant when he or she locates the ball, and then begin to play the game.
7.   This branch may be incorporated into ongoing skill acquisition instruction by implementing it at the beginning and end of the session as well as several times during the session.

Branch for Step 9: Pinball Games

Problem: The participant presses the flipper buttons while the ball is in the upper bumper area or after the ball has rolled out of play. The participant engages in self-stimulatory behaviors with the flipper buttons.

Instructional Objective: The participant will press the flipper buttons only when the ball is in the lower bumper area.

Instructional Procedures:

1. Define the area in which it is permissible for the participant to press the flipper buttons after the ball has entered. A clear decision can then be made as to when the participant is using the flipper buttons as a form of self-stimulation that requires intervention. If necessary, place some tape directly on the face of the machine to separate the upper bumper area from the lower bumper area and further cue the participant as to when flipper use is appropriate within the game.

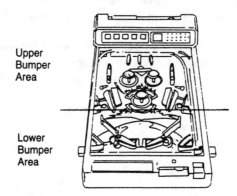

Upper
Bumper
Area

Lower
Bumper
Area

2. Follow the procedures for mass trials (see Table 3.8) and work on Steps 9, 15, and 21. Perform all of the other steps of the task analysis for the participant as quickly as possible.
3. For a participant who responds well to verbal cues:
    a. Cover the flipper buttons with your hands until the ball reaches the lower bumper area.
    b. Pair the removal of your hands with a short verbal cue, such as "now" or "push," to indicate the appropriate time to press the flipper buttons and reinforce the appropriate waiting by the participant.
    c. Fade the physical assist of covering the flipper buttons as soon as the participant indicates that he or she will wait for the verbal cue.
    d. Begin fading the verbal cue when the participant presses the flipper buttons correctly for *three* consecutive balls.
        1) Gradually give the verbal cue with lower intensity and volume, fading to a near whisper.
        2) Give the verbal cue on progressively fewer balls. Give the verbal cue on all three balls in trial 1, on the first and second balls in trial 3, and on the first ball in trial 6.
        3) If an error occurs, reinstate the verbal cue on the next ball.
        4) Begin reinforcing the participant's successful hitting of the ball with the flippers.
4. For a participant whose response to verbal cues is not predictable:
    a. Remove or cut out the machine's top plastic cover with a saw to gain access to the playing area.
    b. Drop the ball in various places on the playing area.
    c. Physically assist the participant in correct flipper use, and provide a generous amount of reinforcement for the participant's efforts and appropriate responses.

Pottery

*P*ottery is an activity that is appropriate for all age groups, from preschoolers to older adults. It encourages creativity and self-expression, and promotes manual dexterity, fine motor skills, eye–hand coordination, and a sense of the aesthetic. Pottery may be adapted for many ability levels. A preschooler may be introduced to pottery by shaping and coiling a long "snake" of clay or Play-Doh to form a bowl or by "pinching" a bowl from a mound of clay. Or, one may engage in pottery by using the traditional potter's wheel, as presented in this activity description. Pottery may be learned as a personal hobby to enjoy by oneself, or it may be learned in a social, classroom environment at a community recreation center or through a community education program. To encourage opportunities for socialization, this pottery activity is described within the context of an ongoing class in the community.

Materials

Clay, bucket of water, sponge, potter's slice (wire cutting tool), needle tool, glaze, tongs, smock, electric potter's wheel, kiln, wax

Additional materials for possible adaptations: Velcro fasteners for smock; adapted tongs for dipping vessel into glaze; tape to build up handles of potter's slice and needle tool

Entry Motor Skill Level and Possible Adaptations

To throw a vessel using a potter's wheel, a participant needs: 1) the ability to hold a stable position, 2) head and trunk control, 3) the ability to manipulate clay with one or two hands, 4) sufficient eye–hand coordination to shape clay, and 5) the ability to use the foot to press and operate foot pedal of an electric potter's wheel.

For a participant who has difficulty with fine motor movements or mobility, the principle of partial participation may be employed. For example, another person (peer, friend, leisure educator) may provide hand-over-hand or finger-over-finger manual guidance to the participant as necessary to facilitate throwing the vessel. Or, another person may assist the participant in carrying a newly shaped, fragile vessel to a shelf to dry, or in carrying a dried vessel to a kiln for firing. A participant who has difficulty operating the foot pedal may need assistance from another person who can synchronize the rotation of the potter's wheel with the participant's manipulation of the clay on the wheel. The leisure educator needs to determine in advance of the class just how much assistance the participant will need and who will provide the assistance.

Instructional Environment

1. To throw a vessel, the participant should sit at a table directly in front of the clay and the potter's wheel. The surface of the table should be at a comfortable level for manipulating the clay.
2. If a participant requires physical assistance, the person providing assistance (peer, friend, leisure educator) should sit or stand next to the participant so that help can be offered easily.
3. Depending on the participant's abilities, he or she may sit in a wheelchair or specially adapted chair. The participant may also stand on a prone stander, in a standing box, or on a tilt table.
4. If a participant uses a wheelchair, the leisure educator should make certain that the community center or community education facility, parking lot, classroom, and materials are physically accessible.

Instructional Procedures

1. A participant may have difficulty completing some steps of the task analysis for pottery independently. In these cases, he or she may participate partially with assistance from a peer, friend, fellow classmate, instructor, or the leisure educator. Care should be taken that any assistance that is provided does not prevent another person from completing his or her vessel.
2. Throwing, firing, and glazing vessels can be a highly intuitive process that requires experience in working with a variety of clays, kilns, and glazes. The instructor is probably aware of the temperamental nature of using certain clays and glazes. He or she should be consulted regarding the finer points of firing particular clays and the results of applying certain glazes.
3. When enrolled in a pottery class that meets over a period of several weeks, a participant will have many opportunities for socialization and making friends. Depending on a participant's needs for social skills instruction, along with the task analysis for learning pottery, a participant could receive instruction on appropriate social skills (e.g., greeting instructor and other classmates, shaking hands when meeting new people, initiating and sustaining conversation when appropriate, complimenting another person's work).
4. Leaded glazes are becoming obsolete; yet, some still remain on the market. When purchasing glazes, be certain that they are lead-free, cadmium-free, and food safe.
5. In addition to throwing traditional vessels, other objects appropriate for all ages may be made from clay. For example, one may make decorative tiles, pinch pots, sculpture, or jewelry (e.g., beads, pins, pendants).

Task Analysis: Pottery

Phase I: *Instructional Objective:* Given enrollment in a pottery class, the participant will prepare for class and for throwing a vessel.

Step 1:   Before leaving home, put on proper attire (old clothes) to participate in the pottery class.
Step 2:   Enter the community recreation center or community education facility.

Step 3   Locate and proceed to the room where the pottery class is being held.

Step 4:   Enter the room.

Step 5:   Acknowledge the other participants and the instructor.

Step 6:   Locate the coat rack and proceed in that direction.

Step 7:   Take off coat and hang it on a coat hanger (or place it with other belongings).

Step 8:   Find a seat in front of a potter's wheel.

Step 9:   While waiting for the class to begin, engage in light conversation with other participants and instructor.

Step 10:   When the class begins, listen to and follow the verbal directions of the instructor.

Skill Level Adaptations: Access to the facility by a participant who uses a wheelchair will need to be screened in advance of the first class meeting. Access to the facility may be provided via a ramp and reserved parking, and access to the classroom may be provided via ramps or elevators. Also, be certain that washrooms and drinking fountains are physically accessible.

A peer or friend may either travel to the facility with a participant or meet a participant at the front door of the facility. This person could initially assist a participant in Step 3 (locating the classroom), Step 6 (finding the coat rack), Step 8 (finding a seat), and Step 9 (modeling interactions with other participants and instructor). As the participant becomes more familiar with the surroundings and the other people, assistance with these steps can be faded and the participant can take the lead in completing these tasks. The peer or friend (or leisure educator) may need to be available to assist the participant in understanding the instructor's directions. This person could provide additional verbal cues, modeling, or physical assists, depending on the type of assistance to which the participant is most responsive. Care needs to be taken so that the participant does not become dependent on additional cues and assistance, but rather attempts to attend and respond to the instructor's directions directly.

Phase II: *Instructional Objective:* Given enrollment in a pottery class, the participant will throw a vessel.

Step 1:   Continue to listen to and follow the instructor's directions throughout the class.

Step 2:   Remove a smock from the sink area and put it on over clothes.

Step 3:   Pick up clay by the sink area.

Step 4:   Carry the clay to the electric potter's wheel and put it down on the surface near the wheel.

Step 5:   Sit at the potter's wheel.

Step 6:   Listen to the instructor's introduction to the class, taking note of the location of the materials and tools as they are pointed out.

Step 7:   Knead the clay until it is of an appropriate consistency.

Step 8:   Cut off a chunk of the clay (approximately 5″ in diameter) with a potter's slice (wire cutting tool).

Step 9:   Shape the clay into a ball.

Step 10:   Put the clay onto the center of the potter's wheel.

Step 11:   Flip the switch of the potter's wheel to "on."

Step 12:   With the preferred foot, apply hard and then lighter pressure to the foot pedal to alternately speed up and slow down the rotation of the wheel. (Do this until you have a good feel for how the wheel responds to varying foot pressures.)

Step 13:   Holding the fingers and thumbs in opposition to each other, shape, open up, and build up the sides of the clay to make a vessel, while simultaneously causing the potter's wheel to spin by operating the foot pedal.

Step 14:   When the vessel is formed, slow down the potter's wheel by easing pressure off the foot pedal.

Step 15:   Finish off the vessel by cutting off the top with a potter's slice.

Step 16:   Stop the potter's wheel.

Step 17:   Remove the vessel from the potter's wheel.

Step 18:   Carry the vessel to the drying rack.

Step 19:   Carefully place the vessel on the drying rack.

Step 20:   Let the vessel dry for the recommended duration (approximately 3–7 days) before firing.

Step 21:   The instructor will fire the vessels in a kiln before the next class session.

Skill Level Adaptations: As noted earlier, a peer, friend, or leisure educator may need to be available to provide physical assistance for the completion of many of the tasks. For example, in Step 2, the participant may need assistance to put on the smock; in Step 11, to turn on the electric potter's wheel; in Step 12, to operate the potter's wheel; and in Step 13, to shape the vessel. The participant may also need extra cues to follow the instructor's directions. For Step 11, the participant may use a pincer grasp, modified pincer grasp, or clenched fist to flip the switch of the potter's wheel to "on." For Step 13, a participant may use either one hand or two hands to shape the vessel. When learning to operate the foot pedal of the potter's wheel (Step 12), the leisure educator may choose to first teach the participant to operate the wheel without clay. Once the participant is familiar with how the machine works, then clay can be added to the wheel.

From a technical standpoint, before firing the vessel, it must be completely dry. The amount of time required for drying varies (approximately 3–7 days) depending on several factors: the amount of moisture in the clay, the size of the vessel, and the amount of humidity in the atmosphere. Be certain that the piece is cold to the touch and that all moisture has evaporated before firing. If a participant wishes to carve designs into the sides of the vessel or incise his or her name and date into the bottom of the vessel, this may be accomplished while the clay is "leather hard." That is, the vessel has been allowed to dry enough so that it is firm, yet it is still soft enough to carve into it with a needle tool. (As a warning, once the vessel is completely dry, do not try to make an incision as the clay is very brittle and may crack or break.)

In an introductory class, the instructor will most likely complete the firing of the vessels in a kiln. He or she will be aware of the correct temperature and length of time for firing depending on the type and quality of the clay (e.g., earthenware and stoneware require a low fire; porcelain requires a high fire). The kiln will need to be cooled sufficiently so the vessel can be handled and removed from the kiln. After the vessel has cooled completely, it is ready to be glazed.

Phase III: *Instructional Objective:* Given enrollment in a pottery class, the participant will glaze the vessel.

Step 1:   Check that the vessel is cool enough to glaze.

Step 2:   Pick up a stick of wax with the preferred hand.

Step 3:   Rub the stick of wax against the bottom of the vessel, as well as 1/4″ around the base of the vessel, so the clay will resist the glaze in these areas.

Step 4:   Set the stick of wax on the table and off to the side.

Step 5:   With the preferred hand, pick up a pair of tongs.

Step 6:   With the other hand, pick up the vessel and tilt the base of the vessel toward the ends of the tongs.

Step 7:   Use the tongs to pick up the vessel by its base.

Step 8:   Extend the arm holding the vessel by the tongs toward the top of the container of glaze.

Step 9:   Hold the vessel directly over the container of glaze.

Step 10: Slowly lower the arm to dip the vessel top first into the glaze. (Glaze should approach no closer than 1/8″–1/4″ from the base of the vessel.)

Step 11: Slowly raise arm to lift the vessel from the container of glaze.

Step 12: Continue holding the vessel over the container of glaze to allow excess glaze to drip off.

Step 13: Slowly lower the vessel to dip it in glaze a second time.

Step 14: Slowly raise the vessel from the container of glaze, allowing excess glaze to drip off.

Step 15: Slowly lower the vessel to dip it in glaze a third time.

Step 16: Slowly raise the vessel from the container of glaze, allowing excess glaze to drip off.

Step 17: Rub off any drops of glaze that may have collected on the waxed areas.

Step 18: Return the glazed vessel to the kiln for firing. (Firing will be completed by the instructor.)

Skill Level Adaptations: A participant with limited mobility and manipulation skills will need assistance from another person to accomplish some of these tasks. This task analysis recommends dipping the vessel into the glaze three times. The first time the vessel is dipped, much of the glaze is absorbed into the clay; the second time, the color of the glaze begins to show through; the third time, the glaze builds up to produce a shiny, lustrous finish. Glazes may also be brushed or sprayed on, in which case care must be taken that the vessel is evenly coated with glaze. Because glazes react differently to different kinds of clay, it would be wise to fire a sample of the glaze to be sure the desired affect will be achieved. To create a design on the surface of the vessel, a wax resist may be applied before glazing. (Note: Because most glazes contain metallic compounds, it is recommended that glazed vessels not be used in microwaves.)

In most cases, the instructor is responsible for firing the glazed vessels. When firing glazed vessels, care should be taken so that vessels do not touch each other in the kiln, and that the glaze from one vessel will not drip onto another vessel. Wait until the kiln is sufficiently cool before opening it to remove the vessel. If the kiln is opened when it is too hot, you may hear a "ping" sound that means the glaze is cooling too quickly, causing the glaze to crack.

Phase IV: *Instructional Objective:* Given enrollment in a pottery class, the participant will prepare to leave and exit class.

Step 1: Clean up pottery area.

Step 2: Wash hands in sink.

Step 3: Dry hands with towel.

Step 4: Take off smock and return it to sink area.

Step 5: Interact socially with the other participants and the instructor.

Step 6: Locate the coat rack and proceed in that direction.

Step 7: Remove coat from the coat hanger and put coat on.

Step 8: Say good-bye to the instructor and the other participants.

Step 9: Exit the community recreation center or community education facility.

Remote Control Vehicle

*R*adio-controlled toys are enjoyed by children, youths, and adults without disabilities. Cars, trucks, vans, robots, and airplanes that use a remote control device to activate and manipulate their movements are only a few of the widely available objects. These age-appropriate vehicles are particularly suitable for participants with significant disabilities because they produce movements that most players find novel. In addition, they may be adapted to varying skill levels and environments. Remote control vehicles range in price from about $15 to $40 or more.

Materials

Radio-controlled vehicles are available from manufacturers such as Asahi, New Bright, or Mattel.

Additional materials for possible adaptations: wooden base; stick, large juice can, or pie tin; masking tape; cones; milk cartons; cardboard boxes

Entry Motor Skill Level and Possible Adaptations

To play with the remote control vehicle as intended by the manufacturer, a participant must have: 1) the ability to hold a stable posture, 2) head and trunk control, 3) use of both hands—one to hold the hand control device and press the forward/reverse button and one to turn the wheel, 4) a three-finger grasp of the wheel, and 5) the ability to turn the wheel.

Most radio-controlled vehicles are very sensitive and will turn sharply even when the participant turns the wheel on the hand control only slightly. To better regulate the vehicle's turns, the leisure educator can loop two pieces of strong string around the front axle, pull the two pieces toward the back of the car, tie the two pieces together so that they are equal in length, and secure the string on the tail bar with tape so that the string is held tight and the vehicle moves straight ahead. To secure the string even more firmly, it can be taped to the underside of the vehicle as well.

If the player has difficulties manipulating the hand control device, the leisure educator may mount the device in a large wooden base so that the control would not have to be hand held. A stick may be added to the right or left side of the wheel (depending on which hand the participant prefers to use); the wheel may then be turned with a gross arm movement rather than a hand grasp. Or, the wheel may be adapted to hold a large juice can on top. The juice can may then be manipulated by open hands holding it, using large shoulder motions instead of finger motions. These movements in themselves tend to be relaxing and encourage reduction of hypertonicity if it is present. For a player with somewhat finer hand control, a pie tin mounted over the hand control device may be used as a steering wheel adaptation to simulate actual driving.

If the participant has difficulties following the track and directing the vehicle, the leisure educator may mark with masking tape the path the vehicle should take and the start and finish lines. If necessary, the leisure educator may also mark with an "X" the spots where the cones should be placed. All of these instructional cues should eventually be faded.

If cones are included with the remote control vehicle set and they are too small for the participant to steer the vehicle around, the leisure educator may substitute milk cartons or other larger objects. A participant who has difficulty with mobility may need cardboard boxes to form a boundary around the play area to keep the vehicle from going under furniture and becoming inaccessible.

Instructional Environment

1. The remote control vehicle should be placed on a hard surface such as concrete or tile. Carpeted areas and surfaces having a slope will not permit the vehicle to move freely; carpet might also jam the vehicle's mechanism and is not recommended by the manufacturer.
2. This activity requires a minimum area of $4' \times 8'$; an area of $6' \times 15'$ would be ideal. The cone (or other obstacle such as a milk carton) in Phases II and III should be placed about $3'-5'$ from the start at equal distances from the finish line. The four cones form the square track in Phases IV, V, and VI and should be placed about $5'$ from each other.
3. If at all possible, the participant should be instructed to follow the vehicle through its maneuvers because it is easier to see which way the vehicle should turn when he or she is facing the same direction as the front of the vehicle. The participant should walk a few steps directly behind the vehicle and look down on its roof. The leisure educator should stand close enough to the participant to give any necessary assistance but should not block the vehicle's path.
4. If the participant cannot walk or stand, several alternate positions are possible. The participant may sit in a wheelchair or any specially adapted seat, or he or she may stand on a prone stander, in a standing box, or on a tilt table. The participant may also lie on his or her side, or prone on a gurney.

Instructional Procedures

1. The use of reverse is taught in Phase I-B so that when the vehicle goes off its path, the participant may self-correct by pressing the button on the hand control to "reverse" and therefore move the vehicle back on its path. If the player has difficulties in manipulating the hand control for this reverse movement, the leisure educator may instead have the player simply pick up the vehicle with his or her hands and replace it on its path. The participant should not be prevented from proceeding to Phase II if he or she lacks the skill to reverse the vehicle with the hand control.
2. In order for the participant to independently perform the steps in all phases of the task analysis, he or she must be able to execute a variety of right and left turns, varying from 30° to 360°. These turns are gradually introduced in phases (Phase II—30°, 45°, 90° turns;

Phase III—180° turns; Phase VI—360° turns) as the player learns to manipulate the vehicle through increasingly difficult maneuvers (see Figure 4.1).

Even though the participant can successfully perform the steps in Phase II when he or she executes any one of a variety of angles, it is important that the player become proficient at turning the vehicle at a 30°, 45°, and 90° angle. Therefore, in Phase II, the leisure educator should first instruct the player on how to make a 30° turn, the angle that requires the slightest movement of the wheel on the hand control. After the player successfully executes two successive 30° turns, the leisure educator should instruct the player on how to make a 45° turn, and so forth. To teach the participant to make the appropriate turns, the leisure educator has only to vary the placement of the finish line. The angle on which the participant is working should be recorded in the "Number/Score" column at the bottom of the Participant Performance Data Sheet (Form 4.1).

3. It may be difficult for a participant to press the forward/reverse button and turn the wheel on the hand control simultaneously. If this is the case, the leisure educator may have the participant do only one motion at a time—releasing the button when the vehicle comes to a cone, turning the wheel when the vehicle is not moving, holding the wheel in that position while pressing the button to "forward," releasing the button after the vehicle completes the turn, and turning the wheel to straighten out the vehicle's path while the vehicle is not moving. The results will be more steps to perform and will create somewhat jerky vehicle movements, but this procedure can give the participant better control over the vehicle's movements and the angles of the turns.

4. If the participant independently executes a required turn on his or her first attempt, the leisure educator should simply put a slash through the step number on the data sheet. If the player makes an error (moving straight ahead rather than turning, bumping into a cone, and so forth), but independently self-corrects that error on his or her second attempt, the leisure educator should place an "E" for error as well as a slash on the step number (𝐄̸). This would indicate that the player stopped the vehicle, reversed it, and performed the maneuver successfully. The leisure educator should ensure that the second attempt is successful, giving a physical assist if necessary. If the leisure educator does give assistance, he or she should not score the step number, thus indicating no or only partial independence.

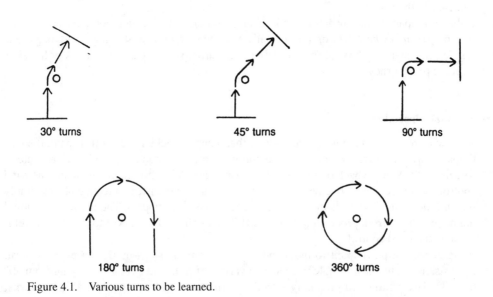

Figure 4.1.   Various turns to be learned.

Participant Performance Data Sheet

Participant: Dana Johnson   Activity: Remote Control Vehicle

Date	9/12	→			4/13	→		
Trainer	AS	AS	AS	AS	AS	AS	AS	AS
Number/Score	45° 45°	90°	180°	45°	90°	90°	180°	360°

Task Analysis: Remote Control Vehicle

Phase I: *Instructional Objective:* Given a remote control vehicle, the participant will manipulate the controls to move the vehicle forward and backward.

Phase I-A: *Instructional Objective:* The participant will manipulate the controls to move the vehicle forward.

Step 1:   Slide the power switch located under the vehicle to "on."
Step 2:   Place the vehicle on the ground.
Step 3:   With the nonpreferred hand, press the button on the hand control to "forward."
Step 4:   Hold the button in that position until the vehicle has moved straight ahead for 3'–5'.
Step 5:   Release the button.
Step 6:   Slide the power switch to "off."

Phase I-B: *Instructional Objective:* The participant will manipulate controls to move the vehicle forward and backward.

Step 1:   Slide the power switch located under the vehicle to "on."
Step 2:   Place the vehicle on the ground.
Step 3:   With the nonpreferred hand, press the button on the hand control to "forward."
Step 4:   Hold the button in that position until the vehicle has moved straight ahead for 3'–5'.
Step 5:   Release the button.
Step 6:   With the nonpreferred hand, press the button to "reverse." (The front of the vehicle should still be facing the same direction as it was when moving forward.)
Step 7:   Hold the button in that position until the vehicle has moved straight backward for 3'–5'.
Step 8:   Release the button.
Step 9:   Slide the power switch to "off."

Phase II: *Instructional Objective:* Given a remote control vehicle and one traffic cone (or other obstacle such as a milk carton), the participant will manipulate the controls to move the vehicle forward and will turn it right and left at varying angles (30°, 45°, 90°).

Phase II-A: *Instructional Objective:* The participant will position the cone and will manipulate the controls to move the vehicle forward and to the right.

Step 1:   Place the cone on the ground.
Step 2:   Slide the power switch located under the vehicle to "on."
Step 3:   Place the vehicle on the ground.
Step 4:   With the nonpreferred hand, press the button on the hand control to "forward" and continue to hold it in that position during the maneuver.
Step 5:   As the vehicle is passing the cone on the vehicle's right side, turn the wheel on the hand control slightly to the right with the preferred hand so that the vehicle makes a right turn around the cone.
Step 6:   Turn the wheel slightly to the left so that the vehicle moves straight ahead again.
Step 7:   After the vehicle has moved 3'–5', release the button.
Step 8:   Slide the power switch to "off."

Phase II-B: *Instructional Objective:* The participant will manipulate the controls to move the vehicle forward and to the left.

Step 1: Place the cone on the ground.

Step 2: Slide the power switch located under the vehicle to "on."

Step 3: Place the vehicle on the ground.

Step 4: With the nonpreferred hand, press that button on the hand control to "forward" and continue to hold it in that position during the maneuver.

Step 5: As the vehicle is passing the cone on the vehicle's left side, turn the wheel on the hand control slightly to the left with the preferred hand so that the vehicle makes a left turn around the cone.

Step 6: Turn the wheel slightly to the right so that the vehicle moves straight ahead again.

Step 7: After the vehicle has moved for 3'–5', release the button.

Step 8: Slide the power switch to "off."

Phase III: *Instructional Objective:* Given a remote control vehicle and one traffic cone (or other obstacle such as a milk carton), the participant will position the cone, will manipulate the controls to move the vehicle forward, and will maneuver the vehicle through U-turns (180°).

Phase III-A: *Instructional Objective:* The participant will position the cone and will manipulate the controls to move the vehicle forward and through a right U-turn.

Step 1: Place the cone on the ground.

Step 2: Slide the power switch located under the vehicle to "on."

Step 3: Place the vehicle on the ground.

Step 4: With the nonpreferred hand, press the button on the hand control to "forward" and continue to hold it in that position during the maneuver.

Step 5: As the vehicle is passing the cone on the vehicle's right side, turn the wheel on the hand control to the right with the preferred hand so that the vehicle makes a semicircle around the cone and faces the opposite direction.

Step 6: Turn the wheel to the left so that the vehicle continues to move straight ahead.

Step 7: After the vehicle has completed a U-turn, release the button.

Step 8: Slide the power switch to "off."

Phase III-B: *Instructional Objective:* The participant will manipulate the controls to move the vehicle forward and through a left U-turn.

Step 1: Place the cone on the ground.

Step 2: Slide the power switch located under the vehicle to "on."

Step 3: Place the vehicle on the ground.

Step 4: With the nonpreferred hand, press the button on the hand control to "forward" and continue to hold it in that position during the following maneuver.

Step 5: As the vehicle is passing the cone on the vehicle's left side, turn the wheel on the hand control to the left with the preferred hand so that the vehicle makes a semicircle around the cone and faces the opposite direction.

Step 6: Turn the wheel to the right so that the vehicle continues to move straight ahead.

Step 7: After the vehicle has completed a U-turn, release the button.

Step 8: Slide the power switch to "off."

Phase IV: *Instructional Objective:* Given a remote control vehicle and four traffic cones (or other obstacles such as milk cartons), the participant will position the cones to form a square track and will manipulate the controls to move the vehicle forward and in a square pattern (90°).

Step 1:   Place the cones on the ground.
Step 2:   Slide the power switch located under the vehicle to "on."
Step 3:   Place the vehicle on the ground.
Step 4:   With the nonpreferred hand, press the button on the hand control to "forward" and continue to hold it in that position during the maneuver.
Step 5:   As the vehicle is passing cone 2 on the vehicle's left side, turn the wheel on the hand control slightly to the left with the preferred hand so that the vehicle makes a left turn around the cone.
Step 6:   Turn the wheel slightly to the right so that the vehicle moves straight ahead again.
Step 7:   As the vehicle is passing cone 3 on the vehicle's left side, turn the wheel on the hand control slightly to the left with the preferred hand so that the vehicle makes a left turn around the cone.
Step 8:   Turn the wheel slightly to the right so that the vehicle moves straight ahead again.
Step 9:   As the vehicle is passing cone 4 on the vehicle's left side, turn the wheel on the hand control slightly to the left with the preferred hand so that the vehicle makes a left turn around the cone.
Step 10:   Turn the wheel slightly to the right so that the vehicle moves straight ahead again.
Step 11:   After the vehicle has passed by cone 1 and completed a square pattern, release the button.
Step 12:   Slide the power switch to "off."

Phase V: *Instructional Objective:* Given a remote control vehicle and four traffic cones (or other obstacles such as milk cartons), the participant will position the cones to form a square track and will manipulate the controls to move the vehicle forward and in an "S" pattern (180°).

Step 1:   Place the cones on the ground.
Step 2:   Slide the power switch located under the vehicle to "on."
Step 3:   Place the vehicle on the ground.
Step 4:   With the nonpreferred hand, press the button on the hand control to "forward" and continue to hold it in that position during the following maneuver.
Step 5:   As the vehicle is passing cone 2 on the vehicle's left side, turn the wheel on the hand control to the left with the preferred hand so that the vehicle makes a semicircle around the cone and faces the opposite direction.
Step 6:   Turn the wheel to the right so that the vehicle continues to move straight ahead.
Step 7:   As the vehicle is passing cone 4 on the vehicle's right side, turn the wheel on the hand control to the right so that the vehicle makes a semicircle around the cone and faces the opposite direction.
Step 8:   Turn the wheel to the left so that the vehicle continues to move straight ahead.
Step 9:   After the vehicle has passed by cone 3 and completed an "S" pattern, release the button.
Step 10:   Slide the power switch to "off."

Phase VI: *Instructional Objective:* Given a remote control vehicle and four traffic cones (or other obstacles such as milk cartons), the participant will position the cones to form a square track and will manipulate the controls to move the vehicle forward in a "figure 8" pattern (360°).

Step 1: Place the cones on the ground.

Step 2: Slide the power switch located under the vehicle to "on."

Step 3: Place the vehicle on the ground.

Step 4: With the nonpreferred hand, press the button on the hand control to "forward" and continue to hold it in that position during the following maneuver.

Step 5: With the preferred hand, turn the wheel on the hand control to the left so that the vehicle makes a complete circle around cones 1 and 2.

Step 6: With the preferred hand, turn the wheel on the hand control to the right so that the vehicle makes a complete circle around cones 4 and 3.

Step 7: After the vehicle has completed a "figure 8" pattern, release the button.

Step 8: Slide the power switch to "off."

Simon

Simon is an electronic game of concentration that has captured the attention of children, teenagers, and adults. It is chronologically age appropriate for teens and adults, yet its novel light and sound patterns are also attractive to and appropriate for younger children. Several variations of Simon are now available commercially, and the following instruction procedures and task analysis may be adapted to these variations to teach participants to play with them.

Playing with Simon does require color matching and sequencing, making it more suitable for participants who demonstrate those skills. However, the game and the task analysis have been adapted for players with varying skills.

Materials

Simon by Milton Bradley

Additional materials for possible adaptations: construction paper or plastic; tape or glue; pieces of paper that match the colors of the lenses

Entry Motor Skill Level and Possible Adaptations

To use the activity as intended by the manufacturer, a participant must have: 1) the ability to hold a stable position, 2) head and trunk control, 3) sufficient eye–hand coordination to accomplish visually directed reaching, and 4) sufficient strength to activate the game when pushing on the colored lenses.

If the participant is distracted by all the buttons and switches on the central control panel, the leisure educator can set the game selector and skill level switches for the player (thus eliminating Steps 2 and 3 of the task analysis), and cover all of the switches, except for the on/off switch and the start button, with a piece of construction paper or plastic. The paper or plastic can be cut into a circle (minus a triangular wedge for the button and switch) and attached to the control panel with tape or glue.

If the participant lacks the strength to activate the game when he or she pushes on the colored lenses with one hand, the leisure educator can have the participant use two hands, an elbow, a foot, or even a stick held in his or her hand(s). As a last resort, the player can either point to colored pieces of paper that correspond to the colors of the lenses or even call out the colors, and the leisure educator or another player can assist by pressing on the lenses as directed.

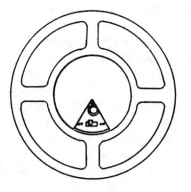

Instructional Environment

The participant should be seated at a table or desk with the on/off switch centered directly in front of his or her body. The leisure educator should be close enough to provide any necessary assistance.

Depending on the participant's abilities, he or she may sit in a wheelchair equipped with a tray or in a specially adapted chair with a table, or he or she may stand on a prone stander, in a standing box, or on a tilt table. The participant may also lie prone over a wedge or a roll.

Instructional Procedures

1. To play Simon as intended by the manufacturer, a participant must be able to match at least one signal by pressing the same colored lens that lights up and emits a sound. For a participant who fails to make progress in the task analysis because he or she does not match the signal, the leisure educator should first implement the Branch for Step 6 of the task analysis. If the participant still does not learn to match one signal correctly, the participant can enjoy Simon through partial participation with someone else matching the signals.

2. The number of signals Simon naturally gives increases following each correct match; if the player matches one signal correctly, Simon gives two consecutive signals to match, then three, and so forth. If the player successfully matches all the signals, he or she wins the game; if the player does not match them all correctly, or if he or she takes longer than 5 seconds to respond, Simon gives a "razz" sound and the player loses the game. The player then presses the start button to begin a new game. These game rules can present the leisure educator with a difficult teaching situation because few participants with significant disabilities demonstrate the ability to recall and then match a long sequence of signals. Also, many individuals may have difficulties making the auditory discrimination between the "razz" sound and the other sounds emitted by Simon. Furthermore, the player must learn how to respond to an "if–then" situation that may not occur frequently— "If I *do not* match the signal correctly, then I have to press the start button."

   To address some of these difficulties, the following task analysis artificially limits the number of signals presented to the player. In Phase I, the player is taught to turn the machine off immediately after matching one signal; in Phase II, after matching two signals. (If the machine were not turned off at this point, Simon would add another signal to the sequence.) The participant then starts another game, and the leisure educator starts a new trial by turning the machine on and matching the same number of signals designated for the phase the participant is on. If the player does not match the signal(s) correctly, he or she is taught to press the start button and to try to match the designated number of signals again. Whether the player matches the signal(s) correctly on the first or second attempt (the leisure educator ensures success on the second attempt), a trial ends only after the participant has correctly matched the designated number of signals and has turned Simon off.

3. To play Simon independently, the participant must learn what to do when he or she matches correctly and what to do when he or she does not match correctly. The leisure educator, therefore, should make certain that the player is exposed to both possibilities by: 1) teaching the task analysis, or 2) first teaching the player only to match correctly and then teaching the task analysis. If the leisure educator starts with the task analysis, it is assumed that the participant will naturally match some signals and will naturally make some errors; whenever these two situations occur, the leisure educator should simply give the player enough assistance so that he or she learns to handle both possibilities. If the leisure educator starts with the Branch for Step 6 and only correct matches, he or she should give whatever assistance is necessary for the player to learn to independently match 70% of the time over a period of 2 consecutive days. Then the leisure educator should follow the task analysis, allowing the participant to make whatever errors he or she would naturally make, providing enough assistance so that the matching response generalizes and the participant learns what to do when an error is made.

4. Regardless of how carefully the leisure educator fades assistance, matching errors will be made by the participant from time to time. When such an error occurs, the leisure educator should inform the participant that he or she did not match correctly and should assist the player in self-correcting that error. When the player makes a matching error in Phase I, he or she must: 1) press the start button, 2) look at the lighted colored lens, and 3) press the same colored lens within 5 seconds. The number of steps involved in this self-correction grows progressively larger as the player progresses through the higher phases because Simon always goes back to one signal after an error occurs. The leisure educator should make certain that the participant's second attempt at matching the signal(s) is successful; otherwise, the task analysis varies too much from trial to trial. (As it is, the leisure educator will have some variation between the trials in which the participant matches correctly and the trials in which the participant makes a matching error.) In addition, a trial can become too long if the leisure educator does not limit the number of matching errors, and the participant may also learn an inappropriate rule (it is not necessary to match the signal at all if the player presses the start button all the time).

    To ensure that the participant's second attempt at matching Simon's signals is successful, the leisure educator should provide assistance in making the correct response immediately, using a physical assist if necessary. Gradually, as the player makes fewer and fewer matching errors, the leisure educator should delay providing assistance and give the player the opportunity to initiate self-correction. Assistance should be delayed for 1 second, then 2 seconds, and so forth, until the leisure educator gets as close as possible to the 5-second maximum allowed by Simon. The leisure educator must assist the participant before the 5-second time limit; otherwise, Simon will indicate another error by making a "razz" sound.

5. Besides matching errors, other errors may occur due to machine malfunctions or inadequate and/or inaccurate pressure applied to the colored lenses. The difference between the matching error and the other errors should be made clear to the participant as soon as such situations occur. The leisure educator should explain that the machine is not working right or that

the participant is not pressing hard enough in a specific area and should then restart the game. Every effort should be made so that no error is regarded by the participant as a "punishing" situation.

6. Once the participant reaches Phase III, he or she already knows how to play Simon and can match two signals. In Phase III, the objective is to increase the number of consecutive signals the player can match correctly. On skill level 1, Simon gives a maximum of eight sets of signals for the player to match. While it is unlikely that a participant with significant disabilities will learn to match all of these sets, during field tests several players did learn to match up to four or five sets.

7. The use and positioning of the hands are important parts of playing Simon successfully. The leisure educator should decide in advance if the player should use one or two hands to press the colored lenses. For participants who have physical disabilities, two hands may be more effective. If the participant is able to use only one hand, it should, of course, be his or her preferred hand. The hand being used should be positioned next to the machine on the table or desk. Resting the playing hand on or over the machine will prevent the player from seeing all of the signals in the correct sequence; resting it in the player's lap will prevent the person from responding with the necessary speed. The hand not being used to play the game should remain in the player's lap to eliminate the temptation to use both hands during play. (When participants began switching hands during the field tests, many errors occurred.)

8. As with the other activities in this curriculum, data may be collected by placing a slash through the steps of the task analysis performed independently by the player on the Participant Performance Data Sheet (see Form 4.1 in the Remote Control Vehicle Activity). However, the leisure educator needs more than a slash to record what the participant actually does on the steps that require the participant to match the signal(s) or to correct a matching error. If the player independently matches the signal on the first attempt, the leisure educator should place an "M" for match as well as a slash on the step number (M̸). If the player independently presses an incorrect colored lens and independently self-corrects by pressing the start button and matching the signal on the second attempt, the leisure educator should place an "E" for error as well as a slash on the step number (E̸). Rather than writing the additional steps involved in correcting an error in the task analysis every time an error occurs, the leisure educator need only associate "E" with these additional steps. If the player does not independently match the signal on the first or second attempt, or if the leisure educator has to assist the player either in matching the signal or in correcting a matching error, the leisure educator should not score the step number, thus indicating no, or only partial, independence by the participant. If the participant shows partial independence, the leisure educator should note which parts of the step (matching a signal, pressing the start button, looking at the lighted lens, and/or matching the second signal) the participant can perform alone and refer to the appropriate branch for mass trials on the parts the participant is not performing independently.

Task Analysis: Simon

Phase I: *Instructional Objective:* Given Simon, the participant will match one signal and reset the game when errors occur.

Step 1: Slide the on/off switch to "on."
Step 2: Slide the game selector switch to "1."
Step 3: Slide the skill level switch to "1."
Step 4: Press the start button.

Step 5:   Look at the lighted lens and/or listen to its sound.
Step 6:   Press the same lens within 5 seconds. If a matching error occurs, press the start button,
           look at the lighted lens and/or listen to its sound, and press the same lens within 5 seconds.
Step 7:   Slide the on/off switch to "off."

Phase II: *Instructional Objective:* Given Simon, the participant will match two signals and
                 reset the game when errors occur.

Step 1:   Slide the on/off switch to "on."
Step 2:   Slide the game selector switch to "1."
Step 3:   Slide the skill level switch to "1."
Step 4:   Press the start button.
Step 5:   Look at the lighted lens and/or listen to its sound.
Step 6:   Press the same lens within 5 seconds. If a matching error occurs, press the start button,
           look at the lighted lens and/or listen to its sound, and press the same lens within 5 seconds.
Step 7:   Look at the two lighted lenses and/or listen to their sounds. (In some instances, only
           one lens will light up and make the same sound twice.)
Step 8:   Press the same two lenses in the given sequence. (If only one lens lights up, press the
           same lens twice.) If a matching error occurs, press the start button, look at the one
           lighted lens and/or listen to its sound, press the same lens within 5 seconds, look at the
           two lighted lenses and/or listen to their sound, and press the same two lenses in the
           given sequence.
Step 9:   Slide the on/off switch to "off."

Phase III: *Instructional Objective:* Given Simon, the participant will match three (or more)
                  signals and reset the game when errors occur.

Step 1:   Slide the on/off switch to "on."
Step 2:   Slide the game selector switch to "1."
Step 3:   Slide the skill level switch to "1."
Step 4:   Press the start button.
Step 5:   Look at the lighted lens and/or listen to its sound.
Step 6:   Press the same lens within 5 seconds. If a matching error occurs, press the start but-
            ton, look at the lighted lens and/or listen to its sound, and press the same lens within
            5 seconds.
Step 7:   Look at the two lighted lenses and/or listen to their sounds. (In some instances, only
            one lens will light up and make the same sound twice.)
Step 8:   Press the same two lenses in the given sequence. (If only one lens is involved, press
            the same lens twice.) If a matching error occurs, press the start button, look at the one
            lighted lens and/or listen to its sound, press the same lens within 5 seconds, look at
            the two lighted lenses and/or listen to their sounds, and press the same two lenses in a
            given sequence.
Step 9:   Look at the three lighted lenses and/or listen to their sounds. (In some instances, only
            two or perhaps even only one panel will light up and make the same sounds.)
Step 10:   Press the same three lenses in the given sequence. (If only one or two lenses light up,
            press them as many times as indicated by Simon.) If a matching error occurs, press
            the start button, look at the one lighted lens and/or listen to its sound, press the same
            two and press the same three lenses in the given sequence.
Step 11:   Slide the on/off switch to "off."

Branch for Phase I: Simon

Problem: The participant does not manipulate the controls properly and/or look at the lighted lenses.

Instructional Objective 1:   The participant will look at the machine while the leisure educator manipulates the controls.

Instructional Procedures:

1. Eliminate Steps 2 and 3 (sliding the game selector and skill level switches to "1") from the participant's task analysis if he or she is having difficulties with the on/off switch and the start button. The game selector and skill level switches may be set by the leisure educator and then covered with construction paper or plastic along with the last button and the longest button. All these controls will probably never have to be manipulated again.
2. Slide the on/off switch to "on," press the start button, look at the lighted lenses, match the colored lenses, and then slide the on/off switch to "off."
3. Have the participant maintain eye contact with the machine throughout the game.
4. Initially, every instance of eye contact should be reinforced. Then, progressively longer intervals of eye contact should be reinforced until the player can visually monitor the game during the time it takes the leisure educator to match one signal.
5. Encourage the participant to touch the machine and to manipulate the on/off switch and the start button.
6. Keep data on the duration of eye contact with the machine.

Instructional Objective 2:   The participant will press the start button and look at the machine while the leisure educator manipulates the controls.

Instructional Procedures:

1. Slide the on/off switch to "on," prompt the player to press the start button, and then proceed to perform the rest of the steps of the task analysis.
2. Have the player maintain eye contact with the machine and reinforce the player in the same manner as outlined under Objective 1. In addition, the participant should be reinforced every time he or she pushes the start button correctly.
3. Encourage the participant to touch the machine and to manipulate the on/off switch and the start button.
4. Keep data on:
   a.   The duration of eye contact with the machine
   b.   The number of times the player should push the start button
   c.   The number of times the player independently pushes the start button

Instructional Objective 3:   The participant will slide the on/off switch, press the start button, and maintain eye contact with the game.

Instructional Procedures:

1. Prompt the participant to slide the on/off switch to "on" and to press the start button, and then proceed to perform the rest of the steps of the task analysis up to the last step. Prompt the participant to slide the on/off switch to "off."
2. Reinforce the participant every time he or she slides the on/off switch and presses the start button correctly. Reinforcement of eye contact should be on a variable interval schedule.
3. Encourage the participant to touch the machine and to manipulate the on/off switch and the start button.

4. Keep data on:
   a. The duration of eye contact with the machine
   b. The number of times the player should slide the on/off switch to "on" and "off" and press the start button
   c. The number of times the player independently slides the on/off switch to "on"
   d. The number of times the player independently pushes the start button
   e. The number of times the player independently slides the on/off switch to "off"

Branch for Step 6, Phase III: Simon

Problem: The participant does not touch the lens that lights up.

Instructional Objective: The participant will touch the lens that lights up.

Instructional Procedures:

1. Follow the procedures for mass practice (see Table 3.8).
2. Turn on the machine and press the start button.
3. Place the participant's hand lightly on the lens that lights up. Point out to the participant that the lens is lit and is making a sound.
4. Press the start button again and repeat the procedure. If the participant does not press too hard on the lens, the system will not be activated and Simon will continue to function at one signal.

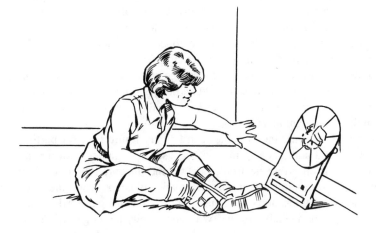

Target
Games

*T*arget games are readily available for use at home or in the community, and they are flexible enough to accommodate any number of players and people of varying skill levels. Target games promote cooperation among players; eye–hand coordination; throwing skills; and, when appropriate, collateral math skills. Velcro ball and dart games may be purchased at a reasonable cost for home use. They are chronologically age appropriate for both children and adults, and they encourage family play. Electronic target games, with darts with plastic tips, may be found in community environments such as pubs, restaurants, and specialty food and game arcades. Activity descriptions and instructional procedures for both Velcro target games (for home use) and electronic target games (for public use) are presented here.

Materials

Velcro target board and either Velcro balls or darts (for home use); or electronic target game and plastic-tipped darts (for community use)

Additional materials for possible adaptations: large, light balls; balloons, Nerf balls, or tennis balls; Velcro; glue; tongs or reaching device; bells; masking tape

Entry Motor Skill Level and Possible Adaptations

To use the activity as intended by the manufacturers, a participant must have: 1) the ability to hold a stable position, 2) head and trunk control, 3) free range of motion at the shoulder and elbow, 4) whole-hand grasp, 5) sufficient eye–hand coordination to accomplish visually directed throwing and removal of darts, 6) sufficient strength to throw darts, and 7) release at the end of an arm swing.

Velcro Target Games: If a participant has difficulty grasping, holding, and/or throwing small objects (e.g., Velcro darts) at the Velcro target game, Velcro balls may be used. Velcro darts are the most difficult to use because they require a fairly refined pincer grasp. (Velcro darts, however, are very similar to standard darts and may help the participant generalize to a standard dart game.) If the player also has difficulty using Velcro balls, larger objects—light balls, balloons, Nerf balls, tennis balls—can be substituted for the Velcro throwing objects. Velcro strips can be glued onto these larger balls so that they will stick to the target.

For a player who has insufficient strength to throw the Velcro objects very far, the leisure educator may place the target within reaching distance, perhaps laying it flat on the ground so that the player is dropping or placing the object on the target rather than throwing it. If the participant has difficulty retrieving the object as well, the leisure educator can not only place the target within reaching distance but also provide tongs or a reaching device.

Leisure materials that provide auditory stimuli often encourage participants with significant disabilities to prolong their engagement in activities. To add auditory stimulation to the Velcro target games, the leisure educator may attach bells to the target, the ball, or the dart so that some sound will be produced when the participant hits the target.

Electronic Target Games: Electronic target games can be very reinforcing for participants who respond well to visual and auditory stimulation because these games light up and make a lot of noise when the target is hit. Most electronic target games that are found in public environments include a computerized monitor screen that automatically keeps score, indicates the player's turn, provides game instructions, and offers opportunities to make game selections. Usually, three darts with plastic tips are available for use with community target games. Additionally, a money rack for depositing coins prior to playing the game is typically situated near the target and indicates the number of people (either an individual or a group/team) who will play the game.

If a participant has difficulty holding an electronic target dart with the required fine pincer grasp, masking tape may be wrapped around the handle of the dart to temporarily build it up. Or, if an even thicker handle is needed, a thin, small rectangle of foam rubber, which can easily slide on and off, may be taped around the handle.

Instructional Environment

1. The Velcro target board should be positioned on the wall at about the participant's eye level. If the player is seated, the target should still remain at about eye level. Because it will probably be impossible to lower and raise the electronic target board at a community site, a participant's ease of throwing the dart or ball may be accommodated by shortening or lengthening the throwing distance from the target (see point 2 below).

2. The distance between the target and the participant should be determined prior to each instruction session and should be based on the player's height and overall throwing ability. Initially, the distance should be at least 1' less than the participant's height. If the participant has not developed an overhand throw, a distance of 1½'–2' between the participant and the target will help to ensure success in hitting the target. As the player's ability to throw the dart, ball, or other throwing object increases, the distance between the player and the target can be increased gradually, until eventually the player is tossing darts or throwing balls from the standard 8' distance.

3. In the early stages of instruction, masking tape may be used to mark a foul line on the ground as a cue to the player. The player should be instructed to stand behind this line while throwing. As instruction progresses, the foul line should be faded and the participant should be taught to stand behind the line without this instructional cue. However, in most environments that house an electronic dart game, a marking will appear on the floor designating the tossing line.

4. Depending on the participant's abilities, he or she may kneel or sit in a wheelchair or a specially adapted chair. The participant may also stand on a prone stander, in a standing box, or on a tilt table.

Instructional Procedures

1. The rules for both the Velcro and electronic target games, as given by the manufacturers, are varied and can sometimes be complicated. For Velcro dart games, different numbers of points are typically awarded for throwing the Velcro balls or darts onto different areas of the target. Similarly, for community electronic games, participants may typically choose from seven different games including Tic Tac Darts, Count-Up, and Cricket—each with different scoring procedures. The preferred game is Cricket, particularly team Cricket, which involves teams consisting of two members each. The following task analyses have been simplified and modified for the skill levels of most participants with significant disabilities. For more skilled participants, the leisure educator can follow standard game rules for darts or the electronic game.

    For the Velcro target games, the participant is given three balls (or other throwing objects) to throw at the target with either an underhand or overhand throw. If she or he hits the target anywhere within the largest circle, it is considered a "hit." If the ball or dart sticks to the space outside the circle, or if it drops to the floor, it is considered a "miss." After the participant has thrown three balls or darts, the trial ends and the leisure educator should tally the number of hits scored independently by the player and record that number in the "Number/Score" column at the bottom of the Participant Performance Data Sheet (see Form 4.1 in the Remote Control Vehicle activity).

    For the electronic target game, the participant is given three plastic-tipped darts to throw at the target with an overhand toss. If the participant hits one of the highest numbers on the dart board (15, 16, 17, 18, 19, 20) or the bull's eye as indicated on the computer monitor, it is considered a "hit." The computer registers the "hit" (visually seen on the monitor) as either a single ring, double ring, triple ring, bull's eye, or double bull's eye. A diagonal line (/) indicates a single hit; criss-cross diagonal lines (X) indicate a double hit; and a criss-cross diagonal line inside a circle (⊗) indicates a triple hit. The bull's eye may be either an "outer" or "inner" hit, to be counted as a single or double bull's eye, respectively. (See Figure 4.2.)

    The following scoring procedure is typically used for electronic target games:

Singles Ring	=	Number shown on dart board × 1
Doubles Ring	=	Number shown on dart board × 2
Triples Ring	=	Number shown on dart board × 3
Outer Bull's Eye	=	Score 25 points automatically
Inner Bull's Eye	=	Score 50 points automatically

    That is, if a dart hits the number 15 within the singles ring, the score would be the number on the board (15) × 1, or 15; if a dart hits the number 15 within the doubles ring, the score would be the number on the board (15) × 2, or 30; and so forth for the triples ring.

    In the game of Cricket, each participant or team must hit each area or number on the board (15, 16, 17, 18, 19, 20, bull's eyes) three times in order to "close out" that number or area. The numbers/areas may be hit in any order. If the dart sticks to the area that borders the scoring area, or if it drops to the floor, it is considered a "miss." After the participant has thrown three darts, the trial ends and the leisure educator should tally the number of hits performed independently by the participant and take note of the points scored (from the computer monitor) and record these numbers in the "Number/Score" column at the bottom of the Participant Performance Data Sheet (see Form 4.1).

    On the Participant Performance Data Sheet (Form 4.1), the leisure educator should also put a slash over the step number if the player hits the target independently on the first attempt. If the player misses the target on the first attempt, *but* independently retrieves the

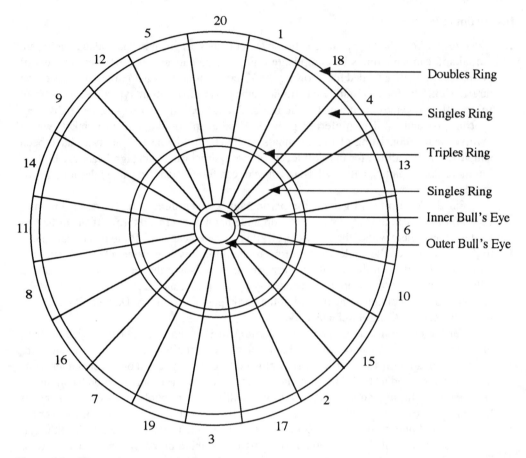

Figure 4.2.   Electronic target scoring board.

dart, ball, or other throwing object, throws it at the target, and hits the target on the second attempt, the leisure educator should add an "M" on the top of the slash (M̸) to indicate a miss on the first throw and extra steps involved in correcting that miss. If the leisure educator provides any assistance on the participant's first or second attempt, the leisure educator should not score the step number, thus indicating no or only partial independence by the player. After the target has been hit six times, the trial ends, and the leisure educator should tally the number of hits scored independently by the participant on either the first or second attempt and should also record that number in the "Number/Score" column at the bottom of the data sheet.

2. Prior to instruction, the leisure educator should determine the most appropriate target game and phase for the participant based on the participant's preferences and skills. If the participant has a good pincer grasp and overhand throw, the leisure educator may consider starting him or her on Phase II with the Velcro darts—the most difficult combination of skill (overhand throw) and material (darts). The easiest combination is Phase I (underhand throw) with Velcro balls or other larger, lighter throwing objects suggested earlier. The leisure educator may, of course, decide to change the phase and throwing object whenever it is appropriate for the individual's needs.

3. Prior to instruction, the leisure educator should decide whether the participant should hold the extra balls or darts in the nonpreferred hand while playing the game, or if the extra

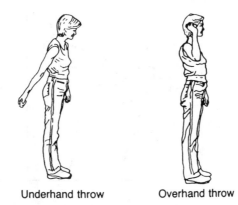

Underhand throw   Overhand throw

throwing objects should be placed on a table or on the ground next to the player during play. As with all of the other activities, the participant should throw or toss the ball or dart with his or her preferred hand. These arrangements should remain consistent throughout instruction.

4. As a general rule, if the dart, ball, or other throwing object does not stick to the target, it is counted as a miss and may not be thrown again. Also, for safety's sake, darts should always be handed to another player with the tips pointed down and away from that player.

Task Analysis: Velcro Target Games (Home Use)

Phase I: *Instructional Objective:* Given a target and three Velcro balls, the participant will throw the balls at the target using an underhand throw and then retrieve them from the target or floor.

Step 1: Pick up the first ball with the preferred hand.
Step 2: Stand at an appropriate distance from the target; face the target.
Step 3: Move the arm backward to an underhand throwing position.
Step 4: While watching the target, throw the ball at the target.
Step 5: Check the target for a hit by looking at the target or at the place where the ball fell.
Step 6: Pick up the second ball with the preferred hand.
Step 7: Stand at an appropriate distance from the target; face the target.
Step 8: Move the arm backward to an underhand throwing position.
Step 9: While watching the target, throw the ball at the target.
Step 10: Check the target for a hit by looking at the target or at the place where the ball fell.
Step 11: Pick up the third ball with the preferred hand.
Step 12: Stand at an appropriate distance from the target; face the target.
Step 13: Move the arm backward to an underhand throwing position.
Step 14: While watching the target, throw the ball at the target.
Step 15: Check the target for a hit by looking at the target or at the place where the ball fell.
Step 16: Pick up any balls on the floor.
Step 17: Go to the target.
Step 18: Remove any balls from the target.

Phase II: *Instructional Objective:* Given a target and three Velcro balls or darts, the participant will throw the balls or darts at the target using an overhand throw and then retrieve them from the target or floor.

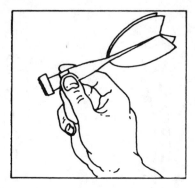

Step 1:   Pick up the first ball or dart with the preferred hand. If using a dart, hold it midway between the dart tip and feathers and point the Velcro tip toward the target.

Step 2:   Stand at an appropriate distance from the target; face the target.

Step 3:   Move the arm backward to an overhand throwing position.

Step 4:   While watching the target, throw the ball or dart at the target.

Step 5:   Check the target for a hit by looking at the target or at the place where the ball or dart fell.

Step 6:   Pick up the second ball or dart with the preferred hand.

Step 7:   Stand at an appropriate distance from the target; face the target.

Step 8:   Move the arm backward to an overhand throwing position.

Step 9:   While watching the target, throw the ball or dart at the target.

Step 10: Check the target for a hit by looking at the target or at the place where the ball or dart fell.

Step 11: Pick up the third ball or dart with the preferred hand.

Step 12: Stand at an appropriate distance from the target; face the target.

Step 13: Move the arm backward to an overhand throwing position.

Step 14: While watching the target, throw the ball or dart at the target.

Step 15: Check the target for a hit by looking at the target or at the place where the ball or dart fell.

Step 16: Pick up any balls or darts on the floor.

Step 17: Go to the target.

Step 18: Remove any balls or darts from the target.

Task Analysis: Electronic Target Game (Community Use)

Phase I: *Instructional Objective:* Given the selection of electronic target games as a community leisure activity, the participant will prepare to play the game at an appropriate community site.

Step 1:   From among a selection of at least two community leisure activities, choose to participate in an electronic target game at an appropriate site in the neighborhood.

Step 2:   Before leaving school or home, make sure the facility is open.

Step 3:   Enter the pub, restaurant, or specialty food/game arcade.

Step 4:   Locate the room or area where the electronic dart board is located and proceed in that direction.

Step 5:   Enter the room or area.

Step 6:   Locate the coat rack and proceed in that direction.

Step 7:   Take your coat off and hang it on a coat rack or hanger (or hang coat around back of chair).

Step 8:   Proceed to the electronic target game.
Step 9:   Prepare to play the game.

Phase II: *Instructional Objective:* Given the electronic target and three plastic-tipped darts, the participant will play the game.

Step 1:   Place coins in money rack. (Request change [e.g., quarters] for a dollar bill from the cashier, if necessary.)
Step 2:   Remove darts from the target board with the preferred hand and put them aside.
Step 3:   One player puts the designated amount of money in the coin slot.
Step 4:   Press the selection button with the finger of the preferred hand.
Step 5:   Watch the computerized monitor screen.
Step 6:   Read the directions for selecting an electronic game.
Step 7:   Decide which game you want to play.
Step 8:   Press the selection button for the game of choice.
Step 9:   Press the selection button until the arrow is pointed at the game of choice.
Step 10:   Press the enter button to start the game of choice.
Step 11:   Walk and stand behind the designated throwing line.
Step 12:   Pick up one dart in the preferred throwing hand.
Step 13:   Raise arm to lift hand to eye level.
Step 14:   Aim the dart at a particular number or area on the target board indicated on the monitor.
Step 15:   Throw the dart toward the target with the preferred throwing hand.
Step 16:   Release the dart at completion of the throwing motion.
Step 17:   Visually track the dart as it approaches the target.
Step 18:   Observe where the dart hits the board.
Step 19:   Repeat Steps 12–16 to throw the second dart.
Step 20:   Repeat Steps 12–16 to throw the third dart.
Step 21:   Proceed toward dart board.
Step 22:   Press the player change button.
Step 23:   Remove darts from the board with the preferred hand. (Pick up any darts that may have fallen to the floor.)
Step 24:   Position darts in the preferred hand with the plastic tips pointed toward you and covered by the fingers and thumb.
Step 25:   Proceed toward the next designated player.
Step 26:   Extend the darts safely toward the next player.
Step 27:   The next player takes the darts and proceeds to take his or her turn.
Step 28:   Repeat task analysis until all players have taken their turns and the points are tallied.

Skill Level Adaptations: Access to the community site by a participant who uses a wheelchair will need to be screened in advance. Access to the site may be provided via a ramp and reserved parking, and access to the game area may be provided via ramps or elevators. A peer or friend may either travel to the site with a participant or meet a participant at the front door of the facility. This person could initially assist the participant in Phase I, Step 3 (entering the site), Step 6 (locating coat rack), and Step 7 (taking coat off and hanging it up). In Phase II, this person could assist a participant in Step 1 (receiving quarters from cashier and placing coins in money rack), Steps 2 and 23 (removing darts from board), Step 3 (putting money in coin slot), and Step 8 (selecting game). As the participant becomes more familiar with the surroundings, game, and other people, assistance in these steps can be faded and the participant can take the lead in completing these tasks.

Branch for Step 4 (Velcro) and Steps 15–17, Phase II (Electronic): Target Games

Problem: The participant does not watch the target while throwing the ball, dart, or other throwing object, and therefore does not hit the target.

Instructional Objective: The participant will watch the target continuously—from the point at which the arm is moved back into the throwing position to the point at which the ball, dart, or other throwing object is released—on four out of five trials for three consecutive sessions.

Instructional Procedures:

1. This branch is designed to be used within the context of the task analysis as a parallel objective to the phase in which the participant is being instructed. Take data on the steps performed independently by the participant and on the number of trials in which the participant watches the target.
2. The leisure educator should stand near and to the side of the target, but certainly not in line of the dart's flight. The target should be positioned at the same distance away from the participant that is currently being used during instruction. On giving the verbal cue, "(Name), watch the target," the leisure educator should touch the target with his or her index finger.
3. The leisure educator should systematically increase his or her distance away from the target until the leisure educator is standing next to the participant.
4. Initially, reinforce the participant every time he or she watches the target while throwing the ball, dart, or other throwing object. As the leisure educator moves closer to the participant, more emphasis should be placed on hitting the target. This can be done by pairing the two responses. For example, "Good watching, (name) . You hit the target with the ball (or dart or other throwing object)." Finally, this continuous reinforcement should be reduced to provide reinforcement only for hitting the target.

Problem: The participant does not release the ball, dart, or other throwing object.

Instructional Objective: The participant will move his or her arm appropriately and will open his or her fingers to release the ball, dart, or other throwing object.

Instructional Procedures:

1. This branch is designed to be used independently of the task analysis. Follow the procedures for mass trials (see Table 3.8) and take data on the number of trials in which the throwing object is released independently.
2. Position the target on the floor and have the participant sit next to the target either on the floor or in a chair.
3. Instruct the participant to hold the throwing object in the preferred hand at eye level.
4. Physically prime the flexing of the wrist and the release of the throwing object. Pair this physical assistance with the verbal cue, "Throw the ball (or dart or other throwing object)." Reinforce the throwing of the object, not the hitting of the target.
5. When the participant begins to release the throwing object without physical priming, incorporate the arm movements for the appropriate underhand or overhand throw the player is using in the skill acquisition instruction sessions. This can be done by physically guiding the participant at the elbow and shoulder to move the arm.
6. When the participant meets the criterion of three out of four successful releases, begin to systematically increase the distance between the participant and the target until the distance is 2'. Begin reinforcing the participant for hitting the target.
7. The target should be returned to the wall. The distance between the player and the target

should be 1½'–2' when the released balls, darts, or other throwing objects fall within 6" from the target on 60% of the trials.

Problem: The participant releases the ball, dart, or other throwing object, but releases it too late so that it hits the floor.

Instructional Objective: The participant will throw the ball, dart, or other throwing object— releasing it at the maximum extension position when the hand is farthest from the body and at about eye level—on two out of three trials for three consecutive sessions.

Instructional Procedures:

1. This branch is designed to be used within the context of the task analysis as a parallel objective to the phase in which the participant is being instructed. No additional data sheet is needed for this branch.
2. Position the participant close enough to the target to ensure success. As the participant's accuracy improves, increase the distance between the participant and the target.
3. For participants who respond well and immediately to verbal cues, a signal such as "now" may be used to teach the participant when to release the ball. Stand as close to the throwing arm as possible to ensure the accuracy of the signal. Prior to beginning this correction procedure, explain to the participant both the nature of the problem and why the cue is being used.
4. For participants who respond better to physical assists, use your own arm to block the follow-through movement of the player's throwing arm. This block should result in the release of the ball, dart, or other throwing object at the appropriate time. The block should be paired with a verbal cue such as "now" and should be faded as quickly as possible.

Problem: The participant does not throw the ball, dart, or other throwing object with enough velocity to hit the target.

Instructional Objective: The participant will throw the ball, dart, or other throwing object with sufficient strength to hit the target on two out of three trials for three consecutive sessions.

Instructional Procedures:

1. This branch is designed to be used within the context of the task analysis as a parallel objective to the phase in which the participant is being instructed. No additional data sheet is needed for this branch.
2. Initially, the distance between the target and the participant should be close enough to ensure success. The distance may be increased as the participant's power increases.
3. Position the participant so that the foot opposite the throwing arm is slightly in front. The participant's body should be angled so that the throwing arm and shoulder are farther from the target than the other arm and shoulder.
4. As the participant brings his or her arm forward to throw the ball, dart, or other throwing object, assist her or him in rotating the shoulder and upper portion of the body on the throwing side as well as in bringing them forward. This should serve to increase the power of the throw.
5. While modeling may be sufficient for those participants with good imitation skills, others may require full physical assistance. Concentrate on developing the shoulder movement prior to coordinating the shoulder and arm movements.

Chapter 5

ENHANCING LEISURE PARTICIPATION BY INDIVIDUALS WITH SIGNIFICANT INTELLECTUAL AND PHYSICAL DISABILITIES

Jennifer York and Beverly Rainforth

*I*ndividuals who have physical disabilities as well as intellectual disabilities present unique challenges for the design of individualized leisure programs. For this population, the tasks of activity selection and instruction discussed in the previous chapters are expanded by considering individual needs related to mobility, positioning, and manipulation of materials to maximize participation. Integrating effective positioning and movement strategies and, when necessary, developing individualized adaptations for leisure instruction require collaboration among team members from many disciplines. This chapter presents a collaborative team approach for addressing mobility, positioning, and physical participation in leisure activities. Adaptation of recreation materials and activities is discussed as well.

A TEAM APPROACH

Professionals with different areas of expertise are involved in the design and implementation of individualized leisure programs to ensure successful participation. Depending on the needs of individual learners, the team includes therapeutic recreation specialists, adapted physical education teachers, occupational therapists, physical therapists, communication specialists, and others. No one discipline has adequate expertise to independently design successful intervention strategies. The challenge is to channel the expertise of each individual team member to the combined efforts of the collaborative team. There are three basic requirements for an effective team process: 1) a unified philosophy, 2) a working organizational structure, and 3) the accomplishment of team goals (Johnson & Johnson, 1987). Rainforth, York, and Macdonald (1992) and York and Wiemann (1991) operationalized these as tenets for the delivery of services to learners

The development of this chapter was supported in part by the Minnesota University Affiliated Program on Developmental Disabilities Grant #G07DD0282/04.

with significant disabilities. The tenets are discussed here with specific application to leisure program design and implementation.

A Unified Philosophy

The diverse opinions and methods of individual team members enrich and strengthen a team. With respect to leisure programs, however, it is important that all team members share certain beliefs. First, all persons, including people with the most significant intellectual and physical disabilities, can enjoy and learn to participate in a variety of age-appropriate recreation activities. Furthermore, leisure opportunities should be available throughout the individual's lifetime, and should include a wide array of those activities enjoyed by persons without disabilities in typical home and community environments. The second aspect of a unified philosophy requires that team members believe that they can achieve better learner results by collaborating in the design and implementation of leisure programs than by working in isolation. In essence, the whole (i.e., a collaborative team) is greater than the sum of all its parts (i.e., divided contributions).

A Working Organizational Structure

An organized structure for team member interactions and program design serves to clarify roles, responsibilities, and expectations. Structure also includes regularly scheduled interaction times that enable team members to work together, conduct joint assessments of learner abilities in the actual leisure environments, and, subsequently, design and implement intervention strategies. Team member roles are defined in terms of both the unique expertise of each discipline and shared responsibilities for program design and implementation.

Occupational and physical therapy and therapeutic recreation expertise is particularly important when designing leisure programs for persons with physical disabilities. Contributions from these disciplines should ensure strategies for: 1) mobility for transitions, 2) positioning, and 3) physical participation. Attention to transitions includes identifying appropriate methods for moving between environments and activities (Rainforth et al., 1992). Once an individual has successfully traveled to the designated area, positions that promote efficient participation in leisure activities are determined. Finally, physical participation strategies to promote maximal participant involvement in the activity are designated. This includes identifying which body parts will be used (e.g., head, hand, arm, foot); efficient movement patterns; and, when necessary, individualized adaptations (York & Wiemann, 1991). A more detailed discussion of these three areas of physical and occupational therapy expertise is provided later in this chapter.

Responsibilities for all team members related to program design and implementation include:

Assessing learners in natural environments and activities
Contributing instructional methods to maximize learner success
Modifying activities and materials
Sharing responsibilities for paperwork (e.g., writing instructional programs, devising data sheets, collecting and graphing data)
Teaching and learning from other team members such that intervention is appropriately executed (role release and expansion)
Monitoring learner performance through data analysis and direct interaction with the learner
Participating in team problem-solving and decision-making efforts to improve learner performance

Thus, each team member is charged with the responsibility to contribute disciplinary expertise and methods for instructional programs to enhance learner performance. This necessarily requires *role release*; that is, team members must share information and skills that are typically considered unique to a particular discipline with others who implement a program. (A discussion of the teamwork logistics to enable such collaboration is beyond the scope of this chapter. Readers interested in teamwork logistics are referred to Rainforth & York, 1991; Rainforth et al., 1992; York, Kronberg, Doyle, & Medwedz, 1993.)

The Accomplishment of Team Goals

The final requirement for effective teamwork is the accomplishment of team goals. This point bears emphasis because collaborative teamwork (e.g., a transdisciplinary model of intervention) is often criticized for the excessive energy spent on team process with minimally enhanced learner outcomes. To be effective, team members certainly must establish a unified philosophy and an operational structure for interactions as described above. The third and most important goal of teamwork, however, is to increase learner participation in leisure environments and activities. The remainder of this chapter discusses the responsibilities shared by all team members to achieve this outcome.

AN ECOLOGICAL INVENTORY
APPROACH TO DETERMINING MOTORIC DEMANDS

Current curriculum development strategies for learners with significant disabilities emphasize starting with an ecological inventory to determine the performance requirements in actual environments (Falvey, 1989; Ford et al., 1989). The first step in conducting the ecological inventory is to identify priority environments for each learner. Then a team member goes to the actual environment and delineates the activities and component skills typical of participation by persons without disabilities. Brown, Evans, Weed, and Owen (1987) and Brown and Lehr (1993) developed a related construct for identifying performance requirements common to activity sequences or routines. They delineated 10 components integral to the performance of most routines. The routine components were initiating, preparing, making choices, participating in core skills, monitoring quality and tempo, problem solving, communicating, socializing, and terminating. Their analysis provides a more concrete basis for identifying generalized competencies appropriate for instructional emphasis in a variety of environments and routines. That is, for learners to be independent in most routines, participation in similar routine components is required. Because it is impossible to provide direct instruction in all natural environments and activities that are conceivably relevant to an individual learner currently or in the future, an emphasis on instruction in generalized routine components at least attempts to prepare learners to use their new skills in a variety of contexts. Slight modification of both the ecological inventory and routine component analysis strategies provides a useful basis for determining the motoric demands in leisure environments and activities. This type of analysis indicates that leisure routines have many common components, which are delineated below.

Participation in most leisure activities requires that the learner travel to the designated environment and activity, assume an appropriate position for the activity, and move body parts to engage in the activity. Using the Brown et al. (1987) routine component approach, mobility skills for traveling to, from, and within leisure environments could be considered part of the *initiation* component of a routine. Positioning would be part of the *preparation* component. Physical participation (i.e., movement of body parts to engage in the activity) would be a critical requisite for execution of the *core routine* component. When conducting an inventory based strictly on the participation of a person without disabilities in an environment or activity, these motoric demands might be easily overlooked. When conducting an inventory of a specific leisure environment intended for use by an individual with physical disabilities, however, attention to transition/mobility, positioning, and physical participation demands becomes critical for successful participation in the routine. An example of a format used to ensure attention to transition/mobility, positioning, and physical participation demands when conducting inventories is presented in Table 5.1 (Rainforth et al., 1992).

DETERMINING TRANSITION/MOBILITY, POSITIONING, AND PHYSICAL PARTICIPATION STRATEGIES

Once the environmental demands of the activity have been identified, the problem-solving task of determining strategies that allow the learner to participate begins. The nature and manifestations of the physical abilities displayed by specific individuals result from a variety of neuromotor and other dysfunctions. It is not necessary to describe what all of these specific disabilities

Table 5.1.   Sample ecological inventory approach to determining mobility, positioning, and participation demands in leisure activities

Activities for Peers without Disabilities	Typical Methods and Acceptable Alternatives		
	Transitions / Mobility	Positions	Participation
Looking at / reading books	TYP: Walk to shelves. ALT: Scoot, crawl, roll. Not much space but small equipment OK.	TYP: Sit on carpeted steps, sit or lie on floor. Children are physically very close, usually touching. ALT: Avoid use of equipment that isolates.	TYP: Manipulate books with hands, read/comment out loud. ALT: Most would be OK. Book holders, sticks to turn pages, taped books.
Talking with friends	TYP: Walk, run to carpeted steps, room corners. Small groups may change location to exclude peers or increase privacy. ALT: Floor method OK, small equipment OK.	TYP: Same as above. Positions may change to exclude peers or be more private. ALT: Avoid use of equipment that isolates, may need to work in position changes.	TYP: Talk, whisper, giggle, point, watch others, interrupt, leave if not included. ALT: Show pictures, activate prerecorded taped messages.
Showing toys to friends	TYP: Walk, skip to cubbies, then return to play area. ALT: Floor method OK, scooter board difficult on surface change, wheelchair OK, friend could get toy.	TYP: Stand or sit on floor or steps, usually very close to each other and touching. ALT: Most upright positions OK.	TYP: Hold, show, exchange, manipulate items. ALT: Point to items, have friend help show item.
Climbing on carpeted stairs / seats	TYP: Walk, skip to steps. ALT: Any method OK, small equipment OK.	TYP: Stand to step, sit to scoot up/down. ALT: Could lie to roll down deep steps.	TYP: Stepping in standing position, scooting seated. ALT: Rolling down deep steps.

From Rainforth, B., York, J., & Macdonald, C. (1992). *Collaborative teams for students with severe disabilities: Integrating therapy and educational services* (p. 198). Baltimore: Paul H. Brookes Publishing Co.; reprinted by permission.
TYP, typical methods displayed by peers without disabilities; ALT, alternatives that may be acceptable.

and diagnoses might be in order to plan the needed adaptations. Instead, we provide a general framework for assessing and effecting motoric functioning that has applications for many individuals with physical disabilities, regardless of specific diagnoses. The framework channels team member attention to the transition and mobility, positioning, and physical participation requirements of activities determined appropriate for each individual. Application to specific individuals with physical disabilities requires collaboration among team members. Again, the roles of the physical and occupational therapists and therapeutic recreation specialists are critical at this point in program design. Purposeful activity as a critical component of intervention design has long been a primary emphasis in the field of occupational therapy (Breines, 1984; Gliner, 1985; Huss, 1981). This focus on transition/mobility, positioning, and physical participation components of activities is consistent with a purposeful activity approach and provides a structure for integrating occupational and physical therapy and therapeutic recreation expertise into the design of leisure programs.

Transition/Mobility Strategies

Transition/mobility strategies address the ways in which individuals move to the location of the designated activity, excluding, for purposes here, transportation methods. These between-activity transition times present excellent opportunities to promote more active learner participation. Unfortunately, the instructional value of transitions is often overlooked. Active participation by the learner in transitions can take many forms, such as keeping the head flexed forward to maintain total body relaxation while being assisted with transition, scooting or rolling across the floor, walking with equipment, and propelling a wheelchair. Selection of appropriate methods (e.g., scooting on the floor, walking, using a wheelchair) depends on environment and activity contexts, as well as an individual's physical abilities. Selection factors include social norms, architectural barriers and terrain, and movement efficiency. In an individual's home, any mobility method that is efficient is likely to be socially acceptable, whereas social norms for public places may be quite different. For example, scooting along the floor in a sitting position to a bookshelf is acceptable at home but might be considered stigmatizing at the public library.

However, attitudes can be changed and social norms should not be allowed to restrict a person's options. Persons with physical disabilities require the use of adaptations to achieve mobility and movement efficiency. Few research efforts have compared the effectiveness among mobility methods in varied situations given individual abilities and environmental demands. In a preliminary investigation of mobility methods found effective by adults with physical disabilities in specific environments, York (1989) found that individuals who used wheeled mobility traveled much longer distances in outside environments before resorting to the use of a motor vehicle than did individuals who walked using equipment. The implication is that while walking may be considered more "normal," other methods of mobility may be more efficient and functional for some individuals. Another finding was that most individuals who were able to walk and use a wheelchair used both forms of mobility at home, but relied almost exclusively on wheeled mobility in community environments. Different mobility options may be more efficient in different environments and activities. At home, several mobility methods might be employed to transition to leisure activities. In community leisure environments, equipment-assisted mobility methods may be more likely. In all cases, selection of mobility methods must be individualized to the environment, activity, physical abilities, and mobility equipment characteristics.

Other researchers have reported functional benefits for children who were provided with wheelchairs that assisted with positioning and who were allowed more independent mobility functioning. These children traveled to more places outside their home (Hulme, Poor, Schulein,

& Pezzino, 1983), engaged in more social activities with peers during and after school (Kohn, Enders, Preston, & Motloch, 1983), and became more curious about their environment and activities that required physical involvement (Butler, Okamoto, & McKay, 1983; Verburg, Pilkington, Snell, & Milner, 1985). These results emphasize the importance of providing efficient mobility methods for individuals with physical disabilities throughout their lives, beginning as early as possible. Some have advocated use of powered mobility as early as 2 years of age (Butler, 1985; Trefler, 1984). This is particularly relevant to this discussion because young children spend large amounts of time engaged in leisure activities.

To illustrate the application of this transition/mobility discussion, a swimming activity is used as an example. Swimming is advocated as a valued activity to meet leisure, social, and therapeutic needs of individuals with physical disabilities (Harris & Thompson, 1983; Peganoff, 1984). Clearly, a team approach among therapists, therapeutic recreation specialists, and others is necessary (Dulcy, 1983). This example involves John, a 14-year-old who has cerebral palsy with increased flexor muscle tone (i.e., he tends to be bent forward and his muscles are tight) throughout his body. Swimming is one of his favorite physical education and recreation activities. He can walk independently, usually using a rollator walker, but he tires quickly. When John began community instruction one school year, it became very apparent that he needed a wheelchair for long distance and community mobility; this need resulted in acquisition of a wheelchair at the end of the school year.

Participation in swimming requires that John use a variety of mobility and transition methods to accommodate varied environmental and physical demands. He uses his rollator walker to go to the locker room. Once in the locker room, he approaches the bench that stretches the length of the row of lockers in which his locker is located. The space between the lockers and the bench is too narrow to enable easy use of his walker. To get to his locker, he parks his walker at the end of the aisle and either walks with a hand against the lockers for balance or, if no other students are using the bench, sits on the bench and scoots to his locker. After changing his clothes, John walks to the pool office to obtain the wheelchair kept for emergency use. He uses the wheelchair because walking with or without his rollator is very dangerous on the slippery pool deck. Using the wheelchair, he propels himself onto the pool deck to the bleachers on the far side of the pool, which is not usually as busy or wet. After setting the wheelchair brakes, he transfers from the wheelchair to the bleachers, and then proceeds to lower himself to a seated position on the pool deck. Finally, he scoots, in a sitting position, across the deck to the pool edge and lowers himself into the water. Once in the water, John moves between areas of the pool by pulling himself along the pool edge. This example illustrates a variety of mobility and transition methods used in the swimming sequence. Determination of methods was based on movement efficiency, safety due to slippery surfaces, space constraints, and required collaboration among the therapeutic recreation specialist, physical therapist, adapted physical education teacher, and special education teacher.

Positioning Strategies

The importance of positioning for participation in leisure activities cannot be overemphasized. Positioning directly affects which movements are possible and, therefore, increase levels of functioning (Bergman, 1991; Cox, 1987; Fraser, Hensinger, & Phelps, 1990; Trefler, Tooms, & Hobson, 1977; Ward, 1984). People who do not have physical disabilities automatically position themselves efficiently to engage in activities. Individuals who have physical disabilities frequently need assistance in determining, assuming, and then maintaining efficient postures. Frequently, therapeutic equipment is required to assist in maintaining efficient postures for function.

Appropriate positioning has both therapeutic and functional benefits. Several researchers have identified functional benefits realized through use of equipment to assist in the maintenance of appropriate positions. These benefits include greater tolerance for upright postures, which enhances academic and adaptive functioning (Trefler, Nickey, & Hobson, 1983), and improved alignment, which results in better grasping abilities, better social interactions, and less time lying down in the bedroom at home (Hulme et al., 1983). The influence of these types of achievement on participation in leisure programs is considerable.

Positions selected must match the environmental and physical demands of the leisure activity. In addition, optimal positions are those that the individual can assume with minimal assistance, maintain with appropriate alignment and stability, and then coordinate movement of designated body parts to engage in the activity (Rainforth & York, 1987; Rainforth et al., 1992; York & Wiemann, 1991). There are several considerations when selecting appropriate positions and determining whether to use equipment for external support (Piuma & Udvari-Solner, 1993b; York, Nietupski, & Hamre-Nietupski, 1985). Readers are directed to Rainforth and York (1987) or Rainforth et al. (1992) for a comprehensive delineation of the advantages and disadvantages of many different positions. Table 5.2 outlines several considerations in selecting positions and positioning equipment, and illustrates how the considerations guided decision making for Ted, who enjoys cooking, and Joan, who enjoys gardening. In both situations, you will see that there are choices to make about positioning. For Ted, the available choices all have some disadvantages, but the process allows decision makers to recognize the alternatives and make informed choices. In Ted's case, the team originally thought he would sit during cooking activities; however, after analyzing the alternatives, they agreed that standing was preferable when the equipment was available.

Once appropriate positions are selected and equipment is identified, strategies for actually assuming and maintaining the position are determined. The specific procedures utilized will vary depending on the individual, position, and equipment. Several general guidelines are appropriate in most situations (Bergman, 1991; Cox, 1987; York & Wiemann, 1991). First, *a stable base of support* must be achieved before efficient movement is possible. To understand the importance of stability for function, assume a seated position. Then lift your feet from the floor and attempt to write a letter or assemble a jigsaw puzzle. Notice the compensations you must make to achieve stability when you cannot use your feet (e.g., you tighten your abdominal muscles, push your thighs together, or lean on your arms). This exercise helps to demonstrate the importance of the second general guideline for effective positioning: *the pelvis and hips are the "key points"* for achieving the alignment that enables functional movement. For example, when seated, slide your pelvis forward so that your lower back is rounded. Note the resulting compensations in your trunk, head, and neck. Your upper trunk rounds forward forcing your neck to hyperextend in order to maintain your line of vision. If the pelvis and hips are not positioned appropriately, alignment is altered throughout the body. A third general rule is to *position proximal body parts* first (Bergen & Colangelo, 1982; Bergman, 1991). Because alignment and stability of proximal body parts (e.g., those parts close to midline and the center of gravity) affect alignment and function of distal body parts (e.g., arms, hands, head, mouth), optimizing proximal posture enhances distal function. Once appropriate positioning of the pelvis is achieved, the thighs, legs, and feet are positioned to secure the stable base of support. Finally, the upper trunk, head, and neck are aligned and supported with positioning equipment as necessary.

Physical Participation Strategies

Once appropriate positions are achieved, the individual is ready to actively participate in the activity. The nature of participation will vary with the specific leisure activity, type and extent of

Table 5.2.   Considerations in selecting positions and positioning equipment

Considerations	Ted - Baking cookies	Joan - Gardening
Proposed Position	**Sitting**	**Kneeling**
1. What positions do peers without disabilities use when they engage in the activity?	Usually standing/walking. Sometimes sitting (but with hips at height of table/counter).	Standing, stooping, kneeling/hands and knees.
2. Which of these positions allow easy view of and access to activity materials and equipment?	Standing is better than sitting at table.	Kneeling seems most versatile. Could build raised garden bed to allow sitting on edge, transfer from wheelchair.
3. Do the positions allow for proximity to peers?	Yes, for sitting or standing. Peers will probably stand.	Yes, peers can garden in adjoining areas/rows.
4. Do the positions promote efficient movement as needed to perform the task?	Standing/walking much better than sitting/wheeling.	Once sitting or kneeling, Joan can plant/weed/harvest an area, then scoot to next.
5. What positions provide alternatives to overused postures or equipment?	Standing is best. Ted spends too much time sitting.	Kneeling is a good change. Joan sits for most activities.
6. If positioning equipment is required, is it unobtrusive, cosmetically acceptable, and not physically isolating?	Wheelchair and supine stander are both large. Could use kitchen chair but will lose mobility. When stander is vertical, Ted can stand close to counter, tables. Wheelchair allows mobility around kitchen.	Garden kneeling stool is unobtrusive, used by people without disabilities; may assist positioning and transitions.
7. Is the positioning equipment safe and easy to handle?	Positioning in stander requires adult. Then other children can handle safely and easily.	Yes, may need outriggers to prevent tipping.
8. Is the equipment individually selected and modified to match individual learner needs?	A supine stander with individualized adaptations was purchased for Ted.	Team will borrow garden kneeling stool to try it.
9. Is the equipment available in and/or easily transported to natural environments?	Stander available at home and school. Difficult to transport to other environments.	Garden kneeler is lightweight, easy to transport.
Final position	**Standing using equipment to assist.**	**Kneeling using equipment to assist.**

From Rainforth, B., York, J., & Macdonald, C. (1992). *Collaborative teams for students with severe disabilities: Integrating therapy and educational services* (p. 186). Baltimore: Paul H. Brookes Publishing Co.; reprinted by permission.

each individual's capability, and position selected for the activity. Spectator activities such as watching a movie or listening during storytime require the least physical demands for participation. Typically, an individual listens and watches in an upright position. For some people with physical disabilities, attending visually, attending auditorily, and maintaining the head and trunk in an upright posture during a movie or storytime are significant achievements. Offering additional postural support or using other positions provides many individuals with a greater scope of opportunities for participation. For example, if an individual is supported in an upright sitting position instead of being required to maintain the position for extended periods of time without support, he or she might be more able to relax and enjoy the activity, show more affect through facial expressions, and/or use his or her arms to more actively engage in the activity. Readers can appreciate this point when they recall how driving endurance is influenced by the presence and position of the seat back, lumbar support, and head rest, and the distance and position of the seat in relationship to the pedals and steering wheel.

Participation in leisure activities is often conceptualized as the manipulation of materials or tools to complete the core routines of the activities. As discussed previously, the types of participation can be expanded considerably (Brown et al., 1987). Pointing to the picture symbolizing "play" on a communication board, selecting the desired leisure material by looking at the preferred item when two are presented, helping to transport materials to the location where they will be used, taking turns, expressing pleasure, and cleaning up after completing the leisure activity are all important aspects of participation. During these and the core routine components, manipulating the materials can be expanded to also include reaching for, grasping, transferring, and releasing the materials. Even grasping has many variations, with the palmar, radial digital, lateral pinch, and pincer grasps constituting a basis for many complex manipulation schemas. Furthermore, diversity is achieved by using different positions at the wrist, forearm, elbow, and shoulder, and by using one or two hands.

To illustrate how these movement components might be conceptualized in a leisure activity, Table 5.3 delineates a task analysis and a corresponding movement analysis for the core routine of participating in a needlepoint activity. Although participation requires fairly precise movement with the right hand, the patterns of movement are quite repetitious, thereby naturally integrating many opportunities for practicing more efficient movement patterns. The left hand position is relatively imprecise and constant throughout the task.

Consideration of other recreation activities, such as playing with toy cars or assembling jigsaw puzzles, reveals that they require other combinations of movements. Although occupational therapists offer particular expertise in analyzing hand and arm movements, all team members can increase their awareness of these component movements simply by observing themselves and others perform a variety of leisure activities.

Movement analysis, such as that delineated in Table 5.3, provides a general picture of the physical manipulation demands of leisure tasks. When the team agrees to provide instruction on a particular leisure activity to an individual with physical disabilities and the movement demands are delineated, the next step is to conduct a *discrepancy analysis.* In this analysis, the individual is assessed on actual performance of the task. Specific movement abilities and difficulties are noted for each step of the task analysis. It is recommended that an occupational therapist, therapeutic recreation specialist, or other team member knowledgeable about hand function participate in the assessment. In addition to assessing performance, this team member can experiment with a variety of methods to facilitate improved hand use, which becomes valuable information when planning instruction. To devise effective instructional strategies, the team needs to address the following questions:

1. Does the person's current movement repertoire allow independent performance of the task?
2. Can the person learn required movements not in his or her current repertoire?
3. Does the task provide an opportunity to teach and/or reinforce movements needed to perform other priority activities?
4. Does the person use substitute movements that achieve the desired outcome without

producing undesirable or detrimental movement patterns that can ultimately result in decreased function?

5. What handling techniques are effective to facilitate required movements?
6. Would splinting improve performance of this and other tasks without limiting other aspects of participation?
7. Would other adaptations improve participation?

Providing effective instruction to people with intellectual and physical disabilities requires the integration of educational and therapeutic methods. Although the research is not extensive, several single-subject studies suggest that the combination of systematic instruction and therapeutic handling are more effective than either method alone to teach functional tasks to persons with intellectual and physical disabilities (Campbell, McInerny, & Cooper, 1984; Giangreco, 1986; Hester, 1981; R.I. Walker & Vogelsburg, 1985). This supports the assertion that functional movement patterns are learned and applied most successfully when taught within the context where they are needed. Therefore, it is essential that occupational and physical therapists and therapeutic recreation specialists work closely with other members of the leisure team during planning, assist with identification of effective handling and facilitation methods, teach other team members to use these methods, learn systematic instruction meth-

Table 5.3.   Analysis of core components of a needlepoint activity

Task analysis of core components	Movement analysis
1. Hold hoop in left hand, design facing upward.	Gross grasp, elbow bent, position maintained throughout activity. Could rest hand or forearm on furniture for support, or mount hoop on standing frame.
2. Hold needle in right hand.	Pincer grasp.
3. Insert needle in proper hole.	Precise reach with entire arm; fine coordination of shoulder, elbow, forearm, and wrist. Could also rest wrist and forearm on mesh then slide hand toward hole. Once needle is to hole, bend wrist or rotate forearm to insert in hole.
4. Push needle through hole and release needle.	With wrist and forearm resting on mesh, maintain firm pincer grasp at end of needle, then push needle all the way through hole. As it is pushed through, control release then remove fingers from needle so as not to pull needle back out.
5. Grasp needle from below.	Reach under mesh with slightly open hand. Locate needle by touch. Orient needle between fingers. Assume and maintain firm pincer grasp.
6. Pull needle bringing yarn through.	Extend elbow with graded movement until yarn is through.
7. Insert needle in proper hole from below.	Rotate forearm toward mesh to orient needle to holes. Rest wrist/base of thumb against mesh. Slide hand laterally until needle is at hole. Bend wrist or rotate forearm to insert needle in hole.
8. Push needle through hole and release needle.	See Step 4.
9. Grasp needle from above.	Reach across mesh with slightly open hand. Assume and maintain firm pincer grasp at base of needle.
10. Pull needle bringing yarn through.	Bend or extend elbow away from body pulling yarn through hole.
11. Repeat Steps 3–10.	

ods, and deliver at least a portion of therapy services within the leisure environments where individuals are expected to use motor skills.

The integration of therapeutic techniques with systematic instruction can be considered application of specialized types of physical prompts. These specialized prompts take into account the poor postural control and abnormal muscle tone that make movement inefficient for many people with physical disabilities. The goals of using therapeutic handling and facilitation techniques are to: 1) normalize muscle tone (e.g., reduce excessive tension), 2) facilitate upright postures (e.g., head and trunk control), and 3) facilitate movement for function (e.g., to perform leisure tasks). General guidelines can assist with selecting and using handling and facilitation methods to achieve these goals (see York & Wiemann, 1991). First, assisting a person to assume and maintain functional positions, as discussed previously, depends on achieving normalized muscle tone and stable upright postures. However, because good positioning is essential for achieving efficient movement for function, positioning is viewed as an integral component of therapeutic handling and facilitation. Second, the influence of spasticity (increased muscle tone resulting in stiffness) can usually be minimized through slow rhythmic movement. Therapists frequently produce this effect by rocking a child on a large beach ball. Similar effects can be achieved in typical leisure environments (where the beach ball technique would be stigmatizing) by providing adequate support to unstable body parts and by inducing controlled, rhythmic movement. For example, an assistant might firmly hold the person's shoulders in a rounded and forward position while gently moving the trunk slightly forward and backward to reduce tension, thereby making arm movement easier and more controlled. Third, the influence of hypotonia (low muscle tone resulting in floppiness) and athetosis (fluctuating muscle tone resulting in excessive movement) can be minimized by stabilizing the trunk and proximal portions of the limbs. Finally, there are "key points" of the body where typical tone, upright postures, and efficient movements can be elicited most easily when a person has a physical disability (Bobath & Bobath, 1972). These key points are usually at the shoulders, hips, and the most proximal part of the arm or leg where movement is desired. The following two case examples for Regina and Donald illustrate application of these therapeutic handling principles in more detail.

Regina

Regina is a young woman with flexor spasticity throughout her body, especially in her arms. One of her recreation activities is using a punch hook for crafts. The canvas is mounted in a frame that is secured to a table top. Instruction focuses on teaching her to hold the punch hook tool, insert it in the canvas, and remove it. She holds the tool in her right hand using a palmar grasp. The instructor facilitates the required grasp and reach by supporting and providing physical assistance at Regina's right wrist and right arm just above the elbow to avoid excessive turning in and flexion of Regina's arm. Without facilitation about the elbow, Regina develops excessive muscle tension around her shoulder joint, which pulls her arm in toward her body in a nonfunctional position. At times during the craft activity, Regina's entire body becomes tense. In these situations, she bends her trunk forward, bends her elbows and wrists, and pulls both arms to the center of her body. To normalize Regina's muscle tone, the instructor holds her arms just above the elbows, gently lifting her arms out and away from her body. Regina's tone is reduced within a few seconds and she returns to the punch hook activity. Although the instructor still needs two hands to handle and facilitate Regina's movement, the time needed to normalize tone decreased considerably over time. The team eventually integrated the therapeutic handling and movement facilitation techniques with a decreasing assistance prompting strategy to promote Regina's independence in this activity.

Donald

Donald is a 6-year-old boy who enjoys many typical play activities, such as playing with cars and trucks. He has difficulty controlling his arm movements due to athetoid cerebral palsy.

His therapists and teachers found they could stabilize his shoulders, and thus limit erratic arm movement, by having him lean on his elbows or by positioning him lying on his side, which stabilizes the shoulder girdle he lies on. Donald discovered a substitute movement in which he used his legs and feet to push the cars. He demonstrated a strong preference for using his feet for manipulation purposes. This has proven to be very functional for many children and adults with athetoid cerebral palsy. Because of possible social stigma, however, the team agreed to continue efforts to teach Donald to stabilize his arms to promote more efficient use of his hands, as well as allowing some play with his feet.

This section emphasizes therapeutic handling and facilitation techniques to promote manipulation of leisure materials and tools. Although many leisure tasks may be performed from stationary positions such as sitting in a chair, activities such as swimming, biking, horseback riding, gardening, or playing with toys on the floor entail use of the entire body. Individuals must not be eliminated from these activities simply because of physical disabilities. The handling and facilitation guidelines offered in this section have equal application when recreation programs require greater mobility and total body use.

LEISURE ADAPTIVE DEVICES

Once the educational team assesses learner performance in the actual leisure environment and activity, skills that the learner was unable to perform appropriately or independently are analyzed to make decisions about how to teach him or her to participate to a greater degree in the activity. Essentially, there are two instructional options: 1) the learner can be taught to perform the activity in the same way that a person without disabilities might, or 2) adaptations can be developed and implemented. The instructional option of developing individualized adaptations became more widely advocated as a result of formal conceptualization of the "principle of partial participation" by Baumgart and her colleagues (1982). The principle asserts that partial participation in age-appropriate and valued activities is more advantageous than exclusion, even if participation must be modified through adaptation of rules, materials, or task sequences. Personal assistance is another aspect of partial participation that might be considered while a person is learning to use other adaptations or when other adaptations do not seem feasible. Personal assistance can be provided by a friend, parent, or professional who performs or assists with steps of the activity that the individual does not currently perform. The person with a disability can also request assistance. At a movie theater, for example, the person might present the cashier with a wallet and a note saying, "I would like one ticket. Please take the money from my wallet."

With so many options for partial participation, there is no justification for concluding that a person is incapable of enjoying leisure activities. The remainder of this chapter focuses on one strategy—the use of adaptive devices to enhance leisure participation. Responsibility for achieving learner participation in leisure environments and activities rests with the education/habilitation team. They function as problem solvers to achieve inclusion, rather than allowing learner difficulties to result in exclusion. This is an affirmative, creative approach to leisure curriculum and instruction that is consistent with the goal of integrated life outcomes for all individuals.

Devices Purchased in Local Stores

Adaptations generally include providing personal assistance, modifying skill or activity sequences, modifying the environment, or using an adaptive device (Baumgart et al., 1982; Wehman & Schleien, 1981). The focus here is on adaptive devices that require simplified movement for leisure participation. Many adaptive devices are homemade. Careful perusal through department store and mail order catalogs, adult toy departments, specialty toy and game stores, music stores, craft stores, and even kitchen stores can yield numerous interesting leisure gadgets that are age appropriate, easy to manipulate, and that actually are not adaptive devices at all. A recent stroll through these types of stores resulted in the purchase of several leisure items for three teenagers with severe intellectual and physical disabilities: a wood carved kaleidoscope, two hand-held adult puzzles (variations of the Rubik's cube), a table-top organ that can be programmed for activation by a microswitch, a moving sand art design, and a basketball game requiring simple activation of levers to shoot the ball. In addition, pets that demand relatively easy care, at least on a daily basis, also make excellent leisure interests for some individuals.

Homemade Devices

Figure 5.1 depicts eight homemade leisure adaptations that were made for specific individuals with multiple disabilities. All of the adaptations were designed so that individuals with limited upper extremity use could participate. In most cases, elbow movement was the only motoric requirement.

The magazine/book holder (Figure 5.1a) was made for a 5-year-old girl who enjoyed looking at books. The holder held books at a tilt so that she did not have to look down and lose head control. She learned to thrust her arm onto the pages, then turn the page by pushing laterally, although assistance was frequently required.

The card holder (Figure 5.1b) was designed for the simple purpose of holding an array of cards so that all cards could be viewed and removal of a card did not result in dropping all cards. This adaptation was used by several individuals who either had poor hand coordination or were unable to use both hands functionally. The needlework holder (Figure 5.1c) was designed with the same premise in mind. A simpler variation could be constructed by mounting a needlework hoop to a standard base. Some craft stores now have such an adaptation available for purchase.

The grasping mitten (Figure 5.1d) was made for a 4-year-old boy with no grasping strength. Using the mitten, he is able to hold musical instruments (e.g., clackers, bells on sticks) and participate more actively in kindergarten music class. He used the mitt during initial instruction on driving a power wheelchair. The mitt secured his grasp to the joystick.

The next two adaptations (Figures 5.1e, 5.1f) were designed for a teenager whose only controlled movement was elbow flexion. The pulley adaptation with the cup was designed to allow the student to throw dice as part of various board and dice games. The plant watering adaptation was developed for vocational purposes at a public library, but could have leisure applications also.

Remote-controlled cars (Figure 5.1g) were terrific facilitators of interactions between a participant with disabilities and his peers without disabilities. To enable activation by a 4-year-old boy who had only minimal control of elbow flexion and extension, the remote control joystick was extended with a dowel rod and secured at its base with plastic splinting material. When in a kneeling position with the remote control on a table in front of him, the boy could move his forearm to deflect the extended joystick. The remote control could be locked into positions to allow only forward and backward or only circular movement of the car. This feature helped tremendously in that the child could not steer the car. With the eventual purchase of a second car, races became a popular pastime.

Finally, the wheelchair putter adaptation (Figure 5.1h) was developed to facilitate participation in the teeing off component of miniature golf. The putter was secured with a spring clamp purchased at a local hardware store. The shaft of the putter functioned as a long lever. Relatively little movement and power were required to move the putter head. York and Rainforth (1991) described additional details of the design, construction, and use of these specific adaptations.

Microswitches to Activate Devices

The introduction of microswitch technology into the education/habilitation arena has expanded many opportunities for learners with physical disabilities. Microswitches provide a simplified means of activating electronic equipment, such as tape recorders, table-top organs, popcorn poppers, hair dryers, communication equipment, and computers. They have the

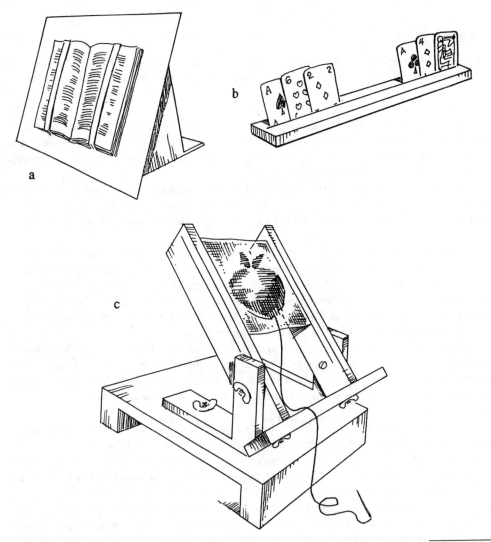

(continued)

Figure 5.1.   Homemade leisure adaptive devices: a) magazine/book holder, b) card holder, c) needlework holder, d) grasping mitten, e) pulley adaptation, f) plant watering adaptation, g) remote-controlled car, and h) wheelchair putter adaptation. (Reprinted with permission from York, J., & Rainforth, B. [1991]. Developing instructional adaptations. In F.P. Orelove & D. Sobsey, *Educating children with multiple disabilities: A transdisciplinary approach* [2nd ed., pp. 267, 277–281, 287]. Baltimore: Paul H. Brookes Publishing Co.)

Figure 5.1. (*continued*)

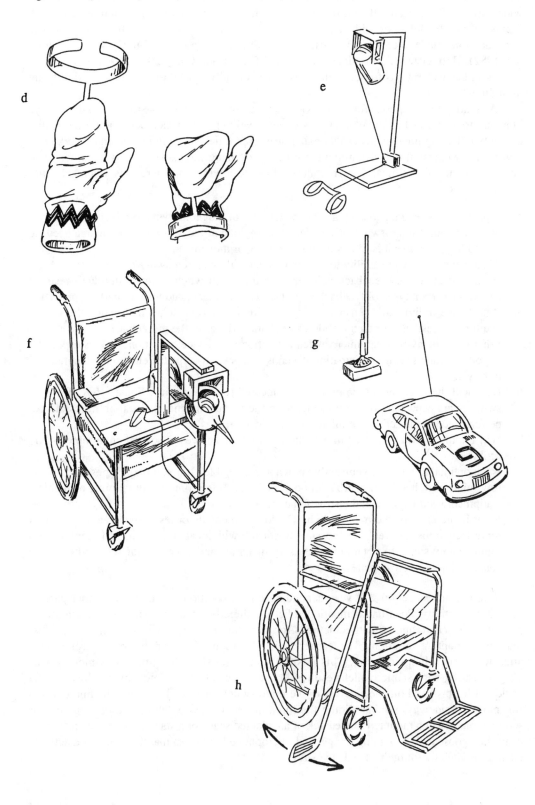

advantage of providing direct and immediate feedback about movements executed. There is a wide variety of commercially available microswitches (from companies such as Able-Net, Prentke-Romich, Behavior Aids, and Adaptive Aids), as well as information about how to construct homemade microswitches (Burkhart, 1980, 1982; Campbell, McInerney, & Middleton, 1982). Hofmeister and Friedman (1986) and Garner and Campbell (1987) discuss applications and considerations for technology use more broadly related to persons with significant disabilities.

Activation mode options for microswitches vary greatly from simple touch pressure, to eye blinking, to sound or breath. With such a variety available, team members should have little difficulty obtaining microswitches that match learner abilities and activity demands. York et al. (1985, p. 218) present a decision-making process for using microswitches with learners who have significant disabilities. They recommend the following considerations when selecting microswitches:

1. What are the strength and accuracy characteristics of the motor behavior the individual will use to activate a microswitch? Consider how large the microswitch activation area needs to be and how sensitive it is to touch, sound, breath, or movement.
2. What is the individual's ability to sustain contact with the microswitch?
3. What type of sensory feedback is inherent in the microswitch? Some individuals respond best when certain types of feedback (e.g., tactile, kinesthetic, auditory, visual) are present.
4. What is the individual's sensory acuity? Are there microswitches that match the visual, auditory, kinsesthetic, or tactile abilities or characteristics of the individual?
5. What is the delay between microswitch activation and device operation? This is especially important when leisure participation depends on a switch-activated electronic communication system.
6. How will the microswitch be mounted or located for the activity? Some types of microswitches are especially difficult to mount in the precise manner or location necessary for performance of the activity or microswitch activation.
7. Will the microswitch be used to activate a variety of devices in several environments and activities?
8. Is the optimal microswitch currently known and available? If not, it may be possible to borrow microswitches from nearby schools, hospitals, electronic supply stores, or medical equipment vendors for initial instruction experiences.
9. What is the price of the microswitch? Could a homemade or less expensive microswitch serve the purpose as well? It is possible to consult with local electricians and radio or electronic supply stores to obtain the necessary materials and expertise for safe and effective construction of microswitches.

Microswitch selection will vary depending on the position in which the learner participates in the activity. Position, as mentioned before, directly affects physical movement that is possible. This can require creative methods for mounting the microswitches. Figure 5.2 illustrates two mounting variations. The learner depicted in Figure 5.2a had the best control of forearm movement when sidelying. This position made the shoulder girdle on which he was weight-bearing very stable, which resulted in more controlled arm movement. However, he could not lift his hand off the sidelyer to the microswitch surface. Therefore, the microswitch was mounted sideways so that sliding the forearm resulted in switch activation. Figure 5.2b shows a microswitch mounted to the back of an adapted seat using standard microphone equipment (i.e., gooseneck, mounting flange, and microphone holder) so that the user could activate the microswitch by tilting his head sideways.

Figure 5.2.   Microswitch mounting variations for: a) positioning in sidelying for activation with arm movement, and b) positioning in upright sitting position for activation with head movement. (Reprinted with permission from York, J., & Rainforth, B. [1991]. Developing instructional adaptations. In F.P. Orelove & D. Sobsey, *Educating children with multiple disabilities: A transdisciplinary approach* [2nd ed., p. 282]. Baltimore: Paul H. Brookes Publishing Co.)

Local Community Resources

When team members identify and design adaptations required for leisure participation, a variety of program and community resources may be available to assist in constructing adaptations. We have previously secured assistance from community business people such as a metalworks expert, a retired electrical engineer who ran a radio store, a plastics expert, and a carpenter. Many programs hire or contract with carpenters to fulfill ongoing needs for adaptations. Custodians, program staff, and families can often provide assistance as well. One program had an annual "work day" during which family members and staff performed several tasks, including construction of adaptations; many valuable talents were discovered.

For many adaptations, sophisticated technology is not required, and for individuals who work professionally with wood, plastic, metal, and electronic materials, only simple applications of their expertise are required. There are four important benefits that can be realized from work with such local community resource personnel: 1) they can individualize adaptations, 2) they are more readily accessible to work with and solve problems than medical vendors or suppliers, 3) their work is more reasonably priced, and 4) a larger community shares the enhancing participation of individuals with disabilities in life's activities.

Written Resources

There are a few written resources related to leisure participation by individuals with significant intellectual and physical disabilities. Schell (1982) developed a manual that illustrates very creative and simple adaptations of young children's toys to make manipulation possible by children with very limited movement capabilities. Levin and Scherfenberg (1986) describe how microswitches can be made and adapted to increase participation in a variety of daily activities. The Nordic Committee on Disability (1985) developed a color monograph of adaptations for individuals with physical disabilities related to each room in the house, as well as community and neighborhood life. Included were several adaptive leisure ideas for children. Wright and Nomura (1985) discuss expansion of simple adaptive electronics beyond activation of toys to interfacing with computer technology. Davis (1981) provides examples of simple adaptations for many aspects of daily life. Two excellent ideas in this manual were elevated gardening and riding a tandem bicycle. A recent visit with friends who have an adolescent son with significant disabilities illustrated the feasibility and enjoyment of tandem bike riding. This adolescent became quite competent at holding on, maintaining balance, and keeping his feet on the pedals. The expression on his face conveyed his sheer delight for this activity. The only minor source of difficulty was occasionally playfully pinching the front rider. Finally, two new monographs are available that illustrate a wide variety of vocational adaptations (some of which could be used at home and in school as well) and a process for adaptation development (Piuma & Udvari-Solner, 1993a, 1993b).

Precautions

In concluding this discussion about adaptations, several precautions are in order. First, adaptations must be selected and designed based on individual learner needs. Too frequently, especially in the case of microswitches, use of adaptations is overgeneralized inappropriately. For example, if a learner can be taught in a reasonable amount of instructional time to turn on a cassette player by directly pushing the "on" button, a microswitch should not be used. Its use would prevent acquisition of more sophisticated skills and more typical, independent operation of the cassette player. Second, adaptations do not replace the need for systematic instruction. Securing an appropriate adaptation is only a preparatory step for skill acquisition. The learner must then receive systematic instruction on how to use the adaptation. Third, there must be ongoing evaluation of the effectiveness of the adaptation. As participant needs and abilities change, adaptations may no longer be necessary or further modification may be required. Finally, maintenance and repairs are an inevitable, recurring need. Whenever possible, use quality materials in final construction and contract with local business personnel so that valuable team member time is not excessively consumed repairing adaptations.

SUMMARY

Designing and implementing individualized leisure programs for individuals with physical disabilities is an important collaborative teamwork effort. For teamwork to be effective, a unified philosophy about integrated leisure outcomes and about collaborative teamwork is necessary. To maximize participant success, special considerations related to mobility, positioning, and physical participation abilities are addressed in leisure environments and activities. In this regard, physical and occupational therapists and therapeutic recreation specialists have an opportunity to contribute valuable expertise in the design of instructional methods. All team members, however, have valuable contributions to make, particularly related to individualized adaptations. The degree of leisure participation by individuals with significant intellectual and physical disabilities is limited only by the extent of collective creativity among team members.

Chapter 6

INSTRUCTION FOR PREFERENCE AND GENERALIZATION

with John Dattilo

*T*he emphasis in Chapter 3 is on teaching individuals how to manipulate leisure activities appropriately through skill acquisition instruction sessions. However, teaching individuals to perform the steps of a task analysis does not ensure their independence during free time—it is equally important that they be taught to *apply* activity skills in naturally occurring leisure situations.

RATIONALE FOR CHOICE INSTRUCTION

Because choice is an important element of leisure participation, it appears logical to encourage participants to make as many choices as possible and take responsibility for their participation (Dattilo, 1994). Providing opportunities for individuals with significant disabilities to cultivate the ability to make choices can be challenging and often requires systematic planning. Dattilo and Kleiber (1993) reported that the goal of enhancing an individual's ability to make a choice has merit because it appears that, when examining leisure participation, it is the participant's perception of freedom and his or her ability to determine personal participation patterns that is more important than the specific recreation activity that he or she chooses.

The opportunities for choice often associated with leisure participation must be systematically provided and taught to individuals with significant disabilities (Dattilo & Rusch, 1985). Wehman and Schleien (1981) identified the ultimate goal of any leisure program as the facilitation of self-initiated, independent use of free time with chronological age–appropriate recreation activities. After examining the current lack of self-determination for people with mental retardation, Wehmeyer (1992) reported that it is apparent there is a need to focus instruction on promoting self-determination among these individuals.

Some teachers make choices for students with significant disabilities rather than allowing their students to decide for themselves. Many school environments are not structured to promote choice making (Wehmeyer, 1992). Students' opportunities to express personal interests and preferences have been prevented when incorrect assumptions are made that they are incapable of making informed choices (Kishi, Teelucksingh, Zollers, Park-Lee, & Meyer, 1988). For example, Houghton, Bronicki, and Guess (1987) reported that classroom personnel (e.g., teachers) responded at very low rates to student-initiated expressions of choice (e.g., gestures) during the school day.

Freedom of choice is vital to the pursuit of enjoyable, satisfying, and meaningful experience, and, according to Hawkins (1993), personal autonomy for people with disabilities has become recognized as an essential aspect of independent functioning and self-reliance. Heyne, Schleien, and McAvoy (1993) emphasized this point when they stated:

> When people with disabilities are allowed to choose activities, they are more eager to learn the skills necessary to participate, they more readily generalize those skills to other settings, and they are more likely to continue to participate in those activities. (p. 46)

When individuals are provided opportunities to make self-determined and responsible choices that reflect their needs to grow, explore, and realize their potential, their ability to experience leisure is enhanced (Dattilo, 1991). Dattilo and Schleien (1994) provided the following example to illustrate this point: A student's favorite recreation activity is doing artwork. When she attends her art class, she is encouraged to select her own paper; she chooses among different colors, sizes, and textures. In addition, she decides to use watercolors one day rather than chalk or markers. After she has her materials, the student is invited to position her easel where she prefers and to begin her chosen project while carefully selecting her color scheme.

Instructors must maintain a delicate balance between facilitating self-determined leisure participation and encouraging development of culturally typical, age-appropriate leisure behaviors for their students (Dattilo & Schleien, 1994). Sometimes individuals choose to exhibit behaviors that society has identified as being offensive or detrimental. At this time, these individuals are often redirected to participate in socially acceptable activities of their choosing that do not bring psychological or physical discomfort to themselves or other people. Leisure instruction related to helping people determine the appropriateness of behaviors is often useful. The appropriateness of behaviors may vary according to location (bedroom vs. public swimming pool), frequency (asking once vs. asking several times in a brief duration), timing (when someone is laughing vs. when someone is crying), and the relationship of people present (brother vs. teacher). All participants must learn that people are rarely completely free to do anything they wish (Wehmeyer, 1992). To experience leisure on an ongoing basis, students must learn to assert their rights as well as respect the other people they encounter (Dattilo, 1994).

Empowering individuals with significant disabilities to make choices and take charge of their lives is important, especially in light of the fact that opportunities and choices are circumscribed by the actual disability (Kelly, 1993) and the attitudes of professionals (Dattilo, 1994). The sooner opportunities for choices are presented to individuals, the more likely it is that they will acquire behaviors associated with self-determination. One area in which individuals with disabilities can begin to make choices is in their play activities and partners (Jolly, Test, & Spooner, 1993). When combined with other social factors (e.g., friendship, residential placement, opportunities for community inclusion), leisure activity choices contribute to life satisfaction and well-being (Schalock, Keith, Hoffman, & Karan, 1989).

The demonstration of choice through selection encourages spontaneous initiation of activity, engagement with elements of the environment, and assertion of a degree of control over one's surroundings (Dattilo & Barnett, 1985). Development of a sense of self-determination facilitates the ability of individuals to make choices and sets the stage for acquisition of more complex decision-making strategies. Individuals with significant disabilities typically need to be taught to make choices and to experience a range of leisure options.

CHOICE INSTRUCTION SESSIONS

The lifelong leisure skills curriculum component emphasizes the importance of the leisure educator's taking a systematic approach to ensuring the individual's generalized application of learned skills and having validated choice instruction sessions to address this need. Choice instruction sessions provide direct programming to teach people how to make activity choices during their free time and to generalize leisure skills from a highly structured instructional environment to a more closely approximating naturally occurring leisure environment. These choice sessions are a critical component of an individual's comprehensive leisure education program.

Choice instruction sessions differ from the skill acquisition instruction sessions described in Chapter 3. During the latter instruction sessions, the *instructor* structures, directs, and determines the range of participant behaviors and activities; essentially, the individual either responds or does not respond to the instructor. Although the instructor attempts to create an atmosphere of fun and enjoyment in these skill performance instruction sessions, participants are not really free to make and enjoy their activity choices or to initiate and direct the interactions between the instructor and themselves. This situation may provide for an optimal learning environment in which consistency and individual performance are maintained, but it bears little relation to leisure or play situations in which choice and self-direction are critical.

In choice sessions, the focus is shifted so that the *participant* directs the interactions with the instructor. Participants either respond or do not respond to the appropriate leisure activities in the classroom, and, from all of the possibilities, participants select the activity they prefer. Their activity choice then determines both how the instructor will interact with the participants and what procedures should be used during these instruction sessions.

To illustrate the importance of choice making associated with leisure participation, Lanagan and Dattilo (1989) observed that most participants in their study who had developmental disabilities were not accustomed to having opportunities for choice, and when given the opportunity to make choices within a leisure activity, many of them experienced difficulty. However, following instruction promoting choice making, these participants increased their autonomy and reported that they enjoyed having choices and input about the activity.

SELF-INITIATED COMMUNICATION: SETTING THE STAGE FOR CHOICES

In many instructional situations with individuals who have significant disabilities, it may be helpful for instructors to take a nondirective approach that strongly considers the individual's preferences and choices (Dattilo, 1993). Nondirective instructional strategies help instructors to avoid instilling a sense of dependency in the participants (Dattilo & Mirenda, 1987). Because a perception of freedom to choose to participate in meaningful, enjoyable, and satisfying experiences is fundamental to the leisure experience (Dattilo & Murphy, 1991), independent leisure participation is achieved more readily when reliance on directive approaches to instruction is avoided.

People with significant disabilities who use alternative communication strategies often take longer to formulate a communication turn than people who rely on speech to communicate their intentions. However, at times, instructors do not provide the participants with adequate time to formulate a communication turn. This unwillingness to wait for participants to take their turn results in the instructor's taking control of the conversation and, often, the entire situation. Time-delay instruction is effective in increasing spontaneous communication (e.g., Ingenmey & Van Houten, 1991). This form of instruction teaches instructors to allow the participants to take up to 10 seconds to formulate a communication turn.

Specific instruction encouraging people with significant disabilities to engage in reciprocal communication is needed. Teaching these individuals to initiate communicative exchanges during social interactions allows them to control situations and communicate their interests and preferences. Matson, Sevin, Box, Francis, and Sevin (1993) stated that because much of daily communication is not verbally prompted, teaching people with disabilities to initiate language is an important goal. As individuals engage in reciprocal exchanges stimulated by their ability to initiate interaction, their ability to communicate preferences, make meaningful choices, and, subsequently, experience leisure is enhanced.

Studies have been conducted to examine the impact of interventions designed to encourage people with significant disabilities to increase their ability to engage in reciprocal communication, and, thus, set the stage for leisure. For example, Dattilo and Camarata (1991) demonstrated the value of incorporating self-initiated conversation instruction for persons with severe communication disorders. Simply providing participants with an alternative form of communication was not sufficient to shift them away from the conversational role of respondent; rather, specific conversation initiation instruction was required before shifts in conversational behavior were observed at home and in a speech clinic. In a similar investigation, Dattilo and O'Keefe (1992) examined implications of an intervention designed to promote reciprocal communication for individuals with significant disabilities. At the conclusion of instruction, and 3 weeks after instruction, all participants were routinely sharing conversations with speaking partners. Results of these studies indicated that instructors may wish to consider teaching reciprocal communication strategies to individuals who exert little, if any, control over their conversations with speaking partners. Engaging in reciprocal communication enhances an individual's ability to communicate preferences, make meaningful choices, and, subsequently, participate in leisure activities.

Not only has research documented the effectiveness of teaching people with significant disabilities to initiate more, but investigations have documented the ability to teach instructors to encourage students to communicate their preferences. For example, Kohl and Beckman (1990) concluded that a teacher-mediated strategy designed to promote reciprocal interactions increased the number and mean length of initiation and response chains with students with severe disabilities. These findings are particularly important in situations where people with and without disabilities are present. In addition, Dattilo and Light (1993) examined the efficacy of instructing facilitators (i.e., significant others) to promote communication with individuals with severe disabilities. Facilitators were instructed to decrease their conversational control and provide more opportunities for the participants to communicate. Following instruction, facilitators decreased their rates of turn taking and initiations and increased the proportion of turns that were responsive. Participants with severe communication disorders increased the frequency of their initiations. These results added strength to the observations of several earlier case reports (Calculator & Luchko, 1983; McNaughton & Light, 1989) suggesting that teaching facilitators interaction strategies was effective in increasing communication opportunities for individuals with significant disabilities.

Because the ability to initiate involvement is critical to the leisure experience, individuals with significant disabilities must be taught how to initiate interactions and share conversations. Dattilo (1993) reported that construction of a supportive environment that is responsive to the communicative attempts of these individuals is important. A supportive environment is created when instructors approach the participant, attend to the participant, and wait at least 10 seconds for the individual to initiate interaction. If the individual does make a communicative initiative, speaking partners can reinforce these attempts (e.g., provide participants with objects they have requested, return greetings to participants, extend and expand their comments); however, if the individual does not initiate interaction, instructors are encouraged to ask open-ended questions beginning with "what" and "how" as opposed to questions that force individuals into a "yes" or "no" response. In conclusion, Wilcox (1993) reported on the importance of consistently recognizing an individual's communicative attempts and responding in a contingent, appropriate, and consistent manner.

CHOICE ACTIVITIES

Prior to conducting a choice instruction session, possible leisure activities from which the individual can choose must be identified. Typically, the more activities that are included in the choice, the more meaningful the individual's choice will be. The instructor must provide at least two different viable activities for there to be any choice.

In our field tests throughout Hawaii, Minnesota, and New York, two questions were repeatedly posed by participating instructors: 1) "Should I include activities as possible choices if the participant demonstrates few (or no) appropriate activity skills?" and 2) "Should I include an activity as a possible choice if it is the only activity the participant ever chooses?" In response to these questions, the criterion was established that before an activity can become a choice option, the participant must receive 10 skill acquisition instruction sessions on that activity *or* the participant must demonstrate appropriate use without the 10 sessions. In addition, to be true to the definition and purpose of leisure, no activity that meets this criterion should be excluded from being a choice option—no matter how many times the participant chooses it during these sessions.

At the beginning of a leisure education program an individual may have only two activities included in the choice instruction sessions. As the participant receives more leisure skill acquisition instruction, the number of viable options should increase.

FREE TIME AND CHOICE CUES

Before individuals can make leisure activity choices, they must realize that free time is present and they must be aware of their leisure activity options. To teach someone to realize that it is free time, the instructor should begin the choice instruction sessions with the same generalized cue indicating free time (e.g., "free time," "go and play") that is used to begin skill acquisition instruction sessions (see "Free Time and Activity Cues" in Chapter 3). Whereas some individuals may choose an activity from those offered in response to this general cue, many individuals with significant disabilities require systematic instruction on how to make a choice (Wehmeyer, 1992).

For people who do not label objects or verbally communicate their desires, an alternative or augmentative communication system (AAC) should be used to indicate preferences for particular leisure activities. Ideally, leisure activity options should be programmed into or included in participants' existing AAC systems so that they may request them via their AAC system. Durand (1993) demonstrated that students with severe communication difficulties who learned to use assistive devices to help them communicate appeared to be happier as a result of their newly acquired communication skills. In addition, as described in Chapter 3 and demonstrated by Mirenda and Dattilo (1987), another approach is to use pictures of the leisure activities, repeatedly pairing these pictures both with the name of the activity and the actual materials during skill acquisition instruction. These same pictures and the process of pairing them with the activity materials are used in choice instruction sessions to provide activity options to the participant. The instructor should help the individual construct a "choice book." To do this, the instructor can take a picture of each leisure activity meeting the criterion for inclusion in choice instruction (pictures of the 10 leisure activities included in this volume appear in Appendix C for the instructor to reproduce), laminate the pictures to increase durability, and compile them into booklet form (a hole may be punched in one corner of each picture and a ring used to hold the pictures together). This choice book can then be used to provide activity options to participants who are taught to point to the picture of the activity with which they would like to play. In addition, the choice book should be easily accessible to each individual in the classroom (and home) so that during naturally occurring free time he or she can initiate making leisure choices. Therefore, making the choice book as portable as possible is important.

In addition to a choice book, other procedures may be employed to encourage participants to indicate their preferences. For example, Dattilo (1986, 1987, 1988) used a computerized assessment procedure to determine leisure preferences of persons with significant disabilities. In addition, Wacker and his colleagues (e.g., Wacker, Berg, Wiggins, Muldoon, & Cavanaugh, 1985; Wacker, Wiggins, Fowler, & Berg, 1988) incorporated microswitches to assess preferences of individuals with significant disabilities and to provide them with communicative control over environmental events. Leisure preference profiles were developed for each individual and opportunities to express these preferences and subsequently engage in preferred leisure activities were provided.

Just as when conducting skill acquisition instruction, prior to choice instruction sessions, the instructor should arrange the environment and acquire any necessary materials and data sheets. Whenever possible, participants should be included in the process of obtaining necessary materials and arranging the environment. Choice instruction sessions should be conducted in the area of the room or facility in which the individuals typically play during free time. To arrange the environment for a choice instruction session, the instructor should ensure that participants have their alternative or augmentative communication systems (e.g., choice book), that the systems include all the necessary activities, and that the activity materials corresponding to each picture are available. Again, when possible, participants should be encouraged to bring or obtain their choice books immediately prior to sessions or to use their AAC systems. If, for some reason, an activity is not available (e.g., a particular activity is being used by someone else), the pictures of the activity should be removed temporarily from the choice book.

To begin a choice instruction session, the instructor gives the individual the generalized cue for free time and a "choice cue." A choice cue tells a participant that he or she has an opportunity to select a leisure activity. The instructor should use a program containing a hierarchy of three choice cues representing three different levels of intrusiveness. These are described in Table 6.1.

The instructor provides whatever choice cue is appropriate for the individual, always striving for the least intrusive cue. After providing the choice cue, the instructor follows similar guidelines as discussed earlier in the chapter encouraging reciprocal communication and waits 10 seconds for the individual to initiate an activity selection. If the participant does not initiate a selection, the instructor gives the cue a second time and assists the participant in making a choice. It is critical that the instructor systematically vary which activities are prompted as choices. By reviewing the Choice Data Sheet (Form 6.1), the instructor can ensure that the same

Table 6.1.   Levels of choice cues

1. General choice cue: The instructor provides the general cue indicating free time and asks, "What do you want to play with?"

2. General choice cue and activity pictures: The instructor provides the general cue indicating free time, asks, "What do you want to play with?" and then presents an illustration of each activity included in the choice session.

3. General choice cue, activity pictures, and activities: The instructor provides the general cue indicating free time, asks, "What do you want to play with?" and then presents an illustration of each activity included in the choice session simultaneously paired with the actual activity materials.

Choice Data Sheet

Participant: __Dana Johnson__

Activity Options
Check all options

A _____	NGB _____
CF _____	Pi __Pinball__
J _____	Po _____
MM _____	RC _____

S __Simon__	
T _____	
(Other) _____	
(Other) _____	

Level of Choice Cues
A. verbal only
B. verbal; activity pic
C. activity pic
D. prompted choice

Date and Time	Instructor	Selection Provided	Level of Cue	Activity Selected	Choice Level*	Time of Instructor Contact	Out of Area	Destructive	Self-stimulatory/ Self-injurious	Failure to Interact	Inappropriately Interacting*	Appropriately Interacting*	Date	Narrative Data
4/1/94 10:00	AS	all	A	S	III	10:02 04 06 08						////		very giggly - laughed each time Simon signaled.
6/5/94	AS	all	A	Pi	III	9:32 34 36 38					/	///		pounded machine with hands when ball dropped out of play
6/6/94	AS	all	A	Pi	III	1:02 04 06 08				/	//	/		pounded machine with hands when ball dropped out of play. Would not reset dial to "3", just sat.

*Used for Choice Teaching Method II only.

A = Aerobic Warm-ups; CF = Connect Four; J = Jenga; MM = Magic Mitts; NGB = Nintendo Game Boy; Pi = Pinball; Po = Pottery; RC = Remote Control Vehicle; S = Simon; T = Target Games.

activity is not continually prompted. The prompted activity choice should be immediately reinforced. Immediate reinforcement is best when it is in the form of a naturally occurring consequence. In the situation of choice instruction, typically the most effective reinforcer the
instructor can provide is the opportunity to engage in the chosen activity.

Once the participant selects an activity (or a choice is prompted), he or she should acquire
the activity materials. If the participant cannot do this, the instructor should assist.

TEACHING METHODS

After a preferred activity is chosen and acquired, the instructor should implement one of the
teaching methods discussed on the following pages. Both of these methods were field tested and
both resulted in participants making choices and applying learned leisure activity skills in nonin-
structional environments.

Choice Teaching Method I

The first teaching method is relatively simple and required minimal effort by the instructors participating in the field tests to successfully implement. In this method, after participants have
acquired the necessary leisure activity materials, they are given a 15-minute time block in which
to interact freely with the chosen activity. During this time, the instructor unobtrusively observes
the participant's behavior and interactions with the leisure activity and records these observations on the Choice Data Sheet (Form 6.1). The instructor describes what the participant does—
whether the individual's behavior is appropriate, whether interactions with the activity
correspond with the steps of the task analysis, and so forth. During the choice session, if the
individual: 1) leaves the area, 2) engages in destructive behavior, 3) engages in self-stimulatory
or self-injurious behavior, and/or 4) fails to interact with the leisure activity, the instructor
should provide an instructor contact. Remaining neutral, the instructor simply interrupts the
inappropriate response and then models and/or prompts the individual to interact appropriately
with the activity materials. This contact should be brief, lasting from 10 to 15 seconds. After the
contact, the instructor should record the time of the contact and put a tally mark on the Choice
Data Sheet in the column corresponding to the behavior that necessitated the instructor contact.
In the narrative data, the instructor should indicate what the individual was doing immediately
prior to the behavior requiring a contact, as well as what the individual did after the contact was
provided. When implementing this choice teaching method, the instructor should not use the
"Choice Level," "Inappropriately Interacting," or "Appropriately Interacting" columns of
the Choice Data Sheet. To terminate the choice session at the end of the 15-minute period, the
instructor tells the participant that free time is over and to put the leisure activity materials away.

This choice teaching method is easy for the instructor to implement and results in the participants learning to make activity choices and to apply learned activity skills to leisure environments in which there is minimal supervision. However, the field tests revealed several
weaknesses. For individuals who displayed a few appropriate leisure activity skills, especially
at the onset of their leisure education program, and/or displayed a high percentage of inappropriate behaviors (e.g., self-stimulation, self-injurious behavior, destructiveness), quite a few
instructor contacts were required to maintain acceptable behavior, particularly during initial
choice sessions. Such a large number of contacts for inappropriate behaviors tended to make
the choice instruction sessions too much like skill acquisition sessions, lessening the "fun and
enjoyment."

Choice Teaching Method II

To address the weaknesses in the first choice teaching method, one can implement a second choice teaching method that systematically programs for: 1) an increase in the duration of appropriate play, 2) a decrease in the number of required instructor contacts, 3) an increase in the appropriate activity interactions, and 4) a decrease in the proportion of inappropriate participant behaviors. In this method, the participant systematically progresses through nine different types of choice instruction sessions or "choice levels," which are listed in Table 6.2. Each choice level is defined by: 1) the length of the choice instruction session, 2) the total number of instructor contacts provided to the individual during the session, and 3) the schedule on which these instructor contacts were provided.

Each of the nine types of choice instruction sessions is conducted for a specific length of time. The instructor always begins a participant's choice instruction sessions at level I (a 5-minute session) and eventually progresses to 15-minute sessions. (The number of instructor contacts listed in Table 6.2 does not include contacts to begin or end a session.)

Instructor contacts refer to interactions between the participant and instructor during the choice session. There are two types of contacts that the instructor can provide: 1) reinforcement of appropriate play behaviors, and 2) intervention for inappropriate behaviors. If the participant is displaying inappropriate behaviors (e.g., leaving the area, being destructive, self-stimulating), the instructor should intervene and immediately remove or turn off the activity for 3 seconds. After this time, the instructor should repeat the general cue indicating free time and prompt an appropriate play behavior.

The schedule of instructor contacts identifies when the instructor should provide the participant with a contact during the choice instruction session. As illustrated in Table 6.2, instructor contacts during choice levels I–IV are provided on a *fixed interval schedule*. If the participant is at choice level I, the instructor would provide a contact every minute of the 5-minute session. If the participant is at choice level IV, the instructor would provide a contact after every 2 minutes of the 15-minute session.

During choice levels V–VIII, the instructor contacts are provided on a *variable interval schedule*. This implies that the contacts are given on an average of however many minutes are listed for the particular choice level under the "Schedule of Instructor Contacts" column of Table 6.2. For instance, at level V, the instructor would give the participant a contact on an average of

Table 6.2.   Choice levels

Level	Length of sessions (in minutes)	Number of instructor contacts	Schedule of instructor contacts (in minutes)
I	5	4	Fixed 1
II	10	9	Fixed 1
III	10	4	Fixed 2
IV	15	7	Fixed 2
V	15	7	Variable 2
VI	15	5	Variable 3
VII	15	3	Variable 5
VIII	15	2	Variable 7
IX	15	0	Nonapplicable

every 2 minutes. The first contact might be after 2 minutes, the second after 4 minutes, the third after 5½ minutes, and so forth, but the contacts would average to every 2 minutes over the session. It is up to the instructor to determine when the contacts will occur and to be sure that they average out to the schedule specified.

In previous choice instruction sessions, the following procedure was used by instructors to determine the exact time of each instructor contact on a variable interval schedule. To determine the random intervals, the instructor marked 13 slips of paper, each with a number from 1 to 13, and then selected the number of slips corresponding to the number of interventions to be given for a specific choice level. For example, if there were to be 5 interventions at level VI, the instructor randomly selected 5 numbers from among the 13 slips of paper and arranged the numbers in order. The resulting sequence represented the minutes *into* the choice session at which the instructor intervened. Thus, if the instructor selected 3, 10, 2, 8, and 5, intervention occurred at 2 minutes, at 3 minutes, at 5 minutes, and so forth.

When implementing this choice teaching method, the instructor determines the appropriate choice levels for each activity and then begins the choice session as previously described. Once the session is underway, the instructor unobtrusively observes the individual's behavior and provides instructor contacts according to the participant's predetermined schedule. During the choice instruction session, the instructor records the time of each contact on the Choice Data Sheet (Form 6.1) and puts a tally mark in the column corresponding to the participant's behavior immediately preceding the contact. This procedure allows the instructor to determine whether the contact was to reinforce appropriate play or to intervene during an inappropriate behavior. The instructor also writes any observations of the participant in the "Narrative Data" column.

At the end of the time specified for the session, the instructor tells the participant that free time is over and asks the individual to put the leisure activity materials away. The instructor should then transfer the data on the contacts he or she provided during the choice instruction session onto the Summary of Instructor Contacts form (Form 6.2). The instructor should record the choice level for the session, the total number of instructor contacts for appropriate play, and the total number of instructor contacts for inappropriate play. This information can then be used to determine when the individual should progress to a higher choice level. The criterion for movement to the next choice level is that the participant receives instructor contacts only for appropriate interactions with an activity across three choice instruction sessions. The individual could, for instance, choose Simon for the first choice session, Simon for the second choice session, pinball for the third choice session, and Simon for the fourth choice session. If the participant then received instructor contacts only for appropriate play during the three choice sessions with Simon, the participant would move to the next choice level.

It is quite likely that individuals will move through the choice levels at different rates for each activity. Because of this, and because the instructor does not know before the choice session begins which activity will be selected, the instructor must review the Summary of Instructor Contacts form for each activity prior to initiating the choice session and be prepared to conduct the session in a variety of ways—the session may last 5, 10, or 15 minutes. The instructor may not have to intervene during the session, or he or she may be required to intervene on several occasions. The instructor may have to adhere to a fixed 1-minute schedule, or he or she may have to create a variable 7-minute schedule.

Selecting a Choice Teaching Method

In our programs' field tests, both choice teaching methods resulted in participants learning to make choices and to apply their leisure skills in situations with minimal supervision. Results of a study comparing the relative effectiveness of the two methods with a subset of individuals sug-

Summary of Instructor Contacts

Participant: **Dana Johnson**

Key:
CA = contacts for appropriate behaviors
CI = contacts for inappropriate behaviors

ACTIVITY: Simon (S)

Choice Level	III															
Date	4/1/94															
Teacher	AS															
CA	4															
CI	0															

ACTIVITY: Pinball (PB)

Choice Level	III	III														
Date	4/5/94	4/6/94														
Teacher	AS	AS														
CA	3	1														
CI	1	2														

ACTIVITY:

Choice Level																
Date																
Teacher																
CA																
CI																

ACTIVITY:

Choice Level																
Date																
Teacher																
CA																
CI																

gest that choice teaching method II resulted in participants engaging in more appropriate play during choice sessions (Graham, 1981); however, these results are preliminary and further investigation is needed.

Because both methods resulted in individuals learning to express their activity preferences and to apply their leisure activity skills, the instructor must decide which of the two methods best meets the needs of the participants. What is crucial to this leisure curriculum component is not which choice instruction method is used, but that the instructor recognizes the importance of systematically teaching the skills these procedures address and implements one of the two options.

DATA EVALUATION

The choice instruction session data provide the instructor with valuable information on a participant's activity preferences. The data can also provide the instructor with information about changes in the "quality" of the individual's behavior during minimally structured periods of time (an index of the success of any leisure education program). For example, during the first few weeks of both skill acquisition and choice instruction sessions, some individuals may require many instructor contacts for self-stimulatory behaviors, but later, after mastering the skill acquisition objective, participants may require very few contacts during choice sessions for the same inappropriate behaviors. The programs have demonstrated that such changes are a function of the leisure activities instruction. Evidence of changes in the percentage of appropriate to inappropriate behaviors as a function of teaching leisure skills argues for attempts to use leisure skills instruction as an alternative to more intrusive behavioral interventions. Such information about the participant's activity preference and changes in the individual's behavior should be shared with family members and friends who may wish to purchase preferred activities to facilitate the individual's ability to enjoy the activity.

Narrative data can also help the instructor identify antecedents that possibly maintain a participant's inappropriate behavior. Finally, choice instruction session data should be evaluated in conjunction with skill acquisition data to facilitate decision making and program revision. If, for instance, skill acquisition data show that some participants have not progressed on the task analysis despite systematic programming, and these participants never select the activity during choice sessions, the instructor may want to consider discontinuing instruction on that activity. Conversely, if the choice data indicate the activity is preferred, the instructor should analyze how participants play with it during choice sessions and develop an alternative task analysis or teaching strategy.

Skill acquisition and choice instruction sessions provide the content of a comprehensive leisure education program. When these sessions are carefully implemented, a participant with significant disabilities can be expected to increase independent leisure participation.

CONCLUSION

When individuals with significant disabilities who receive leisure services are provided with the opportunities and means to freely select activities, spontaneous initiation of activity, engagement with elements of the environment, and assertion of a degree of control over one's surroundings are often the result. In addition to these benefits, teaching individuals to make choices can reduce problem behaviors (e.g., Dyer, Dunlap, & Winterling, 1990), increase interactions with materials that can facilitate leisure, enhance leisure participation, and increase quality of services (e.g., Realon, Favell, & Lowerre, 1990). Because making choices leads to control, and feelings of control are important factors in experiencing leisure, the greater the freedom of choice available to people, the greater the chance that leisure will be experienced (Sylvester, 1987). According to Ficker-Terrill and Rowitz (1991), practitioners must familiarize themselves with best practice strategies that facilitate and encourage informed choice. The intent of this chapter is to help leisure educators adopt best practice efforts associated with leisure instruction by systematically incorporating choice-making instruction.

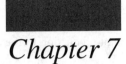

Chapter 7

INCLUSIONARY COMMUNITY LEISURE SERVICES

with John E. Rynders and Nancy A. Staur

*T*he term *least restrictive environment* (LRE) has created a lot of confusion among professionals, agencies, parents, and care providers, and even advocacy groups. Most program leaders have defined this term in their own specific way, using their own criteria. Ironically, the term *least restrictive environment* is really only new to educators; the legal profession has referred to this concept as the doctrine of least restrictive alternative or the doctrine of least restrictive services as far back as the days of John Marshall and Oliver Wendell Holmes. Historically, the concept was meant to convey an intent; that is, any state or federal bureaucracy that was to inflict harm or punishment on a citizen was to do so in the least restrictive way possible. The punishment was supposed to fit the crime, not be overly harsh, and take into consideration the individual's rights. The term *least restrictive environment* is an outgrowth of this intent, specifying that the educational environment within which an individual with a disability is placed should be one that is least restrictive to that individual and does not present a violation to his or her rights (Verhoven, Schleien, & Bender, 1982).

For many individuals with disabilities, exposure to recreation experiences affords them an opportunity to exercise their rights and to interact more fully in typical ways. However, attainment of a full measure of the LRE concept is not easy because a large number of individuals with disabilities have physical, emotional, or cognitive limitations that make it difficult for them to carry out recreation activities independently or interdependently. In many cases, individuals with significant disabilities require special instruction, medical attention, and supportive devices to facilitate their development as well as to increase their functional capacity. Moreover, society tends to stigmatize and stereotype these individuals, creating problems for them that extend far beyond those related directly to the disability.

Positive, direct, and reasonably frequent contact experiences with people who do not have disabilities can stimulate the formation of more positive attitudes, not only for the person with a disability, but for persons without disabilities as well. One viable way to facilitate positive face-to-face encounters is through participation in community recreation activities. Then, as participants with disabilities demonstrate their increased competence in these activities and become more comfortable with their peers without disabilities, public attitudes should reflect a new acceptance of individual differences, narrowing the gap traditionally separating people with and without disabilities in typical life activities. At that point, the LRE concept will be well on its way to influencing the characteristics of inclusive environments in an actual and sustainable way.

In this chapter, the LRE concept is used as an "agenda" for change, contending that recreation leaders need to work together in several areas simultaneously (a type of effort we and others refer to as a "systemic effort"). The four areas identified for LRE attention are: 1) help community recreation agencies become less restrictive in their programming policies, 2) assist leaders to structure the social dynamics of inclusive recreation programming to minimize social restrictiveness, 3) avoid programming pitfalls that hamper the development of less restrictive recreation approaches, and 4) modify recreation environments to promote inclusion in the community.

Before elaborating on these points, the LRE topic should be approached from a very broad or wholistic context—an indicator of quality context. What constitutes an inclusive community recreation program of high quality for a person with a disability? Are there signs that a parent, care provider, or consumer can look for? Are there traits that service providers can strive to include in their programs? Table 7.1 lists indicators of quality in community recreation programs, which were developed from research and demonstration efforts at the University of Minnesota.

Table 7.1.   Quality indicators

Administration

- Statement of mission or philosophy reflects belief in inclusion.
- Staff hiring criteria give credit for education and/or experience that reflect inclusion.
- Adherence to laws and legislation pertaining to serving persons with disabilities in least restrictive environments is apparent.
- Staff instruction priorities emphasize continuing education in topical areas, such as innovations and techniques in inclusion, use of on-site community inclusion consultants, and so forth.
- The effects of inclusionary interventions on participants is documented in logs or other instruments.

Nature of Program

- Features inclusive programming but also may provide alternative programming as "stepping stones" (allows for choice).
- Provides flexible programs that allow for partial participation, if needed.
- Program goals reflect an inclusionary emphasis; for example, interdependent activity provisions and friend-oriented interaction modes are described.

Activities

- Are chronological age appropriate, functional, and have lifelong learning potential.
- Can be generalized across time and environments in the community.
- Allow for personal challenge (dignity of risk) and participant choice of challenge.

Environmental/Logistical Considerations

- Environment is physically accessible. If environment is not accessible (e.g., a remote wilderness area), staff members work with all participants to provide appropriate access, adapting methods and materials as necessary.
- Programming is offered at a time that is convenient and appropriate for participants.
- Cost is reasonable and sponsorships are available to accommodate nontraditional participants.

Techniques and Methods

- Ongoing assessment and evaluation are conducted of participants' inclusionary recreation needs, preferences, skills, and enjoyment levels.
- Parents/care providers and participants are included in assessments and evaluations to maximize inclusionary possibilities.
- Inclusion techniques, such as cooperative learning, environmental analysis, partial participation, and companionship instruction are employed regularly.
- Ongoing program evaluation is conducted, making adaptations if needed to promote inclusion.
- Appropriate involvement of unpaid or paid companions or friends is available to promote the benefits of heterogeneous relationships.

Area 1: Help Community Recreation Agencies

Business and community agencies have worked together to provide less restrictive employment opportunities for individuals with disabilities. They must now unite strongly to accommodate this group with less restrictive recreation activities. Accomplishing this task will require sharing ideas and information while recognizing the needs and concerns of families, transportation providers, architects, recreation professionals, curriculum specialists, health care personnel, legislators, media officials, and others who directly and indirectly affect the planning and delivery of community recreation services. A vigorous united effort will maximize benefits to individuals with disabilities, facilitating their involvement in the leisure and social life of the community. However, given the limited transagency coordination resources of most community agencies and public schools, how does one organize such systemic instruction? One way is to join parents, therapeutic recreation specialists, community recreation professionals, and teachers in a collaborative effort to plan inclusive programs. Because most therapeutic recreation specialists provide leisure skill instruction after school hours and on weekends, such instruction could easily supplement community teaching provided by community recreation professionals, teachers, and parents and care providers at home.

Community's Role in Providing Leisure Education in a Less Restrictive Manner   Several authors (McGill, 1984b; Schleien & Werder, 1985) suggest that the reluctance of community recreation program staff to share responsibility for integrating people with disabilities into their regular programs is understandable when one remembers the emphasis that was placed on the need for highly trained specialists to staff school programs for people with disabilities. Voeltz, Wuerch, and Wilcox (1982) recommended that special educators/recreators seek to remove this "mystique" surrounding people with disabilities by deemphasizing their need for "special" programs and facilities and encouraging their use of generic services.

Community recreation agencies also have a responsibility to ensure that personnel in their agencies are prepared to share the responsibility for integrating participants of varying abilities. Educating staff about the leisure needs of persons with disabilities and teaching them to facilitate successful inclusion is vital. Effective inclusion requires that general recreation programming staff and therapeutic recreation specialists work together, emphasizing the need for generalists and specialists to develop and supervise selected aspects of inclusive programs collaboratively.

To identify contacts to aid in the implementation of community recreation services, Schleien and Ray (1988) developed a networking matrix. This matrix identifies key players' *roles and responsibilities* within the process of inclusive services, affirming that a variety of individuals and agencies concerned with the needs of persons with disabilities, in addition to the community recreator/agency, are critical to the success and sustainability of inclusive recreation services.

Consumers' and Families' Roles in Reducing Restrictiveness   Society's failure to develop inclusive community recreation services is due, in part, to a lack of initiative by citizens with disabilities and their families or care providers. Adults with visual impairments reported (in a survey by Sherril, Rainbolt, & Ervin, 1984) that they desired acceptance into community recreation neighborhood athletic programs; however, only 10% of them participated in community recreation programs and 47% did not even know what their communities offered. Similarly, residents of a large community facility for adults with mental retardation reported a desire for more independence and community involvement (Birenbaum & Re, 1979); however, 83% of them spent much of their leisure time in passive activities within their residence. The number of community activities provided and led by staff members declined during the Birenbaum and Re 4-year study and were not supplanted by resident ventures into the community alone, with friends, or with family members. In a similar vein, residents with mental retardation in group homes and intermediate group residences spent the majority of their discretionary time in their homes, relying almost completely on their supervisors to transport them into the community (Crapps, Langone, & Swaim, 1985). Birenbaum and Re speculated that the decline in community involvement exhibited by the participants of their study may have been due to residents' lack of skills necessary for engaging in community activities, or possibly their reluctance to travel in what they considered to be a "dangerous community." However, Kishi, Teelucksingh, Zollers, Park-Lee, and Meyer (1988) found a clear pattern of fewer choices being made available when the community viewed a person's disabilities as significant. Although it was found recently that residents of small community residences (e.g., group homes) participated in many leisure activities, Hayden, Lakin, Hill, Bruininks, and Copher (1992) discovered that a large proportion of these residents had extremely small leisure repertoires. The researchers reported that residents "practically never" participated in the basic leisure activities of society, such as engaging in hobbies; visiting friends; attending a sporting event; and attending meetings, clubs, and community centers. A high proportion participated in passive activities such as watching television, taking car rides, and listening to the radio or records. Finally, a lack of skills may limit an individual's involvement in the community to passive integration experiences. Rynders and Schleien (1991) and Voeltz, Wuerch, and Wilcox (1982) pointed out that when an individual lacks the skills to participate in recreation options, a full range of choices that may be available become meaningless in light of his or her skill difficulties.

Area 2: Assist Leaders

Guideline A: Structure Activities and Surroundings to Promote Cooperative Interactions
Without structuring an inclusive situation for cooperative interactions, individuals without disabilities may view their peers with disabilities in negative ways, feel discomfort and uncertainty in interacting with them, and sometimes even reject them (Rynders, Johnson, Johnson, & Schmidt, 1980). What does it mean specifically to structure an activity for cooperative interactions? One of three models of activity structure is applied typically when there is a group of people to instruct: competitive, individualistic, or cooperative. Each is legitimate and has strengths in particular situations. Furthermore, sometimes they can be combined in an activity. On the following pages, each of the models is defined and some of their applications are reviewed.

Competitive   Competition, in its traditional application, leads to one person in a group winning, with all other group members placing below the winner. If it is used in a group where some members have disabilities that make competing in that task difficult, it is likely that the participants with disabilities will "come in last." An example of the misuse of competitive structuring may occur during a summer camp where five children, two of whom have movement disabilities, line up at the edge of a lake for a canoe race. Each has a canoe and a paddle to use. The camp director tells them that the person who reaches the other side of the lake first will win a canoe paddle. Clearly, the children with poor coordination and low muscle tone in competition with participants without disabilities do not have much chance of winning. (Note: Informed program leaders would not use a competitive goal structure in this manner, of course, but would rely on one or both of the following structures instead.)

Individualistic   In an individualistically structured situation, each member of a group works to improve his or her own past performance. Potentially, every member of the group, including members with disabilities, can win a prize for improvement if the goals for improved performance are not set too high or are not inappropriately matched with a disability. Using the canoe example again, suppose that the adult leader lines the group up on the shore of the lake and tells them that last week when they paddled across the lake each person's crossing time was recorded. Then, the adult says that each person will win a prize if he or she improves his or her time, even if the improvement is very small. Now everyone can be a winner. This structure is often used in amateur athletics where a child is encouraged to better his or her last time or achieve a personal record.

Cooperative   Cooperatively structured activities are very helpful in many types of inclusive programming, particularly if peer socialization and friendliness are the goals. By its very nature, a cooperative learning structure (if handled properly) creates an interdependence among individuals because the group's attainment of an objective, with everyone contributing something to the outcome, is the quality that determines winning. In the canoe example, the adult leader might have the five children climb into a Voyageur North canoe, give each person a paddle, and tell them that they are each to paddle as well as they can and that they will all win a prize if they work together to keep the canoe inside the floating markers (placed in such a way that perfection in paddling is not required). The adult leader will need to paddle alongside to determine that everyone is paddling, at least a little bit, and that they are encouraging each other and assisting one another as needed.

To promote interactions with an emphasis on *socialization*, the cooperative structure will usually work better than the other two. Why? Because in a competitive situation, each child is concentrating on paddling the fastest; there is no time for socialization. Similarly, in an individualistic structure, each child is concentrating on bettering his or her own past performance. Again, there is no built-in incentive for socialization. In the cooperative structure, however, each person wants to encourage the rest of the group to achieve a group goal that is realistically attainable. This promotes positive social interactions such as encouragement, cheering, and a pat on the back.

Guideline B: Clarify the Purpose of the Activity   Most activities probably promote both skill development and socialization, but there are times when one is given priority over the other. For instance, a 4-H club leader may designate certain periods of the year primarily for completion of projects to enter into competition, such as the months preceding the spring fashion show or county fair. These will be times when participants, especially those without disabilities, will be intent on finishing their individual projects. Socializing will be minimal during these times and may even be regarded as a distraction by 4-H members without disabilities, who are intent on creating the best entry at the county fair. At times such as these, the leader must be clear about the intent of the activity and the needs of participants to avoid creating a situation in which individuals are frustrated by trying to fulfill conflicting objectives. Thus, when skill development is the focus, the program must be organized so that participants both with and without disabilities are able to pursue that objective. One "middle ground" socialization-oriented option is to give participants without disabilities the opportunity to work on their own projects prior to a socialization-focused session with a partner who has a disability. In this way, they have time to develop their project for competition, as well as time to focus on interacting with their companions with disabilities.

Guideline C: Determine the Desired Roles of Participants   The leader must determine whether the peers without disabilities will be interacting as *tutors*, *companions*, or *both*. Each role has a different purpose and fits a slightly different goal; however, all of the roles can be fitted well into a cooperative learning orientation.

The usual purpose of a *peer tutor* program is to have a peer without a disability teach a task skill to a peer with a disability. The relationship of peers in a tutoring program can be thought of as "vertical"; that is, the tutor is in charge ("I'm the teacher, you're the pupil."). A typical example of a peer tutor program is a 12-year-old child without disabilities who comes to a recreation center and works one-to-one on teaching ball-handling skills to a 6-year-old child with a disability. However, the role of the child with a disability in recreation activities should not always be that of the one who receives "help," which is often an expectation when tutoring programs are used. It is important for a child with a disability to experience a giving as well as a receiving role.

The primary purpose of a *peer companion* program is to promote positive social interactions between a child with a disability and a child without a disability. To achieve this, the peers should be approximately the same age, although it is okay if the child without disabilities is 1 or 2 years older than his or her partner. It is not often desirable for the child with a disability to be substantially older than the child without a disability; our research shows that this can create a socially awkward situation. The relationship between two people in a peer companionship program can be thought of as "horizontal"—a relatively equalized, turn-taking relationship. A typical application of this arrangement is two peers, one with a disability and one without, making a pizza by taking turns putting on the ingredients, and later washing the dishes together.

The two peer roles (companion and tutor) raise issues for program leaders to consider. At first, it may appear that the choice of one or the other is easy. The program or activity is tailored according to the outcome desired—skill acquisition or socialization. A peer tutoring approach is used if the primary objective is the acquisition of specific skills, and a peer companionship program is used if socialization is the main objective. However, making a choice between the two may not be necessary; that is, leaders can concentrate on facilitating friendships, at least initially. Then, later, it is typical for one companion to teach another to play a new game, thus allowing the skill acquisition to occur in the natural course of the social relationship.

Guideline D: Recruit Participants Without Disabilities   A helpful tool for recruiting participants without disabilities is a slide presentation[1] that shows people with and without disabilities interacting in natural and interesting ways. This provides a positive pictorial image for prospective participants, many of whom may have negative mental pictures of inclusive programs due to a lack of direct exposure to persons with disabilities, stereotypes of persons with disabilities, or negative experiences with persons who have disabilities. Recruitment presentations that depict positive interactions between people with and without disabilities help create the expectation that prospective participants will have a positive experience in an inclusive program. Such an expectation can go a long way toward creating a successful program.

Guideline E: Strengthen Friendship Skills of Participants Without Disabilities   Why should the recreation leader spend time with instruction in friendship? Don't children without disabilities naturally interact in a friendly way with children who have disabilities? This answer is yes and no. Yes, they usually know how to interact with same-age peers without disabilities in a friendly manner (although their friendship skills may need to be sharpened or expanded). Yet, no, peers without disabilities often do not have the knowledge and skills to interact easily and ably with a person who may be different from them in some manner. Frequently, a significant disability presents interaction challenges never experienced by peers without disabilities. Participants without disabilities need instruction in how to cope with significant communication, movement, and other types of challenges. Meetings involving group members without disabilities and adult leaders should occur frequently, perhaps immediately before or after an inclusive session. During these meetings, discussion can focus on how a particular interaction problem can be overcome, offering new ideas for interacting and providing specific techniques that can be used during one-to-one activities. (See the list of interaction techniques in Table 7.2.)

---

[1] If you photograph your own slides, obtain written photo-use permission from each person who appears in your pictures. (For minors or others unable to legally sign a permission form for themselves, have the parent or guardian sign.) Also, inform all parents or guardians of your intent to provide an inclusive program, and receive consent to have their son or daughter participate. Although this type of permission may not be required technically, it is important to obtain it to avoid any misunderstanding.

Table 7.2. How to be a companion to a peer with a disability

- Welcome your partner and stay close to him or her during the activity.
- Smile, talk pleasantly, and try to maintain eye contact when talking.
- Divide up tasks and encourage your partner to be involved.
- Make the activity enjoyable and let your partner know you are having a good time.
- Take turns—your partner may not be used to this, so be patient. Help as needed, but do not help too much or too soon. If your partner appears to be confused, losing interest, or frustrated, step in. To assist, describe (pleasantly) how to perform the task, then invite him or her to do it. If that does not work, model doing the task as you continue to explain how to do it. Then invite your partner to try it. If that does not work, guide him or her through the task by gently moving his or her arm toward it or by gently moving his or her hand to perform the task while continuing to explain how to do it. Then, invite him or her to do it.
- Say something positive about your companion's efforts.
- Say something pleasant about your time together as the activity ends.

Guideline F: Use a Supporting Curriculum to Enhance Knowledge of Companionship
Use of *The Special Friends Program* curriculum (Voeltz et al., 1983) or one similar to it can be helpful in enhancing the knowledge and motivation of participants without disabilities. Used for short, informal group discussion periods of 15–30 minutes, curricula are often shared with participants without disabilities between interaction sessions. Suggested topics from the curriculum could include:

How do we play together? Discuss how companions take turns, say nice things to each other, help each other out when a task is difficult, stay close to each other when playing, smile at each other, and so forth. In other words, reinforce the interaction techniques that they have been taught to apply during inclusionary activities.

How do we communicate? Discuss communication tips, such as talking slowly, allowing time for a response, trying another way to communicate if your companion does not understand, and not giving up. The use of common, simple manual signs (e.g., "hello," "good," "you," "me") can be introduced, too.

What is a prosthesis? Discuss the use of tools (e.g., ladder, paint brush) that people without disabilities need to do certain tasks (e.g., paint a house). Show examples of prostheses (e.g., artificial limb or piece of adapted equipment) and explain how they are like tools that people with disabilities use.

How does a person with a disability live in the community? Invite a person with a disability to come and talk about how he or she travels from home to work, goes camping, paddles a canoe, and so forth.

What is a best friend? Discuss the nature of friendship. Ask participants to think about similarities and differences in their relationship with their friend with a disability and their best friend (if they are not the same person).

Guideline G: Prepare Yourself to Facilitate Interactions   An adult who assumes an interaction facilitating role is instrumental in determining the success or failure of inclusive activities. Facilitation usually takes two forms:

1. Overall planning and operation of the program, including recruiting participants, structuring activities for cooperation, and preparing peers without disabilities for the inclusive program
2. Facilitating cooperative interactions by modeling appropriate behavior and reinforcing small inclusive groups for interacting well

The following is an illustration of how a leader might facilitate cooperative interactions. The leader of a group engaged in an inclusive art activity could:

Prompt positive interactions when they are not occurring. For example, "Mary, I'll bet that Jennifer would like to paint with you."

Reinforce positive interactions when they are occurring. For example, "Bill and Jim, you both did a really nice job gluing leaves on the mural." Rewarding words should not be given out lavishly or indiscriminately, but should be given right after the desired behavior occurs.

Redirect behaviors if either partner gets off task or is behaving inappropriately. For example, the partner without disabilities may become "sloppy" in his or her interactions by becoming too autocratic, too laissez faire, or sometimes too absorbed in his or her own project. Or, a participant with a disability may wander away (literally) from his or her companion without a disability and might need to be guided back to the interaction environment by the adult.

Step in if a situation is deteriorating. For example, intervene if a child has a tantrum. Sometimes a child needs to be removed for a cooling-off period. The adult leader needs to gauge the seriousness of a problem situation and move in quickly if it is out of control, or, better yet, if it is just beginning to get out of control. The old adage "An ounce of prevention is worth a pound of cure" is well worth remembering.

Area 3: Avoid Programming Pitfalls

Occasionally, even the best intended efforts to extend inclusive program opportunities to people with disabilities turn sour. Nine common problems that can readily be avoided are enumerated below. In offering this outline, the perspective is that the primary intent of an inclusive recreation program is socialization. This perspective does not, however, preclude the legitimacy of a skill tutoring orientation in an inclusive program.

1. **Not aiming for mutuality of benefit**   Inclusion benefits for persons with and without disabilities do not need to be identical; however, both groups need to derive some sort of benefit from the experience to count it as successful (and possibly also to help ensure the long-term acceptance of inclusionary programming by an agency and by society in general). Numerous contemporary studies are showing mutuality of benefit outcomes through inclusive programming.

2. **Asking children without disabilities to assume inappropriate interaction roles**   For safety and social appropriateness reasons, a peer without disabilities should not be expected to do such things as feed a child with cerebral palsy, or teach a peer with a disability how to apply deodorant. These are tasks that are best left to parents or personal care attendants. Making provisions for the safety and mental health of all participants as a first concern for everyone will reap benefits in the long run.

3. **Lack of preparation for peers without disabilities in using social interaction techniques**   As already noted, reliance on physical proximity alone to produce positive interactions usually fails (and may even polarize attitudes of persons of differing ability levels, increasing prejudice unnecessarily). Preparing peers without disabilities in how to interact (e.g., how to model a response, how to cue, how to encourage) in a cooperative, friendly manner is very helpful.

4. **Not providing a child who has a disability with a context sufficient for developing the skill necessary for successful social inclusion**   Sometimes the *context* of an inclusive environment can be the key to inducing a certain desired participatory behavior in a child

with a disability. Occasionally, however, it is virtually impossible to create an inclusive environment so that it provides enough opportunity to learn. Or, on very rare occasions, an inclusive context may actually provoke undesirable (perhaps even dangerous) behaviors because of its unstructured heterogeneous characteristics. Admonitions to do "100% this" or "100% that" will do little to alleviate this problem. When necessary, creative and judicious combinations of contexts can uphold the inclusionary principle while balancing the special needs of children with and without disabilities.

5. **Integrating too quickly** One nonintegrated neighborhood club voted unanimously to bring Janice, a child with mental retardation and significant emotional problems, into their club. Not only did they want her to join, but they wanted her to join immediately and to be included in every activity all of the time. Sadly, their commendable enthusiasm and generosity turned into feelings of guilt when Janice had to be removed because the volunteer leader and the participants did not know how to cope with her inappropriate behavior. Perhaps if they had chosen a short, cooperatively structured, and largely social activity to begin with, they could have moved gradually to the full inclusion plan they all desired.

6. **Emphasizing socialization at the wrong time** Recently, an adult 4-H club leader asked peers without disabilities to devote themselves to socializing with a peer who has disabilities at a time in the club's schedule when every member was trying to finish his or her needlecraft or woodworking project for competition at the county fair. A cooperative "round-robin" system would have allowed them to spend most of the time on their own projects without neglecting (or possibly even resenting) their peer with a disability.

7. **Age mismatch** A younger child without disabilities often feels socially awkward if expected to interact with a substantially older child with a disability, particularly if the interaction is in the form of peer tutoring. A peer tutor model usually works best when the tutor without disabilities is considerably older (about twice as old or more) than the person with a disability. Even a peer socialization model may sometimes operate better when the member without disabilities is somewhat older—even up to 2 years older—than the peer with a disability.

8. **Failure to take advantage of choice-making opportunities** Recreation activity preferences are idiosyncratic. Failure to consider personal preferences undermines even the most noble and enthusiastic inclusion efforts. Included in choice making should be the opportunity to choose one's friends for various times, places, and occasions. This means that a friendship between two people with disabilities is every bit as valid as a friendship between a person with a disability and one without a disability. Indeed, the friendship between two people with disabilities may, in some cases, be more durable than a more heterogeneous friendship. We need to honor and nurture both kinds of friendships. Insistence on only heterogeneous friendships for a person with a disability—to the exclusion of homogeneous friendships—is a form of segregation.

9. **Lack of understanding of when and how to use a particular goal structure** As mentioned earlier, a *cooperative* goal structure ("Everyone needs to add something to this big art mural. If each of you does, we will hang it in front of the principal's office.") promotes positive social interactions and helpfulness. A *competitive* goal structure ("Let's see who can draw the best picture of the school. The person who draws the one that looks the most like our school will have his or her picture hung in front of the principal's office.") promotes task concentration, not social interaction or helpfulness. An *individualistic* goal structure ("I saved each of the pictures that you drew of the school last month. Everyone who improves his or her drawing will get to hang his or her picture in front of the principal's office.") also promotes concentration on the task, not on socialization or being helpful. It is essential that

the activity leader apply the structure that matches his or her instructional intent or to "mix and match" structure to suit the occasion.

Area 4: Modify Recreation Environments

People with disabilities may have functional difficulties seeing, hearing, learning (mental retardation), manipulating objects and moving (physical disability), and socializing (social maladjustment). Other problems may occur in a particular educational situation (learning disability) or may be the result of a health problem such as a heart defect. There are many specific disabilities, such as cerebral palsy, Down syndrome, and cystic fibrosis, and each one affects individuals somewhat differently, but they all have in common the fact that they may hinder an individual's participation in recreation and social activities.

The focus of this section is on facilitating participation by adapting activities to meet the needs of persons with disabilities; that is, making activities more accessible, more "tolerant" of limitations in skill, and more "accepting" of partial participation. A number of guidelines to consider when making adaptations and some specific strategies to achieve them are presented. Underlying these guidelines is the principle that individuals with significant disabilities are entitled to have as much opportunity for choice making in their lives as is feasible. Just as people without disabilities choose to pursue the leisure activities they enjoy, persons with disabilities ought to be able to follow their individual preferences by pursuing activities that appeal to them. For this to happen, two criteria must be met. First, individuals with disabilities must be exposed to different options and allowed to explore those that interest them. Second, community recreation professionals must be willing to make adaptations that will enable an individual with disabilities to participate in and enjoy the activities of his or her choosing.

Adapting an activity can in some ways change its appearance. Consistent with the concepts of social role valorization and least restrictive environment, all persons should learn skills and participate in activities in as typical a manner as possible. Therefore, it is necessary to carefully analyze the total environment before changes are made in an activity. When adaptations are made judiciously, participants with disabilities will not appear too different from their peers without disabilities. The following five guidelines were helpful in assisting program leaders to implement appropriate adaptations in community recreation environments successfully. (See Table 7.3 for an adaptation checklist.)

Guideline 1: Adapt Only When Necessary   Many times, unfortunately, activity leaders use adaptations without considering participants' needs and preferences. Frequently, a material or procedural modification is used because it was purchased with funds difficult to come by, it is

Table 7.3.   Activity leader's adaptation checklist

Ask yourself these questions as you consider making a specific adaptation:

- Is this activity adaptation absolutely necessary to enhance participation, success, and enjoyment?
- Is this activity adaptation viewed as only a temporary change?
- Is this activity adaptation being made on a personal basis to meet one individual's needs?
- Does this activity adaptation help the participant fit in with his or her peers (i.e., is it congruent)?
- Is this activity adaptation of reasonable cost and available in community environments?

All five questions must be answered **"yes"** for a particular adaptation to be considered appropriate and important for implementation in an activity.

For specific adaptations of materials, rules, and task sequences, refer to the "Leisure Adaptive Devices" section of Chapter 5, this volume.

readily available, or the leader is familiar with its application. However, when using such criteria, the ability level of the participant is sometimes overlooked. For example, a simplified version of the activity may not have been necessary; the individual with a disability might have participated successfully using the standard rules and equipment.

A *task analysis* can help a group leader clarify the need for an adaptation by identifying the skills required for successful participation. After conducting a task analysis, the participant's ability to perform the requisite skills of the targeted activity must be assessed. A modification should then be used only if it is positively essential for participation, success, and enjoyment. Adapt only when necessary, but remember that the overall goal of the program is to promote success, so do not hesitate to make a change that helps a participant succeed.

Guideline 2: View Adaptations as Temporary, Transitional Changes   An adaptation should be viewed as a temporary and transitional change in the original activity. Whenever possible, the leader and participant must work toward engagement in the original activity. The acquisition of a skill using modifications in one environment could become a hindrance in other environments. For instance, teaching the necessary skills for newcomb, a simplified version of volleyball, at home would not be sufficient for participation in a typical volleyball game at a community recreation center. Newcomb requires the player to merely catch and throw the ball over the net instead of hitting the ball to a teammate or over the net. In a standard game of volleyball, the participant who is proficient only in the modified game of newcomb may be criticized rather than accepted.

Guideline 3: Adapt on an Individual Basis   An adapted physical education class was observed by an author of this chapter in which 12 students with movement problems were all tossing light-weight Nerf Frisbees. It was noted, however, that all but two of the students had the minimal eye–hand coordination required to throw a standard, hard plastic Frisbee. Nevertheless, when asked why they were all using the modified equipment, the adapted physical education teacher responded: "We recently purchased a carton of Nerf Frisbees for our program, and, also, it would probably be too dangerous for two of my students to be playing with a real Frisbee." Unfortunately, for the remaining 10 students, they never did receive Frisbee instruction commensurate with their ability levels. The solution to this problem would have been to individualize the modification so that only the two pupils would use the Nerf Frisbee while their classmates learned to toss the more age-appropriate models.

Guideline 4: Adapt for Congruence   If it is found that an individual requires a modification to an activity, care should be taken to keep the activity as close to the original or standard version as possible to make it congruent. The implementation of unnecessarily exaggerated adaptations could make the participant stand out by accentuating his or her disabilities. In this manner, others could become more aware of the differences, and not the similarities, between themselves and the individual with disabilities.

Guideline 5: Adapt for Availability   Often an individual learns to use adapted equipment or materials exclusively in one environment, usually an "instruction" environment. The same modifications are usually not found or applicable in other "noninstruction" environments. For example, a person who learns to bowl using a tubular steel bowling ramp may not be able to bowl at a bowling alley where a ramp is not available. It may have been more practical to teach the individual how to use a bowling ball pusher or handle-grip bowling ball, which is less costly, more portable, and makes play accessible in any neighborhood bowling alley. Yet, elaborate and expensive devices such as a bowling ramp may be necessary for persons with more significant disabilities and should be employed in those cases. It is the activity leader's responsibility to consider these factors when making adaptation decisions. Problems with cost and availability may sometimes be overcome by encouraging community facility managers and owners to procure the specialized equipment themselves. The business owner or facility manager could purchase such devices as wise business investments that would make the facility accessible to all citizens of the community. The resulting increase in patronage could easily pay for the equipment many times over in a short period of time.

A SYSTEMIC EFFORT TO PROMOTE
LONG-TERM INCLUSION IN COMMUNITY RECREATION

The fact that an inclusive recreation program produces outstanding outcomes for participants, receives considerable attention from the media, and attracts many dollars from philanthropic sources does not guarantee that the program will maintain itself. In fact, some of the "hottest" programs disappear despairingly quickly and without fanfare. Although we cannot be certain why an apparently successful program begins to disintegrate, we are convinced that one of the major factors leading to program longevity is the quality and quantity of *systemic* efforts that go into and surround the program in supportive ways.

The key to successfully including persons with disabilities into community leisure services *across the lifespan* depends greatly on the amount and quality of networking that takes place. Networking is a process that seeks to establish ongoing and productive working relationships with others who are striving to meet similar ends. Seldom does the recreation professional operate alone as he or she formulates programming at the community center. Networking involves making connections with professionals from various disciplines and organizations, community members, parents, and consumers.

To ensure ongoing, accessible, and inclusive leisure services, one must identify all the "key players" affected and their roles and responsibilities within the community leisure service process. Key players could include parents and/or care providers; participants with and without disabilities; school/day program personnel; allied health professionals, including a therapeutic recreation specialist; advocacy groups; private recreation services (e.g., YMCA, Jewish Community Center, scout organizations); professional/educational resources (e.g., universities, consultants); and the community recreation professional. Each of these key players assumes a significant role by providing access to potential participants and to leisure environments. They provide the community recreator with pertinent information about individual participants, including their needs, preferences, and behavioral characteristics (Schleien & Ray, 1988).

Although social role valorization and LRE concepts have been a guiding force behind efforts to include persons with disabilities into the communities in which they live, adherence to the philosophy does not guarantee that persons with disabilities will be less isolated than if they live in institutions. Providing opportunities for people with significant disabilities to live in residential neighborhoods, work, or go to neighborhood schools is consistent with social role valorization, but is not sufficient to ensure social inclusion into a community on a comprehensive basis. All too often, people with disabilities living in community facilities have minimal contact with people without disabilities in their neighborhoods, spend little time participating in community environments, and may actually decrease their involvement in community activities over time. In contrast to this, true social inclusion in a community may be identified by the way people with disabilities are viewed by people without disabilities, the social environments they share, and the quality and quantity of participation in social interactions that parallel those of people without disabilities. Another indicator of social inclusion into the community includes regular and friendly contacts among citizens with and without disabilities similar to the interactions that occur among acquaintances without disabilities (i.e., horizontal interactions).

Integrated Bocce: An Example of a
Systemic Intervention for Promoting Long-Term Participation

Fortunately, there are several examples of successful community recreation programs designed to promote new skills and relationships between participants with and without disabilities across the lifespan. One such illustration of this systemic change is a neighborhood bocce league that was designed in St. Paul, Minnesota (Staur, 1991). Through the cooperative efforts of young adults with significant disabilities, parents, group home staff members, and members of the Minnesota Bocce Association, the participants learned to play the age-appropriate game of bocce and developed social skills (e.g., turn taking, cheering for one's teammates). As importantly, the bocce league became fully accommodating and may continue as an inclusive bocce program for years to come.

Bocce was selected because it has potential to become a lifelong recreation activity and because it is nonseasonal, can be played in almost any outdoor area, and can be enjoyed by males and females of all ages. Because it is an activity that can be broken down into small, observable steps (i.e., lends itself to task analysis), skill acquisition can be facilitated for individuals with significant disabilities. In addition, bocce is an activity that is naturally inclined toward creating close interaction with teammates, which can lead to increased social inclusion and the development of relationships.

Eight adults with significant disabilities participated in the program, ranging in age from 19 to 28 years. Four of the individuals had autism. Participants with disabilities were recruited from two group homes that were in close proximity to bocce playing areas in the community, providing the possibility for continued bocce play after the termination of this experimental program. Peer partners without disabilities ranged in age from 21 to 32 years.

During a 4-month period, acquisition, generalization, and maintenance of skills were assessed within and across four groups of participants, each group containing two bocce players with disabilities and two players without disabilities. Prior to the program, coaches were instructed on bocce rules, information on instructional and ball-handling techniques, and how to facilitate social interactions and relationships among players. Program sessions occurred once a week for approximately 2 hours each time. Attitudes of the participants without disabilities were assessed prior to the study, after 7 weeks, and at the end of the program to determine if they had changed toward their partners with disabilities who were improving their bocce skills.

Participants were assigned randomly to one of four teams. Participants without disabilities met with a therapeutic recreation specialist to develop sensitivity and skills in interacting more successfully with their teammates with disabilities. Preparation began with a discussion of experiences that the participants without disabilities had with the people with significant disabilities. This discussion was used as an "ice-breaker"; that is, it was used to make participants comfortable in sharing stories and information with each other. Specific concerns about and/or fears in interacting with individuals with disabilities were discussed, and successful techniques that could be used to interact with their peers were identified.

Four of the eight participants with significant disabilities acquired a substantial number of bocce skills. (Bocce skill acquisition was measured as a significant improvement in bocce skills when comparing baseline with intervention performance.) Six of the eight participants with disabilities also generalized these skills across environments and people. Although a positive correlation was not found between bocce skill acquisition by peers with disabilities and the attitudes of the peers without disabilities toward them, several of the responses provided during the attitude assessment indicated significant positive shifts regarding perceptions of participants with disabilities. Most importantly, the Minnesota Bocce Association has undergone systemic change that can now accommodate bocce players of all ability levels. New skills, new friends, and an accessible and ongoing community environment are now available to these "new" and active members of the bocce community.

SUMMARY

The inclusion of people with significant disabilities into community recreation programs is essential if the concepts of congruence and least restrictive environments are to be realized. Successful inclusion requires that those involved in service delivery adopt a philosophy and value system consistent with these principles. Of particular importance is a recognition that people with disabilities are valuable members of the community and have a right to participate in the same recreation programs in which their peers without disabilities participate. Agencies committed to these values must articulate and practice a philosophy of "inclusion" and "zero exclusion." These values must help to replace the creation and provision of segregated recreation programs that are exclusionary, unfair, unequal, and result in the removal of people with disabilities from the rest of society.

The authors' agenda for change—one that improves people's quality of life in their own communities—requires systemic efforts that go well beyond simple, short-term solutions. Long-lasting participation in community recreation requires cooperative efforts of individuals with disabilities, family members, recreation professionals, and others. We believe, and continue to demonstrate, that it is possible and beneficial to alter the way that community agencies think about and serve people with significant disabilities. Activities can be structured and modified to facilitate participation and the development of friendships, and problems that prevent people with disabilities from experiencing success can be avoided. Only when these "pieces of the puzzle" begin to interlock will people with significant disabilities become active and permanent participants in their communities.

Chapter 8

IMPLEMENTATION STRATEGIES FOR CLASSROOM, HOME, AND COMMUNITY

*T*eaching leisure-time skills to a participant with disabilities may well begin as a sequence of systematic instructional sessions carried out during designated times that are programmed within the schedule of daily activities. But the real world of one's leisure time does not take place during scripted sessions or even necessarily in designated locations. We use our leisure repertoire in the variety of settings and situations that occur in an often unplanned series of time periods (as well as planned activities). Because of this, no leisure education program would be complete without specifically addressing the practical issues involved in making certain that the learner can actually enjoy the new skills he or she is being taught. It is critical that the leisure educator keep in mind the learner's criterion leisure environments: For someone who is school age, these will include school, home, and various community environments. This chapter describes some helpful strategies that leisure educators can apply to ensure that leisure skills and activities are available to the learner during actual leisure time in those different environments.

CLASSROOM IMPLEMENTATION

The leisure educator who plans to implement a leisure education or recreation curriculum component in the educational program of one or more participants with disabilities must incorporate various programmatic, environmental, and practical considerations. The leisure educator must: 1) collaborate with the parents and other relevant team members to include one or more leisure instructional objectives in the participant's individualized education program (IEP), 2) arrange the appropriate instructional situations and environments, 3) schedule the necessary opportunities (including elective or "free play" times) to learn and practice the new leisure skills, and 4) establish a monitoring system to evaluate the success of the instructional program without interfering with the basic social and choice characteristics of leisure activities. In addition, the leisure educator must develop and implement a program to ensure that the participant's new leisure skills "generalize" to the many natural environments and situations where such skills are valued and needed—the reason for including leisure instruction in the participant's program in the first place! It would be difficult to imagine, for example, any meaningful leisure activity that is neither available to nor voluntarily chosen by the participant outside the classroom. Unless the leisure skills taught in school become an important and valued part of the participant's leisure time with friends, with family, at home, and in the community, they cannot become a meaningful contribution to the young person's repertoire and daily life.

Collaborating with Parents in Selecting IEP Objectives

In earlier chapters of this book, we have suggested a process for identifying individually appropriate leisure and recreation instructional objectives to include in a participant's IEP. Selecting such objectives follows the same general guidelines that would be followed in selecting any IEP objective. It also incorporates the preferences of the individual and his or her family as well as the skill level that person brings to the activity. Both the parents and professionals on the education team will have a great deal of information about what the participant would like to do and can do during leisure time. A major purpose of this book is to provide explicit instructional programs for a range of leisure and recreation activities that might be identified by the team as most appropriate and preferred for a particular participant. We have emphasized how critical it is that the participant likes the activity and wants to do it, and that his or her family and friends also like the activity and enjoy doing it with the individual. Without these essential ingredients, precious time will be wasted teaching skills that will never be used outside the classroom.

Ford et al.(1989) delineated a *Leisure Scope and Sequence Chart* that comprises five major goal areas that characterize leisure and recreation opportunities: 1) school and extracurricular, 2) activities to do alone at home and in the neighborhood, 3) activities to do with family and friends at home and in the neighborhood, 4) physical fitness, and 5) activities to do with family and friends in the community. The activities included in the curricular component in this book also represent these major goal areas; however, the process delineated in Ford et al. *The Syracuse Community-Referenced Curriculum Guide for Students with Moderate and Severe Disabilities* assists in identifying the objectives that should be priorities for an individual. Form 8.1 illustrates this *Leisure Scope and Sequence Chart* for the five goal areas at the different age levels from kindergarten (age 5) through transition (ages 19–21), with the activities from the curriculum component in this book added to the original chart that appeared in Ford et al. (1989, pp. 333–337).

Parents, teachers, and other members of the education team can reference the *Leisure Scope and Sequence Chart* in the different goal areas for the participant's age to explore a "menu" of leisure possibilities for the individual. Ideally, educational objectives in the leisure domain should address all five goal areas in each age range to adequately prepare someone for leisure time across the lifespan. Yet, in any given school year, a participant's IEP might include only one or two leisure objectives; therefore, priorities must be identified. As we have emphasized throughout this book, individual and family preferences must play a major role in identifying those priorities. The value of having a menu such as the one provided by Ford and her colleagues (1989) is that a family can see the range of possibilities that exist and then make the best choices for their child and themselves.

Arranging the Instructional Situation and Environment

Participants with disabilities may attend school in a variety of instructional arrangements, ranging from full inclusion with special education services provided in a general education classroom with same-age peers to a self-contained classroom including only other students with disabilities. Students with disabilities who are placed in educational programs where they have little to no contact with peers without disabilities are "handicapped" in their opportunities to develop appropriate and enjoyable leisure activity skills. Although students with disabilities can and do learn how to interact socially and spend their leisure time with classmates who have disabilities, the real world includes many peers who do not have disabilities. Learning how to spend enjoyable leisure time with same-age peers who do not have disabilities can greatly expand the recreation opportunities available outside school and across the lifespan to a person

A Leisure Scope and Sequence Chart

	Age and grade levels						
	Elementary school						
Goal areas	Kindergarten (age 5)	Primary grades (ages 6–8)	Intermediate grades (ages 9–11)	Middle school (ages 12–14)	High school (ages 15–18)	Transition (ages 19–21)	
School and extracurricular (*examples*)	Look at books	Read and look at books	Read books and magazines	Read books, magazines, newspapers	Read books, magazines, newspapers	Read books, magazines, newspapers	
	Play computer games, Game Boy	Play computer games, Game Boy	Play computer games, Game Boy	Play computer/electronic games, Game Boy	Play computer/electronic games, Game Boy	Play computer/electronic games, Game Boy	
	Use crayons	Make simple crafts	Take art class	Take elective class in interest area (music, art, pottery)	Take elective class in interest area (photography, electronics, pottery)	Take elective class in interest area (pottery, drama)	
	Play catch	Play catch	Shoot baskets/play catch	Shoot baskets/play catch	Shoot baskets/play catch	Shoot baskets/play catch	
	Engage in imaginary play	Play games at recess	Play games at recess	"Hang out" with friends	"Hang out" with friends	"Hang out" with friends	
			Take instrumental lessons	Take instrumental lessons	Take instrumental lessons	Take instrumental lessons	
			Participate in school musical programs	Participate in school musical programs	Participate in sports/chorus/band	Participate in sports/chorus/band	
				Attend special events as spectator (games)	Attend special events as spectator (sports, shows)	Attend special events as spectator (sports, concerts)	
				Attend school dances	Attend school dances	Attend school dances	
				Participate in clubs/activities (yearbook, newspaper)	Participate in clubs/activities (yearbook, pep rally, assemblies, science fair, student council)	Participate in clubs/activities (pep rally, assemblies, mock U.N.)	
					Participate in aerobics class	Participate in aerobics class	
Activities to do alone: at home and in the neighborhood (*examples*)	Look at books	Read and look at books	Read books and magazines	Read books, magazines, newspapers	Read books, magazines, newspapers	Read books, magazines, newspapers	
	Listen to music	Listen to music	Listen to music	Listen to music	Listen to music	Listen to music	

(continued)

163

Form 8.1 (continued)

		Elementary school		Age and grade levels		
Goal areas	Kindergarten (age 5)	Primary grades (ages 6–8)	Intermediate grades (ages 9–11)	Middle school (ages 12–14)	High school (ages 15–18)	Transition (ages 19–21)
Activities to do alone: at home and in the neighborhood (examples) (continued)	Play computer games, Game Boy Play musical instrument Draw or color pictures	Play computer games, Game Boy Play musical instrument Draw or color pictures Play Simon, pinball, remote control vehicle	Play computer games, Game Boy Play musical instrument Write cards, letters Play Simon, pinball, remote control vehicle	Play computer/electronic games, Game Boy Play musical instrument Write cards, letters Play Simon, pinball, remote control vehicle	Play computer/electronic games, Game Boy Play musical instrument Write cards, letters Cook/bake Play Simon, pinball, remote control vehicle	Play computer/electronic games, Game Boy Play musical instrument Write cards, letters Cook/bake Play Simon, pinball, remote control vehicle
	Watch television/videos	Watch television/videos Ride bike	Watch television/videos Ride bike/skateboard	Watch television/videos Walk/hike/bike/skateboard Take photos Pursue hobby (collecting baseball cards, crafts)	Watch television/videos Walk/hike/bike Take photos/videos Pursue hobby (sewing, painting)	Watch television/videos Walk/hike/bike Take photos/videos Pursue hobby (painting, drawing)
Activities to do with family and friends: at home and in the neighborhood (examples)	Play card games (fish, old maid) Play simple board games (Chutes and Ladders) Use swings/other playground equipment Play Magic Mitts Play table games (Connect Four, Jenga, pinball, Simon) Play target games	Play card games (Uno, war) Play board games (Sorry, Parchesi) Use swings/other playground equipment Play Magic Mitts Play table games (Connect Four, Jenga, pinball, Simon) Play target games Play kickball Play computer games, Game Boy	Play card games (rummy, crazy 8's) Play board games (Jr. Trivia, Monopoly, checkers) Shoot baskets/play catch Play Magic Mitts Play table games (Connect Four, Jenga, pinball, Simon) Play target games Play dodgeball, kickball Play computer games, Game Boy	Play card games (rummy, hearts) Play board games (Pictionary, checkers/chess) Shoot baskets/play catch Play Magic Mitts Play table games (Connect Four, Jenga, pinball, Simon) Play target games Play ball games (softball, basketball) Play computer/video games, Game Boy	Play card games (pinochle, hearts) Play board games (Trivial Pursuit, Pictionary) Shoot baskets/play catch Play Magic Mitts Play table games (Connect Four, Jenga, pinball, Simon) Play target games Play ball games (softball, soccer) Play computer/video games, Game Boy	Play card games (bridge, poker, gin rummy) Play board games (Trivial Pursuit, Pictionary, chess) Shoot baskets/play catch Play Magic Mitts Play table games (Connect Four, Jenga, pinball, Simon) Play target games Play ball games and yard games (croquet, volleyball, Bocce, basketball) Play computer/video games, Game Boy

Physical fitness (examples)					
Swim/play in back-yard pool Watch television/videos	Swim in backyard pool Watch television/videos Ride bike Play bean bag toss Invite friends over Participate in playground program (summer) Participate in exercise routine	Swim in backyard pool Watch television/videos Ride bike/skateboard Play ring toss Invite friends over Participate in playground program (summer) Participate in exercise routine	Swim in backyard pool Watch television/videos Ride bike/skateboard Play ping pong, darts Invite friends over Use local parks Talk on telephone Participate in exercise routine in physical education class Participate in conditioning for team sport (soccer, track, football) Play sport regularly for exercise (volleyball, basketball, cross-country skiing)	Swim in backyard pool Watch television/videos Ride bike Play ping pong, shoot pool Invite friends over/have party Use local parks Talk on telephone Participate in exercise routine in physical education class Participate in conditioning for team sport (soccer, track, football) Play sport regularly for exercise (tennis, basketball) Lift weights Participate in aerobic dance/exercise class Bike/swim/jog/walk regularly for exercise	Swim in backyard pool Watch television/videos Ride bike Play ping pong, shoot pool Invite friends over/have party Use local parks Talk on telephone Participate in exercise routine in physical education class Bike/swim/jog/walk for exercise Play sport regularly for exercise (tennis, basketball) Lift weights Participate in aerobic dance/exercise class Bike/swim/jog/walk regularly for exercise

(continued)

Form 8.1 *(continued)*

Goal areas	Age and grade levels					
	Kindergarten (age 5)	Elementary school		Middle school (ages 12–14)	High school (ages 15–18)	Transition (ages 19–21)
		Primary grades (ages 6–8)	Intermediate grades (ages 9–11)			
Physical fitness (examples) *(continued)*					Do workout routine to videotape/music	Do workout routine to videotape/music
Activities to do alone: in the community *(examples)*			Use public library	Use public library / Ride bike / Walk/hike / Shop	Use public library / Ride bike, all-terrain vehicle (ATV, snowmobile) / Go for drive / Shop	Use public library / Ride bike, ATV, moped, snowmobile / Go for drive / Shop
			Go to video arcade	Go to restaurant with friends / Go to video arcade	Go to restaurant with friends / Go to shopping mall with friends / Go to video arcade	Go to restaurant with friends / Go to shopping mall with friends / Go to video arcade
Activities to do with family and friends: in the community *(examples)*	Use parks and playgrounds / Use public library / Go to shopping malls with family	Use parks and playgrounds / Use public library / Go to shopping malls with family / Use public pool / Take lessons (dance, gymnastics, swimming)	Use parks / Use public library / Go to shopping malls with family / Use public pool / Take lessons (dance, gymnastics, swimming)	Use parks / Use public library / Go to shopping malls with family and/or friends / Use public pool / Take lessons (karate, horseback riding, music)	Use parks / Use public library / Hang out at shopping mall with friends / Use public pool / Take lessons (music, dancing)	Use parks / Use public library / Hang out at shopping mall with friends / Use public pool / Take lessons (music, ceramics)

Go to day camp	Go to summer camp (overnight)	Go to sports camp	Go to camps (sports, band)	Go to retreats, conferences
Participate in Cub Scouts/Brownies	Participate in Boy Scouts/Girl Scouts	Join youth group	Join youth group	Join community group
	Play on recreation team (soccer, football)	Play on recreation team (soccer, baseball)	Play on recreation team (soccer, bowling, swimming)	Play on recreation team (soccer, bowling, swimming)
	Attend spectator events (sports, ice skating shows)	Attend spectator events, sports, concerts	Attend spectator events (sports, concerts)	Attend spectator events (sports, concerts)
		Go camping (family/youth groups)	Go camping with friends (supervised)	Go camping with friends
		Go to teen center	Go to teen center	Go to church group/meeting
		Go boating/fishing	Go fishing/boating	Go fishing/hunting
		Go to movies	Go to movies	Go to movies
			Go dancing: clubs Ski, skate, snowmobile	Go dancing: clubs Ski, skate, snowmobile
				Attend work-related social events
			Participate in aerobics class	Participate in aerobics class

Adapted from Ford, Schnorr, Meyer, Davern, Black, & Dempsey (1989).

Note: Unshaded activities are those that can be incorporated in the school day; shaded activities are those that are better suited to instruction during *nonschool* hours.

with disabilities. In fact, the more significant the disability, the more critical such contact becomes. A group of peers with significant disabilities are simply not in the best position to join together to take advantage of the variety of leisure and recreation activities available in the community. Yet, a peer with a significant disability who has a friend without a disability has a companion who can expand community access in multiple ways. Thus, particularly in the leisure domain, contact with peers without disabilities is essential to the development of a meaningful, lifelong leisure repertoire.

Whatever the educational placement, the leisure educator must identify the appropriate time and place to conduct structured leisure instruction and provide for generalization of learned skills to nonstructured times and places. Typical classrooms are organized for academic activities, with some predictable differences across age ranges. For example, an elementary classroom is typically organized into a main instruction or large group area with other learning sub-areas around the room. In this environment, one of the learning centers might incorporate leisure activities for "choice time" in the classroom, and the leisure educator might use this area for structured leisure instruction with a pair of children several times weekly—a child with disabilities and one or more peers interested in participating in the activity.

At the middle school level, classrooms are typically assigned to subject areas; that is, one room is the location for social studies, another is for English, another is for math, a fourth is for science, and so forth. These "academic" rooms may not be readily amenable to a leisure instructional area; indeed, it might appear so odd for a student with disabilities to be taken aside for leisure instruction in such a room that doing so would further isolate that individual from his or her peers. Instead, leisure instruction might occur in the "home base" time period and room that generally occupies one class period daily in middle schools. In one middle school, for example, a cluster of six subject area teachers plus one special education teacher instruct a subgroup of approximately 135 students at a particular age level to create a smaller sense of community within a large middle school population. Each day, these students are part of one of six (for the six teachers) "Champ" periods, which are like the traditional homeroom time. The major purpose of this Champ period is to foster community and team cohesiveness. The teaching team often conducts special activities during this time period that have been designed by the interdisciplinary team. Leisure instruction could be incorporated into the weekly schedule for a homeroom period such as this one in the majority of middle and junior high schools.

High school and community college environments present different challenges to a leisure educator's efforts to deliver leisure instruction to a participant with disabilities. If a homeroom or team period exists in a high school, the process described for middle schools could also be implemented at the high school level. If not, the leisure educator could, either alone or by teaming with various general education teachers (particularly the physical education staff), offer selected leisure activity electives as part of the curriculum each semester. Peers without disabilities could enroll in such electives or participate for "service" credits for other courses (e.g., government); however, the latter creates a hierarchical structure for leisure activities that unnecessarily stigmatizes social interactions with peers with disabilities as a kind of charitable act or work task. If no other option exists, however, leisure educators can work with the administration to "package" such opportunities in as positive a way as possible, limited only by their own creativity and commitment to do so. A similar process could be utilized at the community college level, although most colleges offer many recreation course options that greatly expand instructional opportunities.

Wherever the physical location of leisure instruction in school, the leisure educator must plan carefully to ensure that the principle of leisure activities as a matter of personal choice during free time—to do as one prefers, alone or with family or friends—is reflected in the program. Participants with severe cognitive disabilities, for example, will not automatically generalize skills and opportunities utilized in structured classroom situations to options available during their free time and in nonschool leisure environments and situations. To ensure that this transfer occurs, the leisure educator must systematically provide opportunities for use of the leisure skills in less structured situations and assist family, friends, and other caregivers outside of school to participate with the individual in leisure activities at home and in community recreation environments.

Thus, instruction on leisure activities should be conducted in the most natural environments at school, within areas of the classroom designated for such activities for all students. In arranging these areas, leisure educators should be certain that: 1) the leisure activities (at least one set of materials for each activity being taught, with enough to provide all participants with options) and any necessary activity pictures are easily accessible and visible to all the participants; and 2) there is enough room for participants to engage in the activities, especially those requiring a lot of space and special floor surfaces. Whenever possible, the area should be large enough to accommodate several participants at once. Scheduling then becomes easier and more flexible and the leisure educator can structure situations to teach such social interactions as sharing, taking turns, and selecting another choice.

If additional free-time environments are available in a classroom or school, the leisure educator should try to conduct instruction sessions in more than one environment. One of the goals of this curriculum component is to have participants with disabilities initiate play with an appropriate leisure activity whenever he or she has free time. When instruction is conducted in multiple environments, individuals are more likely to generalize play skills to other natural environments outside of the school.

While it is advisable to instruct participants in natural, multiple environments, there are some participants for whom an alternative arrangement is more appropriate. For a participant who is extremely distractible, disruptive, and/or who fails to show interest in the leisure activities (at least initially), it may be beneficial to begin by conducting the instruction sessions wherever the individual has performed best in prior educational programs. This may require some "pull-out" instruction at first, perhaps including the involvement of a volunteer peer without disabilities who is interested in becoming a friend and/or helper for the individual with a disability. Then, as the participant is consistently attending and responding to instructional cues and the leisure activity, the environment can be modified to more closely resemble the classroom's actual play area and free-time situation(s). Gradually, as the participant consistently performs the appropriate manipulations with the leisure activity and appears to enjoy it, instructions can be shifted to more natural and multiple environments. It is important to remember that, until the participant performs the skills of the task analysis in multiple, natural free-time environments, the leisure educator should not consider the instruction complete.

Scheduling Opportunities to Learn and Practice

Before the leisure educator can schedule any instruction and choice sessions for all of his or her participants, he or she must decide: 1) how often instruction should occur; 2) how long each session should be; 3) when instruction should occur; 4) who should provide the instruction; and 5) who else, if anyone, should participate (e.g., a peer without disabilities).

Data from our field tests indicate that frequent instruction sessions (with a sufficient number of learning trials in each session) are required if participants with developmental disabilities are to meet with success and acquire new play skills. This implies that instruction on each leisure activity should occur at least two to three times weekly, and that participants need an adequate amount of time during each session to master the activities. At the same time, each instruction session must be tailored to individual participants' attention spans and their tolerance for structured learning situations. This is particularly important if a participant is resistant to any structured situation. Leisure activities are supposed to be preferred activities for one's free time, so perceptions of "compliance" and being forced to engage in something one protests would defeat the purpose of such a curriculum component. Once an activity has taken on a negative tone for an individual, it is difficult to envision how the activity could ever be viewed as something that he or she would prefer or choose to do during his or her free time. For participants with long histories of failure in new skills or activities, instruction, even on an activity they seem to enjoy, may set the stage for a display of challenging behaviors. To constructively deal with participants who display challenging behaviors and/or poor attention, and, at the same time, to provide an enjoyable atmosphere for the sessions, it may be necessary to initially schedule brief instruction sessions at different times throughout the week. The leisure educator might also need to have flexible expectations and be alert for signs that trouble is about to occur; for example, knowing when to stop a session before the participant is aware of losing interest and/or becoming disruptive. Then, as the participant begins to experience success and consistently gains access to the leisure activity's reinforcing characteristics, including enjoying play with a peer, the length of the sessions may be gradually increased to a typical time period for such an activity. Table 8.1 provides a list of guidelines for scheduling structured instruction sessions.

During these sessions, there is the possibility of satiation; that is, continuous and frequent exposure to the same activity may lead to a decrease in a participant's preference for that leisure activity. If this occurs, a participant may then display poor attending or interfering behavior, or may simply indicate a preference to do something else during the sessions. The leisure educator should be aware of this possibility and remain flexible enough to modify the individual's schedule if necessary. At some point, participants should also be made aware of the scheduling of various leisure activities; for example, some events are typically available on weekends and not during the week or during a school day (e.g., spectator sports). Other activities might be allowed during breaks in the school day, but would be highly disapproved of during so-called free time in a classroom after one's work is completed (e.g., playing a computer game on Game Boy). Thus, participants should be encouraged to associate particular days, times, and places with particular leisure activities whenever this is appropriate. At the same time, they should not be made to

Table 8.1.   Guidelines for scheduling instruction sessions

1. Schedule instruction sessions to ensure a sufficient number of learning trials in each session. In general, a skill acquisition instruction session should include a minimum of *15 minutes* of actual instruction time. Choice instruction sessions should initially be 15 minutes if choice teaching method I (see Chapter 6) is implemented, or they should correspond to the time specified for the session by the choice level.

2. Schedule skill acquisition instruction sessions as frequently as possible, with a minimum of *three* sessions per week (i.e., at least every other day) for each activity being taught. Choice instruction sessions should occur at least *twice* a week.

3. Spread out the instruction sessions throughout the school week. Avoid teaching two activities or conducting two sessions for one activity back to back.

4. Schedule instruction sessions to correspond as much as possible to naturally occurring free time, but vary the activities that are taught during that free time from day to day.

5. Accommodate individual participants' attention spans and interest levels. Gradually build sustained attention and tolerance for instruction. (See pp. 27 and 28 on shaping attending behaviors.)

6. Assign instruction sessions so that more than one person or peer teaches each leisure activity.

think that an activity can only be played at one particular time, with a certain individual, and on a certain day; for example, a participant should not be led to believe that he or she can only play pinball games at 1:00 P.M. on Mondays with Mr. Jackson nearby. Such a situation would imply that there is no choice and, therefore, no true leisure.

Just as it is important to teach a leisure skill during various times and in more than one place to facilitate generalization to typical leisure opportunities, it is also important for multiple teachers and/or leisure educators to be available. In addition to varying the activities, the days and times of the instruction sessions, and the instructors (both professional and paraprofessional staff), leisure educators must include opportunities to interact with a peer(s) during leisure instruction and free time, as is appropriate for the activity. A participant learning a particular leisure activity must also learn how to enjoy that activity with family members and one or more friends, and must learn the various social rules and routines for enjoying the activities with different people. A general rule of thumb is that there must be some effort to ensure that leisure activity skills are practiced with people other than paid instructional staff before an instructional program is viewed as complete. This implies that opportunities to engage in an activity with peers and/or family members present and/or participating is essential to any leisure curriculum component.

Establishing a Monitoring System

Teachers responsible for the education of students with disabilities can have an overwhelming number of forms to fill out, data to record, guidelines to follow, and people to whom they must answer about each and every student in their classes. They must, therefore, have some system for keeping track of each student's educational programs and for making certain that these programs are not only being conducted, but that they are being conducted in a consistent, high-quality manner. A traditional data collection system, such as using a student file or clipboard system, could meet such demands, but could also be prohibitively intrusive in various leisure environments. Clearly, continuous data on "leisure trials" would not be appropriate for a leisure curriculum component; furthermore, most educators do not believe that continuous records are necessary to adequately monitor a student's performance. However, deciding on a data monitoring system that will provide information on student performance without interfering with the integrity of the leisure activity situation is important.

In the first version of this curriculum (Wuerch & Voeltz, 1982), teachers were asked to complete extensive data records regarding student performance. Although these were generally "user-friendly" in format and all forms had been extensively field tested, experience has taught us in the past decade that teachers cannot, in fact, keep such systematic data records while functioning as teachers. In addition, at the time the earlier version was published, many students with developmental disabilities were still enrolled in fairly restrictive programs. The students who served as our field-test sample did attend school on general education campuses, but they were typically isolated from peers without disabilities and were enrolled in segregated classrooms only for students with similar disabilities. Today's students with developmental disabilities are far more likely to have opportunities to attend general education classes and to receive community-based instruction. Although it may have been possible for special education teachers to follow students around with clipboards in classrooms only for students with disabilities, to do so in general education classrooms or in the community would represent an intolerable stigmatization for today's students with disabilities. Our expectations for evaluating student performance must, therefore, be reasonable, unobtrusive, and typical, as well as provide a valid measure of whether learning is occurring.

Before beginning any instruction session, the leisure educator should have the following records on file:

1. A Repertoire Chart for the leisure domain appropriate for the participant's age level that has been completed by the parent and team members, with priorities identified. Form 8.2 provides a completed chart for a hypothetical student attending high school. This chart represents one age range for the *Leisure Scope and Sequence* described earlier in this chapter. Keeping such a record across all age ranges allows the family and the education team to coordinate leisure planning to ensure that the participant receives comprehensive leisure instruction opportunities by the time he or she leaves school, as well as a meaningful leisure repertoire.

2. A Participant Interest Inventory (Form 2.3), as described in Chapter 2, that is filled out and has been used in the process of identifying priorities for the current year's instructional activities. As instruction proceeds, other records addressing instructional procedures and sessions should be completed and added to the participant's file, along with any other information that the leisure educator believes is relevant to providing an accurate and helpful record of the participant's progress in acquiring a leisure repertoire.

There are several forms that the leisure educator should design and/or adapt to provide a record of participant performance on leisure activity instructional objectives:

1. A Monthly Instruction Record (Form 8.3) can help the leisure educator schedule whatever activities the participant is playing with during a particular month. The leisure educator should record opportunities for choice, planned sessions with different leisure activities, and actual implementation of both choice opportunities and instruction sessions. The sample Monthly Instruction Record includes a row for each day of the month as well as columns for choice data and up to four leisure activities that can be taught. We suggest that the leisure educator set "schedule goals" for these choices and instruction sessions at the beginning of each month, including assigned responsibilities for supervising such sessions by different instruction personnel. Then, as sessions occur, staff persons responsible can initial that date/session to indicate that choice and/or instruction took place. This form is important for two reasons. First, mapping out the entire month in this way helps the leisure educator to determine whether instruction expectations are reasonable for participants and staff. If the schedule appears unreasonable, modifications should be made to generate a plan that can be implemented. Second, when the month has ended, a visual check of the form will inform the leisure educator whether or not sufficient instruction and/or choice opportunities were in fact made available to a participant. It may well be that lack of progress in learning to express preferences or in mastering a particular leisure activity will be reflected in few actual opportunities to practice and learn such skills. If the participant has had few instruction opportunities, it would be precipitous to abandon a particular objective until those opportunities have indeed occurred.

2. The Participant Information Sheet (Form 8.4) should be designed to include essential individualized information about each participant that would be helpful to anyone carrying out or participating in leisure activity instruction for a participant. Our Participant Information Sheet includes a "brief biography" of the individual that both creates a positive image of the participant and communicates any characteristic that someone who interacts with that individual should know. Thus, in our example, we have communicated that the leisure educator must be aware that Dana may resist physical assistance during transitions. The form is also designed to provide peers, teachers, therapeutic recreation specialists, paraprofessionals, and community agency personnel with information on any

IMPLEMENTATION STRATEGIES

Leisure Repertoire Chart

FORM 8.2

Repertoire chart for: ___High School (ages 15–18)___ Participant: _Shaniqua_

Domain: ___Recreation/Leisure___ Age: _16_ Date: _10/2_

Goal area	Present activities	Performance level — Check one				Critical features — Check all that apply				Note priority goal areas
		Assistance on most steps	Assistance on some steps	Independent	Has related social skills?	Obviously enjoys	Age appropriate	Interacts w/ peers w/o disabilities		
School and extra-curricular (examples)	Attends aerobics class	✓				✓	✓	✓		Needs extra-curricular activity!
	Attends art class	✓				✓	✓	✓		
Activities to do alone: at home and in the neighborhood (examples)	Watches TV		✓			✓	✓			Needs to learn how to use cassette player. Could she learn a computer game?
	Listens to radio		✓			✓	✓			
Activities to do with family and friends: at home and in the neighborhood (examples)	Goes to fast food restaurant w/ family	✓				✓	✓			Could she do this with a school friend? Using a library would be nice!
Physical fitness (examples)										Continue
Activities to do alone: in the community (examples)										Family does not believe this is appropriate now.
Activities to do with family and friends: in the community (examples)										Could she participate?

Monthly Instruction Record for ___April___
(name of month)

Participant: ___Dana Johnson___

Leisure Educators: ___Amy Selemister___
___Sandy Brown___

Date	Choice	Game Boy (name of activity)	Magic Mitts (name of activity)	Connect Four (name of activity)	Target Game (name of activity)
1					
2	AS	SB		AS	
3		AS	SB		
4	AS	AS	SB	AS	
5					SB
6			AS	SB	
7					
8					
9					
10					
11					
12					
13					
14					
15					
16					
17					
18					
19					
20					
21					
22					
23					
24					
25					
26					
27					
28					
29					
30					
31					

Participant Information Sheet

Participant: _Dana Johnson_   Date: _9/7/94_   Completed by: _Amy Selemister_

1. Participant's preferred instructional cues:
   Verbal and modeling

2. Participant's preferred positive reinforcers:
   Verbal praise (eg., "Good job, Dana," "All right!")

3. Participant's functioning language levels:
   How participant listens or understands:
   Understands simple directions and appears to understand classroom conversation.

   How participant talks or communicates:
   Does not initiate spontaneous speech. Usually speaks only when spoken to or when asked a question that demands a verbal answer.

4. Participant's disability: _SMR — seizure disorder_

5. Participant's behavioral problems and leisure educators' intervention procedures:
   often noncompliant — pretends not to hear. Follow-through on all commands is necessary; physical assist is often necessary; however, sometimes she resists.
   It's often helpful to say "Dana, can I help you?"

other characteristics that would be useful to know during free time with Dana. We recommend that the form avoid categories and descriptors that reflect professional jargon or include information that has little or no relevance to leisure-time activity interactions. Thus, rather than using "expressive language," we chose to state "How Dana talks or communicates." The form does include, however, any emergency information, such as what to do in the event that a student engages in a particular behavior that might be dangerous to himself or herself or others. Similarly, information on special equipment needed or movement recommendations would be noted. This would ensure that special supports are available during free time as they would be during structured instruction with a leisure educator or therapist.

3.   The Program Cover Sheet (Form 8.5) provides individualized information on the participant's instructional program for a particular leisure activity. Any given participant will generally require modifications based on individualized needs to the task analysis delineated for the leisure activity presented earlier in Chapter 4. These modifications would include such things as individualized instructional cues; changes or branches in the task analysis; decisions about where, when, and with whom instruction should best occur for that participant; and various additional instruction details relevant for that activity and participant. The form should include sufficient detail to enable a substitute teacher to follow the task analysis with the modifications included on the Program Cover Sheet to deliver the leisure instruction as designed. This detail will also be helpful in the future should the participant fail to progress in a particular program despite an apparent interest in the leisure activity. By examining the information on the Program Cover Sheet, the team can problem solve changes to the program that might better support learning. If, however, no individualized information is recorded regarding how a particular program is actually being taught to a participant, the team has only its intuitions to guide efforts to redesign a "program" that may be poorly individualized and taught inconsistently across staff and situations.

Because instructional environments differ from classroom to classroom, and because the leisure educator should attempt to include multiple instructional environments in most participants' programs, the particular environment(s) should be described on this form. The leisure educator should also list whatever materials and equipment he or she uses to create the instructional environments or to modify the activity. These materials are not the ones that constitute the activity, usually listed in the instructional objective as one of the "givens," but rather the additional materials the leisure educator uses to help the individual read the objective (e.g., masking tape to mark distances, a box to prop up Connect Four).

4.   The Participant Performance Data Sheet (Form 4.1) includes the individualized student steps of the task analysis. This form was introduced and described in detail in Chapter 4 as part of the procedures for skill acquisition instruction. We recommend that the leisure educator review all of his or her participants' files every 2 weeks; informally evaluate the participants' performances; and, based on this informal review, identify programs that require a more formal evaluation. If the necessary information is available in the records to modify a program that is apparently unsuccessful, changes should be decided upon and recorded on the Program Cover Sheet. If insufficient data are available to make changes, the leisure educator should schedule a direct observation of a leisure activity instruction session conducted by another staff member, with time after the session to problem solve with other staff as well as peers without disabilities who might be participating in the program. Ideas for modifying the program should then be recorded on a new Program Cover Sheet and reevaluated after 2 additional weeks of instruction and then

Program Cover Sheet

Participant: Dana Johnson

Activity: Jenga

Date participant baselined: 4/1/94

Date instruction sessions initiated: 4/4/94

Date instruction sessions terminated: _____

1. Instructional objective: Given the tower of Jenga blocks, Dana will take turns with a peer without a disability removing a block from below the top story of the tower and stacking it on top of the tower on 80% of the trials over three consecutive instruction sessions.

2. Any modifications to task analysis: _____

3. Instructional environment(s) and additional materials: Jenga, table and chairs, peer without a disability, leisure instruction area

4. Instructional procedures:

   Teaching method: individual step instruction

   Instructional cues: verbal (Dana often resists physical contact)

   Positive reinforcement: "Good job, Dana!" "Hey, that's great!" "Way to go!"

   Data collection: Use Skill Acquisition Data Record

   Correction procedures: "Oops, try again" — then repeat instructional cue. Reinforce her when she does it correctly.

   Other: _____

5. Behavior interventions: Easily distracted by newcomers in her environment — when this occurs, repeat cue, "Dana, play Jenga."

again after 2 more weeks of instruction. The files should also be summarized every year prior to the annual IEP meeting. They should be shared with the participants' parents to help in selecting priorities for the coming year prior to the design of the next year's goals and objectives.

LEISURE IN THE HOME

Because most of an individual's leisure time is likely to occur outside of school and particularly at home, it is especially critical that the leisure educator coordinate leisure planning with parents, caregivers, and siblings to facilitate a meaningful leisure repertoire for the participant. As mentioned earlier, our model begins with an assessment of the participant's leisure activities and a summary of priorities that would be completed by the parent or caregiver. Parental involvement in selecting activities for inclusion on the IEP and for instruction is an essential first step. If parents are not actively involved in identifying activities that they support for their child, it is unlikely that the necessary out-of-school opportunities to actually enjoy those leisure activities will occur. This is particularly true if the activities are in any way dependent on support from the family, as many activities are. Thus, in addition to assessing the participant's present level of leisure functioning, the Leisure Time at Home Needs Assessment (see Form 9.6) evaluates what parents feel are important leisure activity needs for free time at home. This form is described in detail in Chapter 9. Through collaborative decision making with the parents in identifying leisure education needs, the leisure educator can also assist parents in making decisions regarding appropriate leisure activities for the home and in selecting activities for purchase for their child.

The leisure educator should arrange for time to consult with the family (parents/caregivers and, if possible, siblings) on various aspects of encouraging use of leisure activity skills at home. For example, by teaching parents how to cue their child that he or she has free time as well as how to provide activity options, leisure educators make a major contribution toward ensuring that the concepts of leisure time, activity preferences, and choice making have meaning outside the classroom. A participant's leisure opportunities after school and on weekends offer many natural opportunities to develop understandings of when, where, and with whom one has free time and choices. However, school does not lend itself as readily to teaching the differences between work and play or free time and work time. In fact, it is one's home and time outside of the structured school day or workday that defines free time. Therefore, it is important to keep careful track of an individual's needs and preferences in afterschool and afterwork environments.

Finally, the leisure educator should also be prepared to show a parent or a sibling how their family member with a disability has been taught to play with a particular activity, and then develop their confidence in trying those activities with the participant at home. Many parents and/or siblings may be interested in conducting some systematic leisure instruction at home and in the neighborhood. If this is the case, the leisure educator should teach them how to do so. The choice procedures described in Chapter 6 are easy to implement and provide an excellent and natural opportunity for family involvement in the participant's leisure education. If parents do not feel that they can conduct instruction sessions, they may be encouraged to be involved more informally. We suggest asking the family to use the Home Leisure Data Sheet (Form 8.6) to record any of the self-initiated play behaviors they happen to observe. If the child does not initiate play at all, suggest prompting the child to interact with an activity at least once every 2–3 days. Again, there should be some carry-over of leisure activity availability at home not only to facilitate generalization of the participant's new skills, but, perhaps most importantly, to accom-

Participant's name: __Dana Johnson__

Activities available: __pinball, Nintendo Game Boy, Magic Mitts, Connect Four, Simon__

Date	Initials	Activity was: P = prompted I = child initiated	Activity	Play was: A = appropriate I = inappropriate	Comments and/or what the child did
4/27	SJ	I	pinball	A	Dana pulled the shooter and used the flippers a lot.
4/28	SJ	I	Magic Mitts	A	Handed ball to brother to play with her.
4/29	SJ	I	pinball	I	Kept lifting the machine, dropping it lightly on the table, and laughing.
4/30	SJ	I	Simon	A	Could only match 2 colors. Played for 1 hour.
5/2	SJ	I	pinball	A	warned before play not to drop it, or I would take it away. Did not drop machine.
5/3	SJ	I	pinball	A	played really nicely – no warning.
5/5	SJ	I	Magic Mitts	A	Asked brother to play again.
5/6	SJ	I	Simon	A	matched 3 colors!
5/7	SJ	I	pinball	I	Kept bouncing machine - finally I took it away.
5/8	SJ	I	pinball	A	was good with pinball. Laughed.

plish the true intent of leisure instruction—to give the individual something enjoyable to do during nonstructured time, alone and with family and friends.

Of course, different families have different values and resources regarding their involvement in their child's leisure education. Therefore, the leisure educator must individualize his or her interactions with each family, just as he or she must individualize the participant's educational program. (The home and family involvement component is discussed in detail in the next chapter.)

LEISURE IN THE COMMUNITY

In the past, opportunities for community leisure activities were limited primarily to specialized programs and facilities designed for and including only persons with disabilities; for example, a "special" recreation program at a "special school." Special Olympics also continues to be a major focus of recreation activities for persons with disabilities in many communities. While these programs may accommodate some leisure activity needs of a person with disabilities, they are not a substitute for lifelong leisure activities that are a more natural part of various home and neighborhood environments and situations. An analogy might be a person's involvement in a bowling league: Belonging to and participating in a structured bowling league on a regular basis is no doubt enjoyable and motivating to those who choose to participate, but it is only a small part of the participant's leisure repertoire. Belonging to a bowling league will not help a person to enjoy his or her free time alone, with family members, or with friends. Thus, participation in an activity such as Special Olympics or a "Handicapped Camp" is not a substitute for participation in integrated neighborhood recreation environments and activities.

Within each age range, the leisure educator should collaborate with the family to assess the community for specific environments that will provide the individual with opportunities to apply leisure skills learned in school with peers who do not have disabilities. The Leisure Repertoire Chart (see Form 8.2) assists in this process. Variations of many of the leisure activities included in this curricular component, such as pinball, are widely available in communities (e.g., in shopping centers, video arcades, bowling alleys, waiting areas of restaurants, airports). The leisure educator should structure situations in which the individual can participate in these activities in the community as part of the educational program (see Ford et al., 1989, for one model of implementing community instruction). In fact, unless the leisure educator becomes familiar with these community opportunities to actually enjoy the leisure activities being learned by the participant at school, important related skills needed to access the leisure activity in the community could be overlooked, such as learning to use the coin slot on commercial pinball machines and video games.

Once the participant with disabilities has developed some initial skills with a leisure activity, the leisure educator can also support opportunities to use those new skills while interacting with peers and friends who do not have disabilities in typical community environments. At the middle or high school level in particular, peers without disabilities can be recruited to participate in tutorial activities that involve going with a friend with disabilities to a community environment to learn how to use new leisure skills in that environment. Initially, such joint activities might be directly supported and even supervised by teaching staff. Later, these participants can, if they wish, spend their free time together in the community on their own. Supporting such peer opportunities should be an important part of a comprehensive leisure curriculum component, and evidence that participants with disabilities subsequently do use their leisure skills with friends outside of school would be a sure sign of success for this instructional component.

Most people spend at least some of their free time in the company of another person—usually someone considered a friend. Participants with developmental disabilities may need to be taught to use their leisure skills in a social manner with friends and family members. This requires that the participant be instructed in a variety of complementary skills not specifically included in this leisure activity curriculum component, such as asking someone to play, taking turns, sharing materials, providing reinforcement to the other person, and so forth. To teach these social skills, the leisure educator can incorporate them into the steps of a participant's task analysis and teach a step such as waiting to take a turn just as he or she would teach any other step of the task analysis. Pinball games, video games, target games, and various other recreation activities lend themselves well to dyadic or small group leisure participation involving persons with and without disabilities playing together. Whereas this curriculum component does not include details on teaching these social skills, leisure educators who are interested can reference other materials for guidelines. In addition, we have included the Assessment of Social Competence in Appendix D to assist in this process (Meyer, Reichle, et al., 1985; St. Peter, Ayres, Meyer, & Park-Lee, 1989).

A leisure educator should not underestimate the nature of relationships between participants with even the most significant developmental disabilities and their peers without disabilities. There is evidence that, in the context of leisure activity interactions, teenagers and young adults without disabilities characterize their relationships to peers with developmental disabilities in manners similar to the descriptions offered for more traditional friendships between two peers without disabilities (Green & Schleien, 1991; Kishi & Meyer, in press; Voeltz & Brennan, 1984). Similarly, elementary-age children with and without disabilities express similar reasons why they like each other and are friends: A friend is "someone to have fun with," "someone to eat lunch with," "someone who calls you on the telephone," and "someone who doesn't boss you around" (Heyne, Schleien, & McAvoy, 1993, pp. 1–2). There is also evidence that individuals with developmental disabilities display clear indications of enjoyment and preference for such activities with peers and friends without disabilities (Rynders et al., 1993; Schleien & Ray, 1988; Vandercook, 1991).

USING FOCUS GROUPS TO FACILITATE
HOME–SCHOOL–COMMUNITY COLLABORATION

Thus far, this chapter has addressed the implementation of leisure programs in classrooms, homes, and community environments. Leisure instruction in each of these environments is vital to shaping an individual's lifelong leisure skills and independent leisure lifestyle. How much more powerful could this leisure instruction be if active collaboration and planning occurs among parents, teachers, and community recreation staff on a regular basis? Through coordinated planning among persons in an individual's home, school, and community environments, participants have increased opportunities to practice, generalize, and learn new leisure skills. In this section, we present a vehicle for such collaboration: the use of focus groups.

A focus group is a guided group discussion that brings people together to freely share their perspectives on a given topic without judgment or censorship (Krueger, 1988). Focus groups enable people to express their opinions, discuss issues, exchange ideas, assess needs, generate solutions, plan programs, and evaluate outcomes. Given that the needs of each person are individualized and the situation of each community is unique, focus groups are an effective and flexible means of personalizing people's experiences and applying solutions to meet specific needs and circumstances.

In the area of leisure programming for individuals with disabilities, focus groups may be used to address a variety of questions or concerns across home, school, and community environments. Examples of focus group questions might be:

- What are the individual's leisure needs, abilities, and goals?
- Why is leisure instruction across home, school, and community environments important for the individual?
- In which leisure activities can the individual participate across home, school, and community environments?
- Who is responsible for providing leisure instruction in these environments?
- What community leisure resources are available to the individual?
- How can leisure activities be used to encourage friendships for the individual?
- What obstacles currently prevent friendships from occurring?
- How can friendships be nurtured across home, school, and community environments?

Of course, focus group questions will vary from individual to individual and from community to community, depending on their immediate and long-term needs. Sometimes the questions will revolve around the needs of a particular child and family; at other times, the concerns of groups of individuals or families might be addressed.

To address their specific questions, representatives form the home, school, and community of an individual or individuals with disabilities can come together to meet in a focus group or series of focus groups. Focus group members might include the participant(s) with disabilities; classmates without disabilities; parents or guardians; school personnel (e.g., classroom teacher, inclusion specialist, social worker); neighbors; and community recreation staff (e.g., certified therapeutic recreation specialist or program leader from a local YMCA, YWCA, Jewish community center, or community recreation center). Through the focus group process, these individuals participate in a guided discussion, led by a moderator, to address the questions at hand.

Characteristics of Effective Focus Groups

Whereas no two focus groups are exactly alike, typically they have some common traits. Common characteristics of effective focus groups include:

Participants share a common concern, need, or experience. Regardless of how the various focus group participants know the individual with a disability, each group member is concerned with addressing the leisure needs of the individual.

A warm, supportive, nonjudgmental environment is provided. The atmosphere of the focus group should resemble an "open forum" for free-flowing dialogue and the exchange of ideas.

Participants meet for a specific, well-defined purpose. Whether the purpose is identifying leisure activities for instruction or encouraging friendships, focus group participants clearly understand why they are meeting and what they hope to accomplish.

Meetings take place on a time-limited basis. Focus groups typically meet one time only for a period of 1–2 hours. To monitor progress in learning leisure skills or developing friendships, however, focus group members may wish to meet more regularly throughout the year.

Seven to ten participants are typically involved. If fewer than seven individuals participate, one or two people tend to dominate the discussion; if more than ten individuals are involved, the group tends to fragment into smaller groups and side discussions.

Participants sit in close proximity. Group members usually sit in comfortable chairs around a large conference table or in a circle so that everyone can comfortably see and hear each other.

The moderator is knowledgeable on the subject area and skillful in handling group dynamics. A moderator may be a neutral person from outside the organization, parent or other family member, classroom teacher, school administrator, certified therapeutic recreation specialist, social worker, school psychologist, interested community member, or any individual familiar with the issues and able to manage group interaction.

Open-ended questions are used. To elicit honest, thoughtful, and in-depth responses from group members, open-ended "How?" or "What?" questions are asked.

The discussion resembles a group interview. Through the focused dialogue, group members hear each other's observations, new ideas about leisure programming are stimulated, and enthusiasm about collaboration is generated.

The objective is to hear all opinions, not to reach consensus. Although recurring themes generally emerge from focus groups, the emphasis is not on obtaining general agreement, but on exposing all sides of an issue in an open discussion of pros and cons.

Again, when planning a focus group, it is important to remember not to be too concerned with conforming to these characteristics and guidelines but to adapt the focus group format and process to suit the individual circumstances.

Planning the Focus Group

Before focus group members meet, several *tasks* need to be completed. Although the list of preparatory tasks presented below might give the impression that the tasks occur sequentially, many of the steps could occur simultaneously. Regardless of the order in which tasks are completed, a carefully planned focus group reduces the likelihood that the flow of the actual meeting will be disrupted by any unexpected occurrences.

Clearly define and communicate the purpose of the group. Defining the purpose may be the most difficult task in planning the focus group—it is also the most important. A clearly defined purpose can capture the interest of potential focus group participants, keep the discussion on track, and aid in evaluating the outcomes of the discussion.

Determine whom to include in the focus group. Decide who can best answer the questions related to your purpose. Include those people who know the individual with a disability best and who represent the range of home, school, and community environments.

Develop a written plan. The written plan should begin with a summary of the problem, a statement about why the focus group is needed, and a description of the purpose. A plan of action should be outlined that describes how participants will be recruited, who will be responsible for which tasks, and where and when the focus group(s) will take place. In addition, a meeting agenda, realistic budget, and timeline for conducting and evaluating the focus group needs to be developed.

Recruit focus group members. As a general rule, one recruits by overrecruiting. Because only a limited number of people are appropriate to address the leisure needs of an individual with a disability, focus group members should be hand-picked and personally asked to participate. Participants should be called in advance and meetings should be scheduled when participants are able to attend. Personalized confirmation letters, with an explanation of the purpose of the meeting and clear directions, along with follow-up phone calls, are necessary for a high participant turnout.

Formulate the interview questions. To develop the questioning route for the discussion, make a list of general areas of concern about the individual's leisure lifestyle, formulate questions about these areas, then arrange the questions in a logical sequence. Usually, between 5 and 10 questions are sufficient for one meeting.

Obtain a meeting site. Select a site that is accessible to individuals with disabilities, is easy to locate, and has free, convenient parking. To establish a sense of belonging and equal ownership, choose a site that is familiar to all the participants. Focus groups may take place at schools, community recreation centers, private homes, libraries, restaurants, churches, or synagogues.

Arrange for recording equipment and materials. Focus groups are generally audiotaped to record responses accurately—unless doing so would be obtrusive to group dynamics. Always ask participants for their permission to record and ensure them of the confidentiality of their responses. Other materials that might be useful when conducting focus groups include a flip chart, markers, name tags, note paper, handouts, written surveys, and pens or pencils. In addition, light refreshments add a touch of hospitality to the meeting and help group members feel at ease.

Conducting the Focus Group

When group members arrive, the moderator should greet people in a friendly manner, engage them in light conversation, and have refreshments available. When beginning the discussion, it is important to create a nonthreatening, accepting environment. The moderator should introduce himself or herself and invite all participants to introduce themselves. As introductory remarks, the moderator should restate the purpose of the discussion, clarify the agenda, mention any housekeeping concerns, and establish any ground rules. These remarks could address the confidential handling of responses, point out the necessity of an audio recorder to gather information accurately, ask for participants' permission to record the session, invite group members to ask questions, indicate how long the discussion will last, and remind participants that there are no right or wrong answers.

When leading the group interview, the moderator must be keenly aware of group dynamics, observe nonverbal messages, and anticipate the flow of the discussion. Tips for effective moderators include:

• Create a warm, friendly atmosphere.
• Know the individual with a disability and his or her leisure needs.
• Dress similarly to the participants.
• Maintain control of group dynamics in an unobtrusive manner.
• Memorize the interview protocol so you can look directly at the participants, not at your notes.
• Emphasize that every opinion is important.
• Listen empathetically and with genuine interest.
• Allow group members ample time to respond (wait at least 10 seconds after asking a question).
• Probe participants' answers early so they will provide precise information. Typical probes include: "Could you explain that further?" "Do you have an example?" and "What experiences make you feel that way?"
• Avoid expressing personal opinions or evaluating participants' comments. Be neutral, or "beige," in all reactions.
• Be flexible, but keep the discussion on track. Gauge when to explore an issue more fully and when to move on to a new question.
• Maintain a sense of humor.

When concluding the discussion, a "wrap-up" question may be useful for summarizing information and lending a sense of closure to the meeting. Inviting participants to offer additional comments or questions can also uncover information that might have been overlooked. If appropriate or necessary, plans for subsequent meetings can be made. Finally, the moderator should thank the participants for their time and input, and, as they leave, be available to answer any questions they might have.

Evaluating the Focus Group

After conducting the focus group, it may seem difficult—if not impossible—to pull together the diverse opinions and draw accurate conclusions about the discussion. To digest, interpret, and evaluate the numerous comments, ask yourself the following questions:

• What was the general mood or tone of the meeting?
• What did the participants' body language, nonverbal communication, or other behaviors suggest?
• What common themes, comments, or opinions emerged from the discussion?
• What divergent viewpoints were expressed?
• What shifts in mood, philosophy, or opinions occurred during the course of the meeting?
• What new questions or information arose?
• How well did the discussion meet the original purpose of the meeting?
• How will the information be used and disseminated?

While considering these questions, review the audiotape, taking notes and/or transcribing the discussion. To reduce the possibility that the results will be biased by a moderator's opinions, an assistant moderator (e.g., one of the focus group participants or a neutral person) can help conduct and evaluate the focus group. Together, the moderator and assistant can compare observations, cross-check opinions with actual comments made by the participants, and develop a report based on their mutual agreement.

Focus Group Case Study: The Dowling Friendship Program

At a public elementary school in Minneapolis, the Dowling Urban Environmental Learning Center (Dowling School), family focus groups were used to create connections between homes, the school, and neighborhoods to support and strengthen friendships between children with and without disabilities. Many of the focus group guidelines outlined in this chapter were followed to facilitate the focus groups, as well as tailored to suit the individual circumstances of the families who participated in the Dowling Friendship Program.

The need for the family focus groups at Dowling School arose from a situation that is being experienced by many other communities across the country: the long history of segregation of students with disabilities, the recent *physical* inclusion of students with disabilities in regular education classrooms, the unanticipated lack of *social* interaction and friendship between children with and without disabilities, the continued isolation being experienced by students with disabilities, and the lack of opportunities available to students without disabilities to grow in awareness of the abilities and contributions of students labeled as "different." In talking with Dowling School parents, students, and school staff members, three fundamental questions took shape:

• What is the nature of relationships and friendships between children with and without disabilities?
• What obstacles prevent children with and without disabilities from making friends?
• How can friendships between children with and without disabilities be facilitated, supported, and maintained?

To answer these questions, five family focus groups met over a period of 2 years, resulting in many in-depth discussions about friendships within the context of leisure activities. Each family focus group included a child with a disability and his or her family members; two to four classmates without disabilities and their family members; school staff (e.g., inclusion specialist, classroom teacher, social worker); recreation staff (e.g., program leaders, therapeutic recreation specialists); and program staff.

Because of the families' busy schedules, focus group meetings were arranged far in advance (i.e., 3–5 weeks), families' schedules were coordinated so that as many families as possible could attend, and meetings were held at convenient times and at nearby locations. Sometimes, families were available only during the dinner hour, so they met for potluck suppers. On the average, each family focus group met once every 3 months.

At the onset of the Dowling Friendship Program, focus groups met at the school, a common point of reference for all group members. Later, as group members became more familiar with each other, suggestions were made to meet at community recreation centers and invitations were extended to gather in families' homes. The advantages of meeting at community recreation centers were that families who previously had no exposure to these facilities could explore them, learn about recreation options for their children, and peruse the facilities for programmatic and architectural accessibility. Meetings in family homes were also beneficial. The atmosphere was warm and informal, promoting greater disclosure and ease among group members. Families could connect personally and assess whether and how relationships between family members might develop. When the focus group was held at the home of a child with a disability, a parent of a child without a disability could observe the child with a disability on his or her own "turf," observe how the child interacted with others and the environment, and learn from the example of the child's parent how to meet the child's needs. Through this informal education, a parent of a child without a disability could rehearse in his or her mind the considerations and practical logistics of inviting the child with a disability for a home visit or to a community event.

As focus groups began to meet, it became evident that if families were to work together to discuss questions about leisure time and friendship, they first needed to become acquainted. To accomplish this, the format of meetings resembled a social gathering as much as possible. Focus group meetings typically lasted approximately 1–1½ hours. The first 15 or 20 minutes of the focus group was an informal social time. Besides allowing a grace period for latecomers, this social time provided an opportunity for group members to meet each other, engage in light conversation, share information, and enjoy refreshments. Introductory remarks made up the next 5 or 10 minutes of the meeting and included a welcome by the moderator, introductions, and a review of the agenda. For the following 10–15 minutes, an update of the participants' involvement in recreation activities was provided. Updates were presented by recreation program leaders, parents, classroom teachers, the inclusion specialist, and/or the moderator. After the program update, the children were escorted to a separate room to play together in cooperative activities while their parents, school personnel, and recreation staff discussed issues regarding friendship and recreation participation. Depending on group dynamics, the discussions varied from being led, question-by-question, by the moderator to resembling a group conversation. Although the moderator was prepared with specific questions for discussion, the format was kept flexible so that group members felt free to introduce and discuss new information, concerns, or questions. Discussions usually lasted about 30 minutes. Following the discussion, all focus group participants had the option to participate in a *cooperative* activity for all ages (e.g., volleyball, parachute game, craft activity) and/or visit informally with the other focus group members.

The outgrowth of these discussions revealed key information about the nature of relationships and friendships between children with and without disabilities, obstacles to friendship development, and how to encourage and maintain friendships (Heyne et al., 1993). Regarding the nature of the relationships, children with and without disabilities typically identified each other reciprocally as either a "friend" or "best friend," rather than the less familiar descriptors of "classmate" or "helper." Even though many of the interactions between the children were perceived by parents and school staff as resembling a "helper–helpee" dynamic, the children themselves tended to perceive the relationships as friendships, with helping behaviors being a natural component of friendship. In the few cases where children with disabilities identified classmates without disabilities as simply "classmates" or "helpers," the classmates without disabilities also perceived the relationships in the same way.

Through the focus group process, several *obstacles* to friendship development were reported:

• Families' busy schedules made it difficult to find time to nurture children's friendships.
• Lack of accurate information about people with disabilities and how to meet their needs resulted in fearful or stereotypic attitudes about people with disabilities.
• When children did not live in the same neighborhood, arranging home visits was cumbersome.
• Differences existed between children with and without disabilities, such as different social and communication skills, different abilities, and different recreation interests.
• Arranging public transportation for children with physical disabilities to participate in community recreation activities with friends was difficult.
• Relationships between children with and without disabilities were generally not supported at home if their parents were not compatible.
• Families lacked opportunities to become acquainted.

To address these obstacles, focus group participants outlined the roles that parents and school personnel could play to facilitate, support, and maintain friendships between students across home, school, and community environments. Focus group participants recommended that parents could do the following:

• Make friendship development a family priority.
• Become acquainted with other families.
• Take the initiative to invite children and families for informal recreation activities in homes and neighborhoods.
• Learn about the individual needs of children and how to meet them.
• Support and discuss children's friendships at home.
• Volunteer at school to support children's friendships in recreation activities.

Similarly, focus group participants outlined the role that school staff could play in encouraging friendships.

• Provide opportunities for children to participate in recreation activities throughout the school day.
• Assign children who are friends to the same classrooms.
• Include friendship and recreation goals in IEPs.
• Provide opportunities for families to become acquainted.
• Educate children and parents without disabilities about the needs of individuals with disabilities.
• Inform parents when friendships between children with varying abilities develop.
• Continue to provide an accepting, inclusive environment for children with special needs.

Aside from these outcomes, several unanticipated benefits resulted from the family focus groups.

Families had opportunities to meet each other and develop relationships and a level of trust.
New avenues of communication were established among parents, school staff, and recreation personnel.

Parents could observe their children and other children with and without disabilities playing and socializing together, interactions that most parents had no previous opportunity to experience.

Listening to the stories of parents of children with disabilities proved to be an eye-opening, awareness-building, educational experience for parents of children without disabilities who typically had grown up with little contact with peers with disabilities.

Children without disabilities received recognition for their involvement in the program, and parents of children without disabilities experienced a sense of pride that their children had volunteered to take part in the program.

Through sharing their stories with others, parents of children with disabilities felt less isolated and more supported in their experiences.

At Dowling School, family focus groups proved to be an effective means to answer questions about friendship development and recreation participation for students with and without developmental disabilities. Other schools and communities who wish to use the family focus group model will need to assess and adapt the process to ensure the greatest responsiveness to their communities' needs.

Chapter 9

STRATEGIES FOR HOME INVOLVEMENT IN LEISURE EDUCATION

*P*arents and care providers are perhaps the most critical and certainly the first players in developing and supporting a child's leisure repertoire. It is difficult to imagine an area other than the home environment that could be more instrumental in supporting and nurturing a new skill over time.

Today's children are being raised by their birth, adoptive, and foster parents, as well as by a variety of surrogate parents, including siblings, aunts and uncles, and grandparents. In our work in the urban areas of Minneapolis and New York City, for example, we are finding many young children being raised by a grandparent because of the absence of a parent. School personnel are finding that teenage parents may have virtually disappeared from the picture for a variety of reasons, including prison, abandonment, drug addiction, and even death.

It is sobering to reflect that, as teachers and other professionals, we may still need to be reminded that many children do not live in the stereotypical "nuclear family" with a mother and a father; even if two parents are present in the home, both may work or, at the other extreme, they may both be unemployed. We have long since modified the kinds of expectations we might have had for the "family" of the past. As early as 1989, Vincent and Salisbury (1989) reported that 67% of American children will be raised by a single parent at some point in their lives. Our expectations must now be accommodated even further. Today's family is anything but stereotyped; it includes single parents (both "natural" and adoptive), gay couple parents, and a variety of surrogate parent models that teachers and therapeutic recreation specialists must regard as typical if they are to succeed in encouraging meaningful family involvement in the leisure domain. Throughout this chapter, we use the term *parent* to refer to any individual who is fulfilling this role for an individual with a disability. However, we want to emphasize at the outset that the person responsible for input and support on behalf of a child in the leisure domain may not be a mother or a father. To reflect this emphasis, we have chosen to refer to involvement of the home in the title of this chapter rather than to parental involvement as we did in the first version of this curriculum.

THE IMPORTANCE OF HOME INVOLVEMENT

There is a great deal of evidence about the importance of home involvement in the education of individuals with significant disabilities. Family involvement has been related to demonstrations of increased social, emotional, physical, and cognitive growth for the child (Mahoney & Powell,

This is a significantly revised and rewritten version of "Incorporating Parental Involvement," from *Longitudinal Leisure Skills for Severely Handicapped Learners: The Ho'onanea Curriculum Component* (Wuerch & Voeltz, 1982), which was co-authored with input from Amy Stein. We wish to acknowledge her contributions to the earlier version on which this version is based.

1988; Shearer & Shearer, 1972; Singer, Irvine, & Irvin, 1989). This evidence even extends to the impact that siblings have on the social competence of young children with disabilities when they are taught to act as instructors (Fox, Niemeyer, & Savelle, 1992). Specific parent instruction programs have long been promoted because of evidence that skills initially taught at school would be far more likely to maintain (over time) and generalize (to other natural environments and situations) if family members were taught how to encourage these new skills at home and in the community (Baker, 1984; Horner, Dunlap, & Koegel, 1988). Developing parent–professional relationships involving the transfer of skills from one environment to another (e.g., from school to home) has also been viewed as a process for providing "second order" benefits, including improved parent–child and sibling interactions (Lobato & Barrera, 1988), improved adjustment to the child's disability (Singer & Irvin, 1991), and the development of coping skills and the reduction of stress in the family (Baker, 1984). In leisure education in particular—where indicators of program success must surely reference the individual's use of leisure skills independently at home and in the community—parental involvement has been considered to be critical to an effective program (Wehman & Schleien, 1981). Clearly, the home is where most people spend a majority of their free time, and much of that free time involves family interactions that are naturally interdependent.

Until recently, most of the parent or home involvement programs promoted by professionals and in the literature focused on having parents assume the role of educator. This made the home a kind of "second school setting" where parents work on developing specific skills or implementing behavioral interventions designed by educators, recreation professionals, and others. Although many positive outcomes of these efforts have been reported, there is a growing body of work that suggests not all parents want to be involved at this level (Turnbull & Summers, 1987). In fact, for many families, such involvement may actually become a source of additional stress and result in a number of negative effects. These include the disruption of parents' ability to perform their natural, nurturant role (Benson & Turnbull, 1986); encouragement of a "perpetual patient perspective" toward the child with a disability (Gliedman & Roth, 1980); and negative effects on siblings without disabilities who might be deprived of attention and nurturance due to increased parental responsibility toward the child with a disability (Lobato & Barrera, 1988). As early as 1973, Kogan and Tyler found increasingly negative affective interactions between parent and child over a 2-year period following an instruction program to teach parents how to administer physical therapy to their child. Singer and Irvin (1991) summed up the possible negative impact on the family relationship this way:

> Parents may learn to value their child only as an achiever, and thereby diminish parental involvement in nongoal-directed activity such as playing, joking, and enjoying being together. Also, parents must fulfill many other essential roles as wage earners, spouses, homemakers, and parents of siblings; too great a demand on a parent to deliver instruction in addition to the many tasks involved in these many roles may overtax a parent and contribute to caregiver stress.
>
> In the long run, the strength and continuity of affective social ties between family members and individuals with disabilities is vital to positive community outcomes. If an undue emphasis on parents as teachers undermines these ties, then reform is needed. (p. 294)

Thus, our approach to home–school collaboration in the leisure domain is based on Meyer's (1989) work:

> Certainly, what any student can achieve in his or her lifetime will be affected by what he or she knows how to do. But it will also be affected by the extent to which that person has an interdependent support network—including both friends and family. . . . Thus, [the] role of the family to provide support to the individual must be protected and valued—and not sacrificed in our endeavors to teach children more and more skills. . . .
>
> Just as teaching is surely the most critical role the professional plays in the life of a child, being a family to that child is equally critical for parents. Thus, whatever image the school has for parent involve-

ment or participation must recognize the many and extremely important roles of parent and family. . . . any model of home-school collaboration must balance its demands upon the family with the resources and supports that this collaboration provides to the family [and reflect] a careful balance between the *demands* placed upon the family and the *resources* that such participation adds to support the family. (pp. 17–18)

This systems-oriented perspective requires recognition of changes over time based on families' needs and resources. It also acknowledges that families differ a great deal from one another. Two families with the same structural appearance (e.g., both described as "single-parent") might still be very different—what one family views as a resource, another may find to be a cause of great stress (see, for example, Huang & Heifetz, 1984). Any home involvement component must respond to the functioning of the entire family unit and offer flexible, individualized service support options, including the option not to be involved beyond a level that ensures an appropriate program is developed for the child with a disability.

The role of options and choices for family involvement seems particularly critical in leisure education. By nature, leisure implies relaxation, enjoyment, and freedom from stress. Obviously, some level of family involvement is needed if relevant leisure lifestyle goals are to be identified and appropriate activities selected. In addition, at minimum, parents must be willing to provide the context for the child to play—to practice and enjoy the leisure activities taught at school, in organized recreation, and in other environments. However, such parental input and home involvement should be obtained and facilitated in ways that take into account the unique and ever-changing characteristics of individual families and that support the successful inclusion of the child with a disability into his or her family unit (Benson & Turnbull, 1986). When a parent assumes the role of leisure educator, as described in Chapter 1, this volume, he or she must find a personally comfortable balance between the role of teacher and the role of parent.

This chapter describes components of a flexible leisure home involvement program, with emphasis on individualizing methods and activities to meet the needs of families. For parents who wish or can handle only minimal involvement, strategies for obtaining their input in developing appropriate leisure goals, identifying activities for instruction, and evaluating program outcomes are presented. For parents who wish and can handle more involvement, strategies for developing individualized leisure in-home service plans are included. Also, we provide an overview of the *Ho'onanea* In-Home Training Component, a flexible home involvement program that was field validated with 22 families in Hawaii.

COMPONENTS OF A LEISURE HOME INVOLVEMENT PROGRAM: HOME–SCHOOL COMMUNICATION

At the heart of successful home involvement is open, honest communication between family members and persons providing services in or supports to the home. Yet, as Walker and Singer (1993) noted, professionals are trained primarily to work with children and to develop clinical teaching skills. Parallel instruction in communicating with families is typically lacking.

Communication involves both talking and listening. Communication occurs whenever one person sends a message and the content and intent of the message are received and understood by the other person. For this to happen, each person involved must speak a common language, be willing to invest sufficient energy to actively "listen" to the other person, and seek feedback about whether or not the content of the message received was what was intended. Honest communication requires a willingness to set aside preconceptions and accept the other person's right to his or her own belief system. This is not always easy! Most of us find ourselves poorly prepared to meet the requirements of communicating effectively with parents; however, effective communication is essential if there are to be meaningful interactions between home and school (and community) on behalf of an individual.

To improve home–school communications, we must consider that families vary considerably in their abilities to cope with the presence of a child with a disability (Singer & Irvin, 1991; Turnbull et al., 1993). Being the parent of a child with a disability is but one of many roles parents play within their family systems (Meyer, 1989). As a "professional," we are tempted to focus on a child in a very limited role—as educator, therapist, or leisure educator. Parents, however, need to focus on many family members at once in a variety of ever-changing roles—nurturer, disciplinarian, teacher, care provider, economic provider, leisure educator, and friend. A parent's ability to respond to a professional's demands or concerns will vary over time, both because of individual coping mechanisms and as a function of changing demands placed on him or her from within the family system. A parent's lack of enthusiasm or concern at one point in time does not necessarily imply he or she does not want to work with you in the future or does not care about the issue.

Goldfarb, Brotherson, Summers, and Turnbull (1986) offer the following suggestions to improve communications with parents:

• Pay attention and be what is called an "active listener" (if you are really listening, you will find you are directing a great deal of concentration toward the parent with whom you are speaking).
• Take time to confirm your understanding of what is being said (simply rephrase what the parent has communicated, and ask if that is what was meant).
• Accept the parent's right to his or her own individuality even when you do not agree with something (remember, the child is part of that family unit for his or her lifetime, and your own role is by definition going to be time-limited).

Communication among parents, other family members, and service providers can take many different forms. Informal communication includes the exchange of information between an agency and home about things that happened at school or in the community program, program successes, announcements, reminders of upcoming home visits, and so forth. Informal communication is best accomplished either through brief written notes, chance encounters at school or the community agency, or phone calls. In either case, keep a log of home contacts so that you can refer back to them.

Concerns, serious problems, and program failures should be communicated in person whenever possible. Invite the parent to come to school for a meeting or, if the person prefers, schedule a home visit. A log of parent contacts should be kept that briefly documents what was discussed, decisions that were made, and any concerns raised by the parent. This information can be especially useful in future planning and to document program accountability. A variety of forms used in the *Ho'onanea* In-Home Training Component are well suited for this.

Effective communication becomes increasingly important as parents and service providers work together to identify needs, solve problems, and plan leisure education activities. Current approaches to working with families emphasize including parents in planning educational programs and assessing characteristics of family systems that will have an impact on program outcomes. Family interviews typically need to be conducted to obtain certain assessment information; yet, care should be taken to avoid using one assessment method rigidly in all cases. When conducting interviews, establish a rapport with family members by listening intently and with empathic understanding. Be sure the family members understand what you are asking. Avoid using "jargon" and verify responses to questions by either asking the same questions a different way or by asking the parent if that is what he or she meant. Pay attention to nonverbal communication as well—a face-to-face meeting is often better than a phone call for difficult concerns and decisions. A parent who is speaking very fast or fidgeting may indicate that you have touched on an uncomfortable topic or that he or she does not really want to share that information with you. Respect the family's right to privacy. Any and all information obtained about a family should be considered confidential. Information that is irrelevant to developing a leisure education plan, delivering instruction, or providing for home involvement should not be requested and, if offered voluntarily, should not be recorded in the child's written school or program records.

PARTNERS IN PLANNING

The goal of leisure skill instruction is the development of a leisure lifestyle that includes full participation by the individual with a disability in a variety of community environments with his or her family and friends across the lifespan. The types of leisure choices that are available are largely determined by the types of leisure activities valued and enjoyed by the people with whom time will be spent. Because of this, family participation in identifying leisure education goals, as well as in selecting specific leisure skills for instruction, is essential even when the family wants no further involvement in the leisure education program. Most parents are likely to feel comfortable assuming a role in this process (Voeltz & Apffel, 1981; Voeltz, Wuerch, & Wilcox, 1982), and participation in IEP planning is reported to be one of parents' preferred forms of involvement (Turnbull, Turnbull, Bronicki, Summers, & Roeder-Gordon, 1989). Chapter 2, this volume, describes the parent–educator planning process in detail. What follows here is a description of those aspects of the planning process that provide the context for many home involvement activities where parental input is particularly important.

The selection of specific leisure skills for instruction involves two levels of assessment that require family participation: 1) assessment of family characteristics and preferences, and 2) assessment of the participant's preferences for particular leisure activities.

Assessing Family Characteristics and Preferences for Leisure Activities

As discussed earlier, family systems vary considerably and a family's unique set of characteristics will influence program outcomes. Powers and Handleman (1984) identified eight assessment domains that can be used to determine a family's ability to participate effectively in behavioral change: 1) ability, 2) values, 3) ideas, 4) circumstances, 5) timing, 6) obligations, 7) resistance, and 8) flexibility. Benson and Turnbull (1986) recommended that the assessment of family characteristics include information about the structure of the family, including membership characteristics; cultural style, including ethnicity, religion, socioeconomic status, and geographic location; and ideological style, including beliefs, values, coping behaviors, and family interactions.

Many of these characteristics will have a direct impact on whether or not certain types of leisure activities will be made available to the participant with a disability, now and in the future. For instance, a family may live near a beach, but may not allow siblings without disabilities to spend the day there unsupervised because the parents believe it is unsafe. Although it may seem that swimming, beachcombing, and playing "beach" games such as volleyball would be promising leisure activities to include in the individual's educational program, the family's belief system makes it unlikely that the participant could ever actually use these new skills outside the instructional situation.

Thus, leisure education service providers need to obtain information about: 1) what leisure activities the family regularly engages in; 2) what leisure activities the family would like to participate in, but refrains from enjoying because of the behavior or lack of skills of the family member with a disability; 3) what types of leisure activities the family would like to see the individual participate in, independent of the family unit; and 4) what kinds of barriers exist to making preferred leisure activities available, such as financial resources, transportation, or a critical family member's disapproval of participation by the participant with a disability in certain activities or community environments.

Assessing family characteristics can be accomplished through in-home observations, informal conversations, and semistructured family interviews. It is extremely important that service providers consider using a variety of assessment techniques and strive for a "fit" between the method selected, their expertise, and the family's preferences (Benson & Turnbull, 1986). Service providers should plan assessment of family characteristics and preferences thoughtfully, and should individualize specific questions and assessment techniques based on the unique characteristics of individual families. The *Ho'onanea* (the first version of this curriculum) program's parent–leisure educator planning process described in Chapter 2, this volume, details a field-validated Home Leisure Activities Survey (Form 2.1) that can be used in obtaining a partial assessment of family characteristics. Leisure educators and other specialists (e.g., therapists) should supplement the listed questions to obtain other relevant information.

Assessing the Participant's Leisure Preferences

The assessment of the participant's preferences is integral to planning a leisure education program designed to result in the development of a typical leisure lifestyle. Obviously, the individual is more likely to participate in activities that are preferred, and the enjoyment experienced through interactions with preferred activities will enhance generalization and maintenance of learned leisure skills. Assessing these preferences requires spending time with the participant to ascertain whether he or she is already participating in any leisure activities that are experienced as enjoyable, and to observe whether or not the individual appears to enjoy new or infrequently available activities that parents or other family members have identified as important. Because the home and family is the natural context for much leisure time, parents must be involved in assessing their sons' and daughters' leisure preferences whenever possible.

O'Brien's (1987) Life-Style Futures Planning offers leisure educators a model for this process. Leisure educators seeking information about the participant's interests might ask parents to spend time with the participant engaged in a potential leisure activity. Parents should be instructed to look at the world through the participant's eyes and see how he or she experiences the activity. As a starting point, the family can assist in developing lists of interests and summaries of current leisure-time choices of the individual with a disability. Parents can be asked to list all the choices related to play and leisure made by the participant on a daily, weekly, and occasional basis. They can also be asked what decisions are made by family members on a regular basis that relate to leisure activities and that would affect the range of choices actually available (e.g., if the neighborhood park is "off-limits" until the child is older, any preference for activities that might occur at the park may have to be targeted for a later date). In addition, quite simply, family members might be asked to name all the leisure activities they think the participant with a disability might enjoy.

In the *Ho'onanea* program, parents were involved in assessing the participant's preferences by conducting the Participant Interest Inventory (Form 2.3). This procedure is especially well-suited to assessing leisure activities that occur in the home and are being considered for use in home-based instruction that involves solitary play. To use this inventory, parents first provide an opportunity for the leisure activity to occur in the natural environment. The parent arranges a free-time area where it would be appropriate for the activity to occur, such as the individual's bedroom or a play room. Then the parent presents the leisure activity materials to the individual (one activity at a time) and briefly demonstrates how to interact with the materials, paying particular attention to any inherent reinforcing qualities (e.g., sounds, lights, movement). After the demonstration, the parent moves away slightly and observes the participant for a few minutes. The parent then uses the Participant Interest Inventory form to rate the individual's behavior with the activity, assigning one of three possible ratings for each of the five items on the inventory. This process is repeated for each identified activity, and the activities with the highest scores are selected for use in any leisure education program as they are most likely to reflect the participant's preferences.

Details for administering, scoring, and interpreting the inventory are provided in Chapter 2, this volume. We recommend that the leisure educator demonstrate these procedures for the parent by selecting two activities that are likely to be rated quite differently, given what is known about the participant. This demonstration could be given at school or in the home, or, if there is a VCR in the home, it could be videotaped for the parent to view. It is preferable if the leisure educator can view the video with the parent to explain how to rate the questions on the form to reflect what the individual does. When teaching parents how to do these ratings, keep in mind that parents' ratings may be very different from your own. This does not imply that their observations are inaccurate. Parents are more likely to be aware of subtle expressions of interest (e.g., stiffening body), and their participation in the assessment process may provide an invaluable opportunity for the leisure educator to gain insight into the participant's behavioral and affective repertoire.

After this demonstration, parents should be able to complete the Participant Interest Inventory on their own. They may choose to use this procedure for future purchasing and instruction activities. This exposure makes it more likely that they will incorporate a concern for the participant's preferences and interests in future decisions made on his or her behalf.

Assessing Family Needs and Preferences for Home Involvement

Professionals have traditionally regarded parental involvement as desirable and necessary for the implementation of educational services that result in meaningful behavior change. We have operated under the assumption that teaching parents to behave like "us" supports the person with a disability and his or her place in the family system; however, when we take time to ask parents what they think about parent instruction, it becomes clear whether a family regards home involvement as a resource or a source of additional stress (Meyer, 1989). To ensure that whatever services and supports we provide to families are indeed resources rather than stressors, assessment of the family needs and preferences for home involvement is an essential first step. Once family characteristics have been carefully assessed, the family's needs and preferences for home involvement are easily identified and a plan of home involvement activities can be developed.

Benson and Turnbull (1986) suggested that, at a minimum, we need to know the following information about the family: 1) family structure (Who are the family members and what are their unique characteristics? For example, if a child has several siblings only a few years apart, this may greatly increase that child's opportunities for play with age-appropriate activities on a daily basis.); 2) the impact of the child's disability on family activities (Does the family restrict activities because they find it difficult to manage the child in public places?); 3) the nature of family interactions (Is this a large, extended family with relatives who offer additional support and activity to the child?); and 4) the lifestyle stage of the family (Does the family plan to move soon?). Traditional "needs assessment" surveys to determine a family's "strengths" and "weaknesses" across various service options are unlikely to be very useful for obtaining information relevant to these issues. More effective assessment methods would be informal conversations with family members, observations of family interactions even during brief periods (e.g., when the parent comes to pick up the child), and semistructured interviews over the phone or in person.

INDIVIDUALIZED LEISURE HOME INVOLVEMENT SERVICES

As professionals who have been dealing with IEPs and IHPs for nearly 2 decades, we should be well attuned to the concept of individualization and proficient in developing goals and interventions to meet unique needs. Yet, as Turnbull and Turnbull (1982) noted, it is exactly this level of individualization that is lacking in parent instruction and home involvement programs. A useful home involvement program must fit within the complex of a family system and not be designed solely to address an individual's skill development needs in isolation from the context of the family's needs. This shift from a pure focus on the participant's needs to a consideration of family system needs is illustrated clearly by the newer mandate for Individualized Family Service Plans (IFSP) in early childhood programs. Within the area of leisure lifestyle development, such a shift would imply that leisure educators might need to be receptive to working with siblings and family members without disabilities, not only with the individual with a disability. In some instances, the role of the leisure educator may shift entirely from skills development (in the participant) to coordinating various leisure services for the family or advocating for participation in a community recreation program that has previously included only individuals without disabilities and excluded people with severe disabilities.

In Table 9.1, we have listed the five broad treatment goals that Powers and Bruey (1988) suggested be applied to the development of leisure home involvement services, as well as examples of how leisure home involvement activities might address each of these. Leisure educators must always keep in mind that the family is not a static system. Just as we periodically review and revise IEPs and IHPs for people, we need to review and revise services provided to families through home involvement programs. This is not always easy. At times it may appear that parents are constantly changing their minds about what it is they need and want to be involved in, leaving the leisure educator feeling as if nothing of substance is being accomplished. Be aware that this may signal a variety of things, including: 1) the original program did not address the parents' priority concerns; 2) the family system is going through a period of rapid transition or is under a great deal of stress; and/or 3) the family may not really want any involvement, but because they feel pressured to say something, they present a new plan whenever it seems that they will otherwise have to implement the previous one proposed.

INCLUDING PARENTS IN LEISURE EDUCATION PROGRAM EVALUATION

Regardless of how actively a parent chooses to be involved in an individual's leisure education program, his or her satisfaction with the use of leisure time by the participant is an important indicator of program success. A measure of parental satisfaction with a leisure education program is easily obtained using a consumer satisfaction rating sheet such as Form 9.7 (p. 207).

The leisure educator should use the consumer satisfaction rating sheet on a "pre" and "post" basis, beginning by asking the parent to rate the items on the rating sheet before the leisure program is implemented and then again at the end of the program or year (or possibly just prior to a scheduled IEP or IHP reevaluation). Changes in parental satisfaction with how the participant spends his or her free time at home or in the neighborhood revealed by a comparison of the "pre" and "post" ratings should provide a fair assessment of whether or not the program is actually having any impact. In addition, a parent's ratings at the beginning of the program

Table 9.1. Family therapy goals for leisure home involvement

Goals of family therapy and definition	Leisure home involvement activities
1. Facilitating a healthy response to diagnosis: Social role valorization of the family's response to the development of the participant with an emphasis on securing services to support the participant and the family.	1. Consultation regarding appropriate expectations for the participant's leisure-time behavior; helping the family secure access to community leisure/recreation programs.
2. Facilitating functional forms of organization within the family system: Helping the family establish and/or maintain healthy organizational and interactive patterns.	2. Working with siblings to establish typical play interactions; explaining concepts such as age appropriateness to a family member who disagrees with others in the family regarding how the participant should spend free time.
3. Facilitating the development and maintenance of social networks: Helping families build and use family-of-origin and extended support systems.	3. Providing leisure home involvement services in a relative's home who has expressed willingness to assist in providing respite for the family; setting a meeting with parents and community recreation staff.
4. Facilitating service access and coordination: Acting as an information clearinghouse for existing services and communicating with organizations to make them aware of the family's needs.	4. Meeting with school and community program staff working with the family on leisure activities to ensure that efforts are consistent and demands placed on the family are balanced; communicating the family's needs for community recreational opportunities to various programs; discussing participation by the participant in programs accessed by other family members such as public swimming pools, church functions, and so forth, with persons affiliated with these various environments.
5. Facilitating the development of advocacy skills: Helping family members develop needed skills in contacting agencies and encouraging participation with others in advocacy efforts.	5. Providing parents with a community recreation resource list and a format for collecting information on available services; introducing parents who wish to advocate for a particular type of leisure program to others with similar interests.

Adapted from Powers & Bruey (1988).

should reveal valuable information about family priorities and could be used as a starting point for negotiating the focus of leisure education and the relative weight that should be assigned to this area in comparison to other areas on the IEP or IHP. Parents' responses to the pre-instruction rating can also highlight areas where the leisure educator needs to provide information to parents (e.g., the availability of age-appropriate leisure activities for teenagers that can be easily adapted for significant disabilities).

We find that an interview format is best for obtaining these ratings, rather than sending a survey form home for parents to complete and return. This can be done either in a meeting or on the telephone. Parents should be encouraged to offer specific information about their concerns and not simply be asked to rate each item without comment. Anecdotal notes about this conversation can be added to the form to record parental input.

For those families who receive individualized home involvement services, some measure of their satisfaction with the services provided is also important. A rating sheet that specifically addresses the types of services the family received can be developed and used throughout and on completion of a program or year or other relevant period of time. Information obtained should then be used to revise services and approaches taken with that family and to generate ideas about future services for families in general.

OVERVIEW OF AN IN-HOME INSTRUCTION COMPONENT

In the *Ho'onanea* program, home involvement included parental input in selecting leisure education goals and specific leisure activities for instruction along with participation in one of three levels of service delivery: 1) equipment loan with or without consultation, 2) equipment loan with parent instruction, and 3) equipment loan with in-home instruction. The first level represents a mechanism to facilitate the transfer of learned skills to natural home leisure environments by structuring the availability of materials in the home and assisting families to establish appropriate leisure-time expectations for the participant. The second level is an extension of the first where parents are also instructed to conduct leisure education in the home. At the third level, the leisure educator provides this in-home activity instruction rather than instructing the parent or another family member to do so. The particular level selected should correspond to family needs and preferences for in-home services; however, each level requires that the family commit to making leisure materials available to the participant as he or she develops the necessary skills to play appropriately.

The procedures described in the next sections were field tested with 22 families in Hawaii. Most of the participants in the program were teenagers already receiving school-based leisure education using the *Ho'onanea* program. Three individuals who were not enrolled in the school-based portion of the project also participated in just this in-home component field test.

Although the in-home component was designed to be conducted by a classroom teacher or therapeutic recreation specialist, our field testing was conducted by a part-time parent instructor who supplemented existing school staff. Based on our experiences, an estimated 20 hours per month of staff time would allow a teacher to implement the in-home instruction component described here for 10 students, allocating approximately 30 minutes per week per student. We would recommend that one or more of the teaching assistants assigned to students with significant disabilities could be instructed to perform this in-home role as part of their job descriptions. Advantages of assigning this role to teaching assistants could include:

• Creating a responsible role for capable teaching assistants that makes good use of their skills and could greatly increase their own personal motivation to be involved in the students' programs.
• Allowing for a "cultural fit" between the liaison paraprofessional—the teaching assistant—and the family. There is currently a shortage of professional teachers and therapeutic recreation specialists from diverse cultural backgrounds and who speak languages other than English. Thus, the teaching assistant may have been hired specifically to meet some of these needs and may be able to establish a rapport with a family (and speak the same language) in a manner that might never occur with the teacher or therapeutic recreation specialist. Having the teaching assistant serve as a home liaison in this way may be particularly valuable when he or she is the same gender as the student and perhaps closer in age, and can, therefore, encourage positive age-appropriate leisure activities in the home community (e.g., the teaching assistant is an African American man in his 20s and the student is also an African American male).
• Such a model and use of the teaching assistant may further reinforce the need for teachers and other school personnel to properly instruct and supervise their teaching assistants as well as

develop strategies to monitor their instructional support behavior outside the classroom. Such a program could make it more likely that the school building and district will support the necessary staff development activities to teach these personnel to work together on behalf of students and to develop the skills needed to do a good job.

• Demands for teaching assistant time in the school program may fluctuate across the school year, and an in-home component could emphasize these activities at times when there is less need for in-class time at school. For example, in inclusive education programs, more teaching assistant support might be needed at the beginning of a marking period, and later in the marking period the teaching assistant might be deliberately fading physical presence to enable the learner to better connect with the general education teacher and classmates. This might be the time to initiate significant contact with the families. The in-home component could then greatly enhance the school program even as it is informed by the earlier period of intensive in-school contact with the learner.

Getting Started

The first steps to prepare for an in-home leisure education component involve gathering materials and establishing a procedure for the exchange of activity materials and information between school or community agency and the home.

Materials   Some schools may have an ample budget for an in-home component and can readily purchase the additional games and toys needed to loan to families. Most schools and agencies, however, do not. Having a "lending library" of toys is particularly critical when the families have limited resources—not all families can afford to purchase many of the leisure activity materials featured in our task analyses. Whereas most families would probably "invest" in one or more such sets of materials if they were given evidence that the materials had lasting use and value for the participant with a disability as well as his or her siblings, the lending library is a way to provide this evidence before they are asked to buy anything. We found it essential that participants' preferred activities were available to borrow for home use. In general, having two additional sets of all leisure activities used during school-based instruction met this need.

One idea implemented by one of our schools in Brooklyn, New York, was to solicit contributions from local merchants who would exchange something in their stock for every used toy gun turned in by students with parental consent. During the 1993 holiday season, many toy merchants committed gift certificates for toys to adults who turned over real guns, and our school—the Surfside School in Coney Island—used the same principle to discourage the ownership of toy guns as part of children's play. On the first day of the program at this elementary school of nearly 850 students, 180 toy guns were exchanged for a Burger King certificate for a burger, fries, and a soda. Nearly a dozen television and radio stations as well as major educational news publications featured the program within a few days, as more and more toy guns were turned into school along with the required parent permission for the exchange. We think that schools could use this same principle to solicit commitments from several nearby local or chain merchants who would contribute a dollar amount for each returned toy gun toward the purchase of a set of "positive toys" that would be part of a lending library for individuals with disabilities and their families. Such a campaign could establish a lending library and be viewed as positive publicity by merchants in the area. The campaign may also encourage parents to examine the nature of the toys the participants are using and explore positive alternatives. This, of course, is just one idea; having a focus for contributions of merchandise, in this case toys, can be an effective strategy for building community involvement and responsibility toward educational and community recreation programs, as well as meeting a real need for materials procurement by agencies with limited budgets.

The Materials Lending Library System   Once at least two sets of each of the leisure education materials have been organized, a simple but systematic check-out system must be developed for family use. We used library-type cards with the name of the leisure material printed across the top of the card, which were then glued onto the activity materials boxes. These cards were then placed into pockets mounted on a piece of tag board we referred to as the "equipment loan-out board." Cards might just as easily be filed in a plastic file box (agencies with the computer expertise could develop a computer scan system). When the activity was returned, the card was replaced into the pocket mounted on the box.

Parent Involvement Files   A Parent Involvement File can be established for each participating family and used to document home involvement activities. The following forms were developed and used during our field tests. As they were completed, they were organized within the Parent Involvement Files.

- The Home Information Sheet (Form 9.1) provides information related to family characteristics and helps the parent instructor structure initial home contacts and plan for future activities. This form is completed prior to or during the parent instructor's first contact with the family. The form should be periodically updated.
- Several forms can be used to document home contacts: the Home Contact Log (Form 9.2), the Home Telephone Log (Form 9.3), the Home Visit Report (Form 9.4), and the Home Visit Appointment form (Form 9.5).
- Several assessment instruments relevant to home involvement can be included: the Leisure Time at Home Needs Assessment (Form 9.6), the Home Leisure Activities Survey (Form 2.1), the Leisure Activity Selection Checklist (Form 2.2), the Participant Interest Inventory (Form 2.3), and the Parent/Caregiver Leisure Education Survey (Form 9.7).
- The Leisure Home Program Procedures (Form 9.8) describe specific participant play behaviors and what families should do to consequate them and attempt to substitute more appropriate behaviors over time. This form can be completed in duplicate, with one copy going to the parents and the second kept in the Parent Involvement File.
- Three data sheets are also kept in the Parent Involvement File: the Home Leisure Data Sheet (Form 8.6) and the Participant Activity Update (Form 9.9) and Leisure Time in the Home: Strengths and Needs Assessment (Form 9.10).

We found it useful to have multiple copies of frequently used forms available at all times. Copies of these forms are provided in Appendix B for duplication by school and community agency personnel.

Home–School Information Exchange System   During the program, the parent instructor should review each participant's Parent Involvement File at least once monthly to compare information with the individual's classroom instructional data. Any discrepancies on performance or activity preferences should be taken to the team meeting for discussion, and program modifications should be made as needed. Parent Involvement Files should be available for parental review at any time and should be periodically updated.

Assessment and Program Planning

As noted throughout this chapter, assessment of family characteristics and preferences about leisure for the son or daughter, as well as for participation in an in-home involvement component, is critical. We incorporated these activities into our field test of the in-home component. The Leisure Time at Home Needs Assessment (Form 9.6) was adapted from a measure originally used with a large number of care providers in Hawaii and Washington (Stein, 1981). It was used to give us information about the specific concerns of individual family members. Ratings

Home Information Sheet

Participant: _Dana Johnson_
Address: _4643 Duncan St._
Minneapolis, MN 55455
Phone #: _748-0674_

Participant's birthdate: _10/12/82_
Date form completed: _4/4/94_
Completed by: _Amy Selemister_
Information from: _Suzanne Johnson_

1. What are preferred days and times of day for leisure educator to call on the phone:

   M-F, 7-8 am. and 6-9 pm.

2. With whom should leisure educator discuss participant's program:

   mother

3. Preferred days and times of day for home visit by leisure educator:

   _M-F, 6-9 pm._

4. Preferred days and times of day for school visit by parent:

   Very difficult for parent to come to school (works), but possibly early Tuesday mornings.

5. List siblings' names and ages, listing those most likely to interact with participant:

   Leah - 9, Jesse - 14, David - 15

6. Are there any children in the neighborhood who either do now or might play with participant (describe briefly):

   An 11-year-old girl comes in and reads to Dana and puts on puppet shows. Dana seems to enjoy them. When I say, "Jennie is coming," she shakes her head up and down.

7. Additional comments:

201

Leisure Educator: __Amy Selemister__

Participant: __Dana Johnson__

Page _____ of _____ pages

Date	Type*	Who	Brief Description
4/19/94	LEP	mother	Dana is playing appropriately with activities
4/25/94	HV	mother	Progress with "Star Wars" Nintendo Game Boy activity

* LEP = phone call from leisure educator to parent; PP = phone call from parent to leisure educator;
HV = home visit by leisure educator; SV = school visit by parent; O = other (describe).

Home Telephone Log FORM 9.3

Home called: _Mr. & Mrs. Johnson_   Participant's name: _Dana Johnson_
Date/Time: _3/18/94   7:30 a.m._

1. Has your child, _Dana_, independently initiated play activities?
   yes

2. Have you had to prompt _Dana_ to play with activities?
   Sometimes

3. How long does _Dana_ play?
   20-30 minutes

4. Does _Dana_ seem to enjoy the activities? If so, how can you tell?
   Yes, she smiles, shows us what she is doing.

5. Does _Dana_ play with one activity more than the other? Which one?
   Computer game

6. Do any other persons play with _Dana_ while he (she) is playing with activities?
   Jennie - a friend, and Leah - her sister (sometimes)

7. Where did _Dana_ play with the activities?
   Living room or bedroom

Comments:
   Dana needs a lot of help to get the Game
   Boy started. If Jennie or Leah are there,
   things go well, but she gets frustrated if no
   one is with her.

---

were assigned according to both experience and importance. The rationale for this was that, although "importance" ratings do provide a measure of family values that must be considered in program planning, they may not accurately reflect consultation needs because they indicate a family is saying they do not consider something important because they know little about it. If a concern was rated high on both importance and experience, it probably did not reflect a priority area for consultation. Yet, if an item was rated high on importance and low on experience, the parent instruction would include consultation to give the parent more experience in this area.

As with most needs assessments, this survey had its limitations. For families with little or no information on specific items, it is difficult to interpret the validity of their "importance" ratings (How does one know what one does not know?). When this rating pattern appeared during field testing, our parent instructor systematically probed the family for more input. In some cases the parents' ascribed importance for the particular leisure education dimension showed an increase once more information was provided. Thus, the family should be asked to reevaluate items when this occurs to check whether their importance ratings have changed.

Perhaps above all else parents must be involved in selecting the specific leisure activities that will be taught to their son or daughter, and they must be involved in the assessment of the individual's preferences, as they often may be the only ones who can accurately tell what the participant really enjoys. After a variety of potential leisure activities are selected, parents are involved in assessing the appropriateness of each activity according to lifestyle, individualiza-

Home Visit Report

Leisure Educator: *Amy Selemister*

Participant's name: *Dana Johnson*

Date/Time: *4/25/94*

1. Materials taken to home: *none*

2. Materials returned from home: *Jenga*

3. Objectives/goals for this visit: *Work with Dana on playing "Star Wars" Nintendo Game Boy. Show Mrs Johnson how to do this.*

4. Persons present during visit: *Mrs. Gracia Johnson and Dana*

5. Outcome of visit:

   Progress made: *Dana learned to manipulate the Game Boy system controls to advance the starship.*

   Problems identified: *Dana sometimes self-stimulates with the Game Boy system - picks it up and waves it in the air.*

6. Comments: *Mrs. Johnson is very surprised that Dana has initiated interactions with her brother by means of Connect Four and Magic Mitts. This pleases her, as she encourages Dana to interact with siblings; however, this does not occur. She says Dana prefers to be "left alone," and when asked to join the family in a group activity she refuses - sits and won't move.*

Home Visit   FORM 9.5
Appointment

Date/Time of next visit: _____4/25/94_____

_____6:00 pm._____

Any questions, changes or problems, please call

_____Amy Selemister_____

at _____833-5680_____

tion, and environmental considerations using the Leisure Activity Selection Checklist (Form 2.2) (chap. 2, this volume, discusses this procedure). During our field testing, we found it particularly important for the teacher or parent instructor to work with the parents in completing the form until the parents were comfortable with the various items and criteria. The form also proved useful as a means of familiarizing parents with concepts such as the promotion of typical lifestyles and age appropriateness, and thus puts them in a far better position to support Life-Style Futures Planning (O'Brien, 1987). Parental input can also be critical in assessing participant interest in specific activities using the Participant Interest Inventory (Form 2.3).

THREE SERVICE OPTIONS FOR AN IN-HOME INSTRUCTION COMPONENT

As we stress throughout this chapter, parents should be given the opportunity to participate (or not participate) in whatever level of home involvement they feel best meets their needs. In recognition of this, the *Ho'onanea* program offered parents three different levels of service: 1) equipment loan with or without consultation, 2) equipment loan with parent instruction, and 3) equipment loan with in-home instruction provided by a parent instructor.

During the field test and after completion of assessments, the teacher or parent instructor should describe the three options to parents, taking special care to describe the features of each level of involvement with equal enthusiasm and not create any impression that one level is somehow more beneficial to the individual than another. When describing level 2 (equipment loan and parent instruction), special attention should be given to avoid any implication that "good" parents ought to have sufficient time and energy and/or should prefer this service option. We found that the transfer of leisure skills to the home environment occurred for the activities regardless of which of the three levels of involvement the parents selected.

For the families who choose not to be involved in any of the three service options, the parent instructor should try to obtain some feedback regarding the reasons for this decision so that any concerns hindering any involvement they might actually want could be addressed in future programming efforts. Yet, once parents have clearly expressed an interest to not be involved, our role is not to "convince" them of what they are supposed to do; it is their choice and we may not know the various contingencies that make a decision the right one for any particular family.

Leisure Time at Home Needs Assessment

Participant: _Dana Johnson_   Date completed: _4/7/94_

In order to plan a leisure-time activities program with you for your child at home, we need to know what you feel are important needs. Please take a few minutes to let us know which of the issues in the sentences below are most important to you and whether you have had experience in this area.

For each sentence below, check how important this is to you and your child (check one of the three boxes to the left) and how much experience you have had in that area (check one of the three boxes to the right).	How important is this for you and your child?			How much experience have you had in this area?		
	Not Important	Of Some Importance	Very Important	None	Some	A lot
1. Setting aside an area at home where my child can play independently during leisure time, and providing him or her with appropriate and enjoyable materials and activities for this time.			✓	✓		
2. Knowing how to develop my child's independent use of leisure time in the community, including some time with other children with and without disabilities.		✓		✓		
3. Selecting toys and activities that are appropriate for my child and that he or she will enjoy.			✓		✓	
4. Knowing what to do when toys and activities for my child do not work.		✓			✓	
5. Knowing the effects of play and free-time behavior on my child's future development.			✓		✓	
6. Arranging materials in my child's room so that he or she can readily play with an activity on his or her own.			✓	✓		
7. Knowing what I can expect my child to do during his or her free time, and how often and for how long.		✓				
8. Making leisure activities easily available at home so my child can begin to play on his or her own.		✓			✓	
9. Using leisure-time activities as a reward for positive behavior.			✓	✓		

Participant: _Dana Johnson_   Respondent: _Mrs. Gracia Johnson_
Date completed: _4/21/94_   Relationship: _mother_

Directions: *After each question below, check the blank that best describes your child's behavior.*

1. How important do you think play is for your child's well-being?

_____	_____	_____	_____	_✓_
Not at all important	Not very important	Don't know	Somewhat important	Very important

2. Are you satisfied with the way your child spends his or her leisure time at home?

_____	_____	_____	_✓_	_____
Not at all	Not very	Don't know	Somewhat	Yes, very

3. Do you think your child enjoys spending his or her free time with the leisure activities available to him or her at home?

_____	_____	_✓_	_____	_____
Not at all	Hardly ever	Don't know	Often	Yes, definitely

4. When your child begins an activity during his or her free time at home, can you trust him or her to play independently for 15 minutes or more?

_____	_____	_____	_____	_✓_
Never	Hardly ever	Don't know	Often	Yes, definitely

5. Can your child play with materials with a sibling or friend without a disability?

_____	_✓_	_____	_____	_____
Never	Probably not	Don't know	Probably	Yes, definitely

6. Is your child likely to damage or destroy materials and toys during free time at home unless you watch him or her?

_____	_✓_	_____	_____	_____
Never	Hardly ever	Don't know	Often	Almost always

7. Do you think that appropriate and enjoyable toys and activities are available for children with disabilities like yours?

_____	_____	_✓_	_____	_____
No	Probably not	Don't know	Probably	Yes, definitely

8. When you need to be busy at home, can your child entertain him- or herself with an activity until you are available?

_____	_____	_____	_✓_	_____
Never	Hardly ever	Don't know	Sometimes	Yes, definitely

9. Does your child recognize when he or she has free time and begin to play in an acceptable way on his or her own?

_____	_____	_____	_✓_	_____
Never	Hardly ever	Don't know	Sometimes	Yes, definitely

(continued)

10. Do you think that the activities your child usually engages in during free time are constructive and/or supportive of his or her further development?

No	Probably not	✓ Don't know	Probably	Yes, definitely

11. How important do you think each of the following behavior and curriculum areas are to your child's overall development and adult adjustment? Please check the rating that matches your opinion:

	Not at all important		Don't know		Very important
Adaptive skills (eating, bathing, dressing, toileting)	——	——	——	——	✓
Motor skills/mobility	——	——	——	✓	✓
Preacademic and academic skills	——	——	——	——	✓
Prevocational and vocational skills	——	——	——	——	✓
Leisure-time skills	——	——	——	——	✓
Behavior management	——	——	——	——	✓
Language development	——	——	——	——	✓

LEVEL ONE: EQUIPMENT LOAN WITH OR WITHOUT CONSULTATION

Most families in our field test selected the first level of home involvement. Some key points for implementing this service option were:

1. Only those leisure activities for which the participant was receiving instruction or the participant had previously mastered were loaned out to that family.
2. The parent instructor made certain that the participant demonstrated his or her use of the activity materials in the home in the presence of the parents.
3. The parent instructor explained exactly the purpose and appropriate use of each leisure material and what type of play behaviors the parents should expect. This was especially important when activities were individualized for a participant's specific needs.
4. The parent instructor gave parents examples of self-initiation and how this should be rewarded.
5. Periodic contacts between parents and the parent instructor (and school) were made and documented.

LEVEL TWO: EQUIPMENT LOAN AND PARENT INSTRUCTION

The second level of home involvement required a substantial commitment from parents, as they were actually involved in skill development and facilitating self-initiated play. Parents were instructed in general strategies to help the participant learn (e.g., reinforcement, prompting). The parent instructor would model these various techniques and observe and provide feedback to the parent as he or she worked with the individual. This occurred over several different in-home sessions that included the parent instructor, family members, and the participant. Parents were also instructed in how to use the Home Leisure Data Sheet (Form 8.6) and how to use the cue "free time" every 3 days if the participant did not self-initiate play with the activities. Key points for implementing this service option were:

1. The Leisure Home Program Procedures (Form 9.8) were used to carefully describe specific participant behaviors and what parents should do when they observe them.

2. Parent descriptions of the participant's play behavior on the Home Leisure Data Sheet were regularly reviewed and used to target specific play objectives for future instruction (e.g., self-initiation, playing for longer durations of time, positive interactions with siblings and peers in the neighborhood, increased skill acquisition).
3. Home visits occurred at least every 2 weeks and were prescheduled using the Home Visit Appointment Form (Form 9.5).
4. Siblings and other family members were given instruction in how to implement the program.

LEVEL THREE: EQUIPMENT LOAN AND IN-HOME INSTRUCTION

The third level of in-home services recognizes the importance of community instruction if skills needed in the natural environment are to be elicited in the presence of natural cues and correction procedures, and if they are to be maintained by the presence of natural reinforcers (Falvey, Brown, Lyon, Baumgart, & Schroeder, 1980; Schleien & Ray, 1988). More and more school programs serving individuals with significant disabilities have incorporated both home and community instruction into their curricula. For families who do not wish to or cannot participate in providing instruction themselves, but welcome another leisure educator (e.g., therapeutic recreation specialist, teacher) into their homes, this level of home involvement ensures skills taught in the classroom generalize to the natural environment of the home and neighborhood.

During the field testing of *Ho'onanea* for families who selected this level of services, the parent instructor implemented the same instructional strategies used during the school day in the home, with a particular focus on the choice instruction described in earlier chapters.

Program Evaluation

All parents whose sons or daughters participated in the *Ho'onanea* project were asked to complete a measure of consumer satisfaction at the beginning (pre) and end (post) of 1 of 2 school years during which their children received classroom instruction with leisure activities. Results of our survey were mixed. In some cases, parents perceived their child's behavior more positively following leisure instruction at school and had become more aware of the availability of age-appropriate materials for learners with significant disabilities, particularly teenagers. In most cases, however, parent ratings remained much the same, and in a small number of cases even declined. This may reflect an increased awareness of leisure activity possibilities for their children after a year of exposure to a leisure education program. Leisure behavior may be significantly improved during free time in school as a function of leisure education, but may actually remain unchanged in the home environment; this is the familiar problem of generalization and maintenance. This was less likely to occur when the leisure activities were available to the participant in the home through participation in the in-home component, or simply because the family had the materials.

Several evaluation studies conducted in our work did support an increase in participants' skill levels as a function of school-based leisure education, and those behavioral changes were documented not only during instruction sessions but also during unstructured free time in the classroom (Meyer, Evans, Wuerch, & Brennan, 1985; Voeltz & Delong, 1981). In a study of social validity, in which parents rated pre- and postinstruction videotaped free-time vignettes, we found that parents rated the postinstruction vignettes significantly higher (Voeltz, Wuerch, & Bockhaut, 1982). Our findings suggest that in addition to increased skill levels as a function of instruction, parents were able to perceive significant postinstruction changes during free-time situations that occurred in school. If parents do not perceive the same types of changes in the participant's behavior at home, this emphasizes the importance of home involvement to facilitate transfer of skills to that criterion environment.

Leisure Home Program Procedures

Participant: __Dana Johnson__

Activity: __Pinball__

Stored where: __Dana's bedroom__

Who will conduct program: __Mom__

Most likely day(s): __M-F__

Most likely time(s): __after school – 4:00 pm.__

Where will activity occur: __in bedroom, pinball machine on desk__

How should activity begin: __"Dana, free time, get your pinball machine. Remember, Dana, if__
__you bounce the pinball machine, I'll have to take it away for a while."__

	If participant does:	Parent will (describe procedures for positive and negative behavior):
Positive	doesn't bounce pinball machine	Give verbal praise. "What a terrific pinball player. You can really make those bells go off without bouncing it." Physical praise, etc. – whatever Dana likes (hugs, pats, etc.)
Negative	bounces pinball machine to make bells go off without shooting ball into playing area.	Take machine away for 30 seconds and say, "OK, Dana, you bounced it. I'll have to take it away for a while." If she bounces it again, "Sorry, Dana, you're not playing with it the right way – you're not supposed to bounce it. Maybe next time you'll play nicely." Take away.

How should activity end: __If Dana played appropriately, praise her. If she played inappropriately (bounced__
__pinball machine), explain why pinball machine was taken away – Dana should put activity away.__

Participant Activity Update

Leisure
Educator: _Amy Selenister_   Participant: _Dana Johnson_

Date	Activities* available	Activity preference	Activity(ies) in instruction and skill level	Comments (reinforcers used, adaptations, etc.)
5/1/94	Pi, NGB, CF, MM	Pi, NGB, CF	Pi – can pull shooter, turn ball reset tracks, but does not always put both hands on flippers or set ball on "3."	Encourage Dana to use index finger to rest ball, and not thumb. Use verbal reminders "Dana, both hands on the flippers" before beginning.

*A = Aerobic Warm-ups; CF = Connect Four; J = Jenga; MM = Magic Mitts; NGB = Nintendo Game Boy; Pi = Pinball; Po = Pottery; RC = Remote Control Vehicle; S = Simon; T = Target Games.

211

In order to plan a leisure-time program for your child at home, we need to know what you feel are important objectives in this area. Please take a few minutes to let us know how important you consider each of the following statements and how much experience you have had in the area. On the left side of the page, using the key at the top of the column, place a circle around the number that shows how important each statement is to you and your child. On the right side of the page, using the key at the top of the column, place a circle around the number that shows how much experience you have had with each statement. Please make sure you have circled a number in both the left and right column for each statement.

How important is this
for you and your child?
1. Not important
2. Somewhat important
3. Important
4. Very important

How much experience
have you had with this?
1. None
2. Very little
3. More than a little
4. A lot

Importance					Statement	Experience			
1	2	3	4	1.	Making leisure activities easily accessible so my child can initiate play on his or her own.	1	2	3	4
1	2	3	4	2.	Knowing what I can expect my child to do during his or her leisure time.	1	2	3	4
1	2	3	4	3.	Understanding the importance of leisure activities instruction as a part of my child's educational program.	1	2	3	4
1	2	3	4	4.	Developing ways to involve siblings with their brother or sister with a disability.	1	2	3	4
1	2	3	4	5.	Knowing what demands I can be placing on my child at home for appropriate behavior during leisure time.	1	2	3	4
1	2	3	4	6.	Structuring a weekly or daily period of time to work with my child on how to use his or her leisure time more independently/enjoyably.	1	2	3	4
1	2	3	4	7.	Knowing how to decide what types of toys/activities are appropriate for my child.	1	2	3	4
1	2	3	4	8.	Knowing how to "introduce" a new toy/leisure activity for my child so he or she will see how it works.	1	2	3	4
1	2	3	4	9.	Motivating my child so he or she will select a toy/activity and play alone for a period of time.	1	2	3	4
1	2	3	4	10.	Deciding whether my child likes or dislikes a particular toy/activity.	1	2	3	4
1	2	3	4	11.	Knowing where to buy or find toys/activities that are appropriate for my child.	1	2	3	4
1	2	3	4	12.	Working with my child's teacher in developing appropriate leisure-time behavior.	1	2	3	4
1	2	3	4	13.	Getting my child to play alone for longer periods of time.	1	2	3	4
1	2	3	4	14.	Keeping my child interested in a toy/activity.	1	2	3	4
1	2	3	4	15.	Understanding how leisure-time instruction relates to my child's IEP.	1	2	3	4
1	2	3	4	16.	Getting my child to initiate play with a toy/activity.	1	2	3	4
1	2	3	4	17.	Arranging materials in my child's room so that he or she can readily play with a toy/activity on his or her own.	1	2	3	4
1	2	3	4	18.	Selecting toys/activities that are appropriate for my child and that he or she enjoys.	1	2	3	4
1	2	3	4	19.	Knowing how much time I can spend with my child in leisure-time activities.	1	2	3	4
1	2	3	4	20.	Knowing how often and for how long my child can be expected to play independently without help.	1	2	3	4
1	2	3	4	21.	Knowing how to teach my child to play appropriately with a new toy/activity.	1	2	3	4

(continued)

1. Not important		1. None
2. Somewhat important		2. Very little
3. Important		3. More than a little
4. Very important		4. A lot

1 2 3 4			1 2 3 4
1 2 3 4	22.	Making reasonable demands on my child's siblings in terms of how much time his or her brother(s) and/or sister(s) can be expected to spend with him or her.	1 2 3 4
1 2 3 4	23.	Knowing the effects of play behavior on my child's future development.	1 2 3 4
1 2 3 4	24.	Knowing how to increase my child's independence during leisure time.	1 2 3 4
1 2 3 4	25.	Making leisure-time toys/activities available at home for my child.	1 2 3 4
1 2 3 4	26.	Structuring an area at home where my child can play independently during leisure time.	1 2 3 4
1 2 3 4	27.	Knowing what leisure-time activities are available in the community for my child.	1 2 3 4
1 2 3 4	28.	Knowing how to increase my child's independent use of leisure time in the community.	1 2 3 4
1 2 3 4	29.	Prompting my child to play with leisure toys/activities.	1 2 3 4
1 2 3 4	30.	Getting my child to spend his or her leisure time appropriately with peers with and without disabilities.	1 2 3 4
1 2 3 4	31.	Handling situations when toys/activities fail to work.	1 2 3 4
1 2 3 4	32.	Handling situations when toys/activities get broken accidentally.	1 2 3 4
1 2 3 4	33.	Handling situations when toys/activities get broken purposefully.	1 2 3 4
1 2 3 4	34.	Handling situations when my child wants leisure time but cannot have it.	1 2 3 4
1 2 3 4	35.	Using leisure time as a reward for other behaviors.	1 2 3 4
1 2 3 4	36.	Knowing how to work on play activities with my child.	1 2 3 4
1 2 3 4	37.	Knowing how I can expect my child to play with certain leisure-time toys/activities.	1 2 3 4
1 2 3 4	38.	Knowing how to develop my child's independent use of leisure time in the community.	1 2 3 4

Please answer the following questions by filling in the blank or circling the appropriate response.

1. How old is your child? _____

2. What sex is your child? _____

3. What type of disability does your child have?

4. How does your child communicate?

    a. Verbal   b. Nonverbal

    If your child is nonverbal, does he or she sign?

    a. Yes   b. No

5. What is your child's current educational environment?

    a. Self-contained special school (no children without disabilities enrolled)
    b. Self-contained classroom (special class for children with disabilities located in a regular school)
    c. Resource room (part-time special class and part-time regular class)
    d. Residential care facility (explain: _____)
    e. Other _____

(continued)

6. Does your child have access to peers with disabilities after school?

    a. Yes   b. No

7. Does your child have access to peers without disabilities after school?

    a. Yes   b. No

8. What is your relationship to your child?

    a. Parent
    b. Guardian
    c. Foster parent
    d. Group home manager
    e. Other _____

Home Involvement to Support Children's Friendships

Just as a parent can play a vital role in influencing a child's leisure education goals and support-ing in-home play, a parent can be instrumental in encouraging a child's social relationships and friendships (Asher & Williams, 1987; Hartup, 1992). In the previous chapter, we described how family focus groups were used in the Dowling Friendship Program (Heyne, Schleien, & McAvoy, 1993) to bring family members, school staff, and recreation professionals together to promote relationships and friendships between elementary-age students with and without signif-icant disabilities while involved in leisure-time activities. We would like to close this chapter on home involvement by giving you a closer look at some of the thoughts, opinions, and percep-tions of these Minneapolis parents regarding their children's relationships (Heyne, 1993). Through sharing their impressions, we hope to demonstrate how critical—as well as inspira-tional—parental input can be in understanding issues related to friendship and in collaborating to design leisure education programs that promote social inclusion goals.

Earlier in this chapter we emphasized the importance of listening to parents to gain their in-sights into their children's personalities, communication styles, preferences, and needs. As part of the Dowling Friendship Program, we had the opportunity to hear what parents had to say as they took part in periodic semistructured interviews throughout the 2-year program. To create a trusting, nonthreatening environment in which parents could speak freely about their chil-dren's friendship needs as well as their families' dreams and concerns, interviews were struc-tured informally—as a "conversation with a purpose" (Dexter, 1970; Merriam, 1988). In-terviews were open-ended in nature (to allow parents themselves to choose how they wished to formulate their answers) and took place in families' homes, at the school, or in restaurants—wherever it was convenient for parents to meet. It was this parental input and involvement that guided the direction of the program, served as an impetus for program implementation, and shaped many of the friendship outcomes for the children. Some of the questions that parents of children with disabilities were asked included:

• Why is it important for your child to make friends?
• What hopes and dreams do you have for your child's friendships?
• What fears or concerns do you have about your child's friendships?

• What stands in the way of your child's making friends?
• How does your child benefit from friendships with same-age peers?
• Do you think your child's friendships will last?

These questions served as a springboard for many in-depth conversations with parents about their children's social relationships. The answers to their questions are presented below.

Parents with Children with Disabilities Talk About Their Children's Friendships[1]
When asked, "Why is it important for your child to make friends (with peers without disabilities)?" parents' answers ranged from learning appropriate social play behaviors, to having a confidante, to simply experiencing what it is like to "have and be a friend." In their own words, they responded:

> It is important for the same reasons it is important for any child to make friends. They need someone they can be themselves with, hang out with, share their secrets with—someone to ask how things are going, and encourage and challenge them.

> By playing and making friends with other children, Sam will learn how to act appropriately in a group. He will learn to listen to others, to wait and take his turn, and to pay attention to what is going on around him.

> When our younger child [without a disability] began to make friends earlier than our older daughter, Tracy [who has a disability], we realized Tracy had missed some important milestones in learning to get along with and relate to others. We hope that by being with nondisabled peers she can learn the give-and-take of social relationships and what it means to be and have a friend.

When asked, "What hopes and dreams do you have for your child's friendships?" parents of children with disabilities expressed many of the same wishes that parents of children without disabilities might desire for their children:

> I would like my daughter to make one or two good friends in the neighborhood who will visit her at our house and invite her to their [house] on a regular basis.

> I want my son to be in the "right" crowd, not the "parking lot" crowd.

> I want my son to know that he can have a friend. If John discovers he can have a friend at age 6, then maybe he will realize he can have friends for the rest of his life.

The question "What fears or concerns do you have about your child's friendships?" elicited worries that any parent might have, but ones that these parents of children with disabilities were particularly concerned with—fears of their children's potential isolation and low self-image:

> I am afraid the disability itself will be a barrier to friendship. Even something as minor as having red hair—much less using a wheelchair—can keep people from wanting to get to know a person.

> I am afraid that other children will tease my daughter.

> I am afraid that my son will not be able to make any friends, that no other children will respond or reach out to him.

> I do not want my daughter to feel like she has to apologize for herself.

Parents were also asked, "What stands in the way of your child making friends?" As reported in Chapter 8, this volume, their responses included: 1) families' busy schedules, which

---

[1]In the quotations cited here and in the next section, the children's real names and other identifying characteristics have been changed for confidentiality.

makes it difficult to arrange times for children to play together; 2) stereotypic thinking and lack of accurate information about people with disabilities; 3) children may not live near each other, which makes it inconvenient for children to see each other regularly; 4) differences in children's ability levels (e.g., social skills, communication skills, mobility); 5) arranging public transportation for children with physical disabilities to get together with peers without disabilities; 6) parents of families whose personalities or lifestyles are not compatible; and 7) parents are not acquainted with other families who have same-age peers without disabilities with whom their children could play. Quotations from parents that were representative of some of these obstacles to friendships included:

> Parents' schedules are the biggest barriers to friendships. It is difficult to coordinate everyone's schedules and arrange times to get together.

> The biggest barrier right now seems to be thinking that my daughter may not be accepted by others as an equal partner. I am sure this stems from my having to defend her so often in public.

> Sometimes she talks during the video. They'll ask her, "Can you be quiet, Leah?" but she'll just keep talking. She's like a broken record that just keeps going.

> It is difficult to get together with other families when we live so far apart. If we have to drive, it takes an extra effort to make arrangements to meet.

Despite the barriers to developing relationships and friendships between children with and without disabilities, parents of children with disabilities perceived many rewarding outcomes that resulted from the relationships. When asked, "How does your child benefit from friendships with same-age peers?" parents saw improvements in the areas of self-esteem, social skills, confidence, increased attention span, and general happiness:

> My daughter's self-esteem and self-confidence have improved tremendously. She is initiating conversations, inviting friends over, and greeting other children more appropriately than she used to do.

> She is able to be with a group of kids for a longer period of time without interrupting.

> My son has a better understanding of what it means to be a friend. He knows who his friends are and realizes that he has choices about who he plays with. He realizes that he does not have to play with just anyone.

> She has certainly changed in the last year. She has a longer interest in activities and is able to remember them later and remain excited about them. She's more tuned into the world around her.

> What has really pleased me is that Ben seems happier. He likes to come home and tell me all about what happened [at school] with his friends.

When asked, "Do you think your child's friendships will last?" parents' responses varied considerably. Some parents believed—or wished—their children's relationships would continue throughout the teen years and into adulthood:

> I believe that my daughter's relationships have the potential to last for the rest of her life.

> I guess a tiny corner of my dream is that Julia [peer without disability] will come to my daughter's high school graduation!

Other parents felt that, in the real world, it would be natural for friends to change or go their separate ways:

I have to realize that her circle of friends will change. She may become lifetime friends with one or two of the kids, but that is not necessarily a dream of mine. I do not think that happens a lot in the real world—that people remain friends forever.

Despite these differences in opinion, most parents agreed that, even if their children's current friendships did not endure the test of time, if the children possessed the skills to make a friend, they could continue to make new friends throughout their lives. As one parent explained:

Even if Jenny's friendships do not last, through the friendships she has made, she has learned the skills to make a friend. She will carry these skills with her and continue to make new friends throughout her life.

Listening to parents of children with disabilities express their views about their children's relationships gave professionals a greater understanding of children's needs and characteristics, as well as family perspectives. To gain an even fuller picture of the nature of relationships and friendships between children with and without disabilities, parents of children *without* disabilities were also interviewed.

Parents with Children Without Disabilities Talk About Their Children's Friendships
The impressions of parents of children without disabilities regarding their children's relationships with peers with disabilities were particularly enlightening in two important areas: 1) parents' aspirations for their children's friendships with peers with disabilities, and 2) the actual benefits their children derived from the relationships.

When parents of children without disabilities were asked, "What hopes and dreams do you have for your child's friendships (with children with disabilities)?" several issues came to light. Many parents wanted to "undo the past" they had experienced as children, when contact and interaction with children with special needs were not possible, resulting in a veil of mystery and misunderstanding that surrounded people with disabilities. Parents wanted to see a world in which a better understanding of differences and similarities prevailed. Parents expressed their hopes in these ways:

Our generation did not understand people with disabilities. I would like my child to have an opportunity that I never had, which is to get to know, on a personal level, children with disabilities.

When I was a child, I had relatives who had disabilities. I did not understand what that meant and I was terrified. I was afraid to be around anyone who seemed different. I want Mary to have a different experience. I want her to understand disabilities and be comfortable with people who have them. I want her to be able to see the person, not the disability.

For other parents, friendship transcended issues related to ability or any physical characteristic:

I would like my daughter to learn that color, race, or any degree of disability should not interfere with becoming friends.

I simply want my daughter to learn how to be a friend.

The perceptions of parents of children without disabilities were also very revealing when they were asked, "How does your child benefit from friendships with same-age peers (with disabilities)?" Whereas the parents of children with disabilities generally had difficulty seeing how children without disabilities could benefit from the relationships, parents of children without disabilities saw numerous benefits for their children. Benefits were especially noted in the area of an enhanced awareness and acceptance of differences. Many parents believed their children also matured in their sense of individuality, personal worth, and character development. In their own words:

> She sees people with better eyes than I did [at her age]. She's not afraid to reach out and help someone. She's not afraid of kids in wheelchairs or a kid that can't talk.

> Julia has really opened up. In crowds, she used to hang back. Now she is right up front.

> It is nice to see how comfortable Ben is with Andy. I can barely understand Andy when he talks, but Ben understands him perfectly.

> Getting to know a child with a disability has helped my daughter feel less "different" and excluded. She is an American Indian and does not always know how she "fits in" with others around her.

> He has tapped into a part of himself that he might not have developed otherwise.

Other parents believed their children benefited simply because they made a new friend:

> She never questioned . . . whether anybody was white or black or whatever. They were just becoming friends.

In summary, talking with parents can reveal to professionals a wealth of information about children's needs and family life to which, otherwise, they would have no access. Such one-to-one conversations can form a trusting rapport between the professional and the parent and result in a strong collaborative team from which a child with a disability can benefit tremendously. (For more information about semistructured, in-depth interview techniques, see Henderson, 1991, pp. 71–85; Merriam, 1988, pp. 71–86; Taylor & Bogdan, 1984, pp. 76–105.)

Epilogue

A LOOK TOWARD THE FUTURE IN SERVICE DELIVERY

Ronald P. Reynolds

*T*his epilogue is intended to identify emerging trends that will influence the provision of leisure service delivery to persons with developmental disabilities. Contemporary movements in society and in the field of human services are identified, including developments in the broad disciplines of education, recreation, and the allied health professions. In addition, I cite specific examples of these influences in the actual provision of leisure services, drawing on my background as a therapeutic recreation specialist. Using this information as a foundation, I share my perspectives concerning future actions. During this process, I tried to adopt a "where we were," "where we are," and "where we might be going" approach. My comments are organized around five topical areas, which may be conceptualized as shown in Table E.1.

SHIFT FROM ISOLATED ACTIVITIES TO DEVELOPMENTAL PROGRAMMING

Until recently, much of the programming literature in the recreation, education, and adapted physical education fields was devoted to how to plan and implement (and infrequently evaluate) a specific activity for a client or group of clients. The major goal of these interventions was to have the client(s) perform the activity "successfully." Little thought was given to the developmental nature of the activity. Specifically, little attention was paid to the contribution that this activity would (or would not make) to the participant's overall level of functioning and quality of life; therefore, individuals were frequently led through a variety of random, isolated games and activities based on best guesses and, in many cases, interests of the individual instructor. This approach to activity "planning" resulted in several negative consequences. One of these consequences concerned the age appropriateness of activities. Adults were frequently encouraged to participate in children's

Table E.1. Trends in the provision of leisure services for persons with developmental disabilities

Away from	Toward
Isolated, random activities	Developmental programs
Segregated environments	Inclusive community-based programs
Individual discipline intervention	Interdisciplinary approaches in consort with family
Little accountability for assessment	High degree of internal and external accountability
Little concern for advocacy issues	Greater concern for larger societal barriers

activities when alternative pursuits were readily available. Similarly, adolescents were frequently integrated into the play environments of younger children. As a result of these practices, people with developmental disabilities were often stigmatized by their leisure lifestyles.

Other concerns related to questions of transfer and generalization; specifically, would the skills learned through one activity be useful in the performance of another? Also, would leisure skills transcend specific programming environments? In many cases, these important questions were not addressed. On a larger scale, leisure skill providers revealed little interest in the development of collateral skills, specifically as play behavior relates to social, motor, and educational development. Similarly, little attention was paid to the maintenance of leisure skills. As a consequence, abilities achieved through considerable effort were frequently lost with the passage of time.

Another area of neglect related to the provision of lifelong leisure skills. Clients frequently found themselves without a repertoire of leisure activities as they passed through developmental stages into adulthood. Other concerns related to the quality of interactions present in the instructional environment. For example, there appears to be little emphasis placed on the affective domain in much leisure skill instruction. Until recently, few practitioners or researchers sought to foster cooperation and the development of relationships among persons with developmental disabilities and/or individuals without disabilities through play. Indeed, the socializing aspects of play and leisure were not generally addressed in conjunction with skill acquisition.

Other questions arise concerning the types of activities favored by instructors who work with persons with developmental disabilities. Even a quick perusal of the literature reveals a large reliance on group, large motor, and passive activities. This orientation has detracted from our ultimate goal, which should be self-directed, spontaneous play. Such play should be modulated by cues present in the natural environment. On a related note, some leisure skill instructors have relied on expensive, esoteric play materials to engender responses from clients. This practice has led to concerns regarding generalization and transfer as previously discussed.

Other issues relate to the assumptions made concerning the skill levels of participants. Many approaches to leisure skill development have been predicated on the notion that learners possess similar functional abilities, when, in fact, their levels of functioning may be quite heterogeneous. A final, and most important, point evolves around the failure of leisure educators to capitalize on the participant's inherent leisure interests. In our enthusiasm for teaching leisure skills, we have probably not spent enough time assessing what the participant wishes to learn. We may not exhibit adequate concern for the elements of choice and pleasure that should occur in play and leisure. As a result, we may be limiting the participant's motivation and diminishing the enjoyment that should be inherent in play.

Today, there is ample evidence to suggest that all of these conditions are changing. Although space constraints preclude a more extensive review of current literature, citations on the following pages are illustrative of the shift from isolated skill acquisition efforts to developmental programming for persons with significant disabilities.

Dixon (1980) recognized the need for developmental programming, which greatly transcends the teaching of individual activities when working with learners with developmental disabilities. In his words:

> Leisure education, as a part of therapeutic recreation service, must meet the leisure needs of the mentally retarded, increase independence in leisure participation and facilitate the acceptance and integration of the individual into society. The effectiveness of leisure education intervention with the mentally retarded will depend on the therapeutic recreation professional's selection and use of teaching techniques and how well these strategies complement the individual being served. These teaching techniques need to be individually oriented, complement the activity being taught by preserving its motivating qualities and be efficient in facilitating the individual toward independent leisure participation. (p. 32)

Dixon (1980) suggests the following principles in regard to programming leisure activities in remedial content areas:

introducing new leisure activities;
responding to client preferences for leisure participation;
facilitating client improvement in skills which enhance their potential for leisure participation;
balancing leisure skill acquisition with a playful attitude toward leisure participation. (p. 33)

It is obvious that these steps are designed to capitalize on the client's leisure interests, promote transfer of learning, and encourage self-directed play.

Crawford (1986) designed and experimentally validated a procedure for generalizing lifelong leisure skills acquired by persons with multiple disabilities in segregated environments to natural community environments. Recognizing that leisure skill instruction should be part of a "longitudinal plan" for integrating people with disabilities into society, age-appropriate leisure skills, such as bowling, darts, and stereo operation, would transfer from a segregated instruction room to community-based recreational environments. Because limited generalization of target behaviors were found among the 10 children with significant mental retardation in Crawford's study, this investigation underlined the need for further development of generalization and skill acquisition techniques when working with persons with more severe and multiple disabilities.

In an attempt to overcome these obstacles to generalization of leisure skills to community-based environments, Pollingue and Cobb (1986) developed a three-phase model designed to "provide continuous participation of mentally retarded adults in existing community recreation resources" (p. 57). Phase I (assessment) consisted of the establishment of leisure patterns and determination of community resources and leisure choices. Leisure patterns were determined by using the Leisure Environment Profile, the Leisure Preferences Checklist, and the Adaptive Behavior Scale (Nihira, Foster, Shellhas, & Leland, 1969). The availability of community resources was determined by an individualized inventory of recreational facilities. Selection of leisure skills was based on the criteria of: 1) realistic assessment of the participant's interests and abilities, 2) leisure preferences of the participant's family members, 3) cost of the activity, 4) availability of transportation, and 5) independent functioning level of the participant. Phase II (implementation) involved instructing the individual on the various skills needed in the actual subenvironment (i.e., community) in both supervised and unsupervised conditions. Phase III (evaluation) involved data collected during the implementation phase. The various types of adaptations included: 1) material, 2) rules or procedures, 3) skill sequence, 4) facility, and 5) lead-up activities (Wehman & Schleien, 1981). This approach is but one example of the comprehensive effort that must be made when facilitating the leisure skill development of persons with developmental disabilities.

A more recent intervention addressing the need for generalization of leisure skills was undertaken by Schleien, Cameron, Rynders, and Slick (1988). Using a case study approach, leisure skill instructors taught cooperative play to children with severe multiple disabilities. Parents were then given instruction at home. It was found that the additional instruction facilitated acquisition of skills and generalization and maintenance across time.

In our earlier review of past leisure education practices, therapeutic recreation professionals identified a need for more cooperative types of leisure activities. These should be in sharp contrast to many integrated programs that Hutchison and Lord (1979) found to be "competitive, formal and skill oriented instead of developmental and humanistic, allowing all persons to participate at their level" (p. 23). McGill (1984a) suggested that:

The environment should be one where all children feel free to interact and to play with each other. The environment should be one where all children, regardless of their skill level, are encouraged to participate to the best of their ability. It should be an environment that is fun and that permits each child to develop within his or her own growth and development patterns. The environment should not be one that puts undue stress on skill level or on negatively valued differences. (p. 15)

Two publications have also focused on the need to promote social skills through play and recreation. Sneegas (1989) notes in a review article that social skills are frequently targeted for intervention due to their centrality to the leisure experience. She cites both the cognitive problem-solving approach and the social skills instruction approach as being key tools for therapeutic recreation specialists and other disciplines. Using the latter method, Schleien, Fahnestock, Green, and Rynders (1990) initiated a combined package of leisure and social skills instruction, networking, sociometry, circle of friends, and cooperative learning to reduce the isolation of children with severe developmental disabilities.

As mentioned earlier, past leisure skill education processes have frequently ignored the feelings of participants about activities offered. This has been unfortunate because "the demonstration of choice through selection encourages spontaneous initiation of activity, engagement with elements of the environment and the assertion of control over one's surroundings" (Dattilo & Barnett, 1985a, p. 80). Dattilo and Barnett completed a preliminary study designed to assess the effect of choice on the affective behaviors of nonverbal children with developmental disabilities. Using videotapes to record facial expressions and vocalizations, they were able to establish a link between the ability to control one's leisure environment and mood. Specifically, when children could activate a television program by manipulating an electronic switch, they exhibited less negative affective behavior than when the programs were presented in a noncontingent fashion. Mahon and Bullock (1992) also focused on maintaining self-control during leisure. Using a decision-making model and self-control instruction with four adolescents with mental retardation, they were able to bring about improvements in self-instructed decision making and level of leisure awareness during an 8-week instructional program. Although these programs must be viewed as being tentative, they lend support for the emphasis on self-directed play and provide a promising method for determining when activities for persons with developmental disabilities are perceived as being pleasurable.

FROM SEGREGATED ENVIRONMENTS TO INCLUSIVE COMMUNITY-BASED PROGRAMS

The move away from isolated activity provision toward developmental programming is causing service providers to reexamine the environments in which they offer programs. Today, leisure services professionals and those from other disciplines are becoming aware of the fact that problems associated with the chronological age appropriateness of activities, transfer and generalization of skills, maintenance of ability, provision of lifelong leisure skills, socialization with peers without disabilities, naturally occurring environmental cues, and spontaneous play can only be overcome in inclusive, community-based programs. Since the 1980s there has been a dramatic increase in the number of research publications, program descriptions, textbooks, and reports addressing the provision of leisure skill programs for persons with developmental disabilities in community environments. This practice has generally been termed *recreation integration* or *inclusion*. In reviewing the literature pertaining to this process, Hutchison (1983) offers this general summary of trends:

1. Persons with disabilities and their families have expressed interest in participating in community recreational activities in small groups or with one or two friends rather than in large groups.

2. New skills appear to have the highest probability of transfer to regular environments when activities are meaningful, age appropriate, relevant, and chosen by the participants. The segregated and integrated environments should resemble each other as much as possible in respect to staff–participant ratio. Furthermore, a play/instruction approach may be superior to a therapeutic model.

3. Integration activity in municipal recreation services has increased in terms of the number of special needs coordinators employed, amount of reported programs, and willingness to serve people with disabilities.

4. Residential and day camps have been popular environments for recreation integration efforts and research.

Whereas early efforts to provide leisure services to persons with developmental disabilities in community recreation environments tended to be sporadic and on a small scale, today's efforts are far more ambitious in scope and are carried out in a systematic fashion. For example, within 1 year, one county recreation department fully integrated 262 participants with disabilities, using a progressive four-level challenge program that moved participants through various levels of integration (Richardson, Wilson, Wetherald, & Peters, 1987). Dixon (1980) outlines a similar continuum approach to mainstreaming and leisure education for persons with mental retardation. It should be noted that this process is designed specifically to facilitate choice, leisure satisfaction, and independent leisure participation.

Figure E.1 illustrates the concept of moving an individual with mental retardation from a state of impaired leisure behavior to independent leisure participation. Through effective intervention, the therapeutic recreation professional can reduce his or her role of assistance and

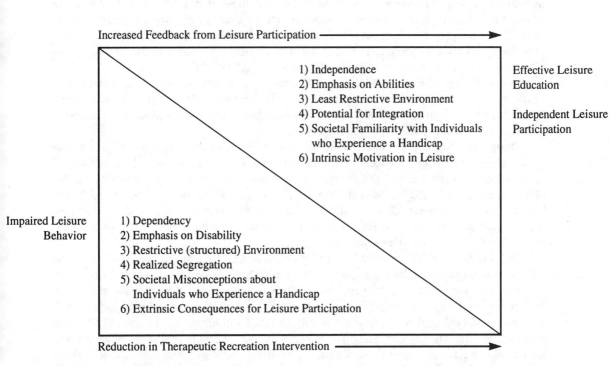

Figure E.1.   Impact of leisure education on mainstreaming concepts. (From Dixon, J.T. [1980]. Mainstreaming and leisure education for the mentally retarded. *Therapeutic Recreation Journal, 14*[1], 30–33; reprinted by permission.)

increase the feedback the individual receives from leisure participation. As a result, the individual demonstrates his or her independence, recreational abilities, and intrinsic motivation in a
least restrictive environment. Thus, society can recognize and become more familiar with special populations and the potential for integration in leisure environments.

In the field of physical education, the integration of children with developmental disabilities into regular activity programs has become so critical that in 1985 a complete issue of
Adapted Physical Activity Quarterly (*APAQ*) was devoted to this topic. Articles ranged from
philosophical and logistical considerations to the effects of mainstreaming on the motor performance of children with mental retardation, learning disabilities, and visual and hearing impairments. Recent issues of *APAQ* have focused directly on integrating children into sports and
physical activity. Nixon (1988) studied how parents encouraged (or discouraged) sports involvement for their offspring with visual impairments, the types of involvement children pursue, and
how parents adjust to the child. In a case study involving a child who was partially sighted,
Nixon (1989) explored the barriers to integrating a soccer league and track and field program.
Schleien, Heyne, and Berken (1988) pilot tested the effects of a collaborative sociomotor,
adapted physical education/therapeutic recreation curriculum on the social play and motor
development of children with autism and their peers without disabilities. Among their findings
were reduced inappropriate play behavior and an increase in two indicators of motor proficiency.
Maddy (1988) initiated a summer residential "close encounters" approach for teenagers with
physical disabilities. The ultimate goal of this program was to increase independence and freedom and to increase the use of community resources.

In the past few years much literature has been devoted to integrated camping for children
with disabilities. Sable (1992) described a collaborative effort to integrate 20 children with disabilities into a camp environment involving 180 peers without disabilities. Anecdotal data are
provided that support positive shifts in attitudes and the benefits of an inclusionary environment.
Camp Easter Seal has also adopted a radical departure from its traditional approach to segregated camping in North Carolina. The elements of this progressive model and the demographics
of those served are described by Bullock, Mahon, and Welch (1992).

Indeed, integrated outdoor education programs have become so much in demand that at
least one entire book has been devoted to this topic. Schleien, McAvoy, Lais, and Rynders
(1993) discuss at length the rationale, administration, adaptations, activity planning, and models
for integrated outdoor education and adventure programs.

Churton (1988) addressed three public laws that were amended to play an even greater role
in the delivery of adapted physical education services. These include the Education for All
Handicapped Children Act of 1975 as amended in 1986 by PL 99-457, the Rehabilitation Act
(RHA) as amended by PL 102-569, and the Developmental Disabilities Assistance and Bill of
Rights Act (DDA) as amended by PL 100-146. Legislature mandate allows the field of adapted
physical education to address issues of qualified personnel, research, transitional impact, appropriate education, and vocational training.

The Americans with Disabilities Act (ADA) of 1990, PL 101-336, has been heralded as the
most far-reaching mandate for the equality of persons with disabilities in this country to date. Its
five titles (i.e., employment, public entities, public accommodations, telecommunications, and
miscellaneous provisions) promise to have a direct positive effect on the approximately 43 mil-
lion people affected by this law. In my opinion, the ADA will improve the leisure lifestyles of
persons with disabilities by increasing discretionary income, expanding the scope of leisure pursuits, facilitating family-oriented recreation, and reducing the stigma that is sometimes associated with certain disabilities.

It seems obvious from this discussion that community leisure environments will serve more
frequently as laboratories to practice recently acquired leisure skills and as the ultimate environ-

ments for persons with developmental disabilities to pursue an independent leisure lifestyle (Schleien & Ray, 1988; Schleien & Werder, 1985).

INCREASING INTERDISCIPLINARY
COOPERATION AND FAMILY INVOLVEMENT

There is every indication that today's "team approach" to the provision of leisure services to learners with developmental disabilities will intensify and that family members will constitute a significant part of this process. Much of the impetus for this trend comes from PL 101-476, Individuals with Disabilities Education Act of 1990 (IDEA), which states that an individualized education program (IEP) be developed for children with special needs. Based on this law, parents, teachers, physical education personnel, and recreation personnel become partners in designing physical activity programs in the public school system. Parents assume responsibility for identifying their child's leisure education needs and for working with their child during afterschool hours. According to Dunn (1983):

> Parents can serve not only to maintain the child's skills learned in physical education, but also can actually accelerate learning so that coordination with parents is an important element in the motor and physical fitness of severely handicapped students. (p. 69)

Similarly, after reviewing the preliminary data related to the effectiveness of parents in implementing supplementary home instruction, Folsom-Meek (1984) concluded:

> When parents and children participate in a supplementary home program, several benefits are possible. Handicapped children's motor proficiency and physical fitness levels are enhanced. Teachers and parents improve communication by working together toward the mutual goal of benefitting handicapped children. Parents become strong advocates of their children's programs when they are part of successful implementation procedures. Parent–child relationships are enhanced because of the time spent together. Most children want to move and to learn, and physical education subject matter offers these opportunities. (p. 280)

Another exciting concept is the notion of family leisure programming. In this model, a leisure education specialist works directly with a small number of families who have children with disabilities in a centrally located, accessible facility on a regular basis. Monroe (1987) describes the family leisure education portion of one such existing program as follows:

> This component addresses the development of leisure attitudes and skills suitable for the home as well as the community. This task is accomplished during the activity portion of each program session. The activities that the therapists choose, to reinforce the goal areas, should also help the family discover new leisure activities that are transferable to daily living and that are within the financial reach of family participants. The general rule of thumb is to choose simple activities that require a minimum of resources and dollar expenditure. It is also helpful to encourage family members to make up their own games out of things that could be found around the house. (p. 48)

She further stated:

> The therapeutic recreation specialist should be constantly aware of helping family members identify ways of modifying activities and finding alternative activities that they can participate in as a family unit. (p. 49)

DeSalvatore (1989) took a similar approach to family therapy. Using a six-phase approach, he proposed techniques whereby activity professionals could involve parents and other family members fully in each phase of the program of children with emotional disturbances.

As the home environment's potential for leisure skill acquisition becomes established and as parents justifiably assert their rights to be involved in educational planning for their children, programs such as these may well become the rule rather than the exception.

THE QUEST FOR ACCOUNTABILITY THROUGH ASSESSMENT

In the past, it was common for leisure services providers to rely on subjective data regarding the success or failure of their interventions. Very often, their "impressions" of participant progress served as the only feedback mechanism to gauge the effectiveness of programs. In other instances, ancillary personnel may have been polled as to their perceptions of participant improvement. When data were collected, they tended to be anecdotal in nature, providing a written narrative of participants' reactions rather than comparing behaviors to objective standards. Today, there is ample evidence that this situation has changed. One rarely sees a journal article describing a leisure skill program or technique that does not have an evaluative component. Likewise, assessment has become a chief concern of leisure services practitioners. Much of the impetus for improving assessment techniques has come from the mandate of regulatory bodies, including agencies of the government, third-party reimbursers, and independent organizations such as the Joint Commission on Accreditation of Healthcare Organizations (JCAHO). These organizations have become increasingly concerned with cost containment in health care services, which has in turn prompted a demand for increased accountability or quality assurance on the part of all persons providing services to persons with disabilities. Joswiak (1980) summarized this need for accountability as follows:

> In terms of professional concerns, the most important rationale for assessment is improved accountability and services to clients. Related to these areas, assessment:
>
> is the tool for identifying the client's baseline of skills, knowledge and abilities;
> is essential in order to identify program and service objectives for clients;
> provides a vehicle to plan relevant teaching strategies or therapeutic interventions;
> furnishes the basis for identifying at a later date whether the client has made progress within recreation therapy programs. (p. 29)

Developing effective assessment procedures, however, is not a simple task. Witt, Connolly, and Compton (1980) have identified several key issues that must be addressed before a meaningful assessment process can be initiated. These include:

> What is the purpose of the assessment procedure or why is the assessment being conducted?
> How and by whom will the assessment data be utilized?
> What techniques will be utilized to accomplish the assessment process? (p. 6)

In addressing these questions, Wehman and Schleien (1980b) made the point that assessment should be made on two planes. In their words:

> Two major forms of assessment influence the success of an individual's program. The first is *baseline assessment*, an initial observation of the client's ability level before actual implementation of a program. A second form of assessment is *instructional assessment*, an ongoing evaluation of the progress which the client is making throughout the program. Both forms of assessment are crucial in a leisure skills program because a) without baseline assessment, it will be impossible to determine the individual's skill level on the activities or skills which are to be taught, and b) without instructional assessment, it may be difficult to verify the progress made by clients. (p. 9)

Riley and Wright (1990) provided a method for developing such quality assessment monitors. Using a modified delphi technique, they were able to identify several key elements as well as an exhaustive list of indicators for each of these elements in a clinical, therapeutic recreation environment. As the trend toward accountability in leisure skill provision intensifies, it appears obvious that assessment procedures that meet both these criteria will be in critical demand.

TOWARD THE ASSUMPTION OF AN ADVOCATE ROLE

Professionals involved in the provision of leisure services to persons with disabilities have not traditionally assumed a strong advocate role. Busy with day-to-day programming within an agency, they have, on many occasions, been content to let parents and voluntary advocate associations assume the major responsibility for improving the overall quality of leisure services. In recent years, however, more and more advocate activity has taken place on the part of human services personnel. Edginton and Compton (1975) have identified the following advocacy roles that may be assumed by leisure services providers:

Initiator or organizer: This function centers around designing strategies for improving the recreational services the disability group currently receives.

Investigator or ombudsman: The practitioner becomes involved in fact finding, data gathering, and identification of the current status of recreation services received.

Mediator or negotiator: The professional deals with situations in which no response has been received from the recreation services delivery system.

Lobbyist: The practitioner gains attention for the leisure concerns of the group and persuades appropriate decision makers.

Counselor: The professional offers guidance regarding the quality of leisure and recreation services to the group.

Resource assistant: The professional is responsible for coordinating logistics associated with the process of improving the quality of recreational services.

Educator: This role calls for improving the level of societal awareness of the recreational needs of persons with disabilities.

Critic or evaluator: The professional assists the organization in determining whether or not they have met the goal of improving the quality of leisure services provided.

Weiner (1975) outlined the roles that professionals may play in integrating persons with disabilities into community-based leisure programs. These include placing the participant in the appropriate program, monitoring progress, assisting the participant in managing "red tape" associated with participation, evaluating the program through feedback from agency and participant, and educating the public and other groups as to participants' needs.

In calling for educators to assume an increased role in the elimination of physical, cultural, and social barriers to persons with disabilities, Darling and Darling (1982) stated:

> If professionals do not act as advocates, who will? Society simply does not have enough interested, knowledgeable, altruistic citizens. Professionals who work closely with the handicapped and their families and who are committed to a "collectivity orientation" (involvement in all aspects of a client's life rather than only in-class instruction) are natural advocates for their clients. Unresponsive systems must somehow be changed to eliminate the "advocacy dilemmas" that are so prevalent in the professional role today. Even professionals who do not choose to become directly involved in advocacy themselves can become effective organizers of parent action. (p. 253)

Noting the lack of leisure education that has taken place in the public schools to date, Collard (1981) has called on educators to assume an increased advocacy role in initiating this type of programming. She suggests that the following questions be asked before approaching parent groups, administrators, nonprofit advocate associations, and governmental agencies:

Is recreation included in your state's special education laws and/or regulations?

Are any leisure related programs currently offered in the schools in your community? How extensive are they?

What are your resources and who are your allies?

Can disabled citizens and parents of disabled children be located to assist? (p. 13)

If the overall leisure lifestyle of persons with developmental disabilities is to be improved, regular and special educators, therapeutic recreation specialists, and others must transcend their traditional professional roles and assume the broader responsibility of consumer advocate as outlined in this text.

SUMMARY

At this point, it may be useful to assess the degree to which this text is reflective of service delivery trends. First, in respect to viewing leisure skill acquisition as a developmental process, this book begins with the premise that the ultimate goal is independent, self-motivated play with preferred leisure activities. Attention is then given to identifying appropriate free-time situations where such play can occur. Participants are taught to indicate activity preferences and attention is given to the quality of interactions between the participant and leisure educator. The authors of this volume recognize that play is related to success in other areas, thus they address the issue of collateral skill development. Indeed, they have stressed a balance among educational, vocational, and avocational pursuits. Traditional shortcomings of other leisure skill development approaches have been overcome. These include the problems of overly specialized play environments, emphasis on group activities versus individual leisure pursuits, reliance on high entry-level skills, chronological age–inappropriate toys, reliance on esoteric play materials, and ignoring the attitudes of parents and teachers.

The emphasis of this text has been on the development of a repertoire of lifelong leisure skills. Consequently, it has consistently addressed the maintenance, not just the acquisition, of behaviors. The instructional activities focus on the abilities of the learner and are designed to provide participants with a sense of mastery at each step of the process. In summary, it recognizes that persons with developmental disabilities have the right to engage in preferred activities. Because of this premise, this book goes far beyond traditional "play instruction."

In regard to its orientation to community-based programming, this text's emphasis is consistent with the notion of integrating individuals into the least restrictive environment possible. Activities are also featured that would appeal to peers and other persons without disabilities. The natural environments of the home and community are continually stressed and attention is given to identifying the naturally occurring cues that exist in these environments. As is consistent with the "dignity of risk" tenet of social role valorization, the authors recognize that mistakes are a natural part of the play process. Consequently, they provide appropriate methods for correcting these errors. Finally, the text has avoided the pitfalls of labeling and relying on stereotyped activities.

The emphasis of this text has also centered heavily on an interdisciplinary approach to leisure skills instruction. Its information is of equal value to parents, teachers, therapeutic recreation specialists, and other individuals promoting leisure development. It strongly recognizes the role of the family in the development and maintenance of preferred leisure activities. All of the workshop materials provided could also be readily adapted for use with individuals of varying abilities.

In this volume, Schleien, Meyer, Heyne, and Brandt have addressed the issue of accountability admirably by field testing their curriculum in an empirical fashion. This technique was used to validate the activities as being typical in field situations and to test the adaptations in actual use. Furthermore, the method provided for structuring the activities ensures accountability on the part of the leisure instructor for both the process and the outcome, thus addressing both the baseline and instructional methods of assessment discussed earlier.

In relation to advocacy, the authors of this volume have identified these broad areas of concern that must be addressed by parents, teachers, and others who work with persons with developmental disabilities. These include social role valorization, individualization, and environmental barriers. The assessment materials related to these three areas appear to be excellent vehicles for identifying obstacles to successful leisure participation in natural environments and can serve as the basis for effective advocacy efforts to remove these barriers.

REFERENCES

Adapted Physical Activity Quarterly. (1985). 2(4).

Asher, S.R., & Williams, G.A. (1987). Helping children without friends in home and school contexts. In S. Asher, G. Williams, C. Burton, & S. Oden (Eds.), *Children's social development: Information for teachers and parents* (pp. 1–21). Urbana: ERIC Clearinghouse on Elementary and Early Childhood Education, University of Illinois.

Baker, B.L. (1984). Intervention with families with young, severely handicapped children. In J. Blacher (Ed.), *Severely handicapped young children and their families* (pp. 319–375). Orlando: Academic Press.

Baumgart, D., Brown, L., Pumpian, I., Nisbet, J., Ford, A., Sweet, M., Messina, R., & Schroeder, J. (1982). Principle of partial participation and individualized adaptations in educational programs for severely handicapped students. *Journal of The Association for Persons with Severe Handicaps, 7*(2), 17–27.

Bellamy, G.T., Horner, R.H., & Inman, D.P. (1979). *Vocational habilation of severely retarded adults: A direct service technology.* Austin, TX: PRO-ED.

Benson, H.A., & Turnbull, A.P. (1986). Approaching families from an individualized perspective. In R.H. Horner, L.H. Meyer, & H.D.B. Fredericks (Eds.), *Education of learners with severe handicaps: Exemplary service strategies* (pp. 127–157). Baltimore: Paul H. Brookes Publishing Co.

Bergen, A., & Colangelo, C. (1982). *Positioning the handicapped client with central nervous system deficits.* Valhalla, NY: Valhalla Rehabilitation.

Bergman, J.S. (1991). *How to position people with severe disabilities.* St. Paul, MN: Governor's Planning Council on Developmental Disabilities.

Birenbaum, A., & Re, M. (1979). Resettling mentally retarded adults in the community—Almost 4 years later. *American Journal of Mental Deficiency, 83,* 323–329.

Bobath, K., & Bobath, B. (1972). Cerebral palsy. In D.H. Pearson & C.C. Williams (Eds.), *Physical therapy servies in the developmental disabilities* (pp. 31–185). Springfield, IL: Charles C Thomas.

Breines, E. (1984). The issue is . . . an attempt to define purposeful activity. *American Journal of Occupational Therapy, 38*(8), 543–544.

Brown, F., Evans, I.M., Weed, K.A., & Owen, V. (1987). Delineating functional competencies: A component model. *Journal of The Association for Persons with Severe Handicaps, 12,* 117–124.

Brown, F., & Lehr, D. (1993). Making activities meaningful for students with severe disabilities. *Teaching Exceptional Children, 25*(4), 79–83.

Bullock, C.C., Mahon, M.J., & Welch, L.K. (1992). Easter Seals' progressive mainstreaming model: Options and choices in camping and leisure services for children and adults with disabilities. *Therapeutic Recreation Journal, 26*(4), 61–70.

Burkhart, L. (1980). *Homemade battery powered toys and educational devices for severely handicapped children.* Millville, PA: Author.

Burkhart, L. (1982). *More homemade battery devices for severely handicapped children with suggested activities.* Millville, PA: Author.

Butler, C. (1985). Effects of powered mobility on self-initiative behavior of very young, locomotor-disabled children. *Developmental Medicine and Child Neurology, 27,* 112.

Butler, C., Okamoto, G.A., & McKay, T.M. (1983). Powered mobility for very young disabled children. *Developmental Medicine and Child Neurology, 25*(4), 472–474.

Calculator, S., & Luchko, C. (1983). Evaluating the effectiveness of a communication board training program. *Journal of Speech and Hearing Disorders, 48,* 185–191.

Campbell, P., McInerney, W., & Cooper, M.A. (1984). Therapeutic programming for students with severe handicaps. *American Journal of Occupational Therapy, 38*(9), 594–602.

Campbell, P., McInerney, W., & Middleton, M. (1982). *A manual of augmented sensory feedback devices for training severely handicapped students.* Akron, OH: Children's Hospital Medical Center of Akron.

Certo, N., Schleien, S., & Hunter, D. (1983). An ecological assessment inventory to facilitate community recreation participation by severely disabled learners. *Therapeutic Recreation Journal, 17*(3), 29–38.

Churton, M.W. (1988). Federal law and adapted physical education. *Adapted Physical Activity Quarterly, 5*(4), 278–284.

Cole, D.A., & Meyer, L.H. (1989). Impact of needs and resources on family plans to seek out-of-home placement. *American Journal on Mental Retardation, 93*, 380–387.

Collard, K.M. (1981). Leisure education in the schools: Why, who and the need for advocacy. *Therapeutic Recreation Journal, 15*(4), 8–16.

Cox, E. (1987). *Dynamic positioning treatment: A new approach to customized therapeutic equipment for the developmentally disabled.* Tulsa, OK: Christian Publishing Services.

Crapps, J., Langone, J., & Swaim, S. (1985). Quantity and quality of participation in community environments by mentally retarded adults. *Education and Training of the Mentally Retarded, 20*, 123–129.

Crawford, M.E. (1986). Development and generalization of lifetime leisure skills for multi-handicapped participants. *Therapeutic Recreation Journal, 20*(4), 48–60.

Cunningham, T., & Presnall, D. (1978). Relationship between dimensions of adaptive behavior and sheltered workshop productivity. *American Journal of Mental Deficiency, 82*, 386–393.

Darling, R., & Darling, J. (1982). *Children who are different.* St. Louis: C.V. Mosby.

Dattilo, J. (1986). Computerized assessment of preferences for persons with severe handicaps. *Journal of Applied Behavior Analysis, 19*(4), 445–448.

Dattilo, J. (1987). Computerized assessment of leisure preferences: A replication. *Education and Training in Mental Retardation, 22*(2), 128–133.

Dattilo, J. (1988). Assessing music preferences of persons with severe handicaps. *Therapeutic Recreation Journal, 22*(1), 12–23.

Dattilo, J. (1991). Recreation and leisure: A review of the literature and recommendations for future directions. In L.H. Meyer, C.A. Peck, & L. Brown (Eds.), *Critical issues in the lives of people with severe disabilities* (pp. 171–193). Baltimore: Paul H. Brookes Publishing Co.

Dattilo, J. (1993). Reciprocal communication for individuals with severe communication disorders: Implications to leisure participation. *Palaestra, 10*(1), 39–48.

Dattilo, J. (1994). *Inclusive leisure services: Responding to the rights of people with disabilities.* State College, PA: Venture.

Dattilo, J., & Barnett, L.A. (1985). Therapeutic recreation for individuals with severe handicaps: An analysis of the relationship between choice and pleasure. *Therapeutic Recreation Journal, 19*(3), 79–91.

Dattilo, J., & Camarata, S. (1991). Facilitating conversation through self-initiated augmentative communication treatment. *Journal of Applied Behavior Analysis, 24*(2), 369–378.

Dattilo, J., & Kleiber, D.A. (1993). Psychological perspectives for therapeutic recreation research. In M.J. Malkin & C.Z. Howe (Eds.), *Research in therapeutic recreation: Basic concepts and methods* (pp. 57–73). State College, PA: Venture.

Dattilo, J., & Light, J. (1993). Setting the stage for leisure: Encouraging reciprocal communication for people using augmentative and alternative communication systems through facilitator instruction. *Therapeutic Recreation Journal, 27*(3), 156–171.

Dattilo, J., & Mirenda, P. (1987). The application of a leisure preference assessment protocol for persons with severe handicaps. *Journal of The Association for Persons with Severe Handicaps, 12*(4), 306–311.

Dattilo, J., & Murphy, W.D. (1991). *Leisure education program planning: A systematic approach.* State College, PA: Venture.

Dattilo, J., & O'Keefe, B.M. (1992). Setting the stage for leisure: Encouraging adults with mental retardation who use augmentative and alternative communication systems to share conversations. *Therapeutic Recreation Journal, 26*(1), 27–37.

Dattilo, J., & Rusch, F. (1985). Effects of choice on behavior. Leisure participation for persons with severe handicaps. *Journal of The Association for Persons with Severe Handicaps, 11*, 194–199.

Dattilo, J., & Schleien, S.J. (1994). Understanding the provision of leisure services for individuals with mental retardation. *Mental Retardation, 32*(1), 53–59.

Davis, W.M. (1981). *Aids to make you able: Self help devices for the disabled.* New York: E.P. Dutton.

DeSalvatore, G.H. (1989). Therapeutic recreators as family therapists: Working with families on a children's psychiatric unit. *Therapeutic Recreation Journal, 23*(2), 23–29.

Dexter, L.A. (1970). *Elite and specialized interviewing.* Chicago: Northwestern University Press.

Dixon, J.T. (1980). Mainstreaming and leisure education for the mentally retarded. *Therapeutic Recreation Journal, 14*(1), 30–33.

Dulcy, F.H. (1983). A theoretical aquatic service intervention model for disabled children. *Physical and Occupational Therapy in Pediatrics, 3*(1), 21–38.

Dunn, J.M. (1983). Physical activity for the severely handicapped: Theoretical and practical considerations. In R. Eason, T. Smith, & F. Caron (Eds.), *Adapted physical activity: From theory to application* (pp. 67–73). Champaign, IL: Human Kinetics.

Durand, V.M. (1993). Functional communication training using assistive devices: Effects on challenging behavior and affect. *Augmentative and Alternative Communication, 9*(3), 168–176.

Dyer, K., Dunlap, G., & Winterling, V. (1990). Effects of choice making on the serious problem behaviors of students with severe handicaps. *Journal of Applied Behavior Analysis, 23,* 515–524.

Edginton, C.R., & Compton, D.M. (1975). Consumerism and advocacy: A conceptual framework for the therapeutic recreator. *Therapeutic Recreation Journal, 9*(1), 26–32.

Education for All Handicapped Children Act of 1975, PL 94-142. (August 23, 1977). Title 20, U.S.C. 1401 et seq: *U.S. Statutes at Large, 89,* 773–796.

Education of the Handicapped Act Amendments of 1986, PL 99-457. (October 8, 1986). Title 20, U.S.C. 1400 et seq: *U.S. Statutes at Large, 100,* 1145–1177.

Eyman, R.K., & Call, T. (1977). Maladaptive behavior and community placement of mentally retarded persons. *American Journal of Mental Deficiency, 82,* 137–144.

Falvey, M.A. (1989). *Community-based curriculum: Instructional strategies for students with severe handicaps* (2nd ed.). Baltimore: Paul H. Brookes Publishing Co.

Falvey, M., Brown, L., Lyon, S., Baumgart, D., & Schroeder, J. (1980). Strategies for using cues and correction procedures. In W. Sailor, B. Wilcox, & L. Brown (Eds.), *Methods of instruction for severely handicapped students* (pp. 109–133). Baltimore: Paul H. Brookes Publishing Co.

Ficker-Terrill, C., & Rowitz, L. (1991). Choices. *Mental Retardation, 29,* 63–65.

Folsom-Meek, S.L. (1984). Parents: Forgotten teacher aids in adapted physical education. *Adapted Physical Education Quarterly, 1*(4), 275–281.

Ford, A., Brown, L., Pumpian, I., Baumgart, D., Schroeder, J., & Loomis, R. (1984). Strategies for developing individualized recreation/leisure plans for adolescent and young adult severely handicapped students. In N. Certo, N. Haring, & R. York (Eds.), *Public school integration of severely handicapped students* (pp. 245–275). Baltimore: Paul H. Brookes Publishing Co.

Ford, A., Schnorr, R., Meyer, L., Davern, L., Black, J., & Dempsey, P. (Eds.). (1989). *The Syracuse community-referenced curriculum guide for students with moderate and severe disabilities.* Baltimore: Paul H. Brookes Publishing Co.

Fox, J.J., Niemeyer, J., & Savelle, S. (1992). Contributions of siblings to the development of social competence interventions for young children with disabilities. In S.L. Odom, S.R. McConnell, & M.A. McEvoy (Eds.), *Social competence of young children with disabilities: Issues and strategies for intervention* (pp. 215–244). Baltimore: Paul H. Brookes Publishing Co.

Fraser, B.A., Hensinger, R.N., & Phelps, J.A. (1990). *Physical management of multiple handicaps: A professional's guide* (2nd ed.). Baltimore: Paul H. Brookes Publishing Co.

Garner, J.B., & Campbell, P.H. (1987). Technology for persons with severe disabilities: Practical and ethical considerations. *Journal of Special Education, 21,* 122–132.

Gaylord-Ross, R. (1980). A decision model for the treatment of aberrant behavior in applied settings. In W. Sailor, B. Wilcox, & L. Brown (Eds.), *Methods of instruction for severely handicapped students* (pp. 135–158). Baltimore: Paul H. Brookes Publishing Co.

Giangreco, M. (1986). Effects of integrated therapy: A pilot study. *Journal of The Association for Persons with Severe Handicaps, 11*(3), 205–208.

Gliedman, J., & Roth, W. (1980). *The unexpected minority: Handicapped children in America.* New York: Harcourt Brace Jovanovich.

Gliner, J.A. (1985). Purposeful activity in motor learning theory: An event approach to motor skill acquisition. *American Journal of Occupational Therapy, 39*(1), 28–34.

Goldfarb, L.A., Brotherson, M.J., Summers, J.A., & Turnbull, A.P. (1986). *Meeting the challenge of disability or chronic illness: A family guide.* Baltimore: Paul H. Brookes Publishing Co.

Graham, B. (1981). Analysis of the effectiveness of two alternative choice training procedures on the free time behavior of two severely handicapped youth. In L. Voeltz, J. Apffel, & B. Wuerch (Eds.), *Leisure activities training for severely handicapped students: Instructional and evaluation strategies* (pp. 137–210). Honolulu: University of Hawaii, Department of Special Education.

Green, F., & Schleien, S. (1991). Understanding friendship and recreation: A theoretical sampling. *Therapeutic Recreation Journal, 25*(4), 29–40.

Harris, S.R., & Thompson, M. (1983). Water as a learning environment for facilitating gross motor skills in deaf-blind children. *Physical and Occupational Therapy in Pediatrics, 3*(1), 75–82.

Hartup, W.W. (1992). Peer relations in early and middle childhood. In V. Van Hasselt & M. Hersen (Eds.), *Handbook of social development: A lifespan perspective* (pp. 257–281). New York: Plenum.

Hawkins, B.A. (1993). A exploratory analysis of leisure and life satisfaction of aging adults with mental retardation. *Therapeutic Recreation Journal, 26,* 98–109.

Hayden, M., Lakin, K.C., Hill, B., Bruininks, R., & Copher, J. (1992). Social and leisure integration of people with mental retardation in foster homes and small group homes. *Education and Training in Mental Retardation, 27,* 187–199.

Henderson, K. (1991). *Dimensions of choice: A qualitative approach to recreation, parks, and leisure studies.* State College, PA: Venture.

Hester, S.B. (1981). Effects of behavior modification on the standing and walking deficiencies of a profoundly retarded child. *Physical Therapy, 61*(6), 907–911.

Heyne, L. (1993). Friendship development between children with and without developmental disabilities through participation in school-home-neighborhood recreational activities. *Dissertation Abstracts International, 54,* 09A. (University Microfilms Publication No. 9405328)

Heyne, L., & Schleien, S. (1994). Leisure and recreation programming to enhance quality of life. In E. Cipani & F. Spooner (Eds.), *Curriculum and instructional approaches for persons with severe disabilities* (pp. 213–240). Needham Heights, MA: Allyn & Bacon.

Heyne, L., Schleien, S., & McAvoy, L. (1993). *Making friends: Using recreation activities to promote friendship between children with and without disabilities.* Minneapolis: School of Kinesiology and Leisure Studies, College of Education, University of Minnesota.

Hofmeister, A.M., & Friedman, S.G. (1986). The application of technology to the education of persons with severe handicaps. In R.H. Horner, L.H. Meyer, & H.D.B. Fredericks (Eds.), *Education of learners with severe handicaps: Exemplary service strategies* (pp. 351–367). Baltimore: Paul H. Brookes Publishing Co.

Horner, R.H., Dunlap, G., & Koegel, R.L. (Eds.). (1988). *Generalization and maintenance: Life-style changes in applied settings.* Baltimore: Paul H. Brookes Publishing Co.

Houghton, J., Bronicki, G.J., & Guess, D. (1987). Opportunities to express preferences and make choices among students with severe disabilities in classroom settings. *Journal of The Association for Persons with Severe Handicaps, 12,* 18–27.

Huang, L.N., & Heifetz, L.J. (1984). Elements of professional helpfulness: Profiles of the most helpful and least helpful professionals encountered by mothers of young retarded children. In J.M. Berg (Ed.), *Perspectives and progress in mental retardation: Vol. I. Social, psychological, and educational aspects* (pp. 425–433). Baltimore: University Park Press.

Hulme, J.B., Poor, R., Schulein, M., & Pezzino, J. (1983). Perceived behavioral changes observed with adaptive seating devices and training programs for multihandicapped, developmentally disabled individuals. *Physical Therapy, 63*(2), 204–208.

Huss, A.J. (1981). From kinesiology to adaptation. *American Journal of Occupational Therapy, 35*(9), 574–580.

Hutchison, P. (1983). The status of recreation integration research. *Journal of Leisurability, 10*(4), 26–35.

Hutchison, P., & Lord, J. (1979). *Recreation integration: Issues and alternatives in leisure services and community involvement.* Ottawa, Ontario, Canada: Leisurability.

Individuals with Disabilities Education Act of 1990 (IDEA), PL 101-476. (October 30, 1990). Title 20, U.S.C. 1400 et seq: *U.S. Statutes at Large, 104,* 1103–1151.

Ingenmey, R., & Van Houten, R. (1991). Using time delay to promote spontaneous speech in an autistic child. *Journal of Applied Behavior Analysis, 24*(3), 591–598.

Johnson, D.W., & Johnson, F.P. (1987). *Joining together: Group theory and group skills* (3rd ed.). Englewood Cliffs, NJ: Prentice Hall.

Jolly, A.C., Test, D.W., & Spooner, F. (1993). Using badges to increase initiations of children with severe disabilities in a play setting. *Journal of The Association for Persons with Severe Handicaps, 18*(1), 46–51.

Jones, S., Clarke, S., & Cook, S. (1985). *Adaptive positioning equipment directory of available services.* Atlanta: Georgia Retardation Center.

Joswiak, K.F. (1980). Recreation therapy assessment with developmentally disabled persons. *Therapeutic Recreation Journal, 14*(4), 29–38.

Katz, S., & Yekutiel, E. (1974). Leisure time problems of mentally retarded graduates of training programs. *Mental Retardation, 12,* 54–57.

Kelly, A. (1993). Patient empowerment. *Independent Living, 8*(4), 42–46.

Kishi, G.S., & Meyer, L.H. (in press). What children report and remember: A six-year follow-up of the effects of social contact between peers with and without severe disabilities. *Journal of The Association for Persons with Severe Handicaps.*

Kishi, G., Teelucksingh, B., Zollers, N., Park-Lee, S., & Meyer, L. (1988). Daily decision-making in community residences: A social comparison of adults with and without mental retardation. *American Journal on Mental Retardation, 92*(5), 430–435.

Kissel, R.C., & Whitman, T.L. (1977). An examination of the direct and generalized effects of a play training and overcorrection procedure upon the self-stimulatory behavior of a profoundly retarded boy. *AAESPH Review, 2,* 131–146.

Kogan, K.L., & Tyler, N. (1973). Mother-child interaction in young physically handicapped children. *American Journal of Mental Deficiency, 77,* 492–497.

Kohl, F.L., & Beckman, P.J. (1990). The effects of directed play on the frequency and length of reciprocal interactions with preschoolers having moderate handicaps. *Education and Training in Mental Retardation, 25*(3), 258–266.

Kohn, J., Enders, S., Preston, J., & Motloch, W. (1983). Provision of assistive equipment for handicapped persons. *Archives of Physical Medicine and Rehabilitation, 64*(8), 378–381.

Krueger, R. (1988). *Focus groups: A practical guide for applied research.* Beverly Hills: Sage Publications.

Lanagan, D., & Dattilo, J. (1989). The effects of a leisure education program on individuals with mental retardation. *Therapeutic Recreation Journal, 23*(4), 62–72.

Levin, J., & Scherfenberg, L. (1986). *Breaking barriers: How children and adults with severe handicaps can access the world through simple technology.* Minneapolis: Ablenet.

Lobato, D., & Barrera, R.D. (1988). Impact of siblings on children with handicaps. In M.D. Powers (Ed.), *Expanding systems of service delivery for persons with developmental disabilities* (pp. 43–52). Baltimore: Paul H. Brookes Publishing Co.

Maddy, B.J. (1988). Close encounters: Promoting social independence in adolescents with physical disabilities. *Therapeutic Recreation Journal, 22*(4), 49–55.

Mahon, M.J., & Bullock, C.C. (1992). Teaching adolescents with mild mental retardation to make decisions in leisure through the use of self-control techniques. *Therapeutic Recreation Journal, 26*(1), 9–26.

Mahoney, G., & Powell, A. (1988). Modifying parent-child interaction: Enhancing the development of handicapped children. *Journal of Special Education, 22,* 82–96.

Marion, R.L. (1979, Summer). Leisure time activities for trainable mentally retarded adolescents. *Teaching Exceptional Children,* pp. 158–160.

Matson, J.L., Sevin, J.A., Box, M.L., Francis, K.L., & Sevin, B.M. (1993). An evaluation of two methods for increasing self-initiated verbalizations in autistic children. *Journal of Applied Behavior Analysis, 26*(3), 389–398.

McGill, J. (1984a). Cooperative games as a strategy for integration. *Journal of Leisurability, 11*(4), 14–18.

McGill, J. (1984b). Training for integration: Are blindfolds enough? *Journal of Leisurability, 11*(2), 12–15.

McNaughton, D., & Light, J. (1989). Teaching facilitators to support the communication skills of an adult with severe cognitive disabilities: A case study. *Augmentative and Alternative Communication*, 5, 35–41.

Merriam, S. (1988). *Case study research in education: A qualitative approach.* San Francisco: Jossey-Bass.

Meyer, L.H. (1989). Home-school collaboration. In A. Ford, R. Schnorr, L. Meyer, L. Davern, J. Black, & P. Dempsey (Eds.), *The Syracuse community-referenced curriculum guide for students with moderate and severe disabilities* (pp. 17–24). Baltimore: Paul H. Brookes Publishing Co.

Meyer, L.H. (1991). Advocacy, research, and typical practices: A call for the reduction of discrepancies between what is and what ought to be, and how to get there. In L.H. Meyer, C.A. Peck, & L. Brown (Eds.), *Critical issues in the lives of people with severe disabilities* (pp. 629–649). Baltimore: Paul H. Brookes Publishing Co.

Meyer, L.H. (1992). *Consortium for collaborative research on social relationships: Inclusive schools and communities for children and youth with diverse abilities.* Research proposal funded by USDOE, Syracuse University, Syracuse, NY.

Meyer, L.H., & Evans, I.M. (1989). *Nonaversive intervention for behavior problems: A manual for home and community.* Baltimore: Paul H. Brookes Publishing Co.

Meyer, L.H., Evans, I.M., Wuerch, B.B., & Brennan, J. (1985). Monitoring the collateral effects of leisure skill instruction: A case study in multiple-baseline methodology. *Behaviour Research and Therapy*, 23, 127–138.

Meyer, L.H., & Henry, L.A. (1993). Cooperative classroom management: Student needs and fairness in the regular classroom. In J.W. Putnam (Ed.), *Cooperative learning and strategies for inclusion: Celebrating diversity* (pp. 93–121). Baltimore: Paul H. Brookes Publishing Co.

Meyer, L.H., & Kishi, G.S. (1985). School integration strategies. In K.C. Lakin & R.H. Bruininks (Eds.), *Strategies for achieving community integration of developmentally disabled citizens* (pp. 231–252). Baltimore: Paul H. Brookes Publishing Co.

Meyer, L.H., & Putnam, J. (1988). Social integration. In V.B. Van Hasselt, P.S. Strain, & M. Hersen (Eds.), *Handbook of developmental and physical disabilities* (pp. 107–133). Elmsford, NY: Pergamon Press.

Meyer, L.H., Reichle, J., McQuarter, R.J., Cole, D., Vandercook, T., Evans, I., Neel, R., & Kishi, G. (1985). *The Assessment of Social Competence (ASC): A scale of social competence functions.* Minneapolis: University of Minnesota Consortium Institute.

Mirenda, P., & Dattilo, J. (1987). Instructional techniques in alternative communication for students with severe intellectual handicaps. *Augmentative and Alternative Communication*, 3, 143–152.

Monroe, J.E. (1987). Family leisure programming. *Therapeutic Recreation Journal*, 21(3), 44–51.

National Therapeutic Recreation Society. (1982). *Philosophical position statement of the National Therapeutic Recreation Society.* Alexandria, VA: National Recreation and Park Association.

Nihira, K., Foster, R., Shellhas, M., & Leland, H. (1969). *AAMD Adaptive Behavior Scale.* Washington, DC: American Association on Mental Deficiency.

Nixon, H.L. (1988). Getting over the worry hurdle: Parental encouragement and the sports involvement of visually impaired children and youth. *Adapted Physical Activity Quarterly*, 5(1), 29–43.

Nixon, H.L. (1989). Integration of disabled people in mainstream sports. *Adapted Physical Activity Quarterly*, 6(1), 17–31.

Nordic Committee on Disability. (1985). *The more we do together: Adapting the environment for children with disabilities.* New York: World Rehabilitation Fund.

O'Brien, J. (1987). A guide to life-style planning: Using *The Activities Catalog* to integrate services and natural support systems. In B. Wilcox & G.T. Bellamy, *A comprehensive guide to The Activities Catalog: An alternative curriculum for youth and adults with severe disabilities* (pp. 175–189). Baltimore: Paul H. Brookes Publishing Co.

Peganoff, S.A. (1984). The use of aquatics with cerebral palsied adolescents. *American Journal of Occupational Therapy*, 38(7), 469–473.

Piuma, M.F., & Udvari-Solner, A. (1993a). *A catalog of vocational assistance devices for individuals with severe intellectual disabilities.* Madison: Madison Metropolitan School District and University of Wisconsin–Madison.

Piuma, M.F., & Udvari-Solner, A. (1993b). *Materials and process manual: Developing low cost vocational adaptations for individuals with severe disabilities.* Madison: Madison Metropolitan School District and University of Wisconsin–Madison.

Pollingue, A.B., & Cobb, H.B. (1986). Leisure education: A model facilitating community integration for moderately/severely mentally retarded adults. *Therapeutic Recreation Journal, 20*(3), 54–62.

Powers, M.D., & Bruey, C.T. (1988). Treating the family system. In M.D. Powers (Ed.), *Expanding systems of service delivery for persons with developmental disabilities* (pp. 17–41). Baltimore: Paul H. Brookes Publishing Co.

Powers, M.D., & Handleman, J.S. (1984). *Behavioral assessment of severe developmental disabilities.* Rockville, MD: Aspen Press.

Pukui, M.K., & Elbert, S.H. (1986). *Hawaiian dictionary, revised and enlarged.* Honolulu: University of Hawaii Press.

Putnam, J.W. (Ed.). (1993). *Cooperative learning and strategies for inclusion: Celebrating diversity in the classroom.* Baltimore: Paul H. Brookes Publishing Co.

Rainforth, B., & York, J. (1987). Integrating related services in community instruction. *Journal of The Association for Persons with Severe Handicaps, 12*(3), 190–198.

Rainforth, B., & York, J. (1991). Handling and positioning. In F.P. Orelove & D. Sobsey, *Educating children with multiple disabilities: A transdisciplinary approach* (2nd ed., pp. 79–118). Baltimore: Paul H. Brookes Publishing Co.

Rainforth, B., York, J., & Macdonald, C. (1992). *Collaborative teams for students with severe disabilities: Integrating therapy and educational services.* Baltimore: Paul H. Brookes Publishing Co.

Realon, R.E., Favell, J.E., & Lowerre, A. (1990). The effects of making choices on engagement levels with persons who are profoundly multiply handicapped. *Education and Training in Mental Retardation, 25*(3), 299–305.

Rehabilitation Act of 1973, PL 93-112. (September 26, 1973). Title 29, U.S.C. 701 et seq: *U.S. Statutes at Large, 87,* 355–394.

Rehabilitation Act Amendments of 1986, PL 99-506. Title 29, U.S.C. 701 et seq: *U.S. Statutes at Large, 100,* 1807–1846.

Rehabilitation Act Amendments of 1992, PL 102-569. (October 29, 1992). Title 29, U.S.C. 701 et seq: *U.S. Statutes at Large,* 106 stat 4344.

Richardson, D., Wilson, B., Wetherald, L., & Peters, J. (1987). Mainstreaming initiative: An innovative approach to recreation and leisure services in a community setting. *Therapeutic Recreation Journal, 21*(2), 9–19.

Riley, B., & Wright, S. (1990). Establishing quality assurance monitors for the evaluation of therapeutic recreation service. *Therapeutic Recreation Journal, 24*(2), 25–39.

Rynders, J., Johnson, R., Johnson, D., & Schmidt, B. (1980). Producing positive interaction among Down syndrome and nonhandicapped teenagers through cooperative goal structuring. *American Journal of Mental Deficiency, 85,* 268–273.

Rynders, J., & Schleien, S. (1991). *Together successfully: Creating recreational and educational programs that integrate people with and without disabilities.* Arlington, TX: The Arc–United States; National 4-H; and the Institute on Community Integration, University of Minnesota.

Rynders, J.E., Schleien, S.J., Meyer, L.H., Vandercook, T.K., Mustonen, T.A., Colond, J.S., & Olson, K. (1993). Improving integration outcomes for children with and without severe disabilities through cooperatively structured recreation activities: A synthesis of research. *Journal of Special Education, 26*(4), 386–407.

Sable, J. (1992). Collaborating to create an integrated camping program: Design and evaluation. *Therapeutic Recreation Journal, 26*(3), 38–48.

Schalock, R.L., Keith, D.D., Hoffman, K., & Karan, O.C. (1989). Quality of life: Its measurement and use. *Mental Retardation, 27,* 25–31.

Schell, G. (1982). *Opening the door again: A collection of toys for special children.* Dallas: LTV Aerospace and Defense.

Schleien, S., Cameron, J., Rynders, J., & Slick, C. (1988). Acquisition and generalization of leisure skills from school to the home and community by learners with severe multihandicaps. *Therapeutic Recreation Journal, 22*(3), 53–71.

Schleien, S.J., Fahnestock, M., Green, R., & Rynders, J.E. (1990). Building positive social networks through environmental interventions in integrated recreation programs. *Therapeutic Recreation Journal, 24*(4), 42–52.

Schleien, S., Green, F., & Heyne, L. (1993). Integrated community recreation. In M. Snell (Ed.), *Instruction of students with severe disabilities* (4th ed., pp. 526–555). Columbus, OH: Macmillan.

Schleien, S.J., Heyne, L.A., & Berken, S.B. (1988). Integrating physical education to teach appropriate play skills to learners with autism: A pilot study. *Adapted Physical Activity Quarterly, 5*(3), 182–192.

Schleien, S., Heyne, L., & Dattilo, J. (1995). Teaching severely handicapped children: Social skills development through leisure skills programming. In G. Cartledge & J. Milburn (Eds.), *Teaching social skills to children: Innovative approaches* (3rd ed., pp. 262–290). Needham Heights, MA: Allyn & Bacon.

Schleien, S., Kiernan, J., & Wehman, P. (1981). Evaluation of an age-appropriate leisure skills program for moderately retarded adults. *Education and Training of the Mentally Retarded, 16*(1), 13–19.

Schleien, S.J., McAvoy, L.H., Lais, G.J., & Rynders, J.E. (1993). *Integrated outdoor education and adventure programs.* Champaign, IL: Sagamore.

Schleien, S., & Meyer, L. (1988). Community-based recreation programs for persons with severe developmental disabilities. In M.D. Powers (Ed.), *Expanding systems of service delivery for persons with developmental disabilities* (pp. 93–112). Baltimore: Paul H. Brookes Publishing Co.

Schleien, S.J., & Ray, M.T. (1988). *Community recreation and persons with disabilities: Strategies for integration.* Baltimore: Paul H. Brookes Publishing Co.

Schleien, S.J., & Werder, J. (1985). Perceived responsibilities of special recreation services in Minnesota. *Therapeutic Recreation Journal, 19*(3), 51–62.

Shearer, M.S., & Shearer, D.D. (1972). The Portage Project: A model for early childhood education. *Exceptional Children, 39,* 210–217.

Sherril, C., Rainbolt, W., & Ervin, S. (1984). Physical recreation of blind adults: Present practices and childhood memories. *Journal of Vision Impairment and Blindness, 78*(8), 367–368.

Singer, G.H.S., & Irvin, L.K. (1991). Supporting families of persons with severe disabilities: Emerging findings, practices, and questions. In L.H. Meyer, C.A. Peck, & L. Brown (Eds.), *Critical issues in the lives of people with severe disabilities* (pp. 271–312). Baltimore: Paul H. Brookes Publishing Co.

Singer, G.H.S., Irvine, A.B., & Irvin, L.K. (1989). Expanding the focus of behavioral parent training: A contextual approach. In G.H.S. Singer & L.K. Irvin (Eds.), *Support for caregiving families: Enabling positive adaptation to disability* (pp. 85–102). Baltimore: Paul H. Brookes Publishing Co.

Sneegas, J.J. (1989). Social skills: An integral component of leisure participation and therapeutic recreation services. *Therapeutic Recreation Journal, 23*(2), 30–40.

Staur, N. (1991). *Effects of integrated bocce training on acquisition, maintenance, and generalization by young adults with developmental disabilities.* Unpublished master's thesis, University of Minnesota, Minneapolis.

Stein, A.L. (1981). The development and validation of the leisure time in the home strengths and needs assessment. In L.M. Voeltz, J.A. Apffel, & B.B. Wuerch (Eds.), *Leisure activities training for severely handicapped students: Instructional and evaluation strategies* (pp. 37–69). Honolulu: University of Hawaii, Department of Special Education.

St. Peter, S., Ayres, B.J., Meyer, L.H., & Park-Lee, S. (1989). Social skills. In A. Ford, R. Schnorr, L. Meyer, L. Davern, J. Black, & P. Dempsey (Eds.), *The Syracuse community-referenced curriculum guide for students with moderate and severe disabilities* (pp. 171–188). Baltimore: Paul H. Brookes Publishing Co.

Sulzer-Azaroff, B., & Mayer, G.R. (1977). *Applying behavior-analysis procedures with children and youth.* New York: Holt, Rinehart & Winston.

Sylvester, C. (1987). The politics: Leisure, freedom and poverty. *Parks and Recreation, 22*(1), 59–62.

Taylor, S., & Bogdan, R. (1984). *Introduction to qualitative research methods: The search for meanings* (2nd ed.). New York: John Wiley & Sons.

Tharp, R.G., & Gallimore, R. (1989). *Rousing minds to life: Teaching, learning, and schooling in social context.* Cambridge: Cambridge University Press.

Trefler, E. (1984). Mobility for the young disabled. In E. Trefler (Ed.), *Seating for children with cerebral palsy* (pp. 87–92). Memphis: University of Tennessee, Rehabilitation Engineering Program.

Trefler, E., Nickey, J., & Hobson, D. (1983). Technology in the education of multiply handicapped children. *American Journal of Occupational Therapy, 37*(6), 381–387.

Trefler, E., Tooms, R.E., & Hobson, D.A. (1977). Seating cerebral palsied children. *Interclinic Information Bulletin, 1*(1), 1–8.

Turnbull, A.P., Patterson, J.M., Behr, S.K., Murphy, D.L., Marquis, J.G., & Blue-Banning, M.J. (Eds.). (1993). *Cognitive coping, families, and disability.* Baltimore: Paul H. Brookes Publishing Co.

Turnbull, A.P., & Summers, J.A. (1987). From parent involvement to family support: Evolution to revolution. In S.M. Pueschel, C. Tingey, J.E. Rynders, A.C. Crocker, & D.M. Crutcher (Eds.), *New perspectives on Down syndrome* (pp. 289–306). Baltimore: Paul H. Brookes Publishing Co.

Turnbull, H.R., III, & Turnbull, A.P. (1982). Parent involvement in the education of handicapped children: A critique. *Mental Retardation, 20,* 115–122.

Turnbull, H.R., III, Turnbull, A.P., Bronicki, G.J., Summers, J.A., & Roeder-Gordon, C. (1989). *Disability and the family: A guide to decisions for adulthood.* Baltimore: Paul H. Brookes Publishing Co.

Vandercook, T. (1991). Leisure instruction outcomes: Criterion performance, positive interactions, and acceptance by typical high school peers. *Journal of Special Education, 25,* 320–339.

Van Deventer, P., Yelinek, N., Brown, L., Schroeder, J., Loomis, R., & Gruenewald, L. (1981). A follow-up examination of severely handicapped graduates of the Madison Metropolitan School District from 1971–1978. In L. Brown, D. Baumgart, I. Pumpian, J. Nisbet, A. Ford, A. Donnellan, M. Sweet, R. Loomis, & J. Schroeder (Eds.), *Curricular strategies that can be used to transition severely handicapped students from school to nonschool and post school environments* (pp. 1–177). Madison, WI: Madison Metropolitan School District.

Verburg, G., Pilkington, M., Snell, E., & Milner, M. (1985). Providing powered mobility to two-to-five year-olds: The effects on child and family. *Developmental Medicine and Child Neurology, 27,* 92.

Verhoven, P., Schleien, S., & Bender, M. (1982). *Leisure education and the handicapped individual: An ecological perspective.* Washington, DC: Institute for Career and Leisure Development.

Vincent, L.J., & Salisbury, C.L. (1989). Changing economic and social influences on family involvement. *Topics in Early Childhood Special Education, 8*(1), 48–59.

Voeltz, L.M., & Apffel, J.A. (1981). A leisure activities curricular component for severely handicapped youth: Why and how? *Viewpoints in Teaching and Learning, 57,* 82–93.

Voeltz, L.M., & Brennan, J.M. (1984). Analysis of interactions between nonhandicapped and severely handicapped peers using multiple measures. In J.M. Berg (Ed.), *Perspectives and progress in mental retardation: Vol. I. Social, psychological and educational aspects* (pp. 61–72). Baltimore: University Park Press.

Voeltz, L.M., & Delong, D. (1981). Behaviors of severely handicapped adolescents during free time before and after training. In L.M. Voeltz, J.A. Apffel, & B.B. Wuerch (Eds.), *Leisure activities training for severely handicapped students: Instructional and evaluation strategies* (pp. 243–267). Honolulu: University of Hawaii, Department of Special Education.

Voeltz, L., Hemphill, N., Brown, S., Kishi, G., Klein, R., Fruehling, R., Levy, G., Collie, J., & Kube, C. (1983). *The special friends program: A trainer's manual for integrated school settings.* Honolulu: University of Hawaii, Department of Special Education.

Voeltz, L.M., & Wuerch, B.B. (1981a). A comprehensive approach to leisure education and leisure counseling for the severely handicapped person. *Therapeutic Recreation Journal, 15,* 24–35.

Voeltz, L.M., & Wuerch, B.B. (1981b). Monitoring multiple behavioral effects of leisure activities training on severely handicapped adolescents. In L.M. Voeltz, J.A. Apffel, & B.B. Wuerch (Eds.), *Leisure activities training for severely handicapped students: Instructional and evaluation strategies* (pp. 269–307). Honolulu: University of Hawaii, Department of Special Education.

Voeltz, L.M., Wuerch, B.B., & Bockhaut, C. (1982). A social validation of leisure activities training with severely handicapped youth. *Journal of The Association for Persons with Severe Handicaps, 7*(4), 3–13.

Voeltz, L.M., Wuerch, B.B., & Wilcox, B. (1982). Leisure and recreation: Preparation for independence, integration, and self-fulfillment. In B. Wilcox & G.T. Bellamy (Eds.), *Design of high school programs for severely handicapped students* (pp. 175–209). Baltimore: Paul H. Brookes Publishing Co.

Vygotsky, L.S. (1978). *Mind in society: The development of higher psychological processes* (M. Cole, V. John-Steiner, S. Scribner, & E. Souberman, Eds. & Trans.). Cambridge, MA: Harvard University Press.

Wacker, D.P., Berg, W.K., Wiggins, B., Muldoon, M., & Cavanaugh, J. (1985). Evaluation of reinforcer preferences for profoundly handicapped students. *Journal of Applied Behavior Analysis, 18*, 173–178.

Wacker, D.P., Wiggins, B., Fowler, M., & Berg, W.K. (1988). Training students with profound or multiple handicaps to make requests via microswitches. *Journal of Applied Behavior Analysis, 21*, 331–343.

Walker, B., & Singer, G.H.S. (1993). Improving collaborative communication between professionals and parents. In G.H.S. Singer & L.E. Powers (Eds.), *Families, disability, and empowerment: Active coping skills and strategies for family interventions* (pp. 285–315). Baltimore: Paul H. Brookes Publishing Co.

Walker, R.I., & Vogelsburg, R.T. (1985). Increasing independent mobility skills for a woman who was severely handicapped and nonambulatory. *Applied Research in Mental Retardation, 6*, 173–183.

Ward, D. (1984). *Positioning the handicapped child for function.* Chicago: Phoenix.

Webster's Third New International Dictionary. (1986). Springfield, MA: Merriam-Webster, Inc.

Wehman, P. (1977). *Helping the mentally retarded acquire play skills: A behavioral approach.* Springfield, IL: Charles C Thomas.

Wehman, P., & Schleien, S. (1980a). Assessment and selection of leisure skills for severely handicapped youth and adults. *Education and Training of the Mentally Retarded, 15*(1), 50–57.

Wehman, P., & Schleien, S.J. (1980b). Relevant assessment in leisure skill training programs. *Therapeutic Recreation Journal, 14*(4), 9–20.

Wehman, P., & Schleien, S. (1981). *Leisure programs for handicapped persons: Adaptations, techniques, and curriculum.* Austin, TX: PRO-ED.

Wehmeyer, M.L. (1992). Self-determination and the education of students with mental retardation. *Education and Training in Mental Retardation, 27*(4), 302–314.

Weiner, A. (1975). The recreation advocate: Your leisure insurance agent. *Therapeutic Recreation Journal, 9*(2), 63–68.

Wilcox, M.J. (1993). Partner-based prelinguistic intervention: A preliminary report. *OSERS News in Print, 5*(4), 4–9.

Witt, P.A., Connolly, P., & Compton, D.M. (1980). Assessment: A plea for sophistication. *Therapeutic Recreation Journal, 14*(4), 5–9.

Wright, C., & Nomura, M. (1985). *From toys to computers: Access for the physically disabled.* San Jose, CA: Christine Wright.

Wuerch, B.B., & Voeltz, L.M. (1982). *Longitudinal leisure skills for severely handicapped learners: The Ho'onanea curriculum component.* Baltimore: Paul H. Brookes Publishing Co.

York, J. (1989). Mobility methods selected for use in home and community environments. *Physical Therapy, 69*(9), 736–747.

York, J., Kronberg, R., Doyle, M.G., & Medwedz, L. (1993). *Creating inclusive school communities: Module 4. Adults learning together on collaborative teams.* Minneapolis: University of Minnesota, Institute on Community Integration.

York, J., Nietupski, J., & Hamre-Nietupski, S. (1985). A decision-making process for using microswitches. *Journal of The Association for Persons with Severe Handicaps, 10*(4), 214–223.

York, J., & Rainforth, B. (1991). Developing instructional adaptations. In F.P. Orelove, & D. Sobsey, *Educating children with multiple disabilities: A transdisciplinary approach* (2nd ed., pp. 259–298). Baltimore: Paul H. Brookes Publishing Co.

York, J., & Wiemann, G. (1991). Accommodating individuals with severe physical disabilities. In J. Reichle, J. York, & J. Sigafoos, *Implementing augmentative and alternative communication: Strategies for learners with severe disabilities* (pp. 239–256). Baltimore: Paul H. Brookes Publishing Co.

Appendix A

LEISURE ACTIVITY
VENDORS

*T*he chart on the following page provides a list of vendors for the leisure activities included in this curriculum component. All of these materials should be available locally from community shopping centers and other retail locations. However, you may wish to obtain extra items in an arrangement that differs somewhat from those that are prepackaged (e.g., extra Nintendo Game Boy software), or you may need to obtain information on servicing certain materials (e.g., Simon or a remote control vehicle). The manufacturer may be willing to respond to such inquiries if you write directly to these central offices.

Activity name	Manufacturer's activity name	Manufacturer address	Approximate price ($)[a]
Aerobics[b]			
Connect Four	Connect Four: The Vertical Checkers Game	Milton Bradley Co. Springfield, MA 01101	11.00
Jenga	Jenga	Milton Bradley Co. Springfield, MA 01101	15.00
Magic Mitts (Scatch)	Magic Mitts	Sportcraft Co. Bergenfield, NJ 07621	7.00
Nintendo Game Boy	Basic Video Game System	Nintendo of America, Inc. Box 957 Redmond, WA 98073	85.00
Pinball	Atomic Arcade Pinball	Tomy America, Inc. 427 Northfield Avenue Edison, NJ 08818	45.00
Pottery[b]			
Remote Control Vehicle	Radio Control Porsche Rally Sports Series	Nikko Americana Inc. 2801 Summit Avenue Plano, TX 75074	85.00
Simon	Simon	Milton Bradley Co. Springfield, MA 01101	37.00
Target Games	Soft-Tip Dart Set	Franklin Sports Industries, Inc. 17 Campanelli Parkway Stoughton, MA 02072	23.00

[a]Prices reflect Spring 1994 approximate costs of the activities. Actual prices vary depending on location and purchase date.

[b]Community activity—purchase of equipment and/or materials may be unnecessary, except for appropriate clothing early in instruction.

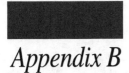

Appendix B

LIFELONG LEISURE
SKILLS AND
LIFESTYLES FORMS

O n the following pages, blank copies of all forms used in this curriculum component are provided for your reference. These samples may be reproduced for use in initiating a leisure skills curriculum component within your program. Completed samples of the forms are included throughout the text and their use explained.

Home Leisure Activities Survey

Participant: _____ Date: _____ Completed by: _____

1. Please list any leisure activities available in your home, including other children's toys and games, in which your child has shown some interest.

2. What are your child's favorite leisure activities?

3. What does your child typically do during his or her free time?

4. Can you list some indoor or outdoor activities your family enjoys doing together? (Please list these by beginning with those you *most prefer*.)

5. Are there any special *space* or *transportation* needs that we should consider in planning leisure or recreation activities for your child?

6. People resources: Are there other people in the home who spend leisure time with your child? Who are they and what would you like your child to be able to do with these persons?

7. Which of these activities are available in the home?

| ___ Aerobics | ___ Jenga | ___ Nintendo Game Boy | ___ Pottery | ___ Simon |
| ___ Connect Four | ___ Magic Mitts (Scatch) | ___ Pinball Games | ___ Remote Control Toys | ___ Target Games |

8. Please assign a rating to each activity to indicate how interesting you think your child would find the activity.

    1 = not very interesting; 2 = somewhat interesting; 3 = very interesting

| ___ Aerobics | ___ Jenga | ___ Nintendo Game Boy | ___ Pottery | ___ Simon |
| ___ Connect Four | ___ Magic Mitts (Scatch) | ___ Pinball Games | ___ Remote Control Toys | ___ Target Games |

9. Which of these activities is your child permitted to play with?

| ___ Aerobics | ___ Jenga | ___ Nintendo Game Boy | ___ Pottery | ___ Simon |
| ___ Connect Four | ___ Magic Mitts (Scatch) | ___ Pinball Games | ___ Remote Control Toys | ___ Target Games |

10. Which of these activities do you feel are appropriate leisure-time activities for your child?

| ___ Aerobics | ___ Jenga | ___ Nintendo Game Boy | ___ Pottery | ___ Simon |
| ___ Connect Four | ___ Magic Mitts (Scatch) | ___ Pinball Games | ___ Remote Control Toys | ___ Target Games |

Leisure Activity Selection Checklist

Participant: _____ Date: _____ Completed by: _____

Instructions: For each activity circle "yes" or "no" for each criterion. Tally the number of "yes" responses for each of these subsections and record them on the appropriate line. Tally the overall score for each activity. Activities that receive a score of 11–14 points are generally considered appropriate for instruction.

	Activity	Activity	Activity
Lifestyle: A concern for selecting activities that are socially valid and that will facilitate typical play and leisure behaviors, as well as provide opportunities for increasingly complex interactions.			
1. *Age Appropriateness.* Is this activity something a peer without a disability would enjoy during free time?	yes no	yes no	yes no
2. *Attraction.* Is this activity likely to promote interest of others who frequently are found in the participant's leisure-time environments?	yes no	yes no	yes no
3. *Environment Flexibility.* Can this activity be used in a variety of potential leisure-time situations on an individual and group basis?	yes no	yes no	yes no
4. *Degree of Supervision.* Can the activity be used under varying degrees of caregiver supervision without major modifications?	yes no	yes no	yes no
5. *Longitudinal Application.* Is use of the activity appropriate for both an adolescent and an adult?	yes no	yes no	yes no
Individualization: Concerns related to logistical and physical demands of leisure activities on current and future environments and free-time situations.			
1. *Skill Level Flexibility.* Can the activity be adapted for low- to high-entry skill levels without major modifications?	yes no	yes no	yes no
2. *Prosthetic Capabilities.* Can the activity be adapted to varying disabilities (sensory, motor, behavior)?	yes no	yes no	yes no
3. *Reinforcement Power.* Is the activity sufficiently novel or stimulating to maintain interest?	yes no	yes no	yes no
4. *Preference.* Is the participant likely to prefer and enjoy the activity?	yes no	yes no	yes no
Environmental: Concerns related to logistical and physical demands of leisure activities on current and future environments and free-time situations.			
1. *Availability.* Is the activity available (or can it easily be made so) across the participant's leisure environments?	yes no	yes no	yes no
2. *Durability.* Is the activity likely to last without need for major repair or replacement of parts for at least a year?	yes no	yes no	yes no
3. *Safety.* Is the activity safe (i.e., would not pose a serious threat to or harm the participant, others, or the environment if abused or used inappropriately)?	yes no	yes no	yes no
4. *Noxiousness.* Is the activity not likely to be overly noxious (noisy, space consuming, distracting) to others in the participant's leisure environments?	yes no	yes no	yes no
5. *Expense.* Is the cost of the activity reasonable? That is, is it likely to be used for multiple purposes?	yes no	yes no	yes no

Area of Concern Scores
1. Lifestyle _____ _____ _____
2. Individualization _____ _____ _____
3. Environmental _____ _____ _____

Total Activity Score _____ _____ _____

Participant Interest Inventory

Participant: _____

	Activity				
Instructions: *For each activity, complete each of the sentences below by placing the number of the description that best matches the participant's behavior in the appropriate box for that activity.*	Date				
	Rater				
A. For this participant's usual level of *interest* in play materials, he or she is: 1. Not as interested as usual 2. About as interested as usual 3. More interested than usual					
B. For this participant's usual level of *physical interaction* with materials (pushing control buttons, turning knobs, putting things together, etc.), he or she is: 1. Not as busy as usual 2. About as busy as usual 3. Busier than usual					
C. For this participant's usual *affective* behaviors (smiling, signs of enjoyment, etc.), he or she seems to be: 1. Enjoying this less than usual 2. Showing about the same amount of enjoyment as usual 3. Enjoying this more than usual					
D. For this participant's usual level of *looking or visual regard* of an activity, object, or person, he or she is: 1. Not looking as much as usual 2. Looking as much as usual 3. Looking more often or longer than usual					
E. Compared to this participant's *usual behavior* during a short period of time with minimal supervision, he or she is: 1. Engaging in more negative behavior than usual 2. Engaging in about the same amount of negative behavior as usual 3. Engaging in less negative (or off-task) behavior than usual					
Activity Interest Scores: *(Total the numbers in each column)*		——	——	——	——

Steps of the Task Analysis

Participant: _____

Activity: _____

1
2
3
4
5
6
7
8
9
10
11
12
13
14
15
16
17
18
19
20
21
22
23
24
25
26
27
28
29
30

Skill Acquisition Data Record

Participant: _____
Skill Sequence: _____
Leisure Educator: _____

Level of Assistance Key	
I = Independent	FP = Full Physical
V = Verbal	X = Partial Physical
PP = Partial Participation	M = Point or Model

Date and Initials[a]

Steps in Activity Sequence												% Correct[b]
10.	10	10	10	10	10	10	10	10	10	10	10	
9.	9	9	9	9	9	9	9	9	9	9	9	
8.	8	8	8	8	8	8	8	8	8	8	8	
7.	7	7	7	7	7	7	7	7	7	7	7	
6.	6	6	6	6	6	6	6	6	6	6	6	
5.	5	5	5	5	5	5	5	5	5	5	5	
4.	4	4	4	4	4	4	4	4	4	4	4	
3.	3	3	3	3	3	3	3	3	3	3	3	
2.	2	2	2	2	2	2	2	2	2	2	2	
1.	1	1	1	1	1	1	1	1	1	1	1	

[a] One data probe should be collected at least once every 2 weeks for each activity sequence.

[b] Percentage of steps performed independently (I).

Participant Performance Data Sheet

Participant: _____

Activity: _____

30	30	30	30	30	30	30	30	30	30	30	30	30	30	30	30	30	30	30	30	30	30	30	30	30	30	30	30
29	29	29	29	29	29	29	29	29	29	29	29	29	29	29	29	29	29	29	29	29	29	29	29	29	29	29	29
28	28	28	28	28	28	28	28	28	28	28	28	28	28	28	28	28	28	28	28	28	28	28	28	28	28	28	28
27	27	27	27	27	27	27	27	27	27	27	27	27	27	27	27	27	27	27	27	27	27	27	27	27	27	27	27
26	26	26	26	26	26	26	26	26	26	26	26	26	26	26	26	26	26	26	26	26	26	26	26	26	26	26	26
25	25	25	25	25	25	25	25	25	25	25	25	25	25	25	25	25	25	25	25	25	25	25	25	25	25	25	25
24	24	24	24	24	24	24	24	24	24	24	24	24	24	24	24	24	24	24	24	24	24	24	24	24	24	24	24
23	23	23	23	23	23	23	23	23	23	23	23	23	23	23	23	23	23	23	23	23	23	23	23	23	23	23	23
22	22	22	22	22	22	22	22	22	22	22	22	22	22	22	22	22	22	22	22	22	22	22	22	22	22	22	22
21	21	21	21	21	21	21	21	21	21	21	21	21	21	21	21	21	21	21	21	21	21	21	21	21	21	21	21
20	20	20	20	20	20	20	20	20	20	20	20	20	20	20	20	20	20	20	20	20	20	20	20	20	20	20	20
19	19	19	19	19	19	19	19	19	19	19	19	19	19	19	19	19	19	19	19	19	19	19	19	19	19	19	19
18	18	18	18	18	18	18	18	18	18	18	18	18	18	18	18	18	18	18	18	18	18	18	18	18	18	18	18
17	17	17	17	17	17	17	17	17	17	17	17	17	17	17	17	17	17	17	17	17	17	17	17	17	17	17	17
16	16	16	16	16	16	16	16	16	16	16	16	16	16	16	16	16	16	16	16	16	16	16	16	16	16	16	16
15	15	15	15	15	15	15	15	15	15	15	15	15	15	15	15	15	15	15	15	15	15	15	15	15	15	15	15
14	14	14	14	14	14	14	14	14	14	14	14	14	14	14	14	14	14	14	14	14	14	14	14	14	14	14	14
13	13	13	13	13	13	13	13	13	13	13	13	13	13	13	13	13	13	13	13	13	13	13	13	13	13	13	13
12	12	12	12	12	12	12	12	12	12	12	12	12	12	12	12	12	12	12	12	12	12	12	12	12	12	12	12
11	11	11	11	11	11	11	11	11	11	11	11	11	11	11	11	11	11	11	11	11	11	11	11	11	11	11	11
10	10	10	10	10	10	10	10	10	10	10	10	10	10	10	10	10	10	10	10	10	10	10	10	10	10	10	10
9	9	9	9	9	9	9	9	9	9	9	9	9	9	9	9	9	9	9	9	9	9	9	9	9	9	9	9
8	8	8	8	8	8	8	8	8	8	8	8	8	8	8	8	8	8	8	8	8	8	8	8	8	8	8	8
7	7	7	7	7	7	7	7	7	7	7	7	7	7	7	7	7	7	7	7	7	7	7	7	7	7	7	7
6	6	6	6	6	6	6	6	6	6	6	6	6	6	6	6	6	6	6	6	6	6	6	6	6	6	6	6
5	5	5	5	5	5	5	5	5	5	5	5	5	5	5	5	5	5	5	5	5	5	5	5	5	5	5	5
4	4	4	4	4	4	4	4	4	4	4	4	4	4	4	4	4	4	4	4	4	4	4	4	4	4	4	4
3	3	3	3	3	3	3	3	3	3	3	3	3	3	3	3	3	3	3	3	3	3	3	3	3	3	3	3
2	2	2	2	2	2	2	2	2	2	2	2	2	2	2	2	2	2	2	2	2	2	2	2	2	2	2	2
1	1	1	1	1	1	1	1	1	1	1	1	1	1	1	1	1	1	1	1	1	1	1	1	1	1	1	1
0	0	0	0	0	0	0	0	0	0	0	0	0	0	0	0	0	0	0	0	0	0	0	0	0	0	0	0

Date

Trainer

Number/Score

Choice Data Sheet

Participant: _____

Activity Options
Check all options

A ____	NGB ____	S ____
CF ____	Pi ____	T ____
J ____	Po ____	(Other) ____
MM ____	RC ____	(Other) ____

Level of Choice Cues

A. _____   C. _____
B. _____   D. _____

Narrative Data

Date and Time	Instructor	Selection Provided	Level of Cue	Activity Selected	Choice Level*	Time of Instructor Contact	Teacher Contacts						Date	Narrative Data
							Out of Area	Destructive	Self-stimulatory/ Self-injurious	Failure to Interact	Inappropriately Interacting*	Appropriately Interacting*		

*Used for Choice Teaching Method II only.

A = Aerobic Warm-ups; CF = Connect Four; J = Jenga; MM = Magic Mitts; NGB = Nintendo Game Boy; Pi = Pinball; Po = Pottery; RC = Remote Control Vehicle; S = Simon; T = Target Games.

Summary of Instructor Contacts

Participant: _____

Key:
CA = contacts for appropriate behaviors
CI = contacts for inappropriate behaviors

ACTIVITY:

Choice Level																	
Date																	
Teacher																	
CA																	
CI																	

ACTIVITY:

Choice Level																	
Date																	
Teacher																	
CA																	
CI																	

ACTIVITY:

Choice Level																	
Date																	
Teacher																	
CA																	
CI																	

ACTIVITY:

Choice Level																	
Date																	
Teacher																	
CA																	
CI																	

Leisure Repertoire Chart

Repertoire chart for: __High School (ages 15–18)__   Participant: _____

Domain: _____ Recreation/Leisure _____   Age: _____   Date: _____

Goal area	Present activities	Performance level — Check one			Has related social skills?	Critical features — Check all that apply			Note priority goal areas
		Assistance on most steps	Assistance on some steps	Independent		Obviously enjoys	Age appropriate	Interacts w/ peers w/o disabilities	
School and extra-curricular (examples)									
Activities to do alone: at home and in the neighborhood (examples)									
Activities to do with family and friends: at home and in the neigh-borhood (examples)									
Physical fitness (examples)									
Activities to do alone: in the community (examples)									
Activities to do with family and friends: in the community (examples)									

252

Monthly Instruction Record for _____ (name of month)

Participant: _____

Leisure
Educators: _____

Date	Choice	(name of activity)	(name of activity)	(name of activity)	(name of activity)
1					
2					
3					
4					
5					
6					
7					
8					
9					
10					
11					
12					
13					
14					
15					
16					
17					
18					
19					
20					
21					
22					
23					
24					
25					
26					
27					
28					
29					
30					
31					

Participant Information Sheet

Participant: _____ Date: _____ Completed by: _____

1. Participant's preferred instructional cues:

_____

_____

2. Participant's preferred positive reinforcers:

_____

_____

3. Participant's functioning language levels:

How participant listens or understands:

_____

_____

How participant talks or communicates:

_____

_____

_____

4. Participant's disability:

_____

_____

5. Participant's behavioral problems and leisure educators' intervention procedures:

_____

_____

_____

Program Cover Sheet

Participant: _____

Activity: _____

Date participant baselined: _____

Date instruction sessions initiated: _____

Date instruction sessions terminated: _____

1. Instructional objective: _____
   _____
   _____

2. Any modifications to task analysis: _____
   _____

3. Instructional environment(s) and additional materials: _____
   _____

4. Instructional procedures:
   Teaching method: _____
   Instructional cues: _____
   Positive reinforcement: _____
   Data collection: _____
   Correction procedures: _____
   Other: _____

5. Behavior interventions: _____
   _____

Participant's name: _____

Activities available: _____

Date	Initials	Activity was: P = prompted I = child initiated	Activity	Play was: A = appropriate I = inappropriate	Comments and/or what the child did

Home Information Sheet

Participant: _____
Participant's birthdate: _____
Address: _____
Date form completed: _____
Completed by: _____
Phone #: _____
Information from: _____

1. What are preferred days and times of day for leisure educator to call on the phone:

2. With whom should leisure educator discuss participant's program:

3. Preferred days and times of day for home visit by leisure educator:

4. Preferred days and times of day for school visit by parent:

5. List siblings' names and ages, listing those most likely to interact with participant:

6. Are there any children in the neighborhood who either do now or might play with participant (describe briefly):

7. Additional comments:

Leisure Educator: _____   Page _____ of _____ pages

Participant: _____

Date	Type*	Who	Brief Description

* LEP = phone call from leisure educator to parent; PP = phone call from parent to leisure educator; HV = home visit by leisure educator; SV = school visit by parent; O = other (describe).

Home called: _____   Participant's name: _____
Date/Time: _____

1. Has your child, _____ , independently initiated play activities?

2. Have you had to prompt _____ to play with activities?

3. How long does _____ play?

4. Does _____ seem to enjoy the activities? If so, how can you tell?

5. Does _____ play with one activity more than the other? Which one?

6. Do any other persons play with _____ while he (she) is playing with activities?

7. Where did _____ play with the activities?

Comments:

Home Telephone Log   FORM 9.3

Home called: _____   Participant's name: _____
Date/Time: _____

1. Has your child, _____ , independently initiated play activities?

2. Have you had to prompt _____ to play with activities?

3. How long does _____ play?

4. Does _____ seem to enjoy the activities? If so, how can you tell?

5. Does _____ play with one activity more than the other? Which one?

6. Do any other persons play with _____ while he (she) is playing with activities?

7. Where did _____ play with the activities?

Comments:

Leisure Educator: _____

Participant's name: _____

Date/Time: _____

1. Materials taken to home: _____

2. Materials returned from home: _____

3. Objectives/goals for this visit: _____

_____

_____

_____

4. Persons present during visit: _____

5. Outcome of visit:

Progress made: _____

_____

_____

Problems identified: _____

_____

_____

6. Comments: _____

_____

_____

_____

Home Visit
Appointment   FORM 9.5

Date/Time of next visit: _____

_____

Any questions, changes or problems, please call

_____

at _____

Home Visit
Appointment   FORM 9.5

Date/Time of next visit: _____

_____

Any questions, changes or problems, please call

_____

at _____

Home Visit
Appointment   FORM 9.5

Date/Time of next visit: _____

_____

Any questions, changes or problems, please call

_____

at _____

Home Visit
Appointment   FORM 9.5

Date/Time of next visit: _____

_____

Any questions, changes or problems, please call

_____

at _____

Home Visit
Appointment   FORM 9.5

Date/Time of next visit: _____

_____

Any questions, changes or problems, please call

_____

at _____

Home Visit
Appointment   FORM 9.5

Date/Time of next visit: _____

_____

Any questions, changes or problems, please call

_____

at _____

Home Visit
Appointment   FORM 9.5

Date/Time of next visit: _____

_____

Any questions, changes or problems, please call

_____

at _____

Home Visit
Appointment   FORM 9.5

Date/Time of next visit: _____

_____

Any questions, changes or problems, please call

_____

at _____

Leisure Time at Home Needs Assessment

Participant: _____   Date completed: _____

In order to plan a leisure-time activities program with you for your child at home, we need to know what you feel are important needs. Please take a few minutes to let us know which of the issues in the sentences below are most important to you and whether you have had experience in this area.

How important is this for you and your child?			For each sentence below, check how important this is to you and your child (check one of the three boxes to the left) and how much experience you have had in that area (check one of the three boxes to the right).	How much experience have you had in this area?		
Not Important	Of Some Importance	Very Important		None	Some	A lot
			1. Setting aside an area at home where my child can play independently during leisure time, and providing him or her with appropriate and enjoyable materials and activities for this time.			
			2. Knowing how to develop my child's independent use of leisure time in the community, including some time with other children with and without disabilities.			
			3. Selecting toys and activities that are appropriate for my child and that he or she will enjoy.			
			4. Knowing what to do when toys and activities for my child do not work.			
			5. Knowing the effects of play and free time behavior on my child's future development.			
			6. Arranging materials in my child's room so that he or she can readily play with an activity on his or her own.			
			7. Knowing what I can expect my child to do during his or her free time, and how often and for how long.			
			8. Making leisure activities easily available at home so my child can begin to play on his or her own.			
			9. Using leisure-time activities as a reward for positive behavior.			

Participant: _____   Respondent: _____

Date completed: _____   Relationship: _____

Directions: After each question below, check the blank that best describes your child's behavior.

1. How important do you think play is for your child's well-being?

_____	_____	_____	_____	_____
Not at all important	Not very important	Don't know	Somewhat important	Very important

2. Are you satisfied with the way your child spends his or her leisure time at home?

_____	_____	_____	_____	_____
Not at all	Not very	Don't know	Somewhat	Yes, very

3. Do you think your child enjoys spending his or her free time with the leisure activities available to him or her at home?

_____	_____	_____	_____	_____
Not at all	Hardly ever	Don't know	Often	Yes, definitely

4. When your child begins an activity during his or her free time at home, can you trust him or her to play independently for 15 minutes or more?

_____	_____	_____	_____	_____
Never	Hardly ever	Don't know	Often	Yes, definitely

5. Can your child play with materials with a sibling or friend without a disability?

_____	_____	_____	_____	_____
Never	Probably not	Don't know	Probably	Yes, definitely

6. Is your child likely to damage or destroy materials and toys during free time at home unless you watch him or her?

_____	_____	_____	_____	_____
Never	Hardly ever	Don't know	Often	Almost always

7. Do you think that appropriate and enjoyable toys and activities are available for children with disabilities like yours?

_____	_____	_____	_____	_____
No	Probably not	Don't know	Probably	Yes, definitely

8. When you need to be busy at home, can your child entertain him- or herself with an activity until you are available?

_____	_____	_____	_____	_____
Never	Hardly ever	Don't know	Sometimes	Yes, definitely

9. Does your child recognize when he or she has free time and begin to play in an acceptable way on his or her own?

_____	_____	_____	_____	_____
Never	Hardly ever	Don't know	Sometimes	Yes, definitely

(continued)

10. Do you think that the activities your child usually engages in during free time are constructive and/or supportive of his or her further development?

No	Probably not	Don't know	Probably	Yes, definitely

11. How important do you think each of the following behavior and curriculum areas are to your child's overall development and adult adjustment? Please check the rating that matches your opinion:

	Not at all important		Don't know		Very important
Adaptive skills (eating, bathing, dressing, toileting)	___	___	___	___	___
Motor skills/mobility	___	___	___	___	___
Preacademic and academic skills	___	___	___	___	___
Prevocational and vocational skills	___	___	___	___	___
Leisure-time skills	___	___	___	___	___
Behavior management	___	___	___	___	___
Language development	___	___	___	___	___

Leisure Home Program Procedures

Participant: _____

Activity: _____

Stored where: _____

Where will activity occur: _____

How should activity begin: _____

If participant does:	Parent will (describe procedures for positive and negative behavior):
Positive	
Negative	

How should activity end: _____

Participant Activity Update

Leisure
Educator: _____   Participant: _____

Date	Activities* available	Activity preference	Activity(ies) in instruction and skill level	Comments (reinforcers used, adaptations, etc.)

*A = Aerobic Warm-ups; CF = Connect Four; J = Jenga; MM = Magic Mitts; NGB = Nintendo Game Boy; Pi = Pinball; Po = Pottery; RC = Remote Control Vehicle; S = Simon; T = Target Games.

Leisure Time in the Home:
Strengths and Needs Assessment

In order to plan a leisure-time program for your child at home, we need to know what you feel are important objectives in this area. Please take a few minutes to let us know how important you consider each of the following statements and how much experience you have had in the area. On the left side of the page, using the key at the top of the column, place a circle around the number that shows how important each statement is to you and your child. On the right side of the page, using the key at the top of the column, place a circle around the number that shows how much experience you have had with each statement. Please make sure you have circled a number in both the left and right column for each statement.

How important is this
for you and your child?
1. Not important
2. Somewhat important
3. Important
4. Very important

How much experience
have you had with this?
1. None
2. Very little
3. More than a little
4. A lot

1 2 3 4	1. Making leisure activities easily accessible so my child can initiate play on his or her own.	1 2 3 4
1 2 3 4	2. Knowing what I can expect my child to do during his or her leisure time.	1 2 3 4
1 2 3 4	3. Understanding the importance of leisure activities instruction as a part of my child's educational program.	1 2 3 4
1 2 3 4	4. Developing ways to involve siblings with their brother or sister with a disability.	1 2 3 4
1 2 3 4	5. Knowing what demands I can be placing on my child at home for appropriate behavior during leisure time.	1 2 3 4
1 2 3 4	6. Structuring a weekly or daily period of time to work with my child on how to use his or her leisure time more independently/enjoyably.	1 2 3 4
1 2 3 4	7. Knowing how to decide what types of toys/activities are appropriate for my child.	1 2 3 4
1 2 3 4	8. Knowing how to "introduce" a new toy/leisure activity for my child so he or she will see how it works.	1 2 3 4
1 2 3 4	9. Motivating my child so he or she will select a toy/activity and play alone for a period of time.	1 2 3 4
1 2 3 4	10. Deciding whether my child likes or dislikes a particular toy/activity.	1 2 3 4
1 2 3 4	11. Knowing where to buy or find toys/activities that are appropriate for my child.	1 2 3 4
1 2 3 4	12. Working with my child's teacher in developing appropriate leisure time behavior.	1 2 3 4
1 2 3 4	13. Getting my child to play alone for longer periods of time.	1 2 3 4
1 2 3 4	14. Keeping my child interested in a toy/activity.	1 2 3 4
1 2 3 4	15. Understanding how leisure-time instruction relates to my child's IEP.	1 2 3 4
1 2 3 4	16. Getting my child to initiate play with a toy/activity.	1 2 3 4
1 2 3 4	17. Arranging materials in my child's room so that he or she can readily play with a toy/activity on his or her own.	1 2 3 4
1 2 3 4	18. Selecting toys/activities that are appropriate for my child and that he or she enjoys.	1 2 3 4
1 2 3 4	19. Knowing how much time I can spend with my child in leisure time activities.	1 2 3 4
1 2 3 4	20. Knowing how often and for how long my child can be expected to play independently without help.	1 2 3 4
1 2 3 4	21. Knowing how to teach my child to play appropriately with a new toy/activity.	1 2 3 4
1 2 3 4	22. Making reasonable demands on my child's siblings in terms of how much time his or her brother(s) and/or sister(s) can be expected to spend with him or her.	1 2 3 4

(continued)

1. Not important	1. None
2. Somewhat important	2. Very little
3. Important	3. More than a little
4. Very important	4. A lot

1 2 3 4	23. Knowing the effects of play behavior on my child's future development.	1 2 3 4
1 2 3 4	24. Knowing how to increase my child's independence during leisure time.	1 2 3 4
1 2 3 4	25. Making leisure-time toys/activities available at home for my child.	1 2 3 4
1 2 3 4	26. Structuring an area at home where my child can play independently during leisure time.	1 2 3 4
1 2 3 4	27. Knowing what leisure-time activities are available in the community for my child.	1 2 3 4
1 2 3 4	28. Knowing how to increase my child's independent use of leisure time in the community.	1 2 3 4
1 2 3 4	29. Prompting my child to play with leisure toys/activities.	1 2 3 4
1 2 3 4	30. Getting my child to spend his or her leisure time appropriately with peers with and without disabilities.	1 2 3 4
1 2 3 4	31. Handling situations when toys/activities fail to work.	1 2 3 4
1 2 3 4	32. Handling situations when toys/activities get broken accidentally.	1 2 3 4
1 2 3 4	33. Handling situations when toys/activities get broken purposefully.	1 2 3 4
1 2 3 4	34. Handling situations when my child wants leisure time but cannot have it.	1 2 3 4
1 2 3 4	35. Using leisure time as a reward for other behaviors.	1 2 3 4
1 2 3 4	36. Knowing how to work on play activities with my child.	1 2 3 4
1 2 3 4	37. Knowing how I can expect my child to play with certain leisure-time toys/activities.	1 2 3 4
1 2 3 4	38. Knowing how to develop my child's independent use of leisure time in the community.	1 2 3 4

Please answer the following questions by filling in the blank or circling the appropriate response.

1. How old is your child? _____

2. What sex is your child? _____

3. What type of disability does your child have?

4. How does your child communicate?

   a. Verbal   b. Nonverbal

   If your child is nonverbal, does he or she sign?

   a. Yes   b. No

5. What is your child's current educational environment?

   a. Self-contained special school (no children without disabilities enrolled)
   b. Self-contained classroom (special class for children with disabilities located in a regular school)
   c. Resource room (part-time special class and part-time regular class)
   d. Residential care facility (explain: _____)
   e. Other _____

6. Does your child have access to peers with disabilities after school?

   a. Yes   b. No

(continued)

7. Does your child have access to peers without disabilities after school?

    a. Yes   b. No

8. What is your relationship to your child?

    a. Parent
    b. Guardian
    c. Foster parent
    d. Group home manager
    e. Other _____

Appendix C

LEISURE ACTIVITY
PICTURES

*T*he following pages contain pictures of 10 leisure activities. These pictures may be reproduced, mounted on heavy paper and laminated, and then used to help determine a participant's leisure activity interests.

Aerobic Warm-Ups

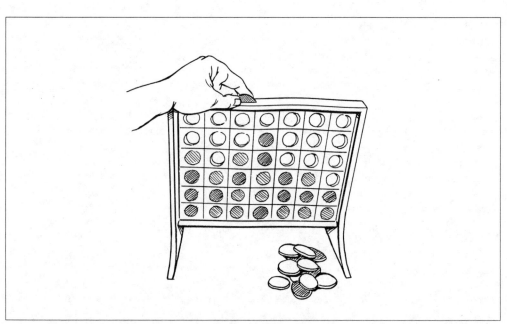

Connect Four

Jenga

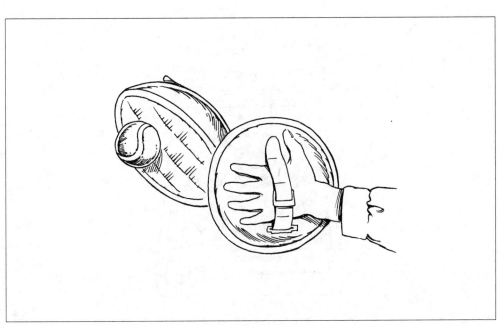

Magic Mitts (Scatch)

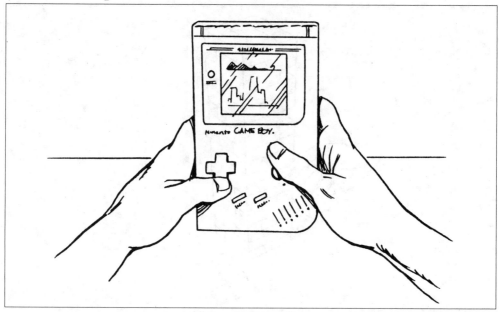

Nintendo Game Boy

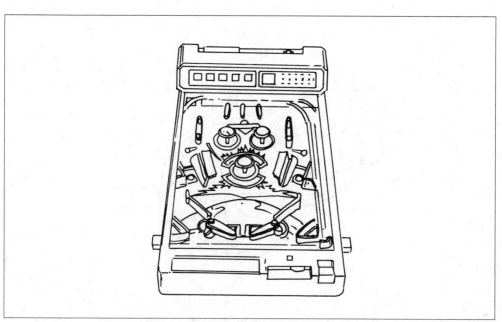

Pinball Games

Pottery

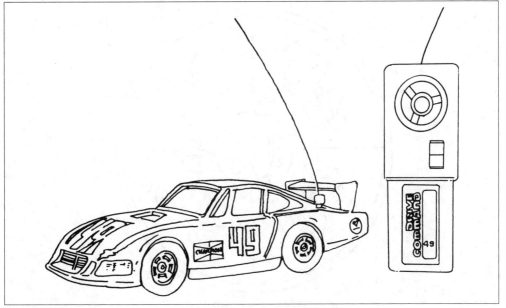

Remote Control Vehicle

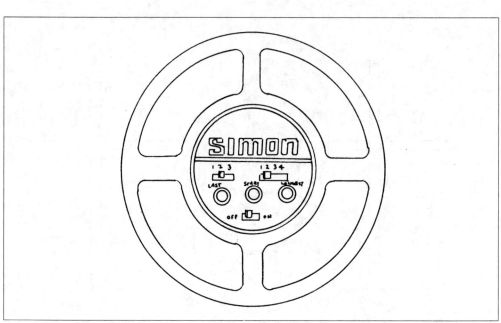

Simon

Target Games

Appendix D

ASSESSMENT OF SOCIAL COMPETENCE

A SCALE OF SOCIAL COMPETENCE FUNCTIONS

Luanna Meyer, Joe Reichle, Ralph McQuarter, David Cole, Terri Vandercook, Ian Evans, Richard Neel, and Gloria Kishi

*T*he Assessment of Social Competence (ASC) assesses 11 highly functional aspects of social competence. Each function is measured by a separate scale, usually completed by a teacher or other adult who is very familiar with the participant. Each subscale consists of eight sets of behavioral examples, except for Function 7. The sets are hierarchically ordered according to level of sophistication. The respondent indicates which behaviors are exhibited by the participant, who "passes" a level if he or she exhibits at least one behavior in the set. Completion of the ASC takes approximately 1 hour.

The ASC is designed for use as a comprehensive measure of social competence functions for participation in naturally occurring activities within integrated community environments. The 11 categories of the ASC were derived from the literature as representative of the skills involved in all social interactions. The categories are referred to as functions rather than as specific skills to emphasize that each category exists to achieve a certain purpose (function) whereas the exact form of the behavior (specific skill) can vary greatly. The learner's individual strategies and abilities at any given time, as well as the specific situation, will influence the behavior form that will be used. Many such forms can achieve similar purposes, regardless of their level of sophistication or even whether most individuals would judge them to be the most socially appropriate strategies.

Another critical feature of the ASC is that within each function the levels are intended to represent a hierarchy of increasing social sophistication. The lower levels differ, however, from the more traditional early test items in that they do not reflect prerequisite skills that are believed to be needed for the later development of an effective skill. Instead, the items in the ASC represent behavior forms that reflect increases in the individual's ability to vary strategies for increasingly complex social situations. At the highest level, the forms are considered to reflect mastery or a representation of adult competence, which might, of course, occur at various levels. Thus, even the items at the lowest levels of the ASC should reflect at least partially effective strategies used by persons of different ages and levels of functioning to accomplish particular critical social interactions.

This work was supported in part by Contract #300-82-0363 from Special Education Programs, U.S. Department of Education, to the University of Minnesota with a subcontract to Syracuse University. This material does not necessarily reflect the position or policies of the U.S. Department of Education, and no official endorsement should be inferred. Please contact Dr. Luanna Meyer, School of Education, 150 Huntington Hall, Syracuse University, Syracuse, NY 13244-2340 for information about the scale and for permission to reprint for use.

The item hierarchies were developed through a series of validity studies. These included traditional item analysis, correlations of items within and across functions (convergent and discriminant validity checks), correlations of the measure with other valid measures of adaptive behavior (i.e., the Topeka Association for Retarded Citizens [TARC] Assessment Inventory for Severely Handicapped Children and the Scales of Independent Behavior [SIB]), and correlations of the measure with skill acquisition during instruction and with observed and rated access to and performance in community environments (predictive validity). The function hierarchies have been utilized in social skills instruction research with learners who display moderate and severe disabilities. In addition, internal consistency test–retest (teacher–teacher) and inter-rater (teacher–parent) reliabilities were computed. The ASC has undergone two major revisions based on these studies. (For an overview of the psychometric validation of the ASC, see Meyer, L.H., Cole, D.A., McQuarter, R., & Reichle, J. [1990]. Validation of the Assessment of Social Competence [ASC] for children and young adults with developmental disabilities. *Journal of The Association for Persons with Severe Handicaps, 15*[2] 57–68.)

The following are the 11 aspects of social competence with definitions and examples.

Functions	General Definition	Sample Level Definitions	Example Items
1. Initiate	Joins an ongoing interaction or starts a new one	Level 2: Consistently initiates behavior with other persons.	Joins an ongoing activity whether or not participation is wanted.
		Level 5: Initiates goal-directed social interaction.	Finds a store clerk in order to pay for an item.
		Level 8: Bases initiations on indirect knowledge and inference.	Invites one friend rather than another based on the judgment that the person likes the type of activity selected.
2. Self-regulate	Manages one's own behavior without instruction from others	Level 2: Uses specific behavior to access a person or event in order to return to a more comfortable state.	Attempts to raise head, orient toward, or look at a specific object (may use reflex pattern, abnormal posture, etc.).
		Level 5: Generates personal strategies to monitor behavior.	Makes lists to remember which tasks to do that day.
		Level 8: Plans ahead for upcoming events; personal values direct certain actions.	Resists peer pressure to do something contrary to one's own values.
3. Follow rules	Follows rules, guidelines, and routines of activities	Level 2: Daily activity routines follow those consistent	Wakes up and demands attention at the same time

Functions	General Definition	Sample Level Definitions	Example Items
		with usual environmental demands, but participant is inflexible so that a break in routine may result in an effort to follow the usual pattern or even in disruptive behavior.	the family usually gets up in the morning, even on weekends or holidays when others sleep late.
		Level 5: Follows well-established rules for specific environments and situations, even though the rules are no longer posted or the person who originally provided the instructions is no longer present.	Chooses correct line and waits appropriately for service in a store or fast-food restaurant.
		Level 8: Helps to make and establish new rules and guidelines for self and others that are based on a thoughtful analysis of relevant facts.	Advocates for changes in eligibility requirements for joining a club or activity so that new members could be recruited.
4. Provide positive feedback	Provides positive feedback and reinforcement to others	Level 2: Positive affect occurs directed to persons in general.	Smiles when someone calls his or her name.
		Level 5: Positive affect appropriately varied for different persons and the environment or situation.	Behaves differently in a classroom than in the hall or outside the building (e.g., may shout outside, but would be quieter inside).
		Level 8: Engages in nonpreferred activities and shares highy preferred, limited	Helps a family member with that person's domestic chores, where such general

Functions	General Definition	Sample Level Definitions	Example Items
		resources on reciprocal basis.	"favors" balance out across time.
5. Provide negative feedback	Provides negative feedback and consequates others	Level 2: Negative affect occurs, directed toward persons in general.	When approached, turns or moves away as if to avoid contact.
		Level 5: Waits until a more appropriate, future time to provide negative feedback.	In a group situation, does not immediately tell a friend that he or she does not want to do something but will wait until later when alone with that friend.
		Level 8: Expresses negative opinions and dislikes in an appropriate assertive way, clearly specifying the source of concern.	Rejects help from someone by politely telling that individual that he or she can do the task without assistance.
6. Obtain cues	Obtains and responds to relevant situational cues	Level 2: Orients directly toward a stimulus in order to better receive information.	Turns and faces someone who begins to talk to him or her.
		Level 5: Seeks out and responds appropriately to signs and other information sources that are not immediately obvious.	Checks temperature of water with finger before stepping under shower.
		Level 8: Solicits information on the guidelines or rules governing behavior in new situations.	Asks fellow workers what the current practices are regarding vacation time.
7. Offer assistance	Provides information and offers assistance to others	Level 2: Directs attention of another person who is nearby toward an ongoing event that is occurring in the	When extremely interested in something on TV, looks to another person while vocalizing and pointing at TV as if to attract

Functions	General Definition	Sample Level Definitions	Example Items
		immediate environment.	attention to what is occurring on the TV.
		Level 5: Tailors information and assistance to the comprehension level of a listener; initiates an offer of help or information in familiar situations.	Talks differently to a younger child (e.g., using "baby talk") than to a peer or adult.
		Level 7: Initiates a conversation to meet an anticipated need for information and/or assistance.	Watches someone using a vending machine and offers help if needed.
8. Accept assistance	Requests and accepts assistance from others	Level 2: Shows signs of distress, discomfort, and other needs that are directed toward someone who might help; tolerates help from another.	When hungry or bothered by something, will tantrum or cry to get help from an adult who is present.
		Level 5: Directs or makes requests to those persons in the best position to provide the needed help.	Asks a store employee rather than another customer for assistance in finding items in the supermarket.
		Level 8: Changes the style of the request depending on the characteristics of the person asked, and refrains from asking for help when the problem can be solved independently.	Makes certain that solutions likely to succeed have been exhausted before asking for help.
9. Indicate preference	Makes choices from among available and possible alternatives	Level 2: Behaves differently depending on what is presented.	Allows people to help with some things but not with others.

Functions	General Definition	Sample Level Definitions	Example Items
		Level 5: Uses a mediator or symbol to communicate choices to others.	Points to a picture of the preferred food item on the display when ordering at a fast-food restaurant.
		Level 8: Uses long-term goals and values to make decisions about choices and preference.	In order to be with a certain friend, engages in a non-preferred activity that the friend really wants to do.
10. Cope with negatives	Exhibits alternative strategies to cope with negative situations	Level 2: Persists in continuing behavior that is bothersome to others.	Continues to give the same incorrect answer even after being corrected.
		Level 5: Responds to negative feedback by switching to well-rehearsed, alternative responses in a trial-and-error fashion until something "works."	Requests second favorite food when told that first choice is gone.
		Level 8: Anticipates negative feedback and switches strategies before it occurs.	Notices that a friend seems disinterested in his or her suggested activity and proposes an alternative.
11. Terminate	Terminates or withdraws from an interaction and/or activity	Level 2: Uses well-rehearsed and prompted strategies to leave situations.	Signals goodbye in appropriate contexts.
		Level 5: Ceases an activity or interaction appropriately in response to cues that another activity is about to occur.	Politely terminates a conversation after noticing that the other person is glancing at his or her watch and otherwise indicating a need to leave.
		Level 8: Negotiates negative and positive relationships,	Diplomatically disengages from a close relationship

Functions	General Definition	Sample Level Definitions	Example Items
		including major role changes and decisions to terminate relationships.	based on the judgment that interests are no longer shared, feelings have changed, and so forth.

(Adapted from Meyer, Cole, McQuarter, & Reichle, 1990.)

Directions for Scoring the ASC

1. For each function, *every* item should be scored on the line next to that item.
2. The listed items are provided as possible examples of behavior that fit within the function and level indicated. If you can think of a similar example that is not listed as an item but is performed by the learner and seems to fit that level, add that item. There is a blank space and scoring space provided at the end of the listed items under each level to add any similar items (please write the "new" item out in this blank space provided).
3. If the behavior that you have observed or that has been reported to you is very similar to one of the listed items but differs somewhat (perhaps due to an adaptation that has been made), edit the item listed and score the edited item. Please be certain that if the behavior you are scoring differs somehow from the listed item, changes are made to the item.
4. In the blank provided next to *each* item (and any item you might add), score that item according to the score key as follows:

   No evidence = 0   The rater has no direct or reported evidence that the learner engages in this behavior.

   Report only = 1   The rater has not observed the behavior, but someone has reported to him or her that the behavior has occurred.

   Direct observation = 2   The rater has directly observed at least one instance of the behavior. Others may also have reported to the rater that they have seen the behavior.

5. After you have scored all the levels and items for a particular function, complete the Function Summary Grid at the end of the function. Mark an "X" for each level column in the box (of the three possible choices) that applies.
6. Repeat this process until all 11 functions are scored.
7. Complete the ASC Summary Score Sheet on the last page of the ASC.

ASC Learner Information Key

Learner's Name_____Birthdate _____Age at Test _____

School or Environment _____District or Agency _____

Program_____Supervisor/Teacher_____

Other test data (test name, date given, scores) _____

_____

ASC Testing Information

Who scored the ASC for this learner? _____

Relationship to learner (e.g., teacher, parent)_____

Disability of learner _____

Related services now being provided to this learner (check all that apply)

_____Physical Therapy   _____Speech Therapy   _____Social Work

_____Occupational Therapy   _____Psychological   _____Other (please specify)

If this individual is school-age and attends any educational programming in regular education, enter the approximate number of hours weekly and the type of program below:

Number of Hours Weekly   Type of Program

_____   _____

_____   _____

_____   _____

_____   _____

_____   _____

_____   _____

FUNCTION 1.   INITIATE: JOINS AN ONGOING INTERACTION OR STARTS A NEW ONE

Level 1: Initiates behavior inconsistently in the presence of others.

_____Sometimes vocalizes in the presence of others.

_____Sometimes moves (changes position) in the presence of others.

Level 2: Consistently initiates behavior with other persons.

_____Consistently vocalizes to obtain attention.

_____Moves or reaches out to obtain attention.

_____Joins an ongoing activity whether or not participation is wanted.

Level 3: Uses common greetings and initiations.

_____Says, "Hi" to greet another person, but may repeat the same greeting a few minutes later.

_____"Hovers" around a peer activity, but joins only when invited.

_____Initiates handshake when introduced, whether it is appropriate or not.

Level 4: Initiates interactions based on the situation.

_____Does not force an unwanted object on someone.

_____Shares an object with another person who wants it.

_____Says, "Hi" only on first greeting and does not repeat greeting again in a few minutes.

Level 5: Initiates goal-directed social interaction.

_____After greeting a peer, gets out a favorite game to play.

_____Invites a peer to the movies.

_____Finds a store clerk in order to pay for an item.

Level 6: Attends to contextual details when initiating a social interaction.

_____Comments on some aspect of the environment to start a conversation with someone new (e.g., "It's sure cold in here," as both wait to see the dentist).

_____When unable to meet with someone, arranges to meet later.

_____Waits until another person is not busy to initiate interaction.

Level 7: Bases initiations on direct experience with similar activities previously done with a particular person.

_____Initiates activity only with those peers who have been friendly in the past.

_____Differentially approaches mom versus dad for a new activity that resembles the activities typically done with that parent.

_____Telephones a friend who had previously invited him or her to do something together.

_____

Level 8: Bases initiations on indirect knowledge and inference.

_____Tags along with higher status peers to increase his or her chances of being allowed to participate in an activity.

_____Invites one friend rather than another based on the judgment that the person likes the type of activity selected.

_____Asks a peer who is visually impaired to go to a rock concert rather than a movie.

_____

Function 1 Summary Grid: Initiate

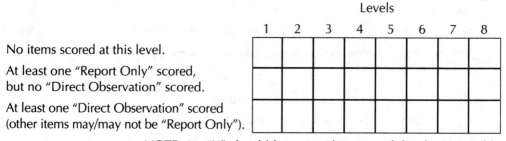

Levels

	1	2	3	4	5	6	7	8
No items scored at this level.								
At least one "Report Only" scored, but no "Direct Observation" scored.								
At least one "Direct Observation" scored (other items may/may not be "Report Only").								

NOTE: An "X" should be entered in one of the three possible choices in each column representing a level within the function.

Comments:

FUNCTION 2.   SELF-REGULATE: MANAGES ONE'S OWN BEHAVIOR WITHOUT INSTRUCTION FROM OTHERS

Level 1: Responds to stimuli in a general way.

_____Responds to irritating stimulus (e.g., insect on arm) with a general movement (a shudder, general flailing of arms, etc).

_____Shows increase in negative behaviors when sick, injured, too hot, and so forth.

Level 2: Uses a specific behavior to access a person or event in order to return to a more comfortable state.

_____Brushes ticklish object off body with hand, scratches an itch.

_____Attempts to raise head, orient toward, or look at a specific object (may use reflex pattern, abnormal posture, etc.)

_____Covers ears to block out loud noise.

Level 3: Modifies a learned behavior based on immediate feedback.

_____Waits for hot soup to cool before eating it.

_____Chooses to take off sweater when too hot.

_____Uses a hot pad to take a dish out of the oven.

Level 4: Delays immediate gratification to get a desired reward later.

_____Finishes chores before taking a break.

_____Saves money now for a bigger purchase later.

_____Puts on sunscreen to prevent sunburn.

Level 5: Generates personal strategies to monitor behavior.

_____Waits at an intersection and says to self, "Don't cross until the light is green."

_____Substitutes a relaxation exercise for self-injurious or stereotyped behavior.

_____Makes lists to remember which tasks to do each day.

Level 6: Using established standard, keeps track of own behavior and changes behavior when appropriate.

_____Weighs self regularly when trying to lose weight.

_____Keeps own record of days worked to guide requests for time off.

_____Coordinates clothes for color and pattern variation.

Level 7: Sets goals for self and rewards self for reaching these goals (rewards may be internal or external).

_____Buys new clothes when reaching weight loss goal.

_____Sets up work schedule (e.g., household chores) so that more pleasant tasks come after less desirable tasks.

_____Shows happiness or pride when reaching a desired goal.

Level 8: Plans ahead for upcoming events; personal values direct certain actions.

_____Shops for groceries before running out of food.

_____Joins an instruction program to enhance a particular skill (e.g., music lessons).

_____Resists peer pressure to do something contrary to one's own value.

_____

Function 2 Summary Grid: Self-Regulate

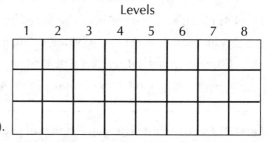

Levels

| | 1 | 2 | 3 | 4 | 5 | 6 | 7 | 8 |

No items scored at this level.

At least one "Report Only" scored, but no "Direct Observation" scored.

At least one "Direct Observation" scored (other items may/may not be "Report Only").

NOTE: An "X" should be entered in one of the three possible choices in each column representing a level within the function.

Comments:

FUNCTION 3.   FOLLOW RULES: FOLLOWS RULES, GUIDELINES, AND ROUTINES OF ACTIVITIES

Level 1: Idiosyncratic biological routines.

_____Urinates and/or has bowel movements on a somewhat predictable schedule.

_____Evidence of hunger is displayed on a somewhat predictable time schedule.

_____Has a predictable sleep–wake cycle, which reflects environmental conditions (e.g., sleeps at night and less often during the day, falls asleep when put into crib or bed with blanket).

_____

Level 2: Daily activity routines follow those consistent with usual environmental demands, but participant is inflexible so that a break in routine may result in an effort to follow the usual pattern or even in disruptive behavior.

_____Even though it is a particularly warm winter day, continues to wear same winter jacket that he or she wears in colder weather.

_____Wakes up and demands attention at the same time the family usually gets up in the morning, even on weekends or holidays when others sleep late.

_____Is upset by a change in schedule or routine in school, at work, or at home.

Level 3: Daily activity routines follow established patterns, but are modified for different situations and environmental demands; follows rules in the presence of authority.

_____Adjusts own behavior according to instructions given by someone else (e.g., will follow a custodian's instruction to walk around an area of the hallway floor that has just been mopped).

_____Expects the schedule of activities on a Saturday or Sunday to be different from the usual events on a weekday.

_____When raining, knows that a planned outing will not take place; anticipates alternative recess activity when weather prohibits going outside.

Level 4: Follows posted rules, signals, and signs independently.

_____Waits until green light over the door goes on before pushing the door open to get off the bus.

_____Follows instructions, such as the "walk/don't walk" lights at intersections.

_____At the movie theater, reads the signs indicating which line to stand in for ticket purchase versus waiting to get in the theater, and responds appropriately.

Level 5: Follows well-established rules for specific environments and situations, even though the rules are no longer posted or the person who originally provided the instructions is no longer present.

_____Brushes teeth or asks for teeth to be brushed (if motorically impaired) after eating.

_____Selects appropriate clothing to wear for the planned activity or place.

_____Chooses correct line and waits appropriately for service in a store or fast-food restaurant.

Level 6: Modifies routines or well-established behaviors to fit a new or different situation.

_____When tissue is not available, will use a paper napkin or toilet paper to blow nose.

_____Selects appropriate alternative eating strategy when the usual rules do not seem to apply (e.g., uses a knife and fork to eat a messy sandwich, uses fingers to eat barbecued ribs or chicken).

_____Varies choice of clothing to match expectations of different persons and environments (e.g., will dress "modestly" or more conservatively when going out with family rather than friends).

Level 7: While still following general rules and guidelines, will disregard those rules when appropriate for unusual circumstances.

_____In case of an emergency, will interrupt others to alert them of the situation.

_____Crosses street when safe to do so at a red light if the light is not working properly.

_____Generally follows "no littering" rules and puts trash in the trash container, but may throw biodegradable items such as an apple core on the ground.

Level 8: Helps to make and establish new rules and guidelines for self and others that are based on a thoughtful analysis of relevant facts.

_____Proposes a change in lunch schedules at work based on individual needs while still providing for needs of work environment.

_____Advocates for changes in eligibility requirements for joining a club or activity so that new members could be recruited.

_____Negotiates with family members to alter schedules or responsibilities based on desire to engage in alternative activities and changes that seem reasonable.

Function 3 Summary Grid: Follow Rules

Levels

	1	2	3	4	5	6	7	8
No items scored at this level.								
At least one "Report Only" scored, but no "Direct Observation" scored.								
At least one "Direct Observation" scored (other items may/may not be "Report Only").								

NOTE: An "X" should be entered in one of the three possible choices in each column representing a level within the function.

Comments:

FUNCTION 4.   PROVIDE POSITIVE FEEDBACK: PROVIDES POSITIVE FEEDBACK AND REINFORCEMENT TO OTHERS

Level 1: Positive affect occurs, but is not consistently related to social events.

_____Smiles or laughs inconsistently in response to events involving people and activities or objects.

_____Does not "mold" to adult's body when being carried, but also does not pull away from touch and contact.

_____ _____

Level 2: Positive affect occurs directed to persons in general.

_____Smiles when someone calls his or her name.

_____"Molds" to adult's body when being carried.

_____Takes on an anticipatory posture (as if getting ready to be picked up) when approached by an adult.

_____ _____

Level 3: Positive affect directed to particular significant others but not to strangers.

_____Generally is positive toward familiar persons but does not approach someone new or unfamiliar (e.g., a substitute teacher or a new babysitter).

_____Would not smile at a stranger unless that person smiled first.

_____Takes on an anticipatory posture (as if getting ready to be picked up) when approached by a primary caregiver, but does not do so when approached by a strange adult.

_____ _____

Level 4: Positive affect appropriately varied for different persons, including efforts to increase interactions with certain significant others.

_____Says, "Thank you" without being told to when given something by parent or teacher.

_____When playing, offers choice of activity or toys to a peer.

_____Hugs mother or father, but not a teacher or therapist.

_____ _____

Level 5: Positive affect appropriately varied for different persons and the environment or situation.

_____Behaves differently in a classroom than in the hall or outside the building (e.g., may shout outside, but is quieter inside).

_____Smiles at a friend in church, but does not laugh or talk with the friend until later when the service is over.

_____ _____

Level 6: Tries to please another person by participation in an activity that the other person selects (does not insist on own preferences).

_____Agrees to go along with an activity suggested by a peer even though he or she prefers something else.

_____Selects a present for another person (e.g., birthday) that he or she knows that person would like, although it might differ from his or her own tastes.

_____Invites a friend to a movie that he or she knows the friend would like, or lets the friend make the decision as to which movie to see.

_____

Level 7: Negotiates own preferences and makes an effort to please others by seeking common preferences.

_____Selects a pizza for a party with friends that anyone attending would like, rather than picking something that matches only one person's preferences.

_____May give personal belongings to a friend on occasion, but would not part with a favorite item just to please the other person.

_____Tries to select a movie that both persons like, rather than simply going along with someone else's choice regardless of own preferences.

_____

Level 8: Engages in nonpreferred activities and shares highly preferred, limited resources on reciprocal basis.

_____Gives personal belongings to friends only on a reciprocal basis and, with rare exception, would not part with a favorite item just to please the other person.

_____Helps a family member with that person's domestic chores, when such general "favors" balance out across time.

_____In order to save enough money to buy a present for a family member or close friend, restricts personal spending for leisure activities, snacks, and so forth.

_____

Function 4 Summary Grid: Provide Positive Feedback

Levels

	1	2	3	4	5	6	7	8
No items scored at this level.								
At least one "Report Only" scored, but no "Direct Observation" scored.								
At least one "Direct Observation" scored (other items may/may not be "Report Only").								

NOTE: An "X" should be entered in one of the three possible choices in each column representing a level within the function.

Comments:

FUNCTION 5.   PROVIDE NEGATIVE FEEDBACK: PROVIDES NEGATIVE FEEDBACK AND CONSEQUATES OTHERS

Level 1: Negative affect occurs but is not consistently related to social events.

_____Seems to dislike physical contact.

_____Cries when something produces a loud, unexpected noise.

Level 2: Negative affect occurs, directed toward persons in general.

_____Increases or continues stereotyped behaviors when someone approaches.

_____Protests or goes limp when picked up and/or carried by someone.

_____When approached, turns or moves away as if to avoid contact.

Level 3: Increased negative affect directed to a particular person in response to a disliked situation or event.

_____Ignores an interruption by a peer, but if interruption continues, might push or hit peer.

_____Grabs toy away when peer begins to play with the same materials.

_____Tantrums during instruction on tasks that he or she does not like or finds difficult to do.

Level 4: Prevents nonpreferred situations from occurring by interrupting them or causing a disruption at the first signs of those events.

_____Protests when parent or teacher puts on coat to leave.

_____Walks across the room to avoid contact with a typically troublesome peer.

_____Says, "No!" when caregiver or teacher starts to set up an activity that he or she does not like to do.

Level 5: Waits until a more appropriate, future time to provide negative feedback.

_____In a group situation, does not immediately tell a friend that he or she does not want to do something but will wait until later when alone with that friend.

_____When invited somewhere, delays making a decision until a time when the peer seems more cheerful to tell him or her that he or she does not want to go.

_____Waits until returning home from the restaurant to tell others that he or she did not like the food.

Level 6: Compensates for negative behavior on an earlier occasion by being positive at a later time.

_____Tries to make up for a tantrum by being particularly nice to parent or other caregiver.

_____After being unpleasant to a parent or teacher, later volunteers to do an extra "clean-up" job for that person.

_____Apologizes to peer, regardless of who was to blame, after getting angry.

Level 7: Explains why he or she behaved in a negative way in a particular situation, and attempts to modify the situation to avoid a repeat of the difficult incident.

_____Tries to explain to supervisor why he or she got angry at a customer.

_____Explains why an appointment was missed or a task was not completed, and plans to remediate the situation.

_____Tries to renegotiate responsibilities around the house following a refusal to do something the day before.

Level 8: Expresses negative opinions and dislikes in an appropriate assertive way, clearly specifying the source of concern.

_____Rejects help from someone by politely telling that individual that he or she can do the task without assistance.

_____After listening to something that a friend complained about, is able to explain to the friend why he or she does not agree with the friend's interpretation of the event.

_____When offered something at a friend's home or restaurant that he or she does not like, is able to refuse graciously.

Function 5 Summary Grid: Provide Negative Feedback

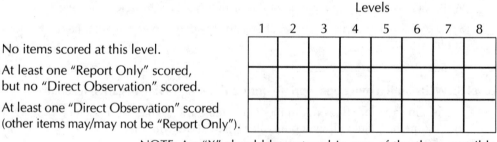

	Levels							
	1	2	3	4	5	6	7	8
No items scored at this level.								
At least one "Report Only" scored, but no "Direct Observation" scored.								
At least one "Direct Observation" scored (other items may/may not be "Report Only").								

NOTE: An "X" should be entered in one of the three possible choices in each column representing a level within the function.

Comments:

FUNCTION 6. OBTAIN CUES: OBTAINS AND RESPONDS TO RELEVANT SITUATIONAL CUES

Level 1: Momentary orientation.

_____Directs a fleeting glance toward a new toy, but does not maintain interest.

_____Glances briefly; eyes may dart toward source of a sound.

_____

Level 2: Orients directly toward a stimulus in order to better receive information.

_____Turns and faces someone who begins to talk to him or her.

_____When using a fork to eat and fails to spear a piece of food, will look down at the plate before trying again.

_____Watches the TV screen when another person is playing a video game.

_____

Level 3: Changes entire body position and/or performs a specific motor response in order to better receive information.

_____Switches on light when it is too hard to see well without it.

_____Turns up the volume on the TV set or radio when it is too low or other noise is interfering.

_____When talking to someone, moves closer in order to hear and see them better.

_____

Level 4: Identifies and responds to immediately visible conventional signs and sources of information.

_____Picks up a cup by the handle rather than the sides, turns doorknob rather than pushing at the door, and so forth.

_____Correctly follows signs designating correct bathroom ("men" and "women"), "in" and "out" doors in stores, and so forth.

_____Notices the "out of order" sign on the soda machine and uses a different machine.

_____

Level 5: Seeks out and responds appropriately to signs and other information sources that are not immediately obvious.

_____Checks temperature of water with finger before stepping under shower.

_____Finds out what the weather is like before dressing to go outside.

_____Watches for soup to boil as a signal to turn down the burner.

_____

Level 6: Gets additional information by communicating with other people or by using conventional means.

_____Asks a friend why he or she recommended a particular restaurant.

_____Finds out how much something costs when the price is not marked.

_____Calls a neighbor or the power company when the lights go out to see if there is a power failure.

_____

Level 7: Uses written and other impersonal sources of information to guide behavior.

_____Follows directions on the package before preparing a new food item as part of the meal.

_____Selects program to watch on television by reading the TV guide for the correct day and time.

_____Checks labels for allergenic substances, number of calories, salt content, and so forth to find items that match diet instructions.

_____

Level 8: Solicits information on the guidelines or rules governing behavior in new situations.

_____Asks fellow workers what the current practices are regarding vacation time.

_____Asks for a discussion of each participant's responsibilities in a new project or task to assist in making health, leisure/recreation, legal, and/or career decisions.

_____Consults several different self-help guides from the library (or those available from friends) to assist in making health, leisure/recreation, legal, and/or career decisions.

_____

Function 6 Summary Grid: Obtain Cues

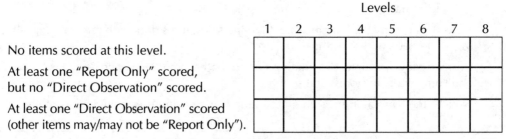

	Levels							
	1	2	3	4	5	6	7	8
No items scored at this level.								
At least one "Report Only" scored, but no "Direct Observation" scored.								
At least one "Direct Observation" scored (other items may/may not be "Report Only").								

NOTE: An "X" should be entered in one of the three possible choices in each column representing a level within the function.

Comments:

FUNCTION 7:   OFFER ASSISTANCE: PROVIDES INFORMATION AND OFFERS ASSISTANCE TO OTHERS

Level 1: Increases rate, duration, and/or intensity of attempts at social contact.

_____Pushes toys or objects toward others, but makes no other effort to socially interact.

_____Vocalizes or gestures to a stranger as if to share information, even though no previous interaction has occurred and the event seems inappropriate.

Level 2: Directs attention of another perosn who is nearby toward an ongoing event that is occurring in the immediate environment.

_____When extremely interested in something on TV, looks to another person while vocalizing and pointing at TV as if to attract attention to what is occurring on the TV.

_____Looks at adult in room and points to the door when the doorbell rings.

_____After playing with a toy, will display the toy to another person who is close by.

Level 3: Seeks out others to show objects of interest and share information; answers simple question appropriately.

_____Goes to another room to get someone to return with him or her to see something (e.g., a spider).

_____If asked in what room someone or something is located, gives the appropriate answer or takes the person there.

_____Seeks out another person to tell him or her that someone has just dropped by for a visit.

Level 4: Adds unsolicited information or extra help.

_____When someone asks, "Did you go outside?" elaborates answer beyond a simple "Yes" or "No" (e.g., "Yes, we played baseball.").

_____Holds door open for someone else whose arms are full of packages.

_____Hands someone else a hot pad when that person is about to remove something from the stove or oven.

Level 5: Tailors information and assistance to the comprehension level of a listener; initiates an offer of help or information in familiar situations.

_____Talks differently to a younger child (e.g., using "baby talk") than to a peer or adult.

_____Volunteers help to a younger child or someone who appears lost.

_____When interacting with a sibling, models how to do something rather than simply doing it for the child.

Level 6: Clarifies, elaborates, or seeks confirmation for ongoing events and conversations.

_____Observes that someone else has a problem and continues to offer possible solutions until the problem is resolved.

_____After giving a message to someone over the phone, asks for the message to be repeated to check for accuracy before hanging up.

_____When explaining to a friend why he or she cannot go somewhere, gives adequate reasons so that the friend is not hurt and does not feel rejected.

Level 7: Initiates a conversation to meet an anticipated need for information and/or assistance.

_____Watches someone using a vending machine and offers help if needed.

_____Initiates a discussion with a friend about a recent event that may be troubling to the friend.

_____Offers to shovel the sidewalk for elderly neighbors after a snowstorm.

Function 7 Summary Grid: Offer Assistance

Levels

	1	2	3	4	5	6	7
No items scored at this level.							
At least one "Report Only" scored, but no "Direct Observation" scored.							
At least one "Direct Observation" scored (other items may/may not be "Report Only").							

NOTE: An "X" should be entered in one of the three possible choices in each column representing a level within the function.

Comments:

FUNCTION 8.   ACCEPT ASSISTANCE: REQUESTS AND ACCEPTS ASSISTANCE FROM OTHERS

Level 1: Shows signs of distress, discomfort, and other needs, although not directed toward anyone.

_____"Fusses" or cries after a period of time in one position; will quiet down if position is changed.

_____Arrives at destination in an irritable mood if he or she has not had his or her usual breakfast or morning routine.

_____

Level 2: Shows signs of distress, discomfort, and other needs that are directed toward someone who might help; tolerates help from another.

_____When hungry or bothered by something, will tantrum or cry to get help from an adult who is present.

_____When in need of help (e.g., buttoning a shirt, opening a door), approaches an adult but simply stands close by without any direct indication as to what is wanted.

_____When having difficulty putting on a coat, allows others to help.

_____

Level 3: Uses differentiated signals to indicate specific needs (e.g., a certain gesture or cry will indicate hunger) to the specific person who could provide help; tolerates help from selected individuals only.

_____Holds up a glass to a particular person to indicate he or she wants a drink.

_____Stands in front of the door and stares at someone likely to open it.

_____Accepts assistance in brushing teeth from one individual but not from others.

_____

Level 4: Uses formal symbols with a variety of individuals to make requests.

_____Uses language (including sign or communication board) to request food at a restaurant.

_____Communicates "help me" when engaged in a task that he or she cannot complete.

_____Expresses need to use and seeks assistance in locating the bathroom when in an unfamiliar place.

_____

Level 5: Directs or makes requests to those persons in the best position to provide the needed help.

_____Asks for help from an adult rather than from a younger child who is also present but is less likely to be able to be of assistance.

_____Asks a store employee rather than another customer for assistance in finding items in the supermarket.

_____Asks the same partner to help complete a joint project that was initiated the previous day.

_____

Level 6: Seeks out a person most able to provide assistance prior to making a request, even though that person may not be immediately present.

_____When an appliance breaks, seeks the person most likely to fix it, even if he or she must wait for that person to return home at a later time.

_____When unsure of the bus schedule, goes to the bus stop and waits for the next bus to ask the driver for the information.

_____When thirsty while shopping, will look for a coffee shop or other similar casual restaurant to order a drink rather than a more formal restaurant or a store that does not serve drinks.

_____

Level 7: Asks for clarification when the initial response to a request for help is not clear.

_____In a supermarket, when told that the fruit is in aisle 4, asks for the location of aisle 4.

_____Raises hand in class to ask for clarification on an assignment.

_____When told to put something away, asks where it should go.

_____

Level 8: Changes the style of the request depending on the characteristics of the person asked, and refrains from asking for help when the problem can be solved independently.

_____Makes certain that solutions likely to succeed have been exhausted before asking for help.

_____Delays asking for help until a "helper" is more likely to provide it (e.g., waiting until someone is not busy or is in a better mood).

_____Uses an individualized strategy to request assistance (e.g., either does or does not offer a favor in return) based on a judgment as to what might motivate another person to help.

_____

Function 8 Summary Grid: Accept Assistance

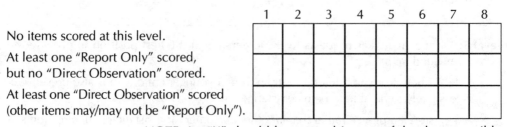

	Levels							
	1	2	3	4	5	6	7	8
No items scored at this level.								
At least one "Report Only" scored, but no "Direct Observation" scored.								
At least one "Direct Observation" scored (other items may/may not be "Report Only").								

NOTE: An "X" should be entered in one of the three possible choices in each column representing a level within the function.

Comments:

FUNCTION 9.   INDICATE PREFERENCE: MAKES CHOICES FROM AMONG AVAILABLE AND POSSIBLE ALTERNATIVES

Level 1: Pays more attention to some things than to others.

_____Consistently looks at or listens to certain objects or noises but not others.

_____Briefly watches a "new" person.

_____Stiffens body when approached by a particular person.

_____

Level 2: Behaves differently depending on what is presented.

_____Allows people to help with some things but not with others.

_____Opens mouth for some foods but not for others.

_____Engages in more stereotyped behavior with certain objects than with others (e.g., tapping or spinning certain items more).

_____

Level 3: Actively makes choices.

_____Whenever possible, manages to find certain objects that were put away when he or she wants them.

_____Selects a favorite item often (e.g., gets out the same shirt to wear whenever it is available).

_____Seeks out favorite person in the room.

_____

Level 4: When presented with alternatives that include at least one preferred item, makes meaningful choices.

_____When given a choice between two toys to play with, consistently selects one rather than the other.

_____When offered a choice between two types of sandwiches, selects one much more frequently.

_____Takes a larger portion of ice cream, which he or she likes, rather than a smaller portion.

_____

Level 5: Uses a mediator or symbol to communicate choices to others.

_____Points to a picture of the preferred food item on the display when ordering at a fast-food restaurant.

_____Asks to watch a desired TV program by name or another symbol.

_____Points to a picture of a preferred leisure activity when presented with two or more pictures of alternative activities.

_____

Level 6: Suggests alternatives to the choices that are offered or immediately available.

_____When offered one or more items, asks for an item that has not been offered but might be available.

_____When asked to perform a nonpreferred task, offers to do something else in its place.

_____When unable to participate in an activity proposed by a friend, suggests an alternative.

_____

Level 7: Gives reasons for preferences based on personal experiences.

_____Tries different brands of a particular food product (e.g., cereal) and will explain why he or she likes one better than another.

_____After listening to a cassette or CD, describes why some songs are preferred over others.

_____Explains why a particular vacation was the best.

_____

Level 8: Uses long-term goals and values to make decisions about choices and preferences.

_____After listening to or reading a movie review, decides that the movie would be too depressing and looks for a comedy instead.

_____In order to be with a certain friend, engages in a nonpreferred activity that the friend really wants to do.

_____Decides to take up a particular sport or exercise because it is healthy, even if it is a lot of work.

_____

Function 9 Summary Grid: Indicate Preference

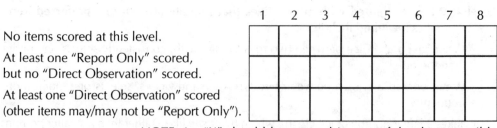

	Levels							
	1	2	3	4	5	6	7	8
No items scored at this level.								
At least one "Report Only" scored, but no "Direct Observation" scored.								
At least one "Direct Observation" scored (other items may/may not be "Report Only").								

NOTE: An "X" should be entered in one of the three possible choices in each column representing a level within the function.

Comments:

FUNCTION 10.   COPE WITH NEGATIVES: EXHIBITS ALTERNATIVE STRATEGIES TO COPE WITH NEGATIVE SITUATIONS

Level 1: Uses generalized avoidance and protest behavior.

_____When tired, becomes irritable and may refuse to engage in any activity; yet, does not attempt to sleep.

_____Continues to eat or drink when probably full, while crying intermittently and seemingly unaware of the source of discomfort.

_____

Level 2: Persists in continuing behavior that is bothersome to others.

_____Continues to give the same incorrect answer even after being corrected.

_____Continues to tug on a person's clothes for attention even though that person has asked him or her to stop.

_____Will not go away when asked to leave by a peer.

_____

Level 3: Responds to negative feedback by stopping ongoing behavior, but waits around rather than engaging in a positive alternative.

_____When told that an answer is incorrect, waits for someone to give the correct answer.

_____Stops tugging on person when told to stop.

_____When corrected at a street crossing, makes no further effort to cross without instruction and may engage in finger flicking while waiting.

Level 4: Responds to negative feedback by stopping ongoing behavior and switching to a "random" alternative behavior; will respond to instructions as to what to do.

_____When told that an answer is incorrect, will guess without thinking about what the answer should be.

_____Refrains from using another selection when told that the first item chosen cannot be used.

_____When a vending machine does not work, moves to another machine and uses the exact same procedure even if it is not appropriate for that second machine.

Level 5: Responds to negative feedback by switching to well-rehearsed, alternative responses in a trial-and-error fashion until something "works."

_____Requests second favorite food when told that first choice is gone.

_____Keeps putting more money into a vending machine until a selection appears.

_____Calls another friend if the first friend called does not answer.

Level 6: Responds to negative feedback by switching to another behavior that appears "safer" based on the situation.

_____When scolded for current behavior, watches others in an attempt to imitate the appropriate behavior.

_____When told not to interfere, asks if there is anything else that he or she could do to participate in the task.

_____Even though there is nothing to do, tries to appear busy when told to find something to do.

Level 7: Changes behavior in response to negative feedback on past experiences.

_____Dresses better for a subsequent job interview after failing to be selected at earlier job interview.

_____After doing poorly on an exam, takes more careful notes in class to better prepare for the next test.

_____Refrains from arguing with a person who has, in the past, been even more harsh following such arguments.

Level 8: Anticipates negative feedback and switches strategies before it occurs.

_____Wants to do well so asks supervisor for instructions before attempting a new job task for which he or she is not specifically trained.

_____Avoids direct interaction with a group of "rowdy" peers who appear on the scene and seem to be acting aggressively.

_____Notices that a friend seems disinterested in his or her suggested activity and proposes an alternative.

_____   _____

Function 10 Summary Grid: Cope with Negatives

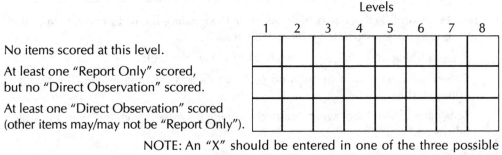

No items scored at this level.

At least one "Report Only" scored, but no "Direct Observation" scored.

At least one "Direct Observation" scored (other items may/may not be "Report Only").

NOTE: An "X" should be entered in one of the three possible choices in each column representing a level within the function.

Comments:

FUNCTION 11.   TERMINATE: TERMINATES OR WITHDRAWS FROM AN INTERACTION AND/OR ACTIVITY

Level 1: Leaves activities and interactions noncontingently.

_____Suddenly stops listening to a story being read to him or her by a caregiver even though the story is not finished.

_____Abandons toys whenever and wherever he or she finishes playing.

_____   _____

Level 2: Uses well-rehearsed and prompted strategies to leave situations.

_____Signals goodbye in appropriate contexts.

_____Leaves the dinner table when the meal is over and everyone else is leaving.

_____Gets coat when other class members get their coats to leave the building.

_____   _____

Level 3: Signals when he or she is about to leave an activity or interaction, but will leave even though the event is still continuing.

_____When done playing with a toy, attempts to give it to someone else before leaving.

_____Says, "All done" and leaves table when finished eating (there may still be food on plate), regardless of whether or not others have finished their meal and the meal is over.

_____Tries to leave an activity by saying, "Time to go" and starting to exit regardless of what others are doing.

_____ _____

Level 4: Waits until activity is completed prior to signaling intent to leave, using informal gestures associated with specific activity.

_____After finishing his or her entire meal, asks to leave the table.

_____Raises hand to obtain permission to leave desk after independent seatwork is completed.

_____Tells parent, "All done" when finished cleaning his or her room and wants to watch television.

_____ _____

Level 5: Ceases an activity or interaction appropriately in response to cues that another activity is about to occur.

_____Politely terminates a conversation after noticing that the other person is glancing at his or her watch and otherwise indicating a need to leave.

_____Stops playing outside or talking on the phone with friends when a family member arrives for a visit.

_____Puts toys away when parent begins to set the dinner table.

_____ _____

Level 6: Plans the length of an activity and terminates an interaction to anticipate leave-taking by others.

_____After a reasonable period of time, suggests taking a break from an activity before others become too tired or bored.

_____Does not monopolize the conversation but allows others an opportunity to participate.

_____On a joint activity, recognizes when a partner is likely to become tired or bored and suggests trading responsibilities for a change of pace.

_____ _____

Level 7: Negotiates new terms for role in activities and tasks.

_____Asks for a promotion based on a judgment that current job is not meeting his or her needs.

_____Asks for an opportunity to try out a different position on a team.

_____Negotiates mowing the lawn in return for no longer having to do the dishes.

_____ _____

Level 8: Negotiates negative and positive relationships, including major role changes and decisions to terminate relationships.

_____Diplomatically disengages from a close relationship based on the judgment that interests are no longer shared, feelings have changed, and so forth.

_____Quits an organized activity (e.g., a club) at the end of the current term based on a decision that the activity is no longer as interesting, conflicts with other needs, and so forth.

_____Leaves a job for a new position when current employment no longer meets needs.

_____ _____

Function 11 Summary Grid: Terminate

Levels

	1	2	3	4	5	6	7	8
No items scored at this level.								
At least one "Report Only" scored, but no "Direct Observation" scored.								
At least one "Direct Observation" scored (other items may/may not be "Report Only").								

NOTE: An "X" should be entered in one of the three possible choices in each column representing a level within the function.

Comments:

ASC SUMMARY SCORE SHEET

Learner's Name _____ Date _____

Name of Scorer _____

After each function, indicate the *highest level* for which at least one item was scored as a direct observation:

Function	Highest Level Directly Observed
1. Initiate	_____
2. Self-regulate	_____
3. Follow rules	_____
4. Provide positive feedback	_____
5. Provide negative feedback	_____
6. Obtain cues	_____
7. Offer assistance	_____
8. Accept assistance	_____
9. Indicate preference	_____
10. Cope with negatives	_____
11. Terminate	_____

Source(s) of "Report Only" Scores _____

General Comments:

INDEX

Page numbers in *italics* denote forms and figures; those followed by "t" denote tables.